Game Research Methods

Game research methods

An overview

Editors: Petri Lankoski and Staffan Björk

ETC Press 2015

978-1-312-88473-1 (Print) 978-1-312-88474-8 (Digital)

Library of Congress Control Number: 2015932563

All submissions and questions should be sent to: etcpress-info (at) lists (dot) andrew (dot) cmu (dot) edu For formatting guidelines, see: www.etc.cmu.edu/etcpress/files/WellPlayed-Guidelines.pdf

Contents

Acknowledgments

We are grateful to Marie Denward, Markku Hannula, Mikko Meriläinen, and Sofia Lundmark for giving feedback on chapter drafts.

Preface

FRANS MÄYRÄ

Finding and following a methods means finding a way. The original etymology of methodology conveys the same message: meta hodos in Ancient Greek meant following a path, as well as finding the way or means to achieve certain goal.

The methodological landscape of games research in some cases may appear as an undisturbed and untrodden terrain, devoid of any paths. In fresh and new research topics there might not be any previous models, set up by successful earlier research, that would provide step-by-step guidance on how to proceed. Trailblazing into unchartered territories is certainly an element in what has made contemporary game studies such an exiting and popular academic field today.

While the being the lone researcher who is the very first to conduct a study on a new game genre, play style, or form of game culture, for example, involves its fair share of innovation and openness towards the unique characteristics of the subject of study, science and scholarship in themselves are not isolated activities. Such key principles as verifiability of claims suggest that all true academic activity is deeply rooted in earlier practices of scholarly community, and closely related to the need of communicating results to other researchers. There are thinkers who advocate method anarchism, claiming that "anything goes" is as good, or perhaps even a better guideline than trying to follow some pre-set formulas to achieve significant scientific discoveries (critical views of Paul Feyerabend are a good example). But even radical breaks or paradigm shifts within science and scholarship are generally created with intimate knowledge about previous research, and its shortcomings. Similarly, Thomas Kuhn is famous for emphasising the role of scientific revolutions that cannot be produced within the regular, accumulative framework of normal science.

The work conducted in games research has both accumulative as well as transformative aspects. In addition, it is characterised by rather exceptional multidisciplinarity and interdisciplinarity, which is rooted on the one hand in the complexity and diversity of its research subjects, as well as on the fact that modern scholarship of digital games is a rather young phenomenon. As humanists, social scientists, design researchers and computer scientists (just to mention a few groups) have turned to study digital games, gameplay, game development, or games' roles in society and culture, they have also brought along theories and research methods from their native disciplines. While it is good to be aware of some Ludologists' warnings about the colonisation of game studies by other, non-games specific disciplines and their individual tilts of perspective, not everything in games research need to be created from scratch. Constant re-inventing the wheel in research methodologies would actually be a rather bad idea: many aspects in games' performative or mediated character can be very well be studied with approaches that have been developed and practiced in other fields for a long time. Joint methodologies also provide bridges between fields of learning that are essential for constructing more comprehensive and holistic comprehension. But game scholars need to be active in evaluating, adapting and re-designing research methodologies so that the unique characteristics of games and play inform and shape the form research takes in this field.

As games related degree programs and researcher training in this field has started, there has been an obvious need of research method textbooks in games research, and this present volume is a very welcome contribution, going a long way towards filling this particular gap. It is obvious that as games, network society and new technologies are all evolving; the research in this field cannot stand still, either. It is important that there is emphasis in games research that is focused on more permanent elements, and the fundamental ontological and epistemological issues that relate to games and play. Solid basis on qualitative and quantitative, games specific and more generally applicable research methods equips researchers to work on contemporary, as well as future, games related research issues. The authors of his volume are welcome travel companions onto the multiple, interconnected pathways of games and play research.

1. Introduction

PETRI LANKOSKI AND STAFFAN BJÖRK

This volume is about methods in game research. In game research, wide variety of methods and research approaches are used. In many cases, researchers apply the method set from another discipline to study games or play because game research as discipline is not yet established as its own discipline and the researchers have been schooled in that other discipline. Although this may, in many cases, produce valuable research, we believe that game research qualifies as a research field in its own right. As such, it would benefit game researchers to have collections of relevant research methods described and developed specifically for this type of research. Two direct benefits of this would be to illustrate the variety of methods that are possible to apply in game research and to mitigate some of the problems; each new researchers has to reinvent how methods from other fields can or need to be adjusted to work for game research.

In our own work, we have been struggling to find suitable literature for courses focusing on game research methods. We have however noticed that researchers have been developing such methods through publications in journals and at conferences. Based on this, we decided to invite game researchers to share their knowledge about these research methods; the book you are now reading is the result of the responses we received to our call for methods. We aim to provide introduction to various research methods in context of games that would be usable to students in various levels. In addition, we hope that the collection is useful to supervisors who are not familiar with the games.

Research, according to Oxford Dictionary, is "[t]he systematic investigation into and study of materials and sources in order to establish facts and reach new conclusions" (Anon, n.d.). A method is a specific procedure for gathering data and analyzing data. Data can be gathered and analyzed in many different ways. Data can be gathered, for example, using questionnaires, interviews, and psychophysiological measurements. Quantitative analysis typically involves building hypothesis prior data gathering and testing those hypotheses using statistical methods to examine relations between measured variables. This means that the typical result is the rejection of a hypothesis or presentation of data that support it. In contrast, qualitative analysis of data involves generating categories based on data, abstracting the data based on these categories and building explanations of studied phenomena based on abstractions. Through this, qualitative research aims to provide rich descriptions of phenomena focusing on meaning and understanding the phenomena. Qualitative and quantitative data and analysis can be integrated in mixed methods approaches to gain richer understanding of a phenomenon.

The objectivity of scientific work and theories has been criticized. Hume's (2006) argument that causation cannot be directly observed and that it is not possible to show things will behave the same way in the future proposed challenge to science in general. Popper (2002) agrees and claims that theories cannot be proven to be true or, in other words, validated but only *falsified*. Popper also maintains that a theory is not scientific if the theory does not produce predictions that can be used to falsify the theory. Popper's account is not without problems because explanatory theories are considered valid scientific theories. Niiniluoto (1993), among others, argues that, for example, the evolutions theory is a good scientific theory that does not really have predictive power.

According to Dewey (2005), a theory is good if one can use it to predict or describe a phenomenon in ways that are useful. However, this does not mean that theories and models should not strive to describe data accurately or provide good predictions how things behave. This means that research is an iterative process where theories are rejected or refined based on new findings.

Yet another challenge to the objective knowledge is that observations are theory-laden (Kuhn, 2012). Observations depend on skills and, in some cases, from biological qualities:

- Visual perception depends on skill and biological factors: seeing certain kinds of dirt in the kitchen tells to some about critter visitors, whereas others see just dirt.
- People living in high altitude areas or near equator have often reduced sensitivity to see blueness (Pettersson, 1982). Hence, these people see colors differently.
- Determining what kind of atmosphere distant planets have. Because the gases of the atmosphere cannot be directly observed, light curves are used to determine the consistent of the atmosphere. Here, the observation is filled with the presupposition coming from the theory of refraction and observation is not independent from the theory.

The above discussion is intended to illustrate some reasons why scientific knowledge can fallible and approximate. However, science is still seen as the most reliable way to form knowledge about the world and observable phenomena. Therefore, it is crucial to be able to discuss about the quality of the results research produces. In all kinds of research, the question of *validity* and *reliability* is important. Procedures for ensuring validity of results should be part of every phase in research. These terms have different definitions in quantitative and qualitative.

Quantitative *reliability* is used to denote that the approach measures the same thing in the same way every time it is used. Validity refers to different related things: *construct validity* refers to that one is measuring X when one intends to measure X (e.g., if measuring zygomaticus major muscle is a good way to evaluate that a person is happy) and *external validity* or generalizability denotes if the results apply to different samples within the same population. In addition, quantitative reliability, validity, generalizability are discussed in more detail in Landers and Bauer (chapter 10) and in Lieberoth, Wellnizt and Aargaard (chapter 11).

Validity in qualitative research can be described as a factual accuracy between the data and the researcher's account. Moreover, validity requires that the inferences made are grounded to data (cf., Maxwell, 1992). *Reliability* can be described as consistency of approach over time and over different researchers. This means, for example, that different researchers should end up with similar codings or categories form the data (Creswell 2014). Saturation is a related concept. *Saturation* means that there is a point in qualitative study when collecting and analyzing data do not reveal new insights to the question in scrutiny (Guest, Bunce and Johnson, 2006). Validation and validity are discussed more in Lankoski and Björk (chapter 3) and Cote and Raz (chapter 7).

The issues of validity and reliability typically become settled in research fields as they mature and various approaches have been explored. However, some phenomena can be approached from several different approaches which all are appropriate and which inform one other. This creates interdisciplinary or multidisciplinary fields where many different views of how research should be conducted coexist. Game research is both a multidisciplinary research field and a new one. It is multidisciplinary because one can conduct research on the games itself and one can study the people who play games: on the actual activity of playing games, one can, in addition, choose many different theoretical and methodological grounding for each of approaches. It is due to this fact that we issued a general call for methods for this book; we wished to present the variety of methods possible and help researchers new to game research navigate which methods will be most appropriate for them.

Next, we provide a short introduction to research design. After that we give an overview on addressing quality of a research. Last, we outline the chapters in this collection.

Recommended reading

- Ladyman, J., 2002. *Understanding philosophy of science*. London: Routledge.

Research design

Research design is a systematic plan for an investigation. Research consists of multiple phases. The research first needs to have an idea about the topic of the research. After having the topic, reviewing research literature about the topic helps to determine if the topic is worth to pursue (e.g., what questions are already covered and how the topics have been studied), building understanding of the research topic, and helping formulating one's research question and framing the problem. In quantitative (and mixed methods) approaches literature review has an additional role where the literature review along with the research question is used when formulating hypothesis for the study.

The research method should be selected based on the research question or topic. What is or what are the good method(s) to approach the area? However, it may also be prudent to be pragmatic and consider what skills various methods require. If there are no researchers in the team that have a prior experience to the method, extra care and time are needed to ensure that that the one knows the limitations and the possibilities of the method in adequate level.

Typical steps before research begins are as follows:

- Identifying the topic of research.
- Review of literature that relates to the topic area.
- Specify research question or hypothesis.
- Specifying what kinds of data are needed to study the question (the unit of analysis and the unit of observation; see below).
- Specifying what kinds of methods are needed to analyze the data.

Not all research designs use all these steps before research begins. For example, a grounded theory approach considers literature as a data for the research among the other types of data. As another example, quantitative explorative designs do not develop hypothesis because the point of the design is to build an initial understanding of a phenomenon.

A very important aspect of research design is the *unit of analysis*. The unit of analysis is the target of the study or more specifically what is the basic data type being studied. Looking at other fields of research, units of analysis can, in many cases, be described as related to the dimension of scale. Physics studies the very miniscule such as atoms while astronomy the large scale objects such as stars and galaxies, with chemistry and geosciences lay in between. Many of the disciplines related to games instead focus on more abstract types of data. The unit of analysis can, for example, be the phenomenological experience of a player, social interactions in cooperative play of a game, formal features of a game, or formal features in a group of games.

The unit of analysis decided upon which level data are collected. For example, collecting data by observing people playing a multiplayer game may be an approach level observation when wanting to investigate social interactions. However, all that is observed may not be part of the unit of analysis. In aforementioned example, the unit of analysis could be the social interaction while playing, and other data gathered might be ignored in this analysis when it is not relevant for the focus of the analysis.

The unit of analysis is closely connected to research questions and methods and often depends on these. Observations might be a more suitable method to gather information about social interactions than interviews. Formal analysis is adequate to understand whether the games in a same genre have some common systemic features or genre can be studied also in using method in linguistic analysis. Adequate method here depends on one's unit of analysis.

Selecting a method is a part of designing ones research process. In more general, the systematic design of research includes planning

- sampling (i.e., what is a target population and how reach informants from that population) and recruiting informants
- how are the data gathered in detail (e.g., interview questions or themes, questionnaire questions, or instrumentation)
- how are the data analyzed
- how are the data stored after study and how it is anonymize, or how the data will be destroyed.

To test that the research design works, a pilot study can be used. In pilot study, the data gathering is tested with a small amount of participants, and the results are analyzed according to the design. The pilot is intended for checking that the design works as intended. After the pilot study, the researchers conduct the actual study, analyze the results (or qualitative studies; gathering and analyzing are iterative process) and report the result. Formats of reporting the results of research vary. Hence, it is recommended to read the earlier (bachelors, masters or doctoral) theses, conference papers, or journal articles and study how studies are reported in that context.

Recommended reading

- Creswell, J.W., 2014. *Research design: Qualitative, quantitative, and mixed method approaches.* 4th ed. Los Angeles: Sage.

Ethical considerations

When conducting a research on people there are always ethical issues to be considered. Care should be taken to set up a study in a way that it does not harm participants. If there are risks, the participants should be aware of that risk before deciding whether to participate in the study. In these kinds of cases, the potential benefits of the study should outweigh the risks. Conducting the study might need approval of ethical committee.

When a study is planned to involve children, a special care should be taken. The guardian consent of the children is needed and the guardian should have details about the study so that they can make educated decision whether their children participation. All games are not suitable to children, and it might not be even legal in some areas to let the children play mature or adult only games. For example, asking children to play *Manhunt* (2003) to study their reactions to violent content is ethically very problematic because it is generally held view that that kind of content is not suitable for children. It is also illegal to let children play mature or adult only game in some countries. One might also require a permit for the study from the ethical committee of ones university.

Even if ones study design does not involve blind experiments[1], anonymizing the data and results is a good practice in most the cases. This is extremely important when conducting studies about sensitive issues such as sexuality to anonymize participants when reporting results. In addition to anonymization the names, the context descriptions of the study should not give away or lead to the participants.

How to deal with ethical issues in interviews are discussed in chapter 7–9.

Ethics apply research throughout the process. In more general level, honesty and standard for the work are an important to keep in mind. Honesty means that the result should reported accurately. Standards of the work means that research procedures follow the established standards of one's discipline. In addition, giving credits to all who were involved in the research is considered good practice.

Recommended literature

- Shamoo, A.E., 2009. *Responsible conduct of research.* 2nd ed. Oxford: Oxford University Press.

What is in this book

This volume is divided in six parts. Outside of those six parts, we have Olsson's (chapter 2) a look at on thesis writing and how to understand or structure argument chain in an essay.

---

1. In blind experiments the researchers are not aware of the subjects identity or conditions (brands, placebo–treatment) to minimize the effects of the preconceptions of the researchers in the study.

Parts I–IV focus on different types of research design. The first two parts focus on qualitative, descriptive research designs. The first part focuses on methods that aim to study games, and the second part focuses on designs for studying players or play. The aim of descriptive designs is to provide rich descriptions about phenomenon. However, the data gathering approaches are different when one is studying games compared with play or players. The third part takes a look at quantitative designs where the aim of the design is to provide quantifiable information about the unit of analysis and relations between the studied variables or examines causal connections. The fourth part looks at mixed methods designs. In mixed methods designs, qualitative and quantitative methods are used in conjunction to study the same phenomenon from multiple perspectives. Part V looks at the role of game development in research.

This collection does not cover all possible methods that can be used to study games, play, or players. We do not cover, for example, methods in platform studies, philosophical design, or historical design. Platform studies focus on the possibilities, limitations and influence of the gaming platforms; for example, see Montroft and Bogost (2009). Philosophical designs are relevant, for example, if one aims to develop definitions or is interested in ontological questions. Historical designs are intended to collect evidence from the past. Although games propose some challenges in these areas, the rich methodologies in these areas apply well to games. A particular area which is not explored in this book is that of research in education; a generic overview of this can be found in Bishop-Clark and Dietz-Uhler (2012), which can then be focused toward games.

Below, we provide overview of each part in this collection.

I QUALITATIVE APPROACHES FOR STUDYING GAMES

The first part looks at *qualitative approaches for studying games*. Games are seen as data and the research build understanding on games and how they work, provide experiences or information to its players. All chapters in this part consider games as systems. The data collection method in these approaches is playing a game or games that is under scrutiny. The methods also make assumptions about players or abstract them in some ways; for example, in Lankoski and Björk (chapter 3), the player is seen only in terms of what actions they can perform. These kinds of methods can arguably be seen as fundamental to much game research. Because in one degree or another, these often are needed to be able to use any of the other approaches; it can, for example, be difficult to understand play or player behavior in a game if one does not know what constitutes the gameplay.

Lankoski and Björk (chapter 3) provide a method for analyzing and describing the core components, or primitives that regulate the gameplay of a game. Zagal and Mateas (chapter 4) present a formal analysis approach that focuses on describing time in games using the concept of temporal frames. Last, Sköld, Adams, Harviainen, and Huvila (chapter 5) describe methodology for analyzing games as information systems.

II QUALITATIVE APPROACHES FOR STUDYING PLAY AND PLAYERS

The second part, *qualitative approaches for studying play and players,* provides methods that focus to actual play or player experiences. The game(s) played provides context but is not the main interest of study when using these methods.

Brown (6) introduces ethnomethodology where players are studied in their natural environments by, for example, observing play making field notes. The natural environment discussed in the chapter is online game worlds and forums. The chapter discusses especially challenges that the researchers encounter when studying intimate situations such as erotic role-play.

The rest of chapters in this part deal with different interview methods. Cote and Raz (chapter 7) covers in-depth interviews, how to plan and conduct interviews, and how to analyze interview data using thematic analysis. The analysis approach is useful for all kinds of qualitative data. Eklund (chapter 8) focuses on group interviews, and Pitkänen (chapter 7) stimulated recall interview approach.

III QUANTITATIVE APPROACHES

The third part provides introduction to *quantitative approaches* in game research.

Landers and Bauer (chapter 10) review the fundamentals of statistical methods in game research. Lieberoth, Wellnitz and Aagaard (chapter 11) discuss limitations challenges of quantitative and how to critically interpret the results of the quantitative studies. Järvelä, Kivikangas, Ekman and Ravaja (chapter 12) provide an introduction to psychophysiology and a practical guide using games as stimulus for psychophysiological studies. Schott and Marczak (chapter 13) discuss various algorithmic solutions to isolate specific audiovisual aspects of a videogame for quantitative analysis. Wallner and Kriglsteinin (chapter 14) provide different methods to visualize gameplay data. Last, Svahn and Wahlund (chapter 15) introduces structural equation modeling as a method to study impact of gameplay.

IV MIXED METHODS APPROACHES

The fourth part focuses on *mixed methods* approaches. In mixed methods research, qualitative approaches are used to build detailed understanding of a phenomenon, and quantitative approaches are used to evaluate magnitudes or references. The approaches are combined to draw strengths of each method.

Lieberoth and Roepstorff (chapter 16) provide introduction to mixed methods research approach, whereas Olsson (chapter 17) focuses on the repertory grid technique. Hook discusses grounded theory approach (chapter 18). Both repertory grid technique and grounded theory can be executed as qualitative or mixed methods design.

V GAME DEVELOPMENT FOR RESEARCH

The fifth and last part discusses *game development for research*.

Mohseni, Pietschmann and Liebold (chapter 19) discuss how to use modding in research. Their approach focuses on modding for experimental quantitative research. On the other hand, Waern and Back (chapter 20) looks at game design research where the design itself and design process are the topic of study. Their methodology is qualitative.

References

Anon, n.d. Research. In: *Oxford dictionaries*. Available at: <http://www.oxforddictionaries.com/definition/english/research>.

Bishop-Clark, C. and Dietz-Uhler, B., 2012. *Engaging in the scholarship of teaching and learning: a guide to the process, and how to develop a project from start to finish* Sterling: Stylus Publishing, LLC.

Creswell, J.W., 2014. *Research design: qualitative, quantitative, and mixed method approaches*. 4th ed. Los Angeles: Sage.

Dewey, J., 2005. *The quest for certainty and human nature*. Kessinger Publishing.

Guest, G., Bunce, A. and Johnson, L., 2006. How many interviews are enough? An experiment with data saturation and variability. *Field Methods*, 18(1), pp.59–82.

Hume, D., 2006. *An enquiry concerning human understanding*. Project Guttenberg. Available at: http://www.gutenberg.org/ebooks/9662.

Kuhn, T.S., 2012. *The structure of scientific revolutions*. 4th ed. Chicago: The University of Chicago Press.

Ladyman, J., 2002. *Understanding philosophy of science*. London: Routledge.

Maxwell, J.A., 1992. Understanding and validity in qualitative research. *Harvard Review*, 62(3), pp.279–301.

Montfort, N., 2009. *Racing the beam: the Atari Video computer system*. Cambridge, Mass: MIT Press.

Niiniluoto, I., 1993. The aim and structure of applied research. *Erkenntnis*, 38(1), pp.1–21.

Pettersson, R., 1982. Cultural differences in the perception of image and color in pictures. *ECTJ*, 30(1), pp.43–53.

Popper, K.R., 2002. *The logic of scientific discovery*. London: Routledge.

Rockstart North, 2003. *Manhunt* [game]. PS2. Rockstar.

Shamoo, A.E., 2009. *Responsible conduct of research*. 2nd ed. Oxford: Oxford University Press.

2. Fundamentals for writing research

a game-oriented perspective

CARL MAGNUS OLSSON

For experienced researchers, constructing the argument chain in an appropriate way based on content intended contribution is central to their success in publishing their work. For junior researchers that lack this experience, the writing process may provide a challenge that drains creativity and reward from what is otherwise an interesting research effort, turning it into a time-consuming and tedious task. While the effect of this on researcher motivation in itself is serious, it is even more serious that high-quality game-oriented research is not presented in a representative way simply due to the lack of experience from the write-up process.

Through examples of relevance to game design and development, this text is presented in a way that makes it particularly easy to adopt for game-oriented researchers. This is done by relying on state-of-the-art publications from methodological approaches that are highly suitable for game-oriented studies, such as design research (Hevner, et al., 2004; Peffers, et al., 2007), experiential computing (Yoo, 2010), and action research (Mathiassen, Chiasson and Germonprez, 2012; Olsson, 2011).

The text holds four sections, following this introduction: The first section explains how to deconstruct the argument chain of established research. This is done in order to identify the elements that are used as building blocks by experienced researchers as they argue, support, and contribute with their research. In the second section, fundamental method elements are described. These act as building blocks for a strong presentation of the research method and research process. The final section presents two styles of outline that are suitable for game-oriented research texts.

When reading this text, it is important to remember that even fundamental elements and structure will never guarantee the relevance of the study itself—only that the text about the study is appropriately presented. Relevance is an illusive notion, and inevitably up to the researcher to understand, present to the reader, and argue for in relation to other research. Fortunately, this argument is part of what should be presented in any text and thereby part of what will be elaborated on in the following pages.

Deconstructing an argument chain

Breaking down how an argument chain is constructed, it is relevant to start from well established research which already does this, and—if needed—adapt it to the specific domain at hand (in our case game-oriented research). Mathiassen, Chiasson and Germonprez (2012) is an example of such a seminal paper; that is, a paper of groundbreaking quality published in a highly acclaimed outlet. Their paper is based on an exhaustive review of top level Information Systems (IS) action research, where they identify structure elements of the reviewed papers. Identifying style compositions, as Mathiassen, Chiasson and Germonprez (2012) are doing, is in itself not tied to action research, however. Instead, it is related to genre analysis of text (cf. Dubrow 1982; Fowler 1982) where style composition is described as the activity a researcher performs as they argue—in text—their contributions using specific elements relevant to the research practice.

By adapting the elements from their review to more generic research terms—developed and extended with additional considerations within this text—we establish a foundation for how to write research text. Chief among our motivations for relying on a genre analysis of action research, is the richness of contribution types that Mathiassen, Chiasson and Germonprez (2012) identify in their review. This is illustrated in the building blocks section below, where we elaborate on each contribution type and show that they translate well to game-oriented research.

ELEMENTS OF RESEARCH

The cross-disciplinary nature of game-oriented research makes for a highly diverse need for building blocks. To name a few interest areas, game-oriented research includes, for example, user studies, community dynamics, game design analysis, design and development techniques, graphics design, tool support, product marketing, and business models. This means that the elements that game-oriented research relies upon must cover a wide array of potential uses, ranging from the *problem-solving cycle* (PS) that focuses on practice outcomes to the *research cycle* (R) which focuses on research outcomes. As with the elements below (based on Mathiassen, Chiasson and Germonprez, 2012, but developed further in this text), these elements are presented to suit all forms of game-oriented research and should not be used to argue for a certain set of elements as 'more important' than others. They are all important in the appropriate context.

The main elements of research (table 1) include the area of concern (A), *real-world problem setting* (P), *conceptual framing of the study* (F), *method of investigation* (M), and *contribution* (C). The area of concern (A) is essentially the positioning of the study in relation to previously published research. This does not mean that game research as a whole is an appropriate A for most studies. Instead, the A should be the particular area *within* game research that the study concerns. For the purposes of this book, the contributions submitted all share the A of research methodology for game research, although the different chapters of the book—as well as the placement of this text—speaks to the potential to narrow down the A further. How specific the A should be depends on the audience that the research contribution is intended.

Element	Definition
PS	The problem-solving cycle. Focused on producing practical outcomes.
R	The research cycle. Focused on producing research outcomes.
A	The area of concern. Represents a body of knowledge in the research domain.
P	The problem setting. Represents real-world practitioner concerns.
F	The conceptual framing. Helps structure actions and analysis.
M	The adopted methods of investigation. Guides the PS and R.
C	The contributions. Positioned towards the P, A, F or M.

Table 1. Main elements of research.

The problem setting (P) is closely related to the problem-solving cycle (PS) and describes the specific practice challenges faced. The P is the specific context within A that the researcher will study.

The conceptual framing (F) is a product of the research cycle (R). It is used as guide to the research efforts during the PS, or for interpretation of data from the P, or emerges as a result of the insight gained during the study. A framework may be based on related research from the specific area of concern (making it an FA), or be independent of the area of research (making it an FI). An FI could be any well-established theory that has been applied successfully in many A.

The method of investigation (M) describes the approach towards both the PS and R (assuming both are within the concern of the study). Meanwhile, the MPS describes the parts of the approach that are concerned with PS, and the MR the parts that are concerned with R. Subsequently, a study that focuses soley on practice problem-solving may be classified as following an MPS, while a study that is strictly theoretical may be classified as following an MR.

Finally, contributions (C) come in four main types. They may be related to the specific problem setting (i.e. a CP) if it is a practice contribution, or related to the area of concern (i.e. a CA). They may also be presented as theoretical frameworks (CF), either associated with the specific area of concern (i.e. a CFA) or independent of it (i.e. a CFI). Finally, they may be related to the method of investigation through which the study was conducted (i.e. CM). Such contributions could be the product of the problem-solving strategy used (CMPS), or the research strategy employed (CMR).

BUILDING BLOCKS OF AN ARGUMENT CHAIN

Mathiassen, Chiasson and Germonprez (2012) break down an argument chain as having three parts to it: (1) a premise style, (2) an inference style, and (3) the contibution type. Using Webster (1994), Mathiassen, Chiasson and Germonprez (2012) describe a premise as a statement or proposition serving as basis for an argument. In other words, it refers to the origin of the argument and as such is used to position where the researcher argues that the contributions (C) are of relevance. Being clear and aiding readers to see this could be one of the—if not *the*—most important things when writing research. It is part of the author responsibility that readers should not have to guess, make assumptions, or simply trust the author when it comes to the relevance of the work and its contributions. This is why an elaborated description of the premise is always relevant.

A *premise style* may be practical or theoretical, where a practical premise is based on an argument regarding challenges that practitioners are facing. This includes practice reports from the research setting in question, or reported practice challenges in previous research that still require further study. In the first case, if a potential research setting is reporting something as a challenge (perhaps through direct contact with the researcher), this does not automatically make it a relevant research subject. In such situations, researchers must identify if existing research already covers the challenge, and if something within this particular setting is likely to provide new insight into the challenge. While confirming previous research findings is relevant, the need for additional studies that test earlier findings must then first be established. The larger the number of other studies already confirming the findings, the less relevant additional testing becomes. The abstraction level of a practical premise may vary and could be specifically related to the P or be based on challenges within A as a whole.

A theoretical premise relies on identified challenges in existing theory, and is typically based on what the author may show (supported by previous research) is currently a gap in A, F, or M. Such a premise is essentially laying a puzzle where the pieces are from previous research. To construct a theoretical premise, the author must find that pieces are missing to complete this puzzle, despite the pieces being related to each other within A, F, or M.

Again relying on Webster (1994), Mathiassen, Chiasson and Germonprez (2012) describe *an inference style* as showing the reasoning from one statement or proposition considered as true to another whose truth is believed to follow from the former. This means that an inference style is the way that the argument chain uses to reach its conclusions. It may be deductive, inductive, or abductive, where deductive reasoning means that researchers take concepts from R and test their validity through evidence from PS. Deductive reasoning is particularly dominating in the natural sciences, where the focus often lies in testing under which conditions a specific reaction and result is triggered.

Inductive reasoning is based on evidence from the PS that suggests (formally: infers) conclusions that may be explained with existing concepts from R. This means that inductive reasoning can be used to infer which concepts (from R) are involved as the outcomes of a problem-solving cycle (PS) are studied. The infered concepts may—if so desired—be tested deductively after to identify the validity of the inference, and degree of effect that these concepts (individually and as a whole) have on the outcome.

Abductive reasoning is best understood in contrast with deductive and inductive reasoning. Peirce (1901) describes induction and abduction as being the reverse of each other, and emphasizes that abduction makes its start from facts without a fully developed theoretical foundation. In other words, abductive inferences suggest new and alternative explanations to phenomena rather than always relying on the existing concepts from R to inductively explain them. It is based on what Apellicon erroneously translated from Aristotle, and Peirce later corrected (cf. 1903), as an inference style that complements inductive and deductive inference:

> Abduction is the process of forming an explanatory hypothesis. It is the only logical operation which introduces any new idea; for induction does nothing but determine a value, and deduction merely evolves the necessary consequences of a pure hypothesis. (Peirce 1903, p.171.)

While Mathiassen, Chiasson and Germonprez (2012) did not find any published action research papers based on abductive reasoning, it remains one of the three accepted forms of inference. Given the highly formalized setting for reviewing research, abductive reasoning without complementing testing of hypotheses risks being considered a weak contribution (or even speculation). Abductive reasoning may, however, serve the important role of outlining research opportunities—something which drives progress and subsequently plays a very important role in research. Such arguments must clearly establish the need for new research by exhaustively outlining the gaps in current research or practice. Related to the premise style we earlier discussed, the positioning and support shown in the text for such research findings are key to what separates speculation from the identification of new and valuable research opportunities.

The third and final building block of an argument chain that Mathiassen, Chiasson and Germonprez (2012) describe is *the contribution type*. They identify five such types: experience report, field study, theoretical development, problem-solving method, and research method. An experience report contains rich insight from practice that could become research contributions. It addresses a P within a particular A and places the emphasis on the practical findings that were made in that context. For game research, this could for instance be the study of a game development company that struggles with creating novel but feasible new games. In focus would then be detailed descriptions of the constructive attempts made, the failures and various explanations given for them, and the resulting dynamics this creates within the company. The contribution of this example would be a CP.

A field study contributes to A in one of two ways. It either provides new empirical insight (a contribution to A itself), or by assessing a framework (F) within A (i.e. an FA contribution). This FA may be an existing F from previous research that is applied and critiqued within A, adapted from an existing F, or developed and assessed by the researchers. For game research, this would for instance include adaptating a theoretical framework that has been used outside A (and possibly from outside game-oriented research) to the particular context within A (and within game-oriented research). As the purpose of the adaptation is to benefit A, this example would be a CFA.

A theoretical development contribution is similar to a field study in what it does, but theoretical development strives towards making contributions that are beyond A. As such, theoretical development typically relies on multiple opportunities to test and revise what may have started as a single field study and FA (but may also be theoretically developed). The argument is thus that the F is a contribution independent of the A, that is, an FI. For game research, we may start from the same example as the previous. However, if the researchers would use the experiences from adapting the F to A, and compare these experiences to other adaptations of F in other A, it would be feasible to synthesize these findings and suggest an FI. This makes the contribution of this example a CFI.

A problem-solving method contribution implies that the research process itself is used as part of a practice oriented problem-solving cycle. The participation may include the M being used as change process through which transformation of practice takes place. This implies that the research approach plays the role of problem-solving method, and is thus a contribution to MPS. For game research, this could for instance include the use of a research technique (e.g., appreciative inquiry) to attempt to stimulate creativity and empower employees in the earlier example of the game development company that struggled with new ideas. Such a contribution would then be a CMPS as it is the research process itself that acts as a mediator for change. A contribution of this type should include both reflections on the PS and the research technique used as problem-solving method.

A research method contribution is primarily concerned with providing guidance for future use of the method itself, regardless of the particular A it is being used in, or P it is being used to address. This implies a contribution to MR and includes critique of existing methods, as well as adaptations of existing methods, and development of new methods. This type of contribution could be related to the philosophical foundation of a method, or methodological tools and techniques that it uses. For game research, this could for instance be to extend a well-established research methodology that is largely inductive or deductive with techniques for negotiating often the abductive creative process of game design. By applying these extensions in domains outside game-oriented research, or hypothesize about the potential impact, the result would constitute a CMR. Applying the extensions would in this case make for a stronger CMR, but hypothesizing about potential impact in a well-informed (inductive) manner is also an appropriate form of contribution to MR.

Method elements

To be considered research, a written text should contain a description of the method of investigation (M) that has been used. This implies both a description of the method itself and the research process that has been followed. The M may be presented in two ways—either as a separate section of the research text, or integrated into the structure of the paper. The first of these alternatives is considerably more common, and therefore what most readers and reviewers look for and expect. In principle, to avoid confusing readers there should be a tangible reason for deviating from this approach, and this reason should be made clear early in the paper.

The action research study by Henfridsson and Olsson (2007) and design research discussion by Peffers, et al. (2007) are both examples where the method of investigation dictates the structure of the majority of the text. In the case of Henfridsson and Olsson (2007), this was done to show the problem-solving (PS) and research cycle (R) of their action research, while Peffers, et al. (2007) used the approach to purposefully suggest an outline that they argue is particularly suitable for design research.

If using a separate method section, the elements in *Table 2* could be presented in the order that they are presented. However, the elements are also valuable to use as a checklist if the M is integrated in the structure of the outline. By following these suggestions for use, authors will have a rich presentation of their M. If there are well motivated reasons for adapting the structure, by all means go ahead and do so, but it is wise to keep an eye out so that no element is changed or removed without strong reason.

Element	Components
	Philosophical foundation
Methodological background	• Origins of the method • Research field it has been used in • Critique of the method • Challenges for the method • Strategies for dealing with the challenges
	Research setting
Applicability	• Previous study settings • Present study setting
	Research approach
Adaptations	• Typical research process • Previous adaptations • Present adaptation needs
	Data collection and analysis
Data treatment	• Previous studies: types of data collected • Previous studies: data collection techniques used • Previous studies: data analysis techniques used • Present study: types of data collected • Present study: data collection techniques used • Present study: data analysis techniques used

Table 2. Method elements and their components.

It is noteworthy that the type of data collected could be quantitative, qualitative, or a mix of both. *Quantitative data* is typically used to support deductive inferences (but can also used in explorative fashion), and the testing of hypotheses that have been inductively or abductively formulated. Inductively formulating hypotheses—as suggested explanations of an observed phenomenon—are interpretations of related literature and the applicability within a new A or P, and thus inherently qualitative. *Qualitative data* is typically used to support inductive or abductive inferences. These inferences are often based on in-depth interviews and interpretation, where the interviews may be ad-hoc (such as researcher field-notes during extended periods of observation or participation with the respondents), semi-structured (typically themes for discussion or open-ended questions with ad-hoc follow-up questions), or structured (with pre-determined questions, and possibly even pre-determined alternatives for answers in particularly strictly formalized—and likely inductive—studies).

Theory-driven research processes start by defining a research model (i.e., an F) that includes research questions derived from F that are tested within a particular P. Particularly when using quantitative data collection, these research questions are often phrased as so called hypotheses. A hypothesis is a statement suggesting what is likely to be true based on previous research. In principle, a theory-driven research process looks to deductively test if the F holds to the exposure of a P which it previously has not been used in. If it stands up, it confirms that the F is generalizable to this new P. If it does not hold this suggests that the F is not an appropriate explanation to the current P. For this testing, quantitative data collection and statistical analysis is the norm to use. It remains feasible, however, to use qualitative data collection techniques and analysis for more exploratory research questions where the F—and subsequently the RQs—has not been well established. In other words, a theory-driven research process strives to explain observations of the world based on existing knowledge. As a result, these studies tend to address 'what can be shown'.

Data-driven research processes focus on understanding *why* a particular phenomenon appears and what effect it has. We refer to this as data-driven as the practice situation—as represented by the data available to researchers—is that which drives the direction of the research. In other words, these studies tend to address 'why something is the case' rather than the 'what can be shown' of a theory-driven process. Data-driven research is typically qualitative in nature and uses inductive reasoning to explain findings using existing knowledge, and abductive inferences to suggest new explanations where needed. While these explanations could possibly be approached in a quantitative manner and be tested, the opposite is also true. In order to understand *why* something that theory-driven research has shown is the case, only data-driven research may suggest the reason for such answers.

Outline and text structure

It is now time to start putting all pieces thus far together and consider how to outline and structure text effectively. We described earlier how the method of investigation (M) may be presented in two ways: as a separate section of a research text, or be integrated into the outline. This means that which M will be used—and if this M holds a certain style of outline—is a leading factor in deciding how to organize a research text.

METHOD OF INVESTIGATION AS A SEPARATE SECTION

Research text is commonly outlined in a similar manner regardless of which domain it is from. This is not a coincidence, but rather motivated by best-practices that have been established over a considerable time. Writing research is different from writing novels. While surprising the reader may still be valid, such surprise should come from the quality and direction of the findings, not from the structure of the text. Deviating from what is expected by readers beyond what is elaborated below is therefore *not* recommended to novice researchers. Or, as Sørensen (1994, p.12) puts it: "Earn your right to deviate from the norm".

The sections of a traditional and generic outline of research includes introduction, theoretical foundation, method, results, analysis, discussion, and conclusions. The introduction section is typically highly structured and lays out the argument chain that the paper will rely upon, for instance by dedicating one paragraph to each of the main elements of the argument chain. The relevance for each part of the chain should be explained as part of the introduction, and the introduction should be kept to the point and only contain the essential parts. Elaboration should be left for later sections, but some examples may be effective to draw reader interest as long as they do not become overly complex.

For a paper based on a theoretical premise style, this means starting from A in the *first paragraph* and moving to the P as part of the *second paragraph*, or at the end of the first. References are a must in the introduction as well as all sections that rely on previous research. The *third paragraph* then moves on with which F will be used to address the P, and ends with the specific RQ (or set of related RQs, such as hypotheses, that are related to the overall research objective). Note, if the hypotheses are difficult to understand without considerable elaboration, it is preferable to develop them as part of the theoretical background. The *fourth paragraph* explains which M will be used, and outlines briefly which research setting, data collection technique and data analysis will be used. After this, the *fifth paragraph* explains what type of contributions that the discussion will be making as the F is contrasted with the analyzed results. This paragraph typically also clarifies for whom these contributions are relevant, even though this is implied by the earlier paragraphs. If at all possible, always avoid having the reader guess at what is implied. Help the reader understand why and for whom the paper is useful. The *final paragraph* of the introduction is typically about the outline of the remaining paper. Even if such a paragraph exists, all main sections after the introduction should still hold a bridge text as the first thing of the section, to explain what the section will contain and why this is relevant.

Most variations of the main sections stem from integrating two of the sections into one. For instance, computer science papers often use deductive experiments (i.e., a part of M) that are defined (through inductive inferences) as direct outcome of the framework (F). This makes it more convenient to present the theoretical foundation within the method section, immediately after the introduction. Research based on practice premises may also choose to present M—which of course includes the research setting—prior to the theoretical foundation.

In fact, such papers have three alternatives for how to approach the theoretical background. First, it may introduce it immediately after M and thus use it as a lense for which data to collect and to drive the discussion. Outside practice contributions (CP), such an approach would assess the usefulness of the F, that is a CFA or CFI depending on if the F is part of A or independent of it. Second, it may wait until the discussion section to identify which related research is relevant to explain the practice-oriented (analyzed) results. This shifts the emphasis heavily towards practice contributions (CP), but would also provide an opportunity for a minor CFA or CFI. Third, by aiming for an experience report alone (a CP), the theoretical background could be removed as a whole. This makes the richness of the CP a vital factor for still qualifying as research. By positioning the findings towards future research opportunities that this CP affords, the risk is reduced.

Further adaptation includes the integration of results and analysis into one section. Similarly, sudies with large amounts of qualitative data (which is more difficult to represent in for instance tables) may choose to leave out the results section and present only the relevant analys and discussion. Overall, we can see that all adaptations in essence still represent the same sections, just in different orders. For all adaptations, it is the argument chain that should dictate what order they are presented in, but starting in the order outlined above is always a good idea if in doubt.

A frequent question from junior researchers is what the difference is between the analysis and discussion sections. The analysis section focuses soley on the P, using statistical analysis for quantitative results, or content analysis (e.g., by categorizing similar results, conflicting results from different respondents, etc) for qualitative results. It is thus common that this section holds the arguments toward practice problem-solving contributions (CP). The discussion section instead focuses on the implications of the analyzed results on A and which contributions this makes (CA). For the sake of symmetry and as a bridge before the conclusion section, all contributions are usually summarized briefly at the very end of the discussion section, even if the CP were developed as part of the analysis section.

Finally, the conclusion section of a research paper should not contain any new discussion that previously was not elaborated on in greater detail. The conclusions should map carefully towards where the paper started, as described in the introduction. For instance, let us assume that the introduction section of our RTS example paper started out by explaining how game design the last decade has changed how it views the role of micromanagement. Instead of suggesting that game design should avoid micromanagement, our hypothetical paper argues, the emergence of expert best-practice support through information communication technology (ICT) channels such as *Youtube*, *TwitchTV*, and forums such as *Reddit* has transformed RTS game design into embracing and taking micromanagement to the next level. Our hypothetical conclusion section should then start from the same A, for example: "This paper set out to assess the impact of expert best-practices through ICTs on RTS design and play." Assuming it followed a traditional outline, it would then proceed with the P and RQ (likely in the same paragraph). After that, the F and M used would be described briefly in terms of which roles they played, perhaps including a couple of sentences about what type of data collection and analysis was used. This would leave the remainder of the conclusions focusing on what the results were, what type(s) of C this is, and what future research opportunities are associated with the study.

METHOD OF INVESTIGATION AS AN INTEGRATED PART OF THE OUTLINE

Two methods where it is common to integrate the M into the outline of the text include action research (Susman and Evered, 1978; Henfridsson and Olsson, 2007) and design-oriented research (Hevner, et al., 2004; Peffers, et al., 2007). The core reason for doing so is that both methods of investigation are iterative between problem identification and action taking. This iteration and gradual exploration of the P means that the argument chain and results tied to each iteration are often more convenient to tell as part of a larger research storyline. While both M contain iteration between practice and theory and may be used to focus on problem-solving (PS) or research (R) (or both), some further tendencies can be observed that are relevant to their use in game-oriented research.

Action research and design-oriented research are presented in this section strictly as an illustration of how an M sometimes is suitable to integrate directly into the outline. For instance ethnography (Van Maanen, 2011) and participatory design (Simonsen and Robertson, 2013) may also effectively be presented in this way, as they tend towards a similar and gradual development of the argument chain. This may also include iteration between results and reflection during the research process in the same principal way that action and design-oriented research does.

The abstraction level of design-oriented research (e.g., Peffers, et al., 2007) makes it useful for design and development of artifacts, e.g. prototype games or extensions and adaptations through end-user development (cf., Lieberman, Paterno and Wulf, 2006). Having said this, it is important to emphasize that Hevner, et al. (2004) show that design research may be used for a wide array of evaluations: observational, analytical, experimental, testing, and descriptive evaluations.

Meanwhile, if the collaborative effort with practitioners is an important aspect—regardless if prototype development is used or not—action research may be a more suitable choice. Action research is widely used and firmly established in many research domains outside game-oriented research. Rapoport (1970) explains that the sociology and psychology roots of action research come from a post World War II era of multi-disciplinary motivation for collaboration. These roots make action research somewhat more suitable than design-oriented research if artifact design and development is not (or at least, as much) in focus. Still, Olsson (2011) illustrates how action research may be used for studies of novel prototypes, as he outlines an adaptation labeled exploratory action research for such purposes.

As explained earlier, Henfridsson and Olsson (2007) as well as Peffers, et al. (2007) are examples where the outline of text has incorporated M. This allows the M to act as a guide through all sections of the text. In principle, using M in this way means that each section of the text is represented by one stage in M. Text within these sections starts by explaining the elements of M that are relevant for the stage. Following this, the relevant parts of P, A and F are identified and presented. Once this is done, the text moves on to the next stage of M in the next section. Not until all stages of the M are completed—sometimes after several iterations between stages—is the sum of all parts of P, A, and F presented. Contributions (C) may be identified either as part of the stages they were reached in, or left for a separate discussion section after the stages of M. Such a separate discussion then looks back at the previous stages—perhaps using an additional literature review or by contrasting with the results of other similar studies—to elaborate on which contributions were made.

Final words

As a whole, these three sections have provided a structured, to-the-point, and hands-on perspective of how to write research using the same fundamentals that experienced researchers do. Readers that embrace this text in their own work—using it as a reference point and check-list for how to compose and structure text—are likely to use their writing-time more effectively while also increasing the likely-hood that their research is presented in a representative way to readers and reviewers.

Recommended reading

- Mathiassen, L., Chiasson, M., and Germonprez, M., 2012. Style composition in action research publication. *MIS Quarterly*, 36(2), pp.347–363.
- Peffers, K., Tuunanen, T., Rothenberger, M. and Chatterjee, S., 2007. A design science research methodology for information systems research. *Journal of Management Information Systems*, 24(3), pp.45–77. DOI=10.2753/MIS0742-1222240302.
- Sørensen, C., 2005. *This is not an article—just some thoughts on how to write one.* London: London School of Economics and Political Science. Available at: <http://mobility.lse.ac.uk/download/Sorensen2005b.pdf>.

References

Björk, S. and Holopainen, J., 2004. *Patterns in game design.* Boston: Charles River Media.

Henfridsson, O. and Olsson, C.M., 2007. Context-aware application design at Saab Automobile: An interpretational perspective. *Journal of Information Technology Theory and Application*, 9(1), pp.25–2.

Hevner, A.R., March, S.T., Park, J., and Ram, S., 2004. Design science in information systems research. *MIS Quarterly*, 28(1), pp.75–105.

Lieberman, H., Paterno, F., and Wulf, V., eds., 2006. *End User development*. Springer Netherlands: Springer.

Mathiassen, L., Chiasson, M., and Germonprez, M., 2012. Style composition in action research publication. *MIS Quarterly*, 36(2), pp.347–363.

Olsson, C.M., 2011. Developing a mediation framework for context-aware applications: An exploratory action research approach. PhD. University of Limerick, Ireland.

Peffers, K., Tuunanen, T., Rothenberger, M. and Chatterjee, S., 2007. A design science research methodology for information systems research. *Journal of Management Information Systems*, 24(3), 45–77. DOI=10.2753/MIS0742-1222240302.

Peirce, C.S., 1901. On the logic of drawing history from ancient documents especially from testimonies. In *Collected Papers of Charles Saunders Peirce*. 7 (of 8), A.W. Burks ed., 1958, Cambridge: Harvard University Press.

Peirce, C.S. 1903. Harvard lectures on pragmatism. In: *Collected papers of Charles Saunders Peirce*. 5 (of 8), In: C. Hartshorne and P. Weiss, eds., 1934, Cambridge: Harvard University Press.

Salen, K. and Zimmerman, E., 2004. *Rules of play: Game design fundamentals*. Cambridge: The MIT Press.

Sicart, M., 2008. Defining game mechanics. *International Journal of Computer Game Research*, 8(2).

Simonsen, J. and Robertson, T., eds., 2013. *Routledge international handbook of participatory design*, New York: Routledge.

Sørensen, C., 1994. This is not an article—just some thoughts on how to write one. In: P. Kerola, A. Juustila, and J. Järvinen, eds, *The proceedings of the information systems research seminar in Scandinavian (IRIS)*, Syöte. pp.46–59.

Susman, G., and Evered, R., 1978. An assessment of the scientific merits of action research. *Administrative Science Quarterly*. 23, pp.582–603.

Van Maanen, J. 2011. *Tales of the field—On writing ethnography*. 2nd ed. Chicago: University of Chicago Press.

Webster, 1994. *Merriam Webster's collegiate dictionary*. 10th ed. Springfield: Merriam Webster Inc.

Yoo, Y., 2010. Computing in everyday life: A call for research on experiential computing. *MIS Quarterly*, 34(2), pp.213–231.

PART I

QUALITATIVE APPROACHES FOR STUDYING GAMES

3. Formal analysis of gameplay

PETRI LANKOSKI AND STAFFAN BJÖRK

Formal analysis is the name for research where an artifact and its specific elements are examined closely, and the relations of the elements are described in detail. Formal analysis has been used, for example, in art criticism, archaeology, literature analysis, or film analysis. Although the context of the studied artifact may complement the research, and different artifacts may be compared with each other, formal analysis can be done on individual artifacts in isolation. Formal analysis can be seen as a fundamental or underlying method in that it provides an understanding of the game system that can in a later step be used for further analysis (cf. Munsterberg, 2009). The results of formal analysis can also be contrasted or tested against other sources, for example, information from players, designers, and reviewers.

Formal analysis of gameplay is a method used in many studies of games, sometimes implicitly. David Myers (2010) use formal analysis of gameplay to study the aesthetics of games, whereas Björk and Holopainen (2005) used it to derive design patterns. In both, formal analysis is used explicitly as a method. The study of psychophysiology in relation to video games by Ravaja, et al. (2005) is an example where formal analysis is used implicitly.

Formal analysis of gameplay in games takes a basis in studying a game independent of context, that is, without regarding which specific people are playing a specific instance of the game. Although a specific group of players can be considered for the analysis, these are descriptions of players used for analyzing the gameplay and not descriptions of their gameplay. Performing a formal analysis of gameplay can be done both with the perspective that games are artifacts and that they are activities; in most cases, it blurs the distinction because both the components of a system and how these components interact with each other often need to be considered. In practice, formal analysis of games depends on playing a game and forming an understanding how the game system works. When analyzing board, card, and dice games, the rule book gives transparent access to the underlying system, and a formal analysis could be done purely by observing these components and together with the understanding gained by playing. Nonetheless, the game dynamics are more easily understood in actual gameplay, so most formal analyses include these, either through researchers playing the game or through observation of others playing the game.[1] This playing may take the form of regular gameplay but may also include specific experiment to understand or explore subparts of a game. Indeed, using cheat codes, hacks, and so on may be motivated because they can allow more efficient exploration or provide more transparency to the game sys-

---

[1] Alternative approaches to understand gameplay include autoethnography (see Brown in this volume) or observations (Linderoth and Bennerstedt, 2007).

tem. Regardless of how gameplay is observed, the understanding should, however, be independent of specific gameplay instances.[2]

Partly because of ease of presentation and partly because games can affect social conventions weakly regarding them, this chapter focuses on the analysis of operational and constitutive rules in contrast to implicit rules[3] (e.g., social norms such as good sportsmanship or cheating).

Formal[4] analysis focuses on describing the formal features of every work. These vary between fields: in visual art form, it consists of lines and colors; in poetry form includes rhythm; and in game form, it is the systemic features of the game such as game elements, rules, and goals. As a more detailed view from another field of games, Bell (2005), in his theory of visual art from 1915, argues the following:

> In each [work], lines and colours combined in a particular way, certain forms and relations of forms, stir our aesthetic emotions. These relations and combinations of lines and colours, these aesthetically moving forms, I call "Significant Form"; and "Significant Form" is the one quality common to all works of visual art. (Bell, 2005.)

Regardless of field, formal analysis focuses on the different elements of a work, that is, asking questions about the elements that constitute the parts of the work and the role of each element in the composition as a whole. Looking at other fields, formalism and structuralism in film and narrative theory have focused on storytelling devices and literary or filmic form: Frazer's (2009) work on myth and religion (1994), Campbell's (2008) monomyth theory, and Propp's (1968) study of Russian folk stories. Borwell, for example, provides an overview of the relation to formal elements in film and how time or space is constructed (1985, pp.74–146). Filmic devices, for example, include cuts and point of view. Myers (2010, pp.40–49) is a good introduction to how formalism and structuralism can be used in games. *Close reading* is a method associated to these formalist approaches in which researchers consciously exclude the interpretations and meanings, depending on materials outside of the work in scrutiny; analyzing games as texts is discussed by Bizzocchi and Tanenbaum (2011) and by Clara Fernandez-Vara (2014). The approach we describe below is leaning more toward formalism in visual arts.[5]

In the next sections, we discuss in more detail what formal analysis is and its history. In Anatomy of Games section, we present a simplified set of concepts that are used in formal analysis. After that, we provide three formal analysis examples. This is followed with discussion on how formal analysis can be combined with other approaches. The chapter ends with concluding remarks about formal analysis.

The anatomy of games

The basis for being able to do formal analysis of games is to have a vocabulary that enables a clear and distinct description of specific games. Although one can imagine a vocabulary that is sufficiently large and expressive to be able to be used for all types of games and for all types of reasons for doing formal analysis, it would be difficult to have a comprehensive overview of such a vocabulary. Furthermore, applying it consistently would likely require much superfluous work as the granularity of such a vocab-

2. Gameplay instance describes whole lifetime of the specific play of a game (Björk and Holopainen, 2005, pp.9–10).
3. Operational, constitutive, and implicit rules are concept introduced by Salen and Zimmerman (2003, p.139).
4. Formal in formal analysis refers to the form of the work, not formalism as in mathematics or in the philosophy of logic.
5. Our approach is also influenced by Björk and Holopainen (2005) who draw on Alexander, et al. (1977) work on patterns in architecture.

ulary is likely to not be matched to the reasons for the analysis. A more pragmatic approach is to either make use of the same smaller vocabulary for groups of related games (or related reasons for making analyses) or even creating or customizing vocabularies for individual analyses.

In this section, we present a small vocabulary that will be used in the case studies below. It is based on aforementioned frameworks. The purpose is to provide one example of a vocabulary that contains design elements likely to be relevant in most formal analyses and can thereby serve as a basis to create or customize other vocabularies.[6] The final case study will exemplify the limits of this vocabulary and how one can address this.

PRIMITIVES

The primitives are the basic types of building blocks of games. Each type of primitive may exist in several different instances and have individual values. During gameplay, the instances of primitives and their associated values define the *game state*. This is not a primitive, but a concept for referring to a game at a specific moment during play. For example, a game state in the chess game would contain whose turn it is and the positions of all game pieces.

Components

Components are the game entities that can be manipulated by players or the game system (Järvinen, 2008). Other names for them include game design atoms (Brathwaite and Schreiber, 2009) and game elements (Björk and Holopainen, 2005), but basically, these all describe individual entities define by a game that has values and can be manipulated. In addition, components are used to define game space. An important aspect of these components is that it also provides the boundaries which game components cannot move outside. Ship, aliens, UFO, bullets, and bunkers in *Space Invaders* (TAITO, 1979) are examples of components. Chess board and the maze walls of *Pacman* (Namco, 1980) are examples of components that define game space.

Components can contain other components or variables such as who has control over the component. Another example of a variable is the number of lives of a player-controlled component in a classical arcade game. In some cases, variables that are not directly linked to any component, such as the score in a single-player game, may be seen as a component to give it a clear position in an analysis.

Actions

Player actions: these are the actions that players initiate. For example, in *Space Invaders* (TAITO, 1979) player actions are move left, move right and shoot. Space Invaders is an example where player actions have direct relation to what a player owned component does. In other games, the relation can be less direct and player builds or buys component and own then, but components are not directly controlled (e.g., as in tower defense games). As another example, most components in the *Sims* (EA 2008) enable players to perform actions but none of them are explicitly player controlled. Sometimes a player action comes available only when certain component is owned or other condition is met. An example of this is in Monopoly (Magie and Darrow, 1933), where one can develop ones properties (e.g., build a house) of one owns all same colored property components.

6. *Time in videogames*, Zagal and Mateas (chapter 4) provide a related example in a case study about game time.

Component actions: these are actions which one perceives as coming from the components themselves. This requires that one is willing to ascribe the component agency and this typically depends not only on the action performed but also on the representation of the component. For example, the aliens in *Space Invaders* move and shoot and this is typically described as actions they themselves perform and for this reason these would be component actions as well as a shot in *Space Invaders* or player shot hitting a cover (removing part of the cover or destroying the ship). As another example, mine that explodes with proximity, the explosion is a component action. Components that can be perceived as intentionally initiating actions will be referred to as *agents*.

System actions: these are the actions not perceived to originate from players or components. They can however directly affect both components under players' control and others. The spawning of enemies, or new tiles in *Tetris* (Pajitnov, 1984), and the handling of scores are both examples of system actions. Timers limiting the play time are a system action.

Goals

Goals are descriptions what overall conditions of the game state have specific significance for the gameplay. Formal goals have relation to the game state: reaching or failing a goal is tracked by the game system. Typically goals are seen as what players should strive for while playing a game, and these exist both as ones that can be achieved or not in the short term (e.g., avoiding a shot in *Space Invaders)* and in the long term (placing the other player's king in checkmate in Chess). However, goals can also be used to explain the strategies of the game system itself or individual components that have agency. The type of goals described here are those that can be identified through formal analysis. This is the main reason why they are directly connected to various game states, players can of course have many other goals while playing games (e.g., having fun, socializing, learning to mastery a technique), but these are beyond the scope of formal analyses to examine. *Rewards* are given for reaching goals. These can be in the form of game components and values in the game state (with points being the archetypical example) but also that the next part of the game becomes available.

Two additional points can be made about goals. The first is that they often are related to each other in *goal structures*. This is basically that the success of one or more goals is requirements for reaching another larger or later goal which create chains or hierarchical structures of goals. The second point is that some goals are obligatory and some are non-obligatory. Obligatory goals are needed for winning the game.[7] Non-obligatory goals typically offer players alternatives in strategies and tactics in that their rewards may help reaching the obligatory goals but requires extra effort or shift in focus of the gameplay. A special case of non-obligatory goals can be when players need to complete one of several goals to complete a larger goal structure but any of the goals suffice.

How-to conduct formal analysis

To provide formal analysis, one needs to play a game carefully and repeatedly to distinguish primitives in the game and, later on, the principles of design. It is important to play the game multiple times and

---

7.   Goals can also be used to judge how well one is playing. Those not trying to reach obligatory goals as efficiently as possible are not seen as playing the game as determined by the game implementation. However, this kind of evaluation use of goals is an extension to formal analysis.

try different things. Discriminating primitives is usually rather straightforward, but understanding the qualities of and relations between primitives requires pushing the system to reveal how it behaves. What happens when one does this? Does the same thing happen every time? What one can do in this situation? What cannot be done in that situation?

The different uses require different levels of descriptions and analyses. The goals of formal analysis determine the needed level of description. In addition, one needs to find a suitable focus and level of detail. Many contemporary games are too big to be described fully. Finding the parts of the games that are relevant for the current focus of interest is the first part of formal analysis. After that, the focus moves to more detailed descriptions.

We can distinguish different levels of descriptions:

1. describing primitives and their relations
2. describing the principles of design
3. describing what is the role of the primitives and principle of design in the game.

The higher level of descriptions depends on the lower level descriptions. This means that to describe the role of elements in a game (level 2 description), one needs to first discriminate and describe the elements (level 1 description).

In addition, games can be compared based on the description and ask how game A is different from game B and is there something unique about how the primitives are used or principles of design compared with other games.

The quality of formal analysis can be described using the concepts of reliability and validity (cf. Creswell, 2014). Reliability and validity relates to the consistency of categorization over time (a primitive A is always described as primitive A) and that different researchers describe the same thing using the same concepts (X is always descried as A) as well as the description has a good fit with to actual game (cf. Morse, et al., 2002; Creswell, 2014).

To maintain reliability and validity, verification is used. Verification, according to Morse, et al. (2002), is: "Data are systematically checked, focus is maintained, and the fit of data and the conceptual work of analysis and interpretation are monitored and confirmed constantly." We can derive from Creswell (2014, pp.202–204) following strategies to maintaining validity and reliability:

- Rich description of the gameplay that is analyzed. Other researchers should be able to follow the researcher's description of research and result to follow the researcher's logic and research as well as understand how the researcher researched to the conclusions.
- Provide descriptions of the researchers' background, interests, etc. to reveal potential biases to the readers.
- Spending prolonged time with the game. The game should be played multiple times, and trying different options to learn how the game system actually works. Better understanding allows better, more nuanced descriptions.
- Constantly checking categories and descriptions in the analysis against their definitions (e.g., against those defined in anatomy of games section).

- Let other researchers check descriptions.

Many contemporary games are too big to be described as whole. For many purposes, first one needs to find a part of the game or parts of games that are analyzed. This require building a rough understanding of the game by playing it and distinguishing the parts that are good candidates for analysis in terms of one's research questions.

Examples

Below, we present two formal analyses of games to exemplify the concepts and method described so far. The games have not only been chosen because they represent different genres but also because they show different levels of applicability to being formally analyzed. For clarity, the components and actions are shown in italics.

PLANT VS ZOMBIES

Plant vs Zombie Online (Popcap, n.d.) is an example of what is typically called a tower defense game where a player tries to hinder zombies from invading his house by placing planting different types of aggressive plants in their way. It is rather simple game regarding game components and is, for this reason, used as an example of a detailed description of the primitives and principles of design. Only levels one to ten are covered, excluding the bowling and conveyor-belt bonus levels and aspects only related to achievements and other meta game issues, but the process for extending the analysis to those levels should be pretty straight-forward from the example.

The game has the following types of components: *plants*, *plant cards*, *zombies*, *items*, *sun tokens*, *lawnmowers*, and *bullets* (in the form of peas and other organic objects). Of these, there exists many different versions of plants and zombies; one new plant version and new zombie every second level are introduced for each of the ten levels examined in this analysis. The game keeps track of *score*, *levels* (how many zombie waves has been cleared), and the amounts of sun available for purchasing plants. The system actions in the game consist of *spawn zombie*, *spawn generic sun token*, and *start new level* after; all zombies have been destroyed. The spawning of zombies is done so that each level has a number of zombie *waves*, in between which the player prepare the defenses.

The environment consists of screen (see figure 1) where there are one to five lanes where zombies can move and the player plant plants. Each lane has a lawnmower component (marked as a box with L). In the first level, only lane A is used. In the next level, track B is added, and in the level after that, track C is added. The player's house is shown left of the lanes before level starts. The area about the environment shows how much sun the player has, the plant cards that are activated to buy plants, and a spade that allows for the removal of existing plants.

Like other tower defense games, player actions is done in response to ongoing or future enemy actions. For this reason, it is logical to start looking at the zombie enemies and their actions. The basic zombie is a component with a health value, and the basic action *move toward the house*, if the access is blocked by some plant, the zombie shifts to the action of *eat plant*. Although the different zombies could have been modelled as different components, these are represented as basic zombies but with extra items

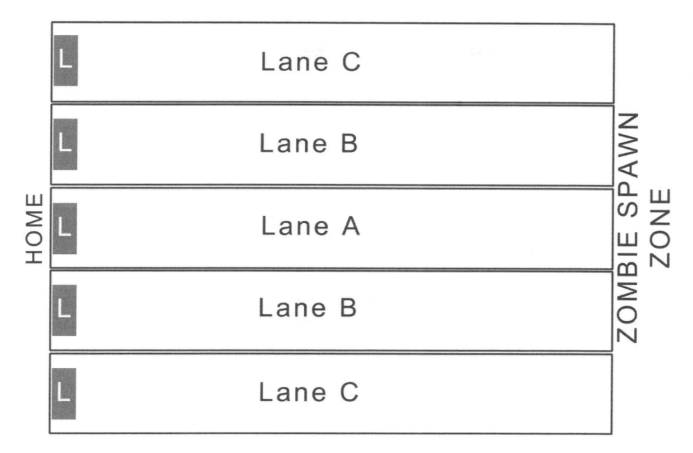

Figure 1. Plant vs Zombies environment.

or different outfit. For this reason, it makes sense to model the zombie component as having a possible item component that changes its behavior. *Road cones* or *iron buckets* worn over zombies' heads are examples of item components that allow the zombies to take more damage, whereas zombies with a flag move slightly faster. Some items provide the zombies with new actions, for example, those outfitted as athletes with pole vaults have a one-time action of *jump over plant*.

Players of *Plants vs. Zombies* have relatively few actions available; much of the complexity in the game comes from making the plants' actions have synergies. One of the most basic actions available to players is to *collect sun tokens*, which intermittently are generated from certain plants (as plant actions) as well as from the environment itself; acquiring sun tokens simply increases the sun value. Sun tokens disappear after some time if they have not been collected (i.e., they have a timed *disappear* action). *Buying and placing plants* is the second most basic action players can do; this is performed by selecting the relevant plant card from above the lanes. Buying a plant activates a *cooldown action* on the card that prevents it to be used again for a certain amount of time depending on the type of plant. This means that the *buying and placing plants* player action is restricted by both having the required amount of sun and the plant card not performing a cooldown action. Besides this, players can activate the spade to remove an existing plant so that another can be put in the place it had.

Component	Component actions
Peashooter	Shoots peas that deals damage to zombies
Sunflower	Creates sun components with certain interval
Sherry Bomb	Explodes when planted and destroys zombies on blast area
Squash	Stops zombies until it is eaten
Wall-nut	Jumps on a zombie near-by and destroys it. The action destroys wall-nut
Snowpea	Shoots peas that slows down zombies in addition to dealing damage
Chomper	Eats a zombie but is vulnerable to the attacks of other zombies while eating
Repeater	Shoots two pies at the same time

Table 1. Component actions in Plants vs. Zombies.

Plant actions depend on the type of plant and are activated independently of the player. Different plants have different component actions. These actions are shown in the table below.

All plant components have recharge time (except Squash and the ones that are destroyed after they have completed their actions). With shooting plants, the recharge time means that the shooters have a rate of fire.

The game ends if a zombie gets to the player's house. The lawnmower component provides a last defense to avoid this in that it has a *move lane*, which is automatically activated if a zombie reaches the end of its lane. This action kills all zombies on that lane, but the lawnmower is then removed from the game until the next level.

Completing a level not only opens up the new level but gives access to a new plant card component. The inventory of plant cards above the lanes has a limited number of slots, so playing on higher levels begin by choosing which plant cards to use. The game difficulty is increased in higher levels by adding lanes (up to a maximum of five), having more zombies and zombie waves, and having zombies with different abilities or qualities in waves.

Some of the gameplay effects of *Plants vs. Zombies* can rather easily be deduced. For example, planting sunflowers to increase the rate at which one can get sun tokens is vital, but the balance between this and placing offensive plants offers clear *directional heuristics,* that is, what strategy to follow when placing different plants.[8] However, the dynamics of the games arises primarily through understanding the efficiency of various types of plants in relation to the zombie types as well as what synergies can be achieved by using combinations of plants in the same lane. Although small synergies (e.g., having a Peashooter component behind a Squash component increases the usefulness of both) can be argued purely from the formal analysis, larger-scale synergies and strategies are not always evident by formal analysis alone.

These kinds of descriptions are good for discussing design and the implications of design choices, for example, when one needs to provide critique to a work. However, the description above is not itself enough for a study. For the study, one needs to have a research question formulated, and the role of description is to help to answer the research question.

8.   About heuristics, refer to Elias, Garfield, and Gutschera (2012).

Next, we discuss *Ico* (Team Ico, 2002). This provides an example of analyzing a game that has a strong focus on narration[9] and shows how one can look at formal game elements via concepts of filmic narrative theory. To do this, we need to augment our vocabulary and use David Bordwell's (1985) theory on narration. He argues that the perceived actions of characters in the film constitute its *events* and that the sequence of these is interpreted as its narrative. This sequence is structured in relation to *time* and *space* (Bordwell, 1985, pp.49–62). We extend the notion of narration to include the goals and the actions of the player-character as well (cf. Lankoski, 2011). It is also important to note that the relation of the events in games and film are not fixed in the same way because the player choices have an impact on the events in the game, whereas audience of (traditional) films cannot influence the events (e.g., the order or the content of events). This example looks at the game from the beginning to the first save point. We begin with the formal description of gameplay and continue to the narration.

Ico, a young man cursed with horns growing from his head, is the central agent in the game and is controlled by the player. The player actions—*move*, *jump*, *climb*, *attack*, *use*—are mapped directly to Ico component's actions. The use action is performed in relation to other components and presented differently, depending on the component interacted with (note that not all components can be used). *Yorda*, a mysterious princess, is another central agent of the game, and after meeting her, the player gets new action: *call Yorda*. If the Yorda component is next to Ico component, this action will cause Ico to hold Yorda's hand (pulling her along if Ico moves), and otherwise, the call will cause Yorda to move toward Ico. Yorda performs also *move actions* without being prompted to do so and initiates *open doors* actions (which Ico initially cannot perform) on her own.

Black portals are important components in the game in that they perform *spawn shadow creature* actions. These *shadow creatures* are agents that perform *move actions* to get close to Yorda or *fight actions* when near Ico; if they succeed, they will *grab Yorda* and move toward a black portal to *disappear with Yorda*. The player can prevent this because Ico can destroy shadow creatures by moving close to and attacking them. The black portals themselves are spawned by the game system.

Important aspects of the game's narration are done through *cut-scenes*, which are the prescribed actions where the player actions are disabled.[10] As short sequences where the player cannot perform actions, these can be approached using Bordwell's theory as they set up a context for evaluating and understanding events in the gameplay. According to Bordwell, film viewers build the story from the events by looking causal, spatial, and temporal links between events (pp.48–53). The first meeting with Yorda serves as an example of the cut-scene. Yorda is imprisoned in a gage that hangs on air supported by a chain. Player can guide Ico to jump on the cage. This action starts the cut-scene. In the cut-scene, the cage falls and breaks open. Ico falls from the top of the cage, and a torch drops on the ground. Yorda comes out from the gage and approaches Ico and says something in a foreign language. Ico looks scared at first. A black portal appears, and a shadow creature appears from the portal while Ico and Yorda try to

9.   A word on the use of narration and narratives. Narratives may point toward the story in many different ways, for example, as the subjective experience one, the one intended by the author, or even the retelling of the experience provided by the game (or other medium). Narration, on the other hand, is more specific in that it focuses on the structural design for telling a sequence of events. Although the possible.

10.   The cut-scenes can allow some limited control over the flow of events as in Mass Effect where you sometimes can initiate a paragon or renegade action.

communicate. The shadow creature grabs Yorda and carries her toward the portal. The cut scene ends, and the player can again control Ico.

However, the events taking place during gameplay are also part of the narration, and here, the game designers have less control. The camera of the game uses the third-person view and is focused on Ico most of the time. Hence, how the animation of Ico's actions and reactions are part of the perceived events and thereby part of the narration of the game. Likewise, Yorda and the shadow creatures are part of the narration in what actions they perform and how they perform them.

Even if the events of the game are not strictly fixed in time, certain events do happen in a predetermined order and with predetermined outcome. If the player reaches the first save point, the following events would have happened:

1. A cut scene showing how Ico is brought to the castle and put into a statue and how the statue falls letting Ico out.
2. Ico used a lever in the first room to open a door.
3. Ico went through that door to the second room.
4. Ico climbed up a chain, jumped to a window, and entered the third room.
5. In the third room, Ico climbed up to a tower.
6. Ico lowered Yorda's cage.
7. Ico jumped on top of the cage, which breaks the cage.
8. A cut-scene showing Ico's and Yorda's first meeting.
9. A black portal appears and shadowy creates emerges from it.
10. Optional: Ico armed himself with a wooden stick.
11. Ico destroyed all creatures with the stick or his horns, thereby preventing them from taking Yorda through the portal.
12. A cut-scene where Ico says that it is too dangerous to be where they are and that they must escape, after which, Yorda opens a magically sealed door leading to the next room.
13. Ico and Yorda entered the next room.
14. Ico helped Yorda to climb up on a ledge.
15. Passing through the door of the room.
16. Save point reached.

The events that exactly happen between these sequences can vary. However, because the space along with the actions of Ico and the actions of NPCs are very limited, there are only limited amount of different kinds of event that can happen in the game. The actions in between are about exploring the space, fighting about the shadow creatures, and guiding as well as helping Yorda through the space. This is assuming that the player is trying to reach the goals given by the game, so the analysis is assuming that the player is playing the game as prescribed by the game and not creating his or her own activity.

We can categorize these events in more general categories:

- Obligatory narrative events: the sequential order of these is predetermined.[11] Some of these

---

11. If we look at other games, such as Mass Effect 2 (Bioware, 2010), we would find that there are also obligatory events, but the order in which the event are encountered can vary based on the player choices.

obligatory events are cut-scenes, and some are points created by level design. The player object needs to perform the action or pass a certain point in the game world.

- Events happening in between obligatory narrative events; sequential order not determined and can vary between the game instances.
- Event that might not happen in a one-game instance (such as Yorda being captured and taken through the portal, which leads to game over and a restart of the game from the last check point).

One question that easily arises when analyzing the narration of a game (or other medium) is to see if it is consistent, that is, it does not contradict itself, and all parts help create a coherent argument. For games, this can easily be problematic because the events caused by players may point toward creating one type of narrative, whereas the cut-scenes may point toward another. In looking at one specific aspect of Ico, a strategy for the player when the shadow monsters arrive is to keep Ico near Yorda and try to keep the shadows away from her. While focusing on hunting and defeating the monster instead can work, it is more difficult and more likely to fail. In this, the gameplay structure subtly encourages the player to behave in a fashion which is aligned with the narration in the cut-scenes. In this way, the gameplay structure and narration can be said to be aligned: the information exposed in gameplay and in cut-scenes have complementary content.

Ico exhibits tightly controlled event structure. This event structure is, in many ways, similar enough to filmic structure as theorized by Bordwell (1985, pp.48–62), and we can consider the story comprehension process the same, linking events in the game causally, spatially, or temporally. Event order in *Ico* is temporally linked, and the player encounters the events in correct temporal order. Events are also temporally and causally connected at the same time.[12]

Again, this example is to demonstrate the steps that one takes in formal analysis, and it is not enough for a study. The study using this approach would need a research question. In this case, a possible research question could be how.

Concluding remarks

In addition to the language for describing primitives, we need a vocabulary to talk about the characteristics of gameplay. Zagal and Mateas (chapter 4) discuss about analyzing game time. Elias, Garfield, and Gutschera (2012) provide comprehensive look at how to describe gameplay such as heuristics available to players, complexity tree growth, randomness, and hidden information.

Although the main use of the formal analysis is to provide detailed description of primitives and principles of design, formal analysis can be used in conjunction with qualitative or quantitative approaches. Björk and Peitz (2007) present an example where formal analysis is combined with clustering. Pitkänen (chapter 8) argues about the importance of understanding the formal feature of the game when designing stimulated recall interview. We indicated above that formal analysis of gameplay works with formal

---

12.   A word of warning. Based on this case study, one should not extrapolate that games are like film in terms of narration. Instead, more research would be needed to understand how story interpretation works in relation to gameplay and when the story interpretation is likely to happen.

analysis of narration. In addition, one could use formal analysis in conjunction with critical theory and look at, for example, how race or gender is portrayed in the systemic level of game.

Recommended reading

- Björk, S. and Holopainen, J., 2005. *Patterns in game design*. Hingham: Charles River Media
- Elias, G.S., Garfield, R. and Gutschera, K.R., 2012. *Characteristics of games*. Cambridge: MIT Press
- Bizzocchi, J. and Tanenbaum, J., 2011. Well read: Applying close reading techniques to gameplay experiences. In: D. Davidson, ed., *Well played 3.0: Video games, value and meaning*. Pittsburgh, PA: ETC Press, pp.289–315.
- Fernández-Vara, C., 2014. *Introduction to game analysis*. New York: Routledge.

REFERENCES

Alexander, C., Ishikawa, S. and Silverstein, M., 1977. *A pattern language: Towns, buildings, construction*. New York: Oxford University Press.

Bell, C., 2005. *Art*. Project Guttenberg. Available at: <http://www.gutenberg.org/ebooks/16917>.

Bioware, 2010. *Mass Effect 2* [game]. Electronic Arts.

Bizzocchi, J. and Tanenbaum, J., 2011. Well read: Applying close reading techniques to gameplay experiences. In: D. Davidson, ed., *Well played 3.0: Video games, value and meaning*. Pittsburgh: ETC Press, pp.289–315.

Bordwell, D., 1985. *Narration in the fiction film*. Madison: University of Wisconsin Press.

Brathwaite, B. and Schreiber, I., 2009. *Challenges for game designers*. Boston: Course Technology.

Björk, S. and Holopainen, J., 2005. *Patterns In game design*. Hingham: Charles River Media.

Björk, S. and Peitz, J., 2007. Understanding pervasive games through gameplay design patterns. In: *Situated Play*. Tokyo. September. Available at: <http://www.digra.org/wp-content/uploads/digital-library/07311.47471.pdf>.

Campbell, J., 2008. *The hero with a thousand faces*. 3rd ed. Novato: New World Library.

Creswell, J.W., 2014. *Research design: qualitative, quantitative, and mixed method approaches*. 4th ed. Los Angeles: Sage.

Elias, G.S., Garfield, R. and Gutschera, K.R., 2012. *Characteristics of games*. Cambridge: MIT Press.

Fernández-Vara, C., 2014. *Introduction to game analysis*. New York: Routledge.

Frazer, J.G., 2009. *The golden bough: a study in magic and religion*. Reissued ed. Oxford: Oxford University Press.

Järvinen, A., 2008. *Games without frontiers: Theories and methods for game studies and design.* PhD. University of Tampere. Available at: <http://urn.fi/urn:isbn:978-951-44-7252-7>.

Lankoski, P., 2011. Player character engagement in computer games. *Games and Culture*, 6, pp.291–311. DOI= 10.1177/1555412010391088.

Linderoth, J. and Bennerstedt, U., 2007. This is not a door: an Ecological approach to computer games. In: *Situated Play.* Tokyo. September. Available at: <http://www.digra.org/wp-content/uploads/digital-library/07312.51011.pdf>.

Magie, E. and Darrow, C., 1933. *Monopoly* [game].

Morse, J.M., Barrett, M., Mayan, M., Olson, K. and Spiers, J., 2002. Verification strategies for establishing reliability and validity in qualitative research. *International Journal of Qualitative Methods*, 1(2).

Munsterberg, M., 2009. *Writing about art.* North Charleston: CreateSpace Independent Publishing Platform.

Myers, D., 2010. *Play redux: the form of computer games.* Ann Arbor: The University of Michigan Press.

Namco, 1980. *Pacman* [game]. Namco.

Pajitnov, A., 1984. *Tetris.* [game].

Popcap, n.d. *Plant vs Zombies Online* [game]. Popcap. Available at: <http://www.popcap.com/games/plants-vs-zombies/online>.

Propp, V.I., 1968. *Morphology of the folktale.* 2d ed. Austin: University of Texas Press.

Ravaja, N., Saari, T., Laarni, J., Kallinen, K., Salminen, M., Holopainen, J., and Järvinen, A., 2005. The psychophysiology of video gaming: Phasic emotional responses to game events. In: *Changing views: Worlds in play.* Vancouver. June. Available at: <http://www.digra.org/wp-content/uploads/digital-library/06278.36196.pdf />.

Salen, K. and Zimmerman, E., 2003. *Rules of play: Game design fundamentals.* Cambridge: The MIT Press.

TAITO, 1979. *Space Invaders* [game]. TAITO.

Team Ico, 2002. *Ico* [game]. SCEE.

4. Analyzing time in videogames

JOSÉ P. ZAGAL AND MICHAEL MATEAS

A number of theorists have analyzed temporal phenomena in games. Some have examined ways in which time playing a game relates to the events in a game (e.g., Benford and Giannachi, 2008; Bittanti, 2004; Eskelinen, 2001; Juul, 2005). Others have identified design challenges such as how to integrate multiple time scales in a single game (e.g., Barreteau and Abrami, 2007; Ford and McCormack, 2000), managing the dynamic complexity of a game (Burgess, 1995), or the pacing and synchronization of activities (Thavikulwat, 1996). Any formal analysis of videogames must account for temporality. One of the dominant experiential effects of videogames as a medium is the sense of agency induced by the player taking meaningful action, action that influences future events in the game. The very concepts of action, event and influence require an account of temporality in games—the myriad ways that temporal structure informs gameplay.

Consider the different temporal structures in *Pac-Man* (Namco, 1980), *Civilization* (Microprose, 1992) and *Animal Crossing* (Nintendo, 2002). In *Pac-Man*, when the player eats a power pellet, a special event is triggered; for a limited time *Pac-Man* can defeat the ghosts that previously had been chasing him. In *Civilization*, the number of turns the player has taken are mapped against a calendar. The game begins in 4000BC and can last through to the year 2100AD, although the player may experience this progression in a few hours. Finally, in *Animal Crossing*, the passage of time in the game is mapped to the passage of time in the real world. If the player plays at 3:00am, he will find his diurnal neighbours asleep while the nocturnal ones are anxious for interaction. As even these limited examples show, any account of game temporality must be able to describe a broad range of phenomena. Concepts such as duration, actions and reactions, timelines, turn-taking, and calendars are just some of the temporal elements commonly seen in videogames.

Our primary contribution is the introduction of a conceptual tool for analyzing videogame temporality, the temporal frame, and a methodology by which new temporal frames can be constructed as needed during analysis. The concept of a temporal frame has been employed by other researchers. For example, it is not uncommon in studies of videogame temporality to examine the relationship between the progression of events within the represented world of the game (what we would call gameworld time), and the progression of clock time as the player plays the game (what we would call real-world time). Many interesting relationships can be discerned between these different temporal flows. What we have done is to recognize the generality of temporal frames. Where previous work has defined specific temporal frames which are assumed to cover the phenomena of game temporality, we have developed a definition of temporal frame uncoupled from any specific event progression. This supports the ability to define many possible frames as needed to perform an analysis of the temporal phenomena in a given game, and also allows one to see the structure that is shared across all temporal frames (that is, why the domain of gameworld events and the domain of real-world events each constitute a flow of time). More broadly, our approach is uncoupled from specific types of videogames and can be useful not only for analyzing current commercial games, but also board games, educational games, serious games, simulations, and so forth.

Our approach is as follows. We first describe our adoption of a relationist definition of time, and discuss the relationship between this relationist definition and the subjective experience of time. This lays the groundwork for the next section, in which we define the concept of a temporal frame, and describe several specific temporal frames that are commonly useful in the analysis of games. Our goal is not to exhaustively enumerate all possible frames, but rather to introduce commonly useful ones as concrete examples. The real power of identifying temporal frames lies in analyzing the relationships between the different flows of time in the different frames. The next three sections give concrete examples from specific games of interesting relationships between frames, including a discussion of temporal anomalies and the explicit manipulation of time as a gameplay mechanic. We conclude with a discussion of related work.

Temporal structure and the experience of time

Our work is situated in the context of the *Game ontology project* (GOP), a hierarchical framework for describing structural elements of games (Zagal, et al., 2005). The GOP generally brackets experiential and cultural concerns. However, perfect bracketing is not possible; structural categories often make (implicit or explicit) reference to experiential categories. This results in a tension between the phenomenological (experiential) and structural (descriptive) accounts of time in games. In order to ease this problem, we chose to adopt a relationist view of time. For the relationist, discourse about time and temporal relations can be reduced to talking about events and the relationships between them. Without change (events), there can be no time. By adopting a relationist view of time, experiential concerns become manifest from the beginning, in the notion of state changes associated with events.

All talk of time can be reduced to talk about the relationships between events, and thus to relationships between state changes in the world. Discussing the temporality of a game requires that a player perceive events and relationships between them. Thus, an experiential category of perception is fundamental to a relationist account of time.[1]

Experiential categories also play a role in both temporal cognition and the socio-cultural references that reinforce a temporal fiction. Most of our understanding of time is a metaphorical version of our understanding of motion in space (Lakoff and Johnson, 1999). Common metaphors include time flowing past a stationary observer (e.g., time flies by) and an observer moving relative to stationary temporal locations (e.g., we have reached September). Experiments have shown that people switch metaphors

---

1. Videogames execute on a computational infrastructure, in which the fundamental state changes are the billions of computational state changes happening per second. Describing events at this granularity would achieve maximal precision, but be incredibly onerous. Further, players cannot perceive events at the level of individual instruction execution; such an analysis would fail to provide a description of game time relevant to players and designers. The execution of instructions in the processor is simply too removed from the player's experience.

depending on the priming provided by spatial experiences (Boroditsky and Ramscar, 2002). Thus, the player's experience of time can potentially be manipulated or influenced through game design via tasks that trigger specific forms of metaphoric temporal cognition. This experiential aspect can be partially captured in a structural framework by developing ontological categories for the various metaphoric relations between embodied spatial experience and temporal cognition.

Social-cultural references can create a temporal fiction within the game world. For instance, videogames can use either the passage of time, or real-world units or dates, to influence the perception of gameworld time. A game that takes place in the year 1492 mediates our understanding of the events that occur in the game. Playing a game where rounds are labeled as "years" also changes the player's experience of time. Inappropriate labels can break the player's suspension of disbelief. If the turns in *Civilization* were labeled as "days", the game would be unrealistic because the player could build the Great Pyramids in mere days. Finally, gameworld events may be experientially notable or significant through their participation in a narrative structure. In the beginning of *Half-Life* (Valve, 1998), the player moves a cart into a machine. This action triggers the disaster that plunges the Black Mesa research facility into chaos, and motivates the rest of the game. Viewed purely as a state change within the game world, pushing the cart is undistinguished from many other player-initiated state changes, like opening doors or firing weapons. However, this event is notable because the player understands that the game happens only because of that specific event. In our model, we capture the experiential aspects of socio-cultural references through a temporal frame we call fictive time.

A deep understanding of temporality in videogames requires multiple simultaneous perspectives, including the purely structural, as well as cognitive and socio-cultural aspects of time. Our relationist approach to time makes it natural to define multiple temporal frames in terms of different domains of reference events. Although the *Game ontology project* is primarily structural and descriptive, temporal frames provide a vehicle for recuperating socio-cultural references and (potentially) cognitive aspects into the model through the introduction of frames specific to those aspects. An analysis of game temporality then turns on identifying the temporal frames operating within a game, and the relationships that hold both within and between frames.

Temporal frames

When playing a game, say, *Kingdom Hearts II* (Square-Enix, 2006b), the player perceives many events. In the bedroom where the player is playing, the hands of a clock turn, street noises come in through the window, and the player's breath moves in and out. Her avatar navigates different game spaces, moving continuously within locations, between locations, or flying in spaceships between worlds. Additionally, she engages in a struggle against the Heartless and Organization XIII, piecing together the complex story that relates these enemies to the player character. Relationships between events constitute time; it follows that all of these events contribute to the temporality of the game. Rather than developing a single temporal domain consisting of the set of relationships between all these events, we have found it useful to identify specific event subsets, define a temporality relative to that subset, and then identify interactions between the times established by these different event subsets. In the example above, we would place the events happening in the bedroom (and the player's body) in one set, those involving the action of the player's avatar in another set, and those involving the story line in a third set. A set of events, along with the temporality induced by the relationships between events, constitutes a temporal frame.

Most games support multiple temporal frames that may overlap or occur sequentially. In the sequential case, different levels or player activities may establish distinct temporal frames. Some *Final Fantasy* games, for example, have distinct temporal frames depending on whether the player is involved in combat or exploration. In combat, gameplay is segmented by rounds; the player has time to decide what actions to perform while everything else is in stasis. When exploring, the game's temporality changes; inaction no longer prevents gameworld events from happening, requiring immediate actions and reactions from the player. When addressing the temporality of a game, it is thus necessary to identify and contextualize the distinct temporal frames that operate in the game.

We have identified four temporal frames commonly relevant for analyzing videogames: real-world time, gameworld time, coordination time, and fictive time.

We have identified four temporal frames commonly relevant Real-world time

Real-world time is established by the set of events taking place in the physical world around the player. These are commonly physical events happening in location in which the game is being played, as well as in the player's body. These events establish a reference temporality outside of the game. This notion is more expansive than play time, or the time taken to play a game (Juul, 2005). Play time addresses the duration of a play session, but does not account for other temporal frame interactions, such as events in a game that depend on specific labeled times in the real world, or on the passage of specific real world durations. For instance, in the web-based game Ikariam (Gameforge, 2008) players build and develop towns to create a mighty island empire. Someone playing the game for a few weeks of real-world time will likely not have more than a few hours of play time because gathering resources and developing buildings requires the passage of real-world time. So, a player may have to wait several days of real-world time for a building upgrade to be completed. Thus, a player actively plays for only a few minutes every day to make progress in the game.

The concepts of cycle and duration are two of the most fundamental relationships established between events in any temporal frame. A cycle is a sequence of repeating events, that is, a sequence of events in which a subset of the world repeatedly re-establishes the same state. Duration is measured by counting events in a cycle. We measure the length of time of a composite event, such as playing in a park, by beginning to count repeated events in some reference cycle at the event initiating playing in the park, stopping counting at the event terminating playing in the park—the number of repeated events we count is the duration of the composite event. In the real-world frame, such counting is facilitated by temporal measuring devices (clocks) that encapsulate reference cycles such as repeated pendulum swings or oscillations of a crystal.

Real-world durations (game world durations are analyzed below) often play a role in videogames. Many games establish their duration in terms of real-world time. A game might last ten minutes segmented in two halves of five minutes each. Alternately, a player may have an amount of time to meet a goal. Many games use a visual representation, like a clock or counter, to communicate a time-limit, literally displaying a reference cycle to the player. Triggers are another mechanism for relating to real-world durations. A trigger is an in-game event performed by the player that initiates a countdown of real-world duration.

An event may occur at the end of the countdown, or the game rules may change during the countdown. In *Alien vs Predator*, the player triggers the self-destruct sequence of a military complex. The player must then make her way to an escape pod before it's destroyed (Rebellion, 1994). As an example of the latter, eating a power pill in *Pac-Man* establishes a countdown during which Pac-Man can eat enemy ghosts. Triggered countdowns may be communicated explicitly via a clock (duration of the countdown is known), or implicitly, such as the ghosts turning blue during the triggered countdown in *Pac-Man* (exact duration of the countdown is unknown).

GAMEWORLD TIME

Gameworld time is established by the set of events taking place within the represented gameworld: this includes both events associated with abstract gameplay actions, as well as events associated with the virtual or simulated world (the literal gameworld) within which an abstract game may be embedded. Some games have multiple gameworld temporal frames defined by selecting subsets of gameworld events. For example, *Wolfenstein: Enemy Territory* (Splash Damage, 2003) has a different temporal frame for each mission. Gameworld time applies to abstract games as well. *Tetris* (Pajitnov, 1984) has a gameworld temporal frame established by event relationships such as the time limit for making decisions about piece placement (before it is placed for you), or the triggering of a new piece falling upon the placement of the previous one.

The gameworld frame can establish its own notions of cycle and duration that are potentially independent of cycles and durations in the real-world frame. For example, many games have a day and night cycle that establishes a new duration measurement in terms of gameworld days. Gameworld days may be used to add atmosphere to a game (but not participate in the abstract rule system), to establish a time limit (which may have variable real-world duration since the passage of days can be affected by player actions), or may play a role in gameplay rules. In *Knight Lore* (Ultimate, 1984), due to the player-controlled avatar's transforming from human to werewolf, the day and night cycle directly affects gameplay. Cycles are also used to describe the behavior of other entities in the gameworld, such as enemy guards who might endlessly walk a patrol path.

COORDINATION TIME

Coordination time is established by the set of events that coordinate the actions of multiple players (human or AI) and possibly in-game agents. Coordination events are the markers that regulate gameplay through moments of synchronization and coordination. These events typically establish periods of play, limit availability of the gameworld, and/or delay the effects of in-game actions. For example, rounds are often used as a basic unit of play. The number of rounds played can trigger in-game events (e.g., reinforcements arrive on round three) or serve as a game goal (e.g., win before round five or best of three rounds). Turn-taking, on the other hand, limits the availability of the game to one player at a time: you only act when it's your turn. Rounds and turn-taking often, but not always, appear together. In Poker, players are dealt cards each round and then take turns placing their bets. In *Monopoly* (Darrow, 1934), players take turns rolling the dice and moving their game piece, but there is no notion of rounds. Sometimes the effects, or resolution, of the player's actions are not immediate. In tick-based games, like *Age of Wonders* (Triumph Studios, 1999), players act simultaneously, but need to wait until everyone completes their actions before a new round may begin (Elverdam and Aarseth, 2007). In *Poker*, players wait until the betting is done before the winner can be determined. These basic building blocks for coordinating and synchronizing appear in many other combinations.

Other games use an abstract timeline for organizing the order of player or character actions. Depending on in-game attributes such as character speed, some characters may act multiple times before slower opponents. Actions can also be assigned a cost in action points (Björk and Holopainen, 2005), with points regained in succeeding turns. Slow or lengthy actions may require a player to wait many turns before they can be carried out.

FICTIVE TIME

Fictive time is established through the application of socio-cultural labels to a subset of events. Labeling the rounds in a game as days or years changes a player's expectations of the granularity of action that can be accomplished in a round. Such expectations are established by activating temporal schemata in a player's mind, that is, cognitive scripts detailing default event sequences and relative durations. *Guitar Hero*'s (Harmonix, 2005) "career mode" relates in-game progress with the temporal schema of a rock star's career path: rock stars start as unknowns playing in small run-down establishments, gradually playing larger venues, and becoming more famous. Many kinds of temporal schemata exist. *Guitar Hero*'s career mode is cultural, while others, such as schemata of activity/recuperation, relate to biological cycles. For instance, characters may have to rest or consume food every so often in order to recover energy.

Representational elements strengthen the fictive frame; labeling the rounds as days or years in a game like *Chess* fails to establish a fictive frame. If a game includes additional representations that refer to socio-cultural labels, such as calendars, day and night cycles, and visual representations that correspond to changes in seasons or centuries, a fictive frame can be established and reinforced.

Fictive temporal frames are also established by association with a historical narrative. Crogan's analysis of *Combat Flight Simulator 2* (Microsoft Game Studios, 2000) describes its gameplay "as play in and with a reconstruction of historical temporality drawn from the narrative modes of more traditional media such as historical discourse, historical archives, war films, and documentaries" (Crogan, 2003). The campaign mode of this game features missions based on conflicts of the Pacific theatre of World War II such that the fictive temporal frame in this game fosters player immersion via historical authenticity.

Games may contain narrated event sequences. We account for this by borrowing temporalities described by narratology and employing them as specific subtypes of the general category of fictive frame. Specifically, narratology establishes a distinction between the chronological order of a series of events (story time), how these events may be narrated (discourse time), and the time of narration (narrative time) (e.g., Bordwell, 1985). Collectively, these are the narrative frames. Narratology identifies these co-existing times and describes how the reader or viewer must actively reconstruct story time from what was represented in the discourse, for example, reconstructing the story event sequence from a discourse sequence that makes use of narrative effects such as flashbacks, flashforwards.

Cut-scenes, character dialogue, flashbacks and other elements are often used to establish the narrative frames. The first-person shooter *XIII* (Ubisoft, 2003) includes levels with playable flashbacks depicting situations encountered by the player character prior to the main narrative of the game. Differences in audio, visual style, and character dialogue help the player understand she is playing a flashback of the main storyline. Narrative can also be established across multiple games. *Half-Life*'s (Valve, 1998) expansions, *Half-Life: Opposing Force* (Valve, 1999) and *Half-Life: Blue Shift* (Valve, 2001), are noteworthy because their fictive temporal frame situates them as occurring simultaneously with the original game. In *Opposing Force*, the player controls a soldier charged with neutralizing Gordon Freeman, the protagonist of the original game. *Blue Shift* presents a third perspective of the Black Mesa disaster, this time through the eyes of a security guard. The player deduces the relationship between the expansions and the original game thanks to shared events, locations, and fleeting glimpses and references of Gordon Freeman's exploits.

Using temporal frames for analysis

We have defined the concept of a temporal frame and described several frames that are commonly useful in the analysis of games (see table 1). The power of identifying temporal frames lies in analyzing the relationships between the different flows of time in the different frames. In the following four sub-sections we give concrete examples from specific games of interesting relationships between frames. First, we explore some phenomena that occur from the interactions of the temporal frames we have identified. For example, we discuss the distinction made between real-time and turn-based games. Following that, we analyze why some games have a sense of temporality that is inconsistent, contradictory, or dissonant with our experience of real-world time. We call these phenomena temporal anomalies and identify some of the more common ones. Next, we examine games with explicit support for player manipulation of temporal frames. From a game design perspective, player agency over a temporal frame offer novel options for gameplay while also introducing additional temporal anomalies. Finally, we illustrate how you can define new temporal frames in order to gain additional insights.

Frame	Definition	Relevant Concepts
Real-world	Real-world time is established by the set of events taking place in the physical world around the player.	Cycle, duration, countdown, trigger
Gameworld	Gameworld time is established by the set of events taking place within the represented gameworld.	Cycle, duration, countdown, trigger
Coordination	Coordination time is established by the set of events that coordinate the actions of multiple players (human or AI) and possibly in-game agents.	Rounds, turn-taking, tick-based, action points
Fictive	Fictive time is established through the application of socio-cultural labels to a subset of events.	Temporal schemata, socio-cultural labels, Story time, narrative time, discourse time

Table 1. Summary of common temporal frames.

INTERACTIONS BETWEEN TEMPORAL FRAMES

Videogames commonly possess multiple temporal frames. Common frame relationships include sequential frames (e.g., different frames for different levels), and co-existing frames (e.g., fictive and gameworld often co-exist in a game). It is important to describe these frames and how they interact. For instance, *Animal Crossing* contextualizes its fictive time with respect to that of the real world. When the player first starts the game, she must enter the current real-world date and time. From that moment, the gameworld tracks time just as a clock in the real world would. The synchronization is such that by not playing on December 25, the player misses all the Christmas day in-game activities. The game also discourages the manipulation of the GameCube's system clock. Whenever a change is detected, the player is chastised by Mr. Resetti, a grumpy mole, for her "temporal manipulation". *Animal Crossing* exhibits a more nuanced relationship between fictive time and the other temporal frames than is commonly found in games.

REAL-TIME AND TURN-BASED

A common temporal distinction made when discussing games is that of *real-time* vs. *turn-based* games. This distinction, often treated as a simple binary, masks a number of related phenomena resulting from the interaction of multiple frames. The theoretical structure of multiple temporal frames allows us to unpack the primitive, binary distinction into a more nuanced collection of related phenomena.

As a player interacts with the gameworld, she physically manipulates a controller (real-world control events) in order to cause events in the gameworld. When, the player is allowed to cause gameworld events, we say that the gameworld is available. When no perceived delay between the control manipulation event (e.g., button press) and the corresponding gameworld event (e.g., character jump) exists, her actions are immediate. In *Pac-Man*, the gameworld is available because the player is always allowed to move Pac-Man, and he moves immediately since there is no delay between input and action.

At times, perceptible events in the real world may not correlate with gameworld events, resulting in a sluggish or non-responsive experience. To the player, the experience does not seem real-time because of a lack of immediacy that was not part of the game's design. For instance, playing over a high latency network can result in lag: an extension of the time between a player's input and a perceived gameworld effect. Some games explicitly use action delays. In the first-person shooter *XIII*, a noticeable real-time delay exists between reloading a weapon and being ready to fire it again, decreasing the immediacy of reload actions. Here, the action delay emulates the physical action of reloading a weapon. However, if there such delays existed for every action, *XIII* would suffer from a loss of immediacy, and would feel less real-time.

If, in the coordination frame, a game makes use of turn-taking, then the gameworld is not always available (Björk and Holopainen, 2005). This loss of availability is also seen in tick-based games, like *Age of Wonders*, where, although they can act simultaneously, players must wait for others in order to continue playing (Triumph Studios, 1999). Loss of availability makes games feel less real-time as well. *Neverwinter Nights* (BioWare, 2002) mitigates this by allowing players to plan and schedule actions at any time. The game has a queued combat system where "you can select special combat actions for your character [...], and these are entered into your combat queue to be performed in the coming round". Players can queue multiple actions, but these are still executed one-per-round and transitions between rounds are determined by the passage of real-time.

Games like *Fallout Tactics* (Micro Forte, 2001) limit the amount of real-time available during rounds. Here, a player's inaction is penalized when it exceeds a certain amount of real-world time. Other games, like *Mario & Luigi: Partners in Time* (Alpha Dream, 2005), although primarily turn-based, allow players to gain bonuses by successfully synchronizing button presses in real-time. These games manage to maintain a certain degree of availability despite being turn-based.

A gameworld has liveliness if gameworld events continue to occur even when the player is not actively participating in the world (Gingold, 2003). Liveliness also contributes to the sense of a game being real-time. When the gameworld is not lively the player may stop taking action for indefinite periods of real-world time and have no gameworld events occur during this period. A game with high availability but no liveliness has some, but not all, of the temporal features we typically associate with a real-time game. *Final Fantasy XII* (Square-Enix, 2006a) lets the player choose between two modes: active and wait. In active mode, the game does not pause while the player issues commands. In wait mode, the player has unlimited time to choose their next move. Here, liveliness is decided by the player!

We argue that the common distinction of real-time vs. turn-based results from a number of distinct interactions between the gameworld, coordination, and real-world temporal frames. Identifying these distinct interactions helps gain a more nuanced understanding of the phenomena that are masked by this binary distinction.

EMBEDDED FRAMES

Temporal frames may appear sequentially, overlap and coexist. They are also often embedded in each other. This occurs with games included within games, such as the case of mini-games. An embedded game may have a distinct temporality that is still related to that of the main game. In *Shenmue* (Sega, 2000), Ryu can visit an arcade and play fully functional versions of classic arcade games. The temporality of the embedded games is distinct, and independent, of *Shenmue*'s. However, the time spent playing them correlates with time spent in the main gameworld. Players can play the arcade games to pass time in the main gameworld since certain places or events only became active at specific gameworld times. In contrast, in *Grand Theft Auto: San Andreas* (Rockstar, 2004), when playing the embedded arcade game Duality, time in the gameworld is on hold. Playing Duality is equivalent to freezing the outside game and playing another one. The temporality of both games can be explained using the notion of embedded temporal frames, the essential difference between them being how they relate to each other.

TEMPORAL ANOMALIES

The relationships between different, often co-existing, temporal frames within one game can result in a sense of temporality that is inconsistent, contradictory, or dissonant with our experience of real-world time. We call these relationships temporal anomalies (see table 2).

Common Temporal Anomalies
Temporal bubble
Temporal warping
Non-uniform temporality
Hardware related anomalies

Table 2. *Common Temporal Anomalies*

Temporal bubbles can occur in the sequential transition between temporal frames. If a game begins in temporal frame A, continues with B, and then goes back to A, a temporal bubble exists when, from the perspective of frame A, no time has passed during the activity in frame B. In *Grand Theft Auto III* (*GTAIII*) (Rockstar, 2001), the gameworld has a day-night cycle that advances as the player's avatar performs actions. However, whenever the player enters a building, time in the outside gameworld stops, regardless of how much real-world, fictive or gameworld time was spent inside the building. In *GTAIII* building interiors have their own gameworld time that is unrelated to that of the outside. Many CRPGs also have temporal bubbles between the temporal frame of combat and general navigation and movement. In combat, regardless of how many rounds a fight lasts, when the player returns to the regular world, no time has passed. Sometimes these anomalies are referred to explicitly in the games' narrative. In *Legend of Zelda: Ocarina of Time* (Nintendo, 2003), when the player first enters Hyrule market, he is informed that while in there, time does not pass outside.

Another common anomaly is temporal warping. This occurs when at least two temporal frames overlap and an inconsistency exists between them. In order to eliminate the inconsistency, it is necessary to warp one temporal system (by compressing, expanding, etc.) to accommodate the other. For instance, in *GTAIII*, it takes roughly the same amount of time to perform in-game actions like shooting or driving, as it would to perform them in the real world. However, the game has a day and night cycle that only lasts a few minutes of real world time. In-game actions take a proportionally longer fraction of a gameworld day to perform than they do in the real world. This anomaly also appears in games with a real-world time limit that is inconsistent with in-game time keeping. Juul describes a mission in *GTAIII* lasting 20 minutes of gameworld time, yet requiring 49 seconds of real-world time, with both times displayed simultaneously on screen (Juul, 2005). This illustrates temporal warping between the gameworld and real-world frames.

A game's temporality is non-uniform when the passage of time is unevenly distributed across different temporal segments (coordination units). For example, consider a game segmented into rounds. If, according to the fictive temporal frame, the duration of each round varies, a non-uniform temporality exists. In *Civilization*, each round initially corresponds to 200 years in the fictive frame. Towards the end of the game, rounds correspond to only one year. This can create an experience of temporal compression where events towards the end of the game are perceived to occur more slowly (it takes longer for a year to pass), despite the fact that in terms of coordination time, no changes occurred (a round is still a round).

Usually the hardware frame is irrelevant to player experience since hardware events are not directly perceived. Occasionally, however, the relationship between gameworld time and real-world time is not uniform across different hardware configurations. Many older videogames are unplayable on faster computers because the amount of real-world time taken by gameworld events directly depends on processor speed (the main game loop is not throttled). On faster computers, these games are unplayable because game entities move too fast. Another anomaly, slowdown, occurs when the complexity of the gameworld exceeds the capacity of hardware resources. In such cases, typically caused when too many objects are on the screen, gameworld events occur in slow motion (take longer in real-world time than usual). Similarly, some players experience network lag that can result in them observing their enemies zooming around them while they can hardly move at all.

Time as gameplay

Some games allow the player to manipulate and affect the temporal frames we have described (see table 3). In these cases, temporality is used as an element of gameplay with the game's temporality defined in part by the player's possible actions. Player agency over a temporal frame can offer novel options for gameplay as well as introduce additional temporal anomalies.

Temporality as Gameplay
Manipulating coordination time
Pausing, starting, and stopping gameworld time
Manipulating the relation between gameworld and real-world frames
Manipulating the relation between gameworld frames
Manipulating the fictive frame

Table 3. Common forms of temporal manipulation

MANIPULATING COORDINATION TIME

Coordination time is established by the events that coordinate the actions of multiple players (human or AI). Games that allow players to manipulate said coordination provide a form of temporal manipulation. For instance, some traditional board and card games allow players to pass, or forgo their turn at play. Similarly, players may be penalized with the loss of a turn or rewarded with additional turns. Manipulations that alter the order of play are essentially about manipulating coordination time. In the board game *Power Grid* (Friese, 2004), the order of play is determined by the current standing in the game and players may strategically try to position themselves so as not to play first.

These concepts also appear in games where player's actions are not directly coordinated (such as in turn-taking). When a player-controlled character is killed in *Team Fortress 2* (Valve, 2007), the player must wait a certain amount of real-world time before she may re-enter (re-spawn in) the game. Meanwhile, the other players continue playing and gameworld time moves along as usual. From the perspective of the player however, she must lose a turn, where turn is equal in this case to an interval of real-world time. In *Wolfenstein: Enemy Territory* (Splash Damage, 2003) players using the medic role can revive characters that have been killed. When killed, a player has the option of "tapping out" and waiting for the next re-spawn interval, or waiting in-game hoping a medic will revive him. Thus, the amount of time spent removed from play is variable, depending on how quickly medics in the vicinity respond.

MANIPULATING GAMEWORLD TIME

Temporarily suspending, or pausing, gameworld time (relative to real-world time), is another common temporal manipulation. The idea is that no events occur in the gameworld while gameworld time is paused. It can be used for gameplay reasons such as allowing the player to perform gameworld actions while the game is paused. Many computer RPG games allow players to access inventory screens and make changes to their characters while the game is paused. Upon un-pausing, the changes come into effect immediately. Similarly, players can often effect changes to the gameworld even as it is paused, for example by healing wounded characters. This notion is not unique to videogames. Some professional sports allow for a time-out that effectively suspends gameworld time allowing coaches to plan or communicate strategies and instructions. In other cases, gameworld time is suspended while players assume certain positions on the field, such as when executing a free-kick in football (soccer).

Players may also have agency while gameworld time is suspended and lose it when it is not. For instance the player may have to organize the gameworld's entities so that when gameworld time is started, gameworld events occur such that the game's goals are met. *The Incredible Machine* and *ChuChu Rocket!* (SonicTeam, 1999) are examples of this. The object of *ChuChu Rocket!* is to guide mice around a board into goal areas by placing tiles with directional arrows on the floor. Gameplay centers on the appropriate placement of the tiles because, when gameworld time is started, the player can only watch as the mice make their way to the goals hopefully avoiding any cats.

The relationship between gameworld time and real-world time is also often manipulated. Sometimes this is accomplished via hardware. The NES Advantage controller for the Nintendo Entertainment System console includes a special button labeled "Slow". Players are instructed to "use this feature to get through difficult portions of games where the action gets too fast" (Nintendo, 1987). The relation between gameworld time and real-world time sometimes changes across different hardware configurations (see hardware related anomalies above). However, here we are interested in game mechanics where the player is provided control over the frame's relationship. For example, players may alter the ratio of events in the real-world with that of the gameworld. If an event occurs in the gameworld every six seconds of real-world time, the player may effect a change so that it occurs every three seconds. In this way, the player has accelerated the gameworld's time (relative to the real-world). Conversely, if the gameworld event where to occur every 12 seconds, the gameworlds' time would have been decelerated. This is like imagining that the gameworld has an internal clock and the player can make it tick faster (or slower), thus speeding up (or slowing down) all of the events in the gameworld relative to the real-world. *Sim City 4* (EA, 2003) provides three settings of simulation speed controls that allow the player to change the speed at which time passes in the gameworld. In *Max Payne* (Remedy Entertainment, 2001), the player can activate "bullet-time", a form of deceleration of gameworld time with respect to real-world time, that allows Max to perform acrobatic combat maneuvers. Since the speed with which the player can move the mouse/cursor remains unchanged, it is easier to aim. This allows the player to be more effective in dispatching opponents in situations that would prove insurmountable in regular time.

A similar form of manipulation exists when players can restore a gameworld's temporal frame to a previous state. Often, such as in *Prince of Persia: Sands of Time* (Ubisoft Montreal, 2003), this manipulation is represented as if gameworld events were recorded on a linear medium like videotape. Here, the prince has the ability to reverse time. While reversing time, all sounds and previous action play backwards, and the gameworld accurately resets to an earlier state (Atkins, 2007). If the prince was struck by an enemy during this period, the health he lost is returned, or a recently destroyed bridge will repair.

The relation between co-existing gameworld temporal frames can also be manipulated. For instance, the player may affect the ratio of events in one gameworld temporal frame with respect to those of another such as when using items that slow down or freeze time only for enemies.

RELATIONS BETWEEN GAMEWORLD FRAMES

Some games present a unique type of overlapping frames where gameworld time, or a subset of gameworld events, from a players' earlier actions in the game overlaps the current gameworld time. Many racing games allow players to race against a visual representation of an earlier version of themselves playing the same game. This visual representation, or ghost racer (ghost player in the context of non-racing games), does not exist in, or affect the gameworld in which it is represented in any meaningful way. So, a player cannot ram a ghost racer, for example (Sandifer, 2006). However, not all the game-world events from the player's earlier play are necessarily overlapped. Gameworld events associated to the interface are typically not included. In other cases, the ghost player, may have an effect on the current player. *Elite Beat Agents* features a multiplayer mode that allows a single player to play against a saved replay that can hinder the current player by making the target markers smaller (iNis, 2006).

More recently, game designers have begun to explore these overlapping temporal frames by adding gameplay significance to the interaction between earlier and current gameplay. Games such as *Braid*, *Cursor*10*, and *Timebot* explore what would it mean if your ghost could interact with you? *Cursor*10* instructs the player to "Click stairs and move" while also cryptically hinting that to be successful, a player must "Cooperate by oneself?!" (Ishii, 2008). In *Cursor*10* the player must reach Floor 16 by finding and clicking on (up) stairs in each room. The player has 10 attempts (or cursors). Each cursor only exists for a limited amount of real-world time. Once that time runs out, the player starts over with the next cursor. However, all the earlier cursors also appear. However, their actions (the player's actions earlier in the game) have an effect in the "present". For instance, some levels have buttons that, when held down, make the stairs appear. In these levels the player must "use up" part of a cursor's lifespan so that when he reaches the same floor, his future cursor can click on the stairs and gain access to the next floor.

MANIPULATING THE FICTIVE FRAME

Sometimes, the fictive frame allows for the player-controlled character to manipulate time. Broadly speaking, these games' narratives incorporate notions of time travel, manipulation of space-time and similar concepts. Usually, the temporal manipulation is framed under the notion of requiring the player to change events in a fictive past so as to affect the fictive future. Games that allow manipulations of the fictive frame include *Chrono Trigger*, *Shadow of Memories*, *Day of the Tentacle*, *Legend of Zelda: Majora's Mask*, and *Time Hollow*.

In *Shadow of Memories* (*Shadow of Destiny* in the USA), the player controls Eike Kusch (Konami, 2001). The game begins as Eike is murdered and the player must prevent his murder in the fictive present while investigating the mystery surrounding it. Over the course of the game the player visits four eras. Eike's survival in the present requires doing things in earlier eras that have an effect on later ones. For example, in 1980 Eike receives an egg clock. If Eike travels to 1908, he can give the egg clock to the owner of a bar. This causes the owner to start a hobby: collecting oval shaped objects. This hobby is then shared by his descendant in the fictive present. When Eike gives the current bar owner another egg, in gratitude he gives Eike a frying pan that ultimately saves his life.

A fictive frame may also contextualize, explain, or otherwise rationalize gameworld events. In his analysis of *Prince of Persia: Sands of Time*, Davidson explains how (most) of the game is situated in the context of the Prince narrating a "tale like none you have ever heard" to a young woman (2008). In keeping with the idea that (most) of the game is a narration of events, when the player is not able to successfully complete an acrobatic feat, "the Prince speaks in voiceover, saying 'Wait, wait [...] that is not how it happened [...] Now, where was I?' and you are reset to the spot right before you accidentally leapt to your demise." (Davidson, 2008). Thus, unsuccessful gameplay events never happened in the fictive frame, they are simply mistakes on the part of the storyteller who mis-remembers what occurred. Once the player successfully completes most of the game, there is a twist wherein, due to "saving the day", everything the player has done in the gameworld is "whirled away within the context of the story" (Davidson, 2008). The character Farah, who had accompanied the prince throughout most of the game, turns out to be the young woman who is being told the story of the events that no longer have happened.

Many games incorporate many (or all) of the temporal manipulations we have discussed. In *Blinx: The Time Sweeper* (Artoon, 2002), the titular character is an anthropomorphic cat dedicated to the locating and correcting temporal glitches throughout the universe. Blinx's raison d'être is manipulating the fictive temporal frame. Blinx wields a device providing him with six different temporal manipulation controls: REW, FF, Pause, REC, Slow and Retry. The REW control, for example, causes gameworld time to run backwards for everything in the gameworld except Blinx. Interestingly, elements previously destroyed can be restored regardless of how long ago they were destroyed. The REC control is used in two phases. The first phase consists of 10 seconds of real-world time during which Blinx is invulnerable to all damage and can move normally. After that, the gameworld and Blinx are rewound by 10 seconds. This temporal frame is then overlapped with the current one. The actions taken by Blinx during the recording are represented by a green ghost that has an effect on the current gameworld. Thus, the player solves puzzles normally requiring two characters.

Using temporal frames for game analysis

One of the contributions of the temporal frames approach is that different temporal frames can (and should) be defined. For instance temporal frames can be used to define and isolate specific phenomenon in a game we want to analyze. For example, consider the cooperative zombie first-person shooter game *Left 4 Dead* (*L4D*) (Valve, 2008). One of the games' design innovations is the AI Director; a system designed to control the pacing and player tension in the game by, among other things, placing enemies and items in varying positions as well as determining when and where key events such as encounters with special enemies will take place (Booth, 2009b). The Director arranges events in order to increase tension while allowing for lulls in between because this helps create a dramatic and exhilarating experience of mounting tension.

From a player's perspective, what elements does *L4D* use in order to help create a sense of mounting tension and how can we describe their temporality? How does *L4D* achieve this while providing an experience for four human players who are doing different things in the game? For the purposes of this limited analysis, we could focus on examining the game's interface and explore which events are communicated to the player and how they are presented. We define the Interface Frame as the set of events that take place in the game's user interface. We argue that the relationship between events in this frame and the gameworld frame play of *L4D* are central to creating intense play experience and promoting player collaboration. In order to perform this analysis we could make two lists of events. The first list includes events that take place in the game's interface and the second list would include events that occur in the game world. We could then try to describe how events in each of those frames relate to each other.

In the game it is possible for players to be rendered helpless and thus require assistance from others. For example, they may be dangling from a ledge or incapacitated on the ground. So, we could consider the following gameworld events: player is helpless (requiring assistance from another player), collaborator begins to assist helpless player, and helpless player is no longer helpless (see figure 1). Next, we examine the events that occur in the interface. When players assist each other, both see an indicator in the middle of the screen that describes the action being carried out, as well as a progress bar that slowly fills up. This serves as an indicator that the assistive action does not occur immediately (compared to, say, picking up ammunition). It also gives players a sense of how much longer, in real world time, before a task is completed. Additionally, since the bar is sometimes reset, for example when attacked, the player is informed that that task is one that is interruptible.

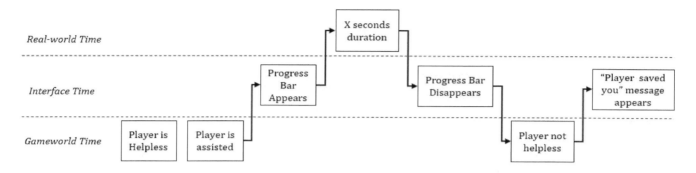

Figure 1. Events related to player being helpless.

The notability of certain gameworld events is reinforced by their appearance in the game's interface. For example, when a player kills a special zombie, a message appears on-screen indicating who killed the monster as well as its type (e.g., "Francis killed Smoker"). If another character saves you, this is also highlighted via the interface ("Francis saved you"). The interface is also used to inform the players of upcoming gameworld events. For instance, the future appearance of the special zombie "The Tank" is preceded by its distinctive non-diegetic music (Booth, 2009a).

Players can also communicate via a standard text-based chat interface with messages that scrolling upwards. In *L4D*, recent messages appear at the bottom and are also brighter. Older messages eventually fade out and disappear. Similarly, when a player is attacked, a red arrow appears on screen indicating the general direction of the attack. Since the arrows eventually fade, the interface also communicates how recent a particular attack was. We can thus see how the game's interface and in particular the Interface Frame mediate the player's experience by serving as a record of the temporality of past events in the gameworld, foreshadowing future gameworld events, and can also recording events that are outside the gameworld.

The above analysis is but a sample of some of the questions and issues that could be examined. A more diligent examination of, say, what happens when a player is rendered helpless, might include additional events and articulate more clearly whether certain events occur simultaneously (e.g., Is the player no longer helpless as soon as the progress bar disappears?), and how the relate to each other (e.g., How long does the "Player saved you" message remain on screen in real-world time?). Hopefully, this serves as an illustration of how this approach can be useful.

Conclusion

Multiple authors are converging on theories of game temporality that involve characterizing event relationships between multiple, simultaneous levels or frames. This indicates that this is a fruitful and productive approach to game temporality. A particular contribution of our paper is an abstract, relationist characterization of temporal frames that supports analysts in creating new frames as they become useful in analysis and design. Much of what makes game temporality unique is the presence of multiple temporal frames and the interactions between them. Temporal frames allow the handling of disparate temporal phenomena under a unifying theoretical framework. Although theorists have introduced temporal categories similar to some of our specific temporal frames, this prior work has treated temporal categories as black boxes, defined once and for all, not viewed as instances of a more general concept. Our work provides a generalization of all event-based frameworks for analyzing game temporality. This framework supports the definition of new temporal frames as needed while performing analyses of specific games, highlighting the importance of analyzing the relationships between the different flows of time present in multiple temporal frames.

Further reading

- Lainema, T., 2008. Theorizing on the treatment of time in simulation gaming. *Simulation & Gaming*, 41(2). DOI=10.1177/1046878108319870.
- Nitsche, M., 2007. Mapping time in videogames. In: A. Baba, ed., *Situated play*. Tokyo. September. pp.145–152. Available at: <http://www.digra.org/wp-content/uploads/digital-library/07313.10131.pdf>.
- Tychsen, A. and Hitchens, M., 2009. Game time: Modeling and analyzing time in multiplayer and massively multiplayer games. *Games and Culture*, 4(2), pp.170–201. DOI= 10.1177/1555412008325479.
- Wei, H., Bizzocchi, J. and Calvert, T., 2010. Time and space in digital game storytelling. *Int. J. Comput. Games Technol.* 2010. DOI=10.1155/2010/897217.

Acknowledgements

This chapter is an abridged version of an article published previously as (Zagal and Mateas, 2010). Please refer to the original article for a more detailed discussion of related work on time and videogames.

References

Alpha Dream, 2005. *Mario & Luigi: Partners in Time* [game]. Nintendo.

Artoon, 2002. *Blinx: The Time Sweeper* [game]. Microsoft Game Studios.

Atkins, B., 2007. Killing time: Time past, time present and time future in Prince of Persia: The Sands of Time. In: T. Krzywinska and B. Atkins, eds., *Videogame, player, text*. Manchester: Manchester University Press, pp.237–253.

Barreteau, O. and Abrami, G., 2007. Variable time scales, agent-based models, and role-playing games: The PIEPLUE river basin management game. *Simulation & Gaming*, 38, pp.364–381.

Benford, S. and Giannachi, G., 2008. Temporal Trajectories in Shared Interactive Narratives. In: *Proceedings of the 26th annual SIGCHI Conference in Human Factors in Computing Systems (CHI 2008)*, pp.73–82.

BioWare, 2002. *Neverwinter Nights* [game]. Atari.

BioWare, 2009. *Neverwinter Nights FAQ v.4.0.* Available at: <http://nwn.bioware.com/about/faq.html>.

Bittanti, M., 2004. Tempo di gioco, tempo in gioco C, *cube*, 5.

Björk, S. and Holopainen, J., 2005. *Patterns in game design.* Hingham: Charles River Media.

Booth, M., 2009a. *Replayable cooperative game design: Left 4 Dead.* Available at: < http://www.valvesoftware.com/publications/2009/ GDC2009_ReplayableCooperativeGameDesign_Left4Dead.pdf >.

Booth, M., 2009b. *The AI systems of Left 4 Dead.* Available at: < http://www.valvesoftware.com/publications/2009/ai_systems_of_l4d_mike_booth.pdf >.

Bordwell, D., 1985. *Narration in the fiction film.* London: Methuen & Co.

Boroditsky, L. and Ramscar, M., 2002. The roles of body and mind in abstract thought. *Psychological Science*, 13(2), pp.185–189.

Burgess, T.F., 1995. Cycle time, decisions, and complexity in business simulation/games. *Simulation & Gaming*, 26(3), pp.376–383.

Crogan, P., 2003. Gametime: History, narrative, and temporality in combat flight simulator 2. In: M.J.P. Wolf and B. Perron, eds., *The videogames theory reader.* New York: Routledge, pp.275–301.

Darrow, C., 1934. *Monopoly* [game].

Davidson, D., 2008. Well played: Interpreting Prince of Persia – The Sands of Time. *Games and Culture*, 3(3–4), pp.356–386.

EA, 2003. SimCity 4 deluxe edition user's manual.

Elverdam, C. and Aarseth, E., 2007. Game classification and game design: Construction through critical analysis. *Games and Culture*, 2(1), pp.3–22.

Eskelinen, M., 2001. Towards computer game studies. *Proceedings of SIGGRAPH 2001, Art Gallery, Art and Culture Papers*, pp.83–87.

Ford, D.N. and McCormack, D.E.M., 2000. Effects of time scale focus on system understanding in decision support systems. *Simulation & Gaming*, 31(3), pp.309–330.

Friese, F., 2004. *Power Grid* [game]. Rio Rancho: Rio Grande Games.

Gameforge, 2008. *Ikariam* [game]. Karlsruhe: Gameforge Productions. Available at: <www.ikariam.org>.

Gingold, C., 2003. *Miniature gardens & magic crayons: Games, spaces, & worlds.* MS. Georgia Institute of Technology. Available at: <http://www.slackworks.com/~cog/writing/thesis/toc.php>.

Harmonix, 2005. *Guitar Hero* [game]. Cambridge: Red Octane.

iNis, 2006. *Elite Beat Agents* [game]. Nintendo.

Ishii, Y., 2008. *Cursor*10* [game]. Available at: <http://www.nekogames.jp/mt/2008/01/cursor10.html>.

Juul, J., 2005. *Half-real*. Cambridge: The MIT Press.

Konami, 2001. *Shadow of Destiny* [game]. Konami.

Lakoff, G. and Johnson, M., 1999. *Philosophy in the Fleshflesh*. New York: Basic Books.

Micro Forte, 2001. *Fallout Tactics: Brotherhood of Steel* [game]. 14 Degrees East.

Microprose, 1992. *Sid Meier's Civilization* [game]. Hunt Valley: Microprose Software Inc.

Microsoft Game Studios, 2000. *Microsoft Combat Flight Simulator 2* [game]. Microsoft.

Namco, 1980. *Pac-Man* [game]. Franklin Park:IL: Midway Mfg. Co.

Nintendo, 1987. *NES Advantage instruction manual*. Nintendo.

Nintendo, 2002. *Animal Crossing* [game]. Nintendo.

Nintendo, 2003. *The Legend of Zelda: Ocarina of Time / Master Quest.* [game]. Redmond: Nintendo.

Pajitnov, A., 1984. *Tetris* [Game]. Moscow: Soviet Academy of Sciences.

Rebellion, 1994. *Alien vs Predator* [game]. Atari.

Remedy Entertainment, 2001. *Max Payne* [game]. Espoo, Finland: Gathering of Developers.

Rockstar, 2001. *Grand Theft Auto III* [game]. Rockstar Games.

Rockstar, 2004. *Grand Theft Auto: San Andreas* [game]. Rockstar Games.

Sandifer, P., 2006. Player epsilon: Demoing a new hermeneutic for games. In: *2nd Annual University of Florida Game Studies Conference*. Gainesville. April. Available at: <http://www.gameology.org/alien_other/player_epsilon>.

Sega, 2000. *Shenmue* [game]. Sega Corporation.

SonicTeam, 1999. *ChuChu Rocket!* [game]. SEGA.

Splash Damage, 2003. *Wolfenstein: Enemy Territory* [game].

Square-Enix, 2006a. *Final Fantasy XII* [game]. Square-Enix.

Square-Enix, 2006b. *Kingdom Hearts II* [game]. Los Angeles: Square Enix.

Thavikulwat, P., 1996. Activity-driven time in computerized gaming simulations. *Simulation & Gaming*, 27(1), pp.110–122.

Triumph Studios, 1999. *Age of Wonders* [game]. Gathering of Developers.

Ubisoft, 2003. *XIII* [game]. Ubisoft.

Ubisoft Montreal, 2003. *Prince of Persia: The Sands of Time* [game]. Montreal, Canada: Ubisoft.

Ultimate, 1984. *Knight Lore* [game]. Ultimate Play the Game.

Valve, 1998. Half-Life [game].Sierra Entertainment.

Valve, 1999. *Half-Life: Opposing Force* [game]. Kirkland: Sierra On-Line Inc.

Valve, 2001. *Half-Life: Blue Shift* [game]. Kirkland: Sierra On-Line Inc.

Valve, 2007. *Team Fortress 2* [game]. Bellevue: Electronic Arts / Steam.

Valve, 2008. *Left 4 Dead*. Valve Corporation.

Zagal, J.P. and Mateas, M., 2010. Time in videogames: A survey and analysis. *Simulation & Gaming*, 41, pp.844–868.

Zagal, J.P., Mateas, M., Fernandez-Vara, C., Hochhalter, B. and Lichti, N., 2005. Towards an ontological language for game analysis. In: S. de Castell and J. Jenson, eds., *Changing views: Worlds in play, Selected Papers of DIGRA 2005*. Mainz: Pediapress, pp.3–14.

5. Studying games from the viewpoint of information

OLLE SKÖLD, SUELLEN ADAMS, J. TUOMAS HARVIAINEN AND ISTO HUVILA

How do players find out what they need to know in order to succeed at the tasks set before them, like defeating a friend in a game of *Starcraft II* (Blizzard Entertainment, 2010) or recruiting competent guild members? How is gameplay behavior and player experience impacted by player interaction with online discussion boards, wikis, in-game chat channels, and gaming friends? In this chapter, our aim is to show how methods and modes of interpretation associated with the notion of *information* can facilitate game research and help answer inquiries like the ones above—and many others. As this chapter shows, several information processes are required for functional, enjoyable gameplay, and they are therefore of interest also to researchers who do not typically analyze information phenomena. Before we proceed to discuss the tools and perspectives implicated in the information-centric study of games, there are however two questions that need to be discussed: what is information, and why is it interesting to consider in relation to game research?

What is information, and why is it of interest in game research?

Information lacks a singular definition. It is a term of broad use in everyday discourse and an important concept in many scholarly disciplines, including the authors' primary discipline of library and information science (LIS). In LIS, information is commonly used to denote potentially meaningful contents that may induce change in our state of knowledge. The process of becoming informed is often construed as complex interactions between the contents' original location (newspaper articles, colleagues, databases), its mode of communication (reading, talking), and the preconfigurations of its origin and destination (skills, preconceptions, functions). Information is thus in close association with terms like meaning, content, knowledge, and communication. Additionally, information is also something related to media, practices, cognition, as well as culture and other contextual phenomena. Key readings on the genealogy, definition, and critique of the concept of information include Buckland (1991) and Day (2001).

As to the question of why it is interesting to bring together the phenomena of games and information, it will be answered—by the means of demonstration—in the main part of this chapter. The chapter consists of a three-section exploration of how the notion of information can be used as an analytic point of entry into the study of games, players, and gameplay. Each section represents different, but interconnected, research perspectives. The first section takes a closer look at recorded player-generated information and online gaming communities. The second section considers game-related information practices and meaning-making. Finally, the third section analyzes games and gameplay using the perspective of information systems.

Archival inquiries: studying artifacts of recorded information, practices, and information infrastructures

This section aims to benefit game research by showing how document-focused research (e.g., Brown and Duguid, 1996; Berg and Bowker, 1997; Frohmann, 2004; 2009) and trace ethnography (Geiger and Ribes, 2010; 2011) can be used to perform 'archival inquiries' of player-generated artifacts of recorded information in context with communities of massive multiplayer online role-playing games (MMORPGs).

ONLINE GAMING COMMUNITIES AND NEW MEDIA

Rehn (2001) characterizes the online warez community in focus of his ethnography by one of its most ubiquitous activities: to discuss and chit-chat, using www and IRC services to communicate. Rehn analyses online small talk not solely as a common activity among the members of the community, but also as a key practice in which community life itself (knowledge, norms, rules, morals, ethics) is reproduced and negotiated (2001). Similar observations of the importance of technologically mediated discussions abound in studies of online gaming communities. For example, Pearce (2009, p.137) argues that the online game worlds are but one, albeit important, part of a larger ludisphere which include all related play spaces online.

As for instance Boellstorff (2008) notes, blogs, discussion boards, and websites are often main sites of interaction in communities relating to virtual worlds. However, there is little research seeking to understand the dynamics between the practices of online gaming communities and the material constitution of their new media environments despite the fact that these are a fundamental part in the communities' communicative infrastructure. How, then, can this crucial relationship between technology and practice in online gaming communities be conceptualized from the viewpoint of information studies? To frame online discussion boards, blogs, and other game-related new media services as the archives of online gaming communities puts into the center of analysis essential aspects of both the material constitution of said sites, and the way in which they are employed.

ARTIFACTS OF RECORDED INFORMATION AND THE ARCHIVE

An important insight in humanities and social science scholarship is that every social formation exists in communion with its archive. This viewpoint, articulated by among others Foucault (1982), Featherstone (2000), and Cook (2012) serves to accentuate two notable and interconnected points. First, artifacts of recorded information like clay tablets, medical journals, and legal documents simultaneously record and play a part in the social formation within which they exist. The archive is a site whose associated processes of storage, organization, retrieval, and use of artifacts of recorded information, tie into productive power relations and other important aspects of sociocultural life (Cook, 2001). Second, the information infrastructure where the artifacts are stored and accessed—the archive, both concretely and metaphorically—is a quintessential place of study for the researcher seeking to gain insight into the social formation in question.

In gaming communities, it can be argued that the function of the archive is filled by the communities' related new media services such as discussion forums, wikis, and blogs; it is here that cultural patterns of consumption and production, gameplay strategies and styles, and other game-related sociocultural practices are negotiated and (re)produced (Rehn, 2001; Hine, 2009; Sköld, 2013). As we shall discuss later, these archives are dispersed and unstructured (in the traditional archival sense), but rich: new media retains a high amount of traces of social interaction that is well-nigh unprecedented in other media forms.

Besides providing a way to theorize the role of recorded information and new media in online gaming communities, the concept of archive is also useful because it frames usage patterns employed by such communities with precision. The practices of information production, consumption, and sharing in game-related new media environments have distinct archive-like diachronic and asynchronous qualities. On online discussion boards, for instance, conversations commonly take place over the span of days, it is expected that old threads are read before a new thread on the same topic is started, and sometimes year-old discussions are resurrected by a newly posted comment and therefore propelled to the front page and the center of community activity. In a study of the activities of the *City of Heroes* (Cryptic Studios, 2004) community on new media-site Reddit, Sköld (in press) shows that threads, much alike the life-cycle of archival records, often are drawn upon to inform matters they were not originally related to.

TOOLS OF INTERPRETATION: THE DOCUMENT PERSPECTIVE

Document-focused research provides an analytic perspective that suits the vein of study outlined above because it provides tools to explore how online gaming communities at the same time shape their new media archives—by posting, commenting, liking, et cetera—and are shaped by them (Sköld, 2013). What is here called the document perspective denotes a range of studies researching documents in professional (e.g., Harper, 1998) as well as leisure social worlds (e.g., McKenzie and Davies, 2010). The study of documentation has its roots in the works of Briet (2006) and Otlet (1989) and is a strand of inquiry in disciplines such as LIS and organization studies. As an interpretative tool, the document perspective highlights how documents function in different cuts of human activity, and furthermore puts into focus the context-bound activities (use, production, circulation) that relate to these documents. To give a few examples, Harper (1998), in his investigation of the IMF, characterizes documents as the outcome, detritus, and structuring agents of work in the organization. Similarly, McKenzie and Davies (2010) find that documents in conjunction with document work—that is, the activities associated with the documents—shape structure, priority, and meaning in everyday life. In document research, documents are furthermore viewed as the underpinnings of communities of both professional and non-professional natures because they provide the means to stabilize and negotiate the social reality of communities (Brown and Duguid, 1996; see also Frohmann, 2004, and Sköld, in press).

The definition of what construes a document is debated (e.g., Buckland, 1997; Frohmann, 2009) and, in practice, often heuristically derived; those artifacts of recorded information that play important roles in the sociocultural interaction of the area under study can be termed documents. Levy (2001, p.23) provides a definition that is useful in relation to the study of new media and online gaming communities. Levy describes documents as "talking things [...] bits of the material world [...] that we've imbued with the ability to speak". From such a definition, and from the many observations of the prominent role of new media in online communities, it follows that blog posts, Facebook likes, discussion board comments, and the activity logs of wikis plausibly can be studied as documentation.

The document perspective accentuates three principal and strongly interconnected venues of analysis and interpretation when applied to the study of online gaming communities and associated new media sites:

1. *The study of documents-as-artifacts*: this line of inquiry focuses on how documents are positioned in the doings and workings of the studied community or context (e.g., Harper, 1998; Berg and Bowker, 1997), which documents are drawn upon to inform and validate actions or viewpoints (e.g., Sköld, in press), and elucidates the material constitution (contents, layout, structure, material substrate) of the document (e.g., Francke, 2008).
2. *The study of doings-with-documents, that is, documentary practices and work*: Berg (1996) and Frohmann (2004) claim that it is what people are doing with documents that grant documents their crucial role in human affairs. Frohmann (2004) suggests that documentary practices should be analyzed as culturally and historically distinct, and as a part of certain sets of social discipline. Research focusing on documentary practices can investigate the reading and writing of documents (e.g., Heath and Luff, 1996), posting, linking, and commenting (as suggested by Sköld, 2013), and how documents are put to use to sustain and demarcate social formations of various kinds (e.g., Brown and Duguid, 1996; Frohmann, 2004).
3. *The study of the affordances of documents*: affordance (as per Gibson, 1979) is a concept seeking to describe how the material constitution of objects connects to what people are doing with them. A specific material constitution may encourage some modes of interaction while discouraging others. The concept of affordances is highly applicable in the study of documents because it can be used to theorize how the material constitution of a document interacts with its related practices, and thus consolidate venues of study 1) and 2) above.

TOWARDS THE STUDY OF GAMING-COMMUNITY INFORMATION INFRASTRUCTURES

Trace ethnography, as formulated by Geiger and Ribes (2010; 2011), is a methodology well suited to document-oriented inquiries of online gaming communities and new media both as a tool of analysis and as a way to prioritize empirical sites of study. Geiger and Ribes (2010; 2011) claim that present-day distributed social formations (organizations, gaming communities) are intimately connected to the information infrastructures they use for the purposes of communication. Often, these information infrastructures prolifically generate traces of the interactions they facilitate. For example, posts and comments are timestamped and linked to a user profile which, in turn, yields further information; activities are recorded in logs (e.g., Wikipedia's revision history); votes and likes are summarized and visibly displayed; thread titles and many other kinds of metadata are searchable and otherwise available for advanced queries. Geiger and Ribes view these traces as both indications of past activities and as recorded information in present use in the sustenance of sociocultural life. Inquiry into these traces can, according to Geiger and Ribes, make visible the activities of users and produce insights into the workings of local social formations. In summation, the perspective of trace ethnography benefits the line of inquiry suggested in the present section by showing how traces of interaction can be fruitfully interpreted as documents and documentary traces of great importance in the constitution of social formations in online environments—and for the researchers that wish to understand them.

Studying information practices and meaning-making in virtual play spaces

When playing in virtual play spaces, such as MMORPGs, players create sometimes fleeting and sometimes elaborate teams, groups and clans in order to succeed. These and other in-game social relationships can be understood in terms of information practice and meaning-making theories. Information practice theories, of course, largely grow from the field of information studies. The meaning-making theories considered in this section originate from a social interactionist perspective (e.g., Goffman, 1959), but relate strongly to the informational aspects of video gaming.

INFORMATION PRACTICES IN VIRTUAL PLAY SPACES

Information practices inside the game, and to a lesser extent in the expanded play space (including outside elements like manuals, blogs, and forums) can be observed similarly to those in any setting, game or non-game. Information practice models such as sense-making (Dervin, 1998) or everyday life information seeking (ELIS) (Savolainen, 1995) are particularly useful in this regard. MacKenzie (2002) offers one model of everyday life information seeking that has proved useful in studying the types of information practices that are used by players in an online environment to get the information needed to succeed there. She outlines "a two dimensional model of the information practices described by participants" (p.25). It includes a continuum of information practices from actively seeking out a known source or planning a strategy to receiving unsolicited advice. An examination of the ways in which players in the virtual play space appear to gather the information they need to succeed both in teaming with others and finding their way through the challenges of the game environment in the MMORPG *City of Heroes* (Adams, 2006) showed that tactics were parallel to those exhibited in real life situations.

The modes of information practice explicated by McKenzie are: *active seeking,* which is the most direct mode; *active scanning,* including semi-directed browsing or scans of the environment; *non-directed monitoring,* which generally includes serendipitous kinds of discovery; and *by proxy,* a situation in which an individual gains the information through the agency or intermediation of another.

Active seeking is the most direct mode of information seeking. In this mode the player seeks out an identified source in order to get answers to specific questions. An example of this type of information seeking is going to the manual or an official forum for information. Players, however, generally search actively in formal sources as a last resort, tending instead to rely on other information practices.

One form of active scanning observed in avatar actions in *City of Heroes* was scanning the environment, being alert for cues and clues. For instance, the blinking and pulsing of objects and the sounds of the enemies are signs to be looked for, and the information they provide is very important to reaching the goals in the game. The pulsing sounds are only evident when an avatar is within a certain pre-determined proximity of the object; so active scanning for the sounds and blinking are necessary.

One form of active scanning observed in avatar actions in City of Heroes was scanning the environment, being alert for cues and clues. For instance, the blinking and pulsing of objects and the sounds of the enemies are signs to be looked for, and the information they provide is very important to reaching the goals in the game. The pulsing sounds are only evident when an avatar is within a certain pre-determined proximity of the object; so active scanning for the sounds and blinking are necessary.

Non-directed monitoring, the third mode, can be compared to serendipitous discovery, encountering or recognizing a source. Often players learn about the interface by this sort of serendipitous discovery. Interestingly, much of this information may be formalized and available in sources such as the game manual, but players often prefer to discover the information by paying attention during exploration. The final mode of this information practice model is having someone else identify a person as being in need of information and offer unsolicited advice or refer that person to a source. MacKenzie (2002) calls this mode information seeking by proxy. In a game environment, the information provider might be another player, but could also be the game developers through use of non-player characters (NPC) and other such devices. For instance in *City of Heroes*, oftentimes an NPC, when assigning a mission to the player, will include some statement such as "You'll meet a lot of resistance there, it might be a good idea to take along some friends". This is piece of information that is supplied by the game creators who see the players as needing the information to succeed.

MEANING-MAKING IN VIRTUAL PLAY SPACES

Bolter and Grusin (1999) observe that some games encourage the player to "look through the surface of the screen and sometimes by dwelling on the surface with its multiplicity of mediated objects" (p.94). The real and the artificial levels of games are considerably blurred, but teasing them apart as far as possible seems vital to exploration of the games from the standpoint of meaning-making.

The combination of seemingly real and frankly artificial elements in the play space gives games a theatrical quality. Staged theater productions have some very real seeming and feeling elements which are affected by the interaction with the audience, just as games do, and likewise they both have some deliberately artificial conventions. While from a certain standpoint the entire game is artificial, it does in fact offer at least the illusion of reality, both visually and in terms of the cultural elements mentioned above. We enter into the game believing that we are about to interact with and be entertained by an alternate environment. As a result, the theatrical nature of game environments lends itself to analysis of meaning-making using a dramaturgical model.

As the name implies, dramaturgical analysis uses a theatrical framework to study sociocultural life. It is particularly concerned with meanings and the making of meaning. "Simply put, dramaturgy is the study of how human beings accomplish meanings in their lives." (Brissett and Edgley, 1990, p.2) Although social dramaturgy specifically is not often used in information studies, the work of Goffman (1959, 1967) from which it emerges appears in the field, particularly the concepts of presentation of self and face work (Burnett, Besant and Chatman, 2001; Ellis, Oldridge and Vasconcelos, 2004).

"Definition of the situation", defined as "the meaning that actors attach to the setting (including the presence or absence of others)" (Hare and Blumberg, 1988, p.154), is an important concept in dramaturgy. Every action begins with a definition of the situation, based on theatrical elements such as role, scene, costume, and so on, and ends with a new definition of the situation derived through social interaction. Thus players make new meanings or understandings. How the situation is defined, and made sense of, is of extreme importance to how the game is played and whether any particular team venture or play session feels successful. In every social situation there is an initial definition of the situation and a final definition of the situation, and meanings may change from one to the other.

This can be seen in *City of Heroes* in an examination of how roles and presentation of self change in social interaction. The player enters through an avatar, as an archetype with certain powers and so forth. The ways in which she has chosen to costume that avatar, the powers chosen, and the mission at hand, among other things, define the situation for the player, as well as others playing with her. However, often a player will play the same mission repeatedly either because she has not yet completed it, or because she is asked to play by a group (for examples, see Adams, 2009).

RELATIONSHIP BETWEEN INFORMATION PRACTICE AND MEANING-MAKING

Much of what we call ELIS is researched by the use of individualized techniques such as interviews, keeping diaries and so on. The model of information practice referred to in above is an ELIS model, as it was created out of the experience of information seeking of a particular group of people (in this case, women pregnant with twins) seeking information in a certain context (MacKenzie, 2002). It, like most forms of ELIS, is considered a micro-sociological approach to studying information practices. Dramaturgy, on the other hand, uses social groups as units of analysis, and tends to foreground the concept of meaning rather than information. The results of dramaturgical analysis are more implicit in nature. In these ways information practices and dramaturgy, as ways of examining the subject of understanding the information practices and meaning-making in the virtual play space, can be seen as quite different from one another. Still, there are ways in which they are quite similar, for instance their micro-sociological nature.

There is a paradox in the fact that even though some ELIS models are built on the individual as the unit of analysis, they can be considered micro-sociological. But, they are built on the presumption that by looking at a number of individuals in a particular group, conclusions can be drawn about the information practices in the group. Dramaturgy is more clearly micro-sociological, because it grows from the roots of symbolic interactionism. It also concerns meaning-making or information in a group. In fact the unit of analysis in dramaturgy is the social group, not the individual. Therefore, it is an essential step toward the understanding of meaning-making in a social context. Dramaturgy has not been employed as a method of analysis in the field of information studies a great deal, but it is just one step from information practices, and a much more social approach to meaning-making in an information studies context. Combining the approaches provides a fuller picture of information practices and meaning-making than other models have done.

Some important similarities between everyday life information practices and the dramaturgical approach are the common concern with the everyday. Both models also consider information practices and meaning-making as situated in time and place. Both models are concerned with the users' definition of the situation (whether an individual or a social group), no matter how it is derived. The situation in either case is vitally important, because it is in context that information practices take place and meaning is both created and understood. Furthermore each of these models lends itself well to an ethnomethodological approach when we consider games spaces as having elements of culture. Individually and in combination they can provide an excellent theoretical and methodological lens for a descriptive analysis of information practices and meaning-making in the virtual play space.

Analyzing games as information systems

In this section, we examine the how the notion of information systems can be used in the study of games. An important reason for employing this approach is that games are both artifacts and processes (Montola, 2012). On one hand there is the designed game itself; an object, a set of codes, or a concept, created by one or more people. On the other, there is the actual play for which the artifact is used. The systemic properties of a game become actualized once one or more players engage with them (Klabbers, 2009), and the game would not function without information that the players themselves bring into play (Crookall, Oxford and Saunders, 1987). A game's designer is therefore simultaneously creating the artifact and the potential play that it facilitates (Wardrip-Fruin, 2009). Nevertheless, players may impose their own play systems on top of the artifact (or at least parts of it), trespassing the limitations expected by the designers (e.g., Myers, 2010).

As game complexity—especially the number of players—grows, a new pattern emerges: the game is not one system, but actually two or more that exist in an interlaced form. At the core is an information retrieval (IR) type of system. It consists of the material input by designers into the game as an artifact, input that exists within the information ecology of the game itself. In an MMORPG, these include things such as item and skill properties, locations, game-internal information sources, quests, and so forth (see Harviainen, Gough and Sköld, 2012). In a live-action role-playing game, they include roughly the same, but instead of existing as code, the information has been distributed to players before play, and is thus more ephemeral and harder to both access and to preserve unchanged (Harviainen, 2007).

The second principal game-information system is a social information system that exists on top of the IR core (Harviainen and Savolainen, 2014). The social information system consists of player interactions, implicit rules, agreed-upon conventions (e.g., "we've decided together that this is a no-fighting zone"), as well as player-to-player economic transactions. This system furthermore extends outside of the play environment itself, as people share their game experiences, discuss rules and content, and so on, through blogs, forums and other channels (Harviainen, Gough and Sköld, 2012; Warmelink, 2014, pp.106–109). Whereas the IR level may be of primary interest to computer science and human-computer interaction, this level draws in researchers or communication, sociology, management, and so forth.

The social system also includes play that takes place beyond the intended or implied use of games. Huvila (2013) describes this as metagames, referring to the established game research concept of game-related second-order activities. Metagames rely on off-script behavior, breaking out of the game in one way or another (Aldred, et al., 2007). They are practices of gaming games, when players attempt to influence the game and, for instance, change its storyline (Jantke, 2010), or "play activities perceived by players as being 'outside' or 'peripheral' to the game, while still being important to the overall game experience" (Carter, et al., 2012, p.11). Metagaming provides also means for players to take over the game they are playing and to use it for their own purposes (Tan, 2011). Steinkuehler (2007) emphasizes that metagaming engages players in theorizing their own game within and outside the limits of the game itself. This theorizing can take place in long and intentional discussions or as a part of game-related hands-on practices.

From an information research perspective, it is apparent that these very diverse informational activities have a major influence on gameplay. The availability, reliability and choice of information when discussing things with co-players, or choosing a guild or strategy to fight an opponent, have direct consequences to the (sometimes relative) success and outcomes of the activity. Further, playfulness, and unconscious and purposeful gaming of these second-order activities have similar influence on information practices and consequently on the primary activity of playing. In this sense, the choice of choosing particular methods of seeking information in the game, using specific types of information or of relying on knowledge that should not be available for a player, can radically change players' fortune.

Relevant research questions can be, for example, how and why players exploit information that comes from outside of the game (see Consalvo, 2007), why certain information sources are preferred, why particular types of information use are perceived as metagaming and others not, and how and why the conceptualizations of metagaming differ from one player to another. The meta-activity is a distinct yet interlinked meaningful activity by itself, instead of being merely a part of the 'use' of information and information systems (Huvila, 2013). While distinct, it nevertheless forms an important part of a game's systemic whole (Harviainen, Gough and Sköld, 2012; see also Myers, 2010).

GAINING ACCESS TO SYSTEMIC INFORMATION

The challenge of applying traditional methods of research on games as information systems is that they both contain artificial limitations (and transgressions of those limitations) not as commonly found in the physical world (Harviainen and Savolainen, 2014), and asymmetric access to information. As the limitations and corresponding information practices have been discussed earlier in this chapter, it is now necessary to focus on information and asymmetry. According to economic game theory, information is either perfect or imperfect. Perfect information means that a participant has access to all relevant data regarding a situation, while imperfect information means that at least something is outside that person's control. This situation can furthermore be asymmetric, so that some parties have access to more information than others.

In games themselves, such game-theoretical assessments nonetheless prove insufficient. While an abstract game of pure skill (e.g., chess) deals with just perfect information, most games contain a mixture of varying information access and possession types, well beyond the dichotomy of perfect versus imperfect. Whereas a player can in theory have access to all information—that is, having a perfect grasp of the game—this does not mean they are able to remember or utilize all of it. Knowledge of a world is always incomplete (Wilson, 1977), and while an artificial world such as a simple game may be easier to comprehend and remember, the very artificiality of such worlds makes information gaps often inevitable. Therefore, a thorough analysis of a game as an information system, we believe, would require a detailed, phenomenographic analysis of the environment and its related practices, combined with a hermeneutical deconstruction of player interpretations of the play-space, game-related information sources, and their own experiences, and a review of all the paratexts and gaming conventions potentially referring to that game. This is rarely possible, so focal points of research are needed.

THE STUDY OF GAME-INFORMATION SYSTEMS: FIVE FOCAL POINTS

The researcher seeking to study games using the notion of information systems can use the following five points of focus. Each of the focal points overlap, and can fruitfully be studied in context with each other.

1. The information retrieval system

The retrieval system can first and foremost be determined by an analysis of the data and code it contains, including access points, emphases, and interfaces (Jørgensen, 2013), as well as the forms in which they are presented (Myers, 2010). Supplementing those are the ways in which operational rules are described in handouts, guidebooks and so forth, which can be analyzed as documents, designer-created paratexts included (cf. Jara, 2013).

Another way of accessing this level of information is through player interviews, on their experiences with the IR system and its rules and interfaces, as well as their ability to analyze that system and compare it with others and the surrounding world, procedural literacy (Bogost, 2007). Some facets of the IR system are furthermore nearly impossible to research without using either ethnographic or interview methods alongside an analysis of the written core. Examples of such include brought-with information needed for the use of the system, as well as the way in which the system is largely spread out between players and organizers in a live-action role-playing game (Harviainen, 2007).

2. The social system(s)

The social information system contains all social interaction that takes place in direct contact with the game environment, but is not one player's interaction with the IR system. As a result, its facets can be studied with the methods of any field that deals with human interaction, including the analysis of information practices.

As the number of players grows, system complexity increases at a rapid pace. Because of this, tools such as collaborative information seeking (CIS), as described by Shah (2012), has become popular. Being task-oriented organizations, especially raid guilds engage in all five facets of CIS: collaboration, cooperation, coordination, contribution and communication (see Vesa, 2013). They also exemplify the ambiguity and tension common to such practices. Such patterns can be found in also other online play organizations, and we believe this to be a particularly fruitful avenue for further research.

Implicit rules of play, including social conventions upon which players have agreed, can be accessed through either interviews or ethnographic methods. To play against the implicit rules can be a (rather provocative) method for revealing and researching said rules (Myers, 2010). The ways in which players intentionally use the system for unintended purposes fall somewhat between the IR and social layers, and for those, we recommend using research methods selected on a case-by-case basis.

3. The expanded system

The way in which gameplay has expanded from the confines of the core systems both eases research and makes it more difficult. On one hand, scholars can now use the aforementioned methods (e.g., documentary analysis) to analyze forums, blog posts and so forth to see what players may have observed and experienced (or claim they have observed and experienced) during, or in relation to, play. On the other, they present a challenge in that their abundance forces a researcher to inevitably select only a part of the available material, effectively risking a bias. Crucial questions are such as what types of information is produced and shared, and on what forums (Harviainen, Gough and Sköld, 2012), and what parts of information are blunted (rejected as unwelcome; Baker, 1996) by players. This leads directly to questions of cheating, information ethics and information overload, that is, spoilers (cf. Consalvo, 2007; Sicart, 2009; Gough, 2013). For this, we recommend especially player interviews, as the lines on what counts as unwelcome information or cheating are very personal.

4. Boundaries

Between system layers and the expanded system is a boundary. It alters the information that is permitted to enter the world of fiction, or blocks it outright (Harviainen, 2012). The barrier is mostly based on a social contract, due to which it is inevitably porous, when players need to access information from outside of play. The exception to this are the interface and code boundaries of videogames, some of which act as the natural laws of the system (i.e., cannot be broken without fundamentally changing the nature of the activity).

As subjects of analysis in that area, we recommend a focus on the functions and porosity of the barrier: what type of information is let through and why. Key questions are, to what extent the participants expect the game world to be self-sufficient, and whether the play is supposed to be a goal in itself or for an external purpose (as in in an educational game). This is an area that requires a combination of document analysis, systems analysis, observation, and interviews, for results of any reliability.

5. Control systems

Crossing all four facets are issues of control. Power to influence game information—its availability, accuracy and applicability—resides primarily in the hands of the game's designers. In a videogame, this can be the studio or the publisher. In a live-action role-playing game, the power is usually in the hands of one or more game masters, as well as the organizers (Harviainen, 2007).

The power can, however, shift to the hands of the players. Examples of these include tacit player agreements and social pressure (Myers, 2010) and intra-game (e.g., guild) leader or core member authority (Vesa, 2013; Warmelink, 2014). These structures, both formal and informal, are particularly well analyzed by way of participant observation, as the differing practices of various groups may not be visible to players, publishers or organizers themselves.

Discussion

This chapter has shown that information is an intrinsic aspect of games, and that inquiries that put information at the center of analytical attention have the potential to elucidate key workings and doings of games, players, gaming, and gaming communities. The three main sections of the chapter have also demonstrated that the study of information in the context of games can—and, indeed, should—be carried out in different ways. In the following, a small example analysis will make clear the distinctions between the three sections in terms of implications for empirical work and analytical focus. A common research scenario will serve as the point of departure:

It is time to write an outline in preparation for your next research project. Putting together a general description of the intended area of study as well as the analytical perspective poses no problems: you have already decided to study the popular and long-running MMORPG World of Warcraft (WoW) (Blizzard Entertainment, 2004) from the perspective of information. However, you also need to reflect on which information-centric analytic perspective to chose and how this particular perspective impacts the future study's focus and choice of empirical sites. Additionally, and perhaps most importantly, you have to elicit how the study of information contributes to the understanding of WoW. This is where you have to put in some work.

The perspective presented in the section Archival inquiries is best suited to study what can be loosely called communal aspects of play and games. Examples are guilds, groups of bloggers, users of a forum or site, and other groups that are an inseparable part of the sphere of WoW. In the study of such groupings, the object of inquiry also becomes that which is shared among individuals: patterns of behavior, the organization of work and responsibilities (e.g., who is tasked with what role at a boss encounter), culture, and practices.

When conducting research seeking to investigate WoW-related communal dealings with recorded information, it is important to identify key sites of interaction in the particular aspect of WoW under study. For instance, a study seeking to investigate the emergence of certain patterns of play in player-versus-player (PvP) combat may be well served by finding influential forums and databases where such strategies are developed and negotiated. If a choice has to be made between several sites of study that are deemed to be of equal importance, the one carrying the most diverse set of traces of user interaction should be prioritized; it will allow for the broadest access to the tapestry of communal sociocultural life. The study of artifacts of recorded information—along with the associated practices and infrastructures (wikis, blogs, forums)—constitutes a fruitful approach in WoW research because it centers attention on what can be considered as the the ground zero of online WoW-related social life. By studying information and its use it is possible to understand how groupings in the WoW-sphere communicate with each other, how they come to know what they know, and how sentiments and opinions and strategies are spread.

The section *Studying information practices and meaning-making* focuses the study of WoW on how players, in the act of play, make use of and gain meaning from formal and informal sources of information in order to succeed in the game environment. Examples of formal information sources include documentation created by the game developer and official game guides, while in-game conversations and player-driven forum discussions are instances of informal sources. Examinations of how WoW players rely on and use such information sources can offer insights about important aspects of WoW culture as well as a way of understanding how the knowledge and know-how critical to the success of guilds, PvP teams, and individuals are formed.

Another choice is to examine the meanings made in the course of playing WoW, whether those meanings are directly game-related or not. One way of doing so is to investigate the context and definition of the gaming situation as a series of theatrical metaphors. For example, what do the costumes of avatars and non-player characters tell others about them? What can we gather about the game world from the scenery (landscapes, architecture, décor)? How do such definitions and meanings change through the course of play? Through observation and conversation with players it is possible to study meanings made about the game world, and what is needed to succeed therein, as well as more personal and lasting redefinitions of self, as for example, how confidence built through gameplay is carried to another context outside of the game.

When planning a study of WoW using the Analyzing games as information systems-approach, the main focus of analysis becomes the game's core information retrieval (IR) system. In the case of WoW (and other videogames), this is the game code and its premier instantiation: the game. Players interact with the IR system continuously as they utilize items, get information from NPCs, and fight monsters. The skills and knowledge of the players are in constant use, as they read the game and react to it, performing various tasks and deciding on best courses of action. What is referred to as the expanded system manifests itself in player discussions, metagaming, rejection of content spoilers and so forth, issues that can be observed using either archival inquiries or practice analyses.

In WoW, all these phenomena are particularly visible right before, during, and slightly after the publication of a new expansion or content patch, as the now extended IR system activates the social system to discuss both what exactly had been added, and how players react to those additions. The study of WoW from the information system-point of view should prioritize key IR systems and empirical sites where such discussions as are mentioned above are the most accessible.

Conclusions

During the course of this chapter, four principal levels of interconnection between the concepts of information and games have emerged. The following strata of information-in-games are, of course, intimately connected and in some cases interdependent.

1. *Artifacts, documents, information infrastructures, and information systems*: As seen in sections one and three, the *information viewpoint* centers the attention of the researcher on the manifold artifacts of recorded information that circulate in and shape the sociocultural life of gaming communities, along with the infrastructures that support the artifacts' creation, retrieval, storage, and dissemination. The information systems perspective shows how people utilize the properties of the system as a basis for social information practices.

2. *Activities*: All of the sections show that the study of information also can entail looking at what players are doing with information, that is, information practices (and related terms found in the literature, such as *information work* and *information behavior*). The information activity-approach sheds light on the strategies players employ to find information to accomplish, for example, gameplay goals, and how this information is shared among peers. The information activity-approach additionally affords the study of how gameplay is shaped by players' patterns of interaction with information sources external to the game.

3. *Knowledge*: Also, all of the sections demonstrate how investigations focusing on information are in a position to explore how knowledge is produced, organized, and managed in a game-related social formation or a field—and consequently, to gain insight into to how local social (gaming) worlds are maintained and negotiated.

4. *Context*: Common in all of the sections is the view of game-related information as something that is never universal or ready-made. Research on information phenomena can therefore put the specific conditions of the area of study into play, acknowledging that information is always both produced and consumed as a part of certain practices and with certain means (e.g., documents), and circulated in differing social worlds.

Taken together, these strata can serve to add to the discussion of how information in games can be understood and, because the conception of a phenomenon has direct implications for how it can be studied, hopefully inform future research in this vein.

References

Adams, S., 2006. *Information behavior and meaning-making in virtual play spaces: a case study of City of*

Heroes. PhD. The University of Texas. Available at: <http://repositories.lib.utexas.edu/handle/2152/2654>.

Adams, S., 2009. What games have to offer: information behavior and meaning-making in virtual play spaces. *Library Trends*, 57(4), pp.676–93.

Aldred, J., Biddle, R., Eaket, C., Greenspan, B., Mastey, D., Tran, M.Q. and Whitson, J., 2007. Playscripts a new method for analyzing game design and play. In: *Proceedings of the 2007 conference on Future Play*, Future Play '07, Toronto. May. New York: ACM.

Baker, L.M., 1996. A study of the nature of information needed by women with multiple sclerosis. *Library & Information Science Research*, 18(1), pp.67–81.

Berg, M., 1996. Practices of reading and writing: the constitutive role of the patient record in medical work. *Sociology of Health and Illness*, 18(4), pp.499–524.

Berg, M. and Bowker, G.C., 1997. The multiple bodies of the medical record: toward a sociology of an artifact. *The Sociological Quarterly*, 38(3), pp.513–537.

Blizzard Entertainment, 2004. *World of Warcraft* [game]. Blizzard Entertainment.

Blizzard Entertainment, 2010. *Starcraft II: Wings of Liberty* [game] Blizzard Entertainment.

Boellstorff, T., 2008. *Coming of age in Second Life: an anthropologist explores the virtually human*. Princeton, NJ: Princeton University Press.

Bogost, I., 2007. *Persuasive games: The expressive power of videogames*. Cambridge: MIT Press.

Bolter, J.D. and Grusin, R., 1999. *Remediation: Understanding new media*. Cambridge: MIT Press.

Briet, S., 2006. *What is documentation?* Translated from French by R.E. Day, L. Martinet and H.G.B. Anghelescu, 1951. Lanham: Scarecrow Press.

Brissett, D and Edgley, C., 1990. *Life as theatre: a dramaturgical sourcebook*. New Brunswick: AldineTransaction.

Brown, J.S. and Duguid, P.,1996. The social life of documents. *First Monday*, 1(1). Available at: <http://firstmonday.org/ojs/index.php/fm/article/view/466/387>.

Buckland, M., 1991. Information as thing. *Journal of the American Society for Information Science*, 42(5), pp.351–60.

Buckland, M., 1997. What is a "document"? *Journal of the American Society for Information Science*, 48(9), pp.804-9.

Burnett, G., Besant, M. and Chatman, E., 2001. Small worlds: Normative behavior in virtual communities and feminist bookselling. *Journal of the American Society for Information Science*, 52(7), pp.536–47.

Carter, M., Gibbs, M., and Harrop, M., 2012. Metagames, paragames and orthogames: A new vocabulary. In: *Proceedings of the international conference on the foundations of digital games* (FDG '12). Raleigh. May–June. New York: ACM, pp.11–17.

Consalvo, M., 2007. *Cheating: Gaining advantage in videogames.* Cambridge: MIT Press.

Cook, T., 2001. Archival science and postmodernism: new formulations for old concepts. *Archival Science*, 1(1), pp.3–24.

Cook, T., 2012. Evidence, memory, identity, and community: Four shifting archival paradigms. *Archival Science*, 13(2–3), pp.95–120.

Crookall. D., Oxford, R. and Saunders, D., 1987. Towards a reconceptualization of simulation: From representation to reality. *Simulation/Games for Learning*, 17(4), pp.147–71.

Cryptic Studios, 2004. *City of Heroes.* [game] NCsoft.

Day, R.E., 2001. *The modern invention of information: discourse, history, and power.* Carbondale: Southern Illinois University Press.

Dervin, B., 1998. Sense-making theory and practice: an overview of user interests in knowledge seeking and use. *Journal of Knowledge Management*, 2(2), pp.36–46.

Ellis, D., Oldridge, R. and Vasconcelos, A., 2004. Community and virtual community. *Annual Review of Information Science and Technology*, 38, pp.145–86.

Featherstone, M., 2000. Archiving cultures. *British Journal of Sociology*, 51(1), pp.161–84.

Foucault, M., 1982. *The archaeology of knowledge and the discourse on language.* New York: Pantheon Books.

Francke, H., 2008. *(Re)creations of scholarly journals: Document and information architecture in open access journals.* Valfrid: Borås.

Frohmann, B., 2004. *Deflating information: from science studies to documentation.* Toronto: University of Toronto Press.

Frohmann, B., 2009. Revisiting "What is a document?". *Journal of Documentation*, 65(2), pp.291–303.

Geiger, R.S. and Ribes, D., 2010. The work of sustaining order in Wikipedia: the banning of a vandal. In: R.H. Sprague Jr., ed., *Proceedings of the 44th Hawaii international conference on system sciences (HICSS-44).* Los Alamitos, CA: IEEE Computer Society, pp.1–10.

Geiger, R.S. and Ribes, D., 2011. Trace ethnography: following coordination through documentary practices. In: R.H. Sprague Jr., ed., 2011. *Proceedings of the 44th Hawaii international conference on system sciences (HICSS-44).* Los Alamitos, CA: IEEE Computer Society, pp.1–10.

Gibson, J.J., 1979. *The ecological approach to visual perception.* Boston: Houghton Mifflin.

Goffman, E., 1959. *The presentation of self in everyday life.* New York: Anchor Books.

Goffman, E., 1967. *Interaction ritual*. New York: Doubleday.

Gough, R.D., 2013. *Player attitudes to avatar development in digital games: An exploratory study of single-player role-playing games and other genre*. PhD. Loughborough University.

Hare, A. and Blumberg H.H., 1988. *Dramaturgical analysis of social interaction*. New York: Praeger.

Harper, R.H.R., 1998. *Inside the IMF: An ethnography of documents, technology, and organisational action*. San Diego: Academic Press.

Harviainen, J.T., 2007. Live-action role-playing environments as information systems: an introduction. *Information Research*, 12(4). Available at: <http://www.informationr.net/ir/12-4/colis/colis24.html>.

Harviainen, J.T., 2012. Ritualistic games, boundary control and information uncertainty. *Simulation & Gaming*, 43(4), pp.506–527.

Harviainen, J.T., Gough, R.D. and Sköld, O., 2012. Information behavior in game-related social media. In: G. Widén and K. Holmberg, eds., 2012. *Social information research*. Bradford: Emerald. pp.149–171.

Harviainen, J.T. and Savolainen, R., in press. Information as capability for action and capital in synthetic worlds. In: *Proceedings of ISIC, the Information Behaviour Conference*. Leeds. September. Available at: < http://InformationR.net/ir/19-4/isic/isic12.html>.

Heath, C. and Luff, P., 1996. Documents and professional practice: 'bad' organisational reasons for 'good' clinical records. In: G.M. Olson, J.S. Olson and M.S. Ackerman, eds., *Proceedings of the 1996 ACM conference on computer supported cooperative work*. New York: ACM Press, pp.354–363.

Hine, C., 2009. How can qualitative Internet researchers define the boundaries of their projects? In: A.N. Markham and N.K. Baym. eds., 2009. *Internet inquiry: conversations about method*. London: Sage, pp.1–20.

Huvila, I., 2013. Meta-games in information work. *Information Research*, 18(19). Available at: <http://www.informationr.net/ir/18-3/colis/paperC01.html>.

Jantke, K.P., 2010. *Extra game play & meta game play*. Erfurt: Fraunhofer IDMT.

Jara, D., 2013. A closer look at the (rule-) books: framings and paratexts in tabletop role-playing games. *International Journal of Role-Playing*, 4, pp.39–54.

Jørgensen, K., 2013. *Gameworld interfaces*. Cambridge: MIT Press.

Klabbers, J.H.G., 2009. *The magic circle: Principles of gaming & simulation*. 3rd rev. ed., Rotterdam: Sense Publishers.

Levy, D.M., 2001. *Scrolling forward: Making sense of documents in the digital age*. New York: Arcade.

McKenzie, P.J., 2002. A model of information practices in accounts of everyday-life information seeking. *Journal of Documentation*, 59(1), pp.19–40.

McKenzie, P.J. and Davies, E., 2010. Documentary tools in everyday life: the wedding planner. *Journal of Documentation*, 66(6), pp.788-806.

Montola, M., 2012. *On the edge of the magic circle: understanding pervasive games and role-playing*. PhD. University of Tampere.

Myers, D., 2010. *Play redux: The form of computer games*. Ann Arbor: University of Michigan Press.

Otlet, P., 1989. *Traité de documentation: Le livre sur le livre, théorie et pratique*. Liège: Centre de lecture publique de la communauté française de Belgique.

Pearce, C., 2009. *Communities of play: emergent cultures in multiplayer games and virtual worlds*. Cambridge: MIT Press.

Rehn, A., 2001. *Electronic potlatch: A study of new technologies and primitive economic behavior*. Stockholm: Kungliga Tekniska Högskolan.

Savolainen, R., 1995. Everyday life information seeking: approaching information seeking in the context of "way of life". *Library & Information Science Research*, 17(3), pp.259–294.

Shah, C., 2012. *Collaborative information seeking: the art and science of making the whole greater than the sum of all*. Dordrecht: Springer.

Sicart, M., 2009. *The ethics of computer games*. Cambridge: MIT Press.

Sköld, O., 2013. Tracing traces: A document-centred approach to the preservation of virtual world communities. *Information Research*, 18(3). Available at: <http://InformationR.net/ir/18-3/colis/paper-C09.html>.

Sköld, O., 2015. Documenting virtual world cultures: Memory-making and documentary practices in the City of Heroes community. *Journal of Documentation*, 71(2),

Steinkuehler, C., 2007. Massively multiplayer online gaming as a constellation of literacy practices. *E-learning*, 4(3), pp.297–318.

Tan, W.-H., 2011. The breaking of the circle: Playing with, through, against medial boundaries. In: S. Sonvilla-Weiss, and O. Kelly, eds., *Future learning spaces*. Aalto University: Helsinki.

Vesa, M., 2013. *There be dragons: An ethnographic inquiry into the strategic practices and process of World of Warcraft gaming groups*. PhD. Hanken School of Economics.

Wardrip-Fruin, N., 2009. *Expressive processing: digital fictions, computer games and software studies*. Cambridge: MIT Press.

Warmelink, H., 2014. *Online gaming and playful organization*. New York: Routledge.

Wilson, P., 1977. *Public knowledge, private ignorance: Toward a library and information policy*. Westport: Greenwood.

PART II

QUALITATIVE APPROACHES FOR STUDYING PLAY AND PLAYERS

6. Awkward

The importance of reflexivity in using ethnographic methods

ASHLEY BROWN

My night elf druid's leather boots gave off a ringing echo as she ran beneath the tracks of the Deep-run Tram. The tram tunnel, which connects the human and dwarven capital cities through an underground passage, was lonely on this particular Saturday night. Other players, like my guildmates, were likely raiding, farming materials, or questing, but I had decided to take my elf exploring. After reading on forums that a rare sea-beast could be seen from a particular point along the tram's journey, I had resolutely dedicated my evening to catching a glimpse of Nessie. As I held down the W key with my left hand to run along the belly of the tram's hollow interior, I used my right hand to sweep the mouse back and forth, looking through the watery windows on the walls of the tram. A rather long run, I had fallen into a monotonous rhythm of sweeping side to side, searching the blue depths of the virtual ocean for any signs of monstrous life. The monotony had caused me to fall into a sleepy placidity until the chat box in the bottom left corner of my screen sprang to life. My elf stopped running as I released the W key and read the text. I hesitatingly moved forward, looking for the characters to which this text belonged. Sweeping the mouse from side to side, changing my view of the surrounding area, I saw the two characters responsible for this sudden outburst of activity: two dwarves. A male dwarf with a long, flame-coloured beard and thinning hair pressed a female dwarf with intricate braids against the windows of the tunnel. With no witnesses, except Nessie and myself, the couple disrobed. As the players clicked on their characters' armour and dragged the items into their inventory, the clothing began to disappear off the avatars. Although the two dwarves stood still, now in only their underwear, the players typed commands, also called emotes, which filled my screen and indicated they were lovingly caressing one another. Unsure of what I was witnessing, but sure that it was not meant for me to witness, I scrambled clumsily to turn my elf around and run back to the city.

This awkward experience in *World of Warcraft* (Blizzard Entertainment, 2004) inspired me to undertake a research project studying erotic role-play. For the purposes of this chapter, it also provides a concrete example of how awkward moments can happen in computer game research. For anyone who has been deeply involved in a computer game, the idea that games are emotional experiences may seem self-evident. More than just discussing emotion, however, this chapter wants to focus on the feelings of discomfort, embarrassment, or awkwardness which stem from ethnographically studying virtual worlds and playful environments. Unlike traditional research settings, conducting research in online computer games presents a set of unique challenges and obstacles for researchers. With a minimised reliance on physicality, many of the social cues normally transferred by environment are lacking in digital surroundings. In my Deeprun Tram experience, for example, there were no walls to prevent me from accidentally stumbling into a virtual *boudoir*.

The overall aims of this chapter are to provide a brief introduction to ethnography as a methodology; discuss some challenges found in participant-driven, ethnographic computer game research; and finally outline some key methods which we, as researchers, can use to be reflexive of the emotions which occur in player research. To do this, the chapter will use the controversial, emotionally charged, and extreme example of the emotions which emerge when studying sex in online computer games. Relying on my own experience, as well as the experiences of other researchers, this chapter will detail how to account for emotions in computer game research through careful boundary maintenance throughout fieldwork (Boellstorff, et al., 2012), the use of autoethnographic methods (Sundén, 2012), and case studies (Brown, 2013). The focus of this chapter is centred on providing concrete and practical advice for all stages of data collection and analysis. As such, it is useful to consider the points of this chapter when designing a new research project, but also when/if an awkward situation occurs in the middle of fieldwork.

What is ethnography?

A working definition of ethnography is needed to begin this chapter. For those unfamiliar, ethnography can be generally described as a qualitative method of knowing a social world by experiencing it. Christine Hine, author of the seminal text Virtual Ethnography, provides a concise and easily accessible definition of ethnography as "[...]a way of seeing through participants' eyes: a grounded approach that aims for a deep understanding of the cultural foundations of the group" (2000, p.21). In an attempt not to conflate methodologies with methods, it is important to point out that ethnography is a methodology which employs more than one method of generating data. Within the field of computer game research, "[...]ethnography is the written product of a palette of methods, but also a methodological approach in which participant observation is a critical element, and in which research is guided by experience unfolding in the field" (Boellstorff, et al., 2012, p.15). The principal defining factor of ethnography as a methodology is that it is organised around an epistemology which considers experience, either the experience of the informants or researcher, as data. Ethnography comes from an anthropological tradition which emphasises attempts to understand an unfamiliar culture through traveling to and living within it. Importantly for fieldwork, "contemporary ethnography thus belongs to a tradition of naturalism which centralises the importance of understanding meanings and cultural practices of people from within the everyday settings in which they take place[...]" (O'Connell, Davidson and Layder, 1994, p.165). Rather than observing the actions of people and players from a distance, ethnography requires researchers to embed themselves into communities in order to gain context and insight into the meanings and practices they exhibit.

Perhaps for reasons of embeddedness, ethnographies have become a popular method for researching virtual worlds and online computer games. Anthropologist Tom Boellstorff (2008) embedded himself in *Second Life* (Linden Research Inc, 2003) to look at how virtual, online environments and cultures shape our selfhood, and anthropologist Bonnie Nardi (2010) used ethnographic methods to explore issues of culture, gender, and addiction in *World of Warcraft* (Blizzard Entertainment, 2004). Ethnography has also been used to explore and provide nuance to marginalised, hard to access, or otherwise unique groups of players. Both tabletop roleplaying groups (Fine, 1983) and online role-playing communities in the past (Turkle, 1995; Taylor, 2006) have been explored using ethnographic methods. In previous research into online gaming communities, ethnographies have been favoured because they "[...]do not claim to generate factual truths that can be generalised from a sample group onto the population as a whole, as in quantitative, survey-based sociology" (Kirkpatrick, 2009, p.21). This is an important facet of ethnography. The aim of the methodology is not to generalise findings to a population, such as gamers as a whole, but rather to provide nuanced descriptions of the actions of players partaking in a particular type of play. Given the diversity of games, both in terms of genres and platforms, ethnography is a useful framework for studying player populations because it allows for nuance.

As a methodology which requires researchers to be embedded within communities of players and actually live (at least virtual) lives within communities of play, ethnography is demanding. It demands that the researcher be present intellectually, and emotionally, from every log in screen until every disconnection. Although rewarding, both in terms of the rich data which emerges from such methods and the personal connections which develop, ethnographies are fraught with social and emotional complications. These complications must be taken into account not only for the validity of data analysis, but also for the emotional health of the researcher and the researched. Since a brief definition of ethnography has now been established, this chapter will move on to detail the subjective and emotional nature of ethnography.

Emotions in ethnography

As hinted at, ethnography is a subjective and emotionally charged methodology which demands that pretences of objectivity be dropped so that emotions can be genuinely accounted for. It is a methodology which understands its own limitations and controversies and openly discusses them. Pretences about objectivity, rationality, and other positivist modes of thinking found in the natural sciences are sacrificed in order to be close enough to an individual or community to gain richly detailed data (Harper, 1992), and to additionally account methodologically for a particular sampling strategy, epistemological stance, or relationship to theory (Paasonen, 2010). This does not mean they are sacrificed without thought or consequence, nor that ethnography is unscientific. This simply means that ethnography acknowledges and takes into account the attachments, emotions, and subjectivities which emerge from embedding oneself into a community. Ethnography acknowledges these subjectivities as part of the human experience of doing research—even in virtual worlds. Before examples of ethnographies in computer games can be discussed, however, we must first account for the subjective nature of ethnographies and how no ethnography can, or should, be value-free.

Prevalent within texts describing the methodology of ethnography are polarisations of social sciences and natural sciences. There is a palpable move away from "the idea that the social scientist should follow the methods of the natural sciences, setting aside all preconceptions and popular opinions and observing the social world rigorously and methodically, [which] sounds sensible enough, yet actually raises a number of rather thorny philosophical problems" (O'Connell Davidson and Layder, 1994, p.22). These thorny philosophical problems stem from associating positivism as scientifically rigorous and interpretivism as generalised. Rarely, for example, does a social scientist employing a positivist methodology need to defend themselves from accusations of impressionistic or journalistic research. As soon as one begins accounting for the presence of the researcher on the research, and the emotions which stem from such an act, one's integrity is questioned.

This questioning of integrity often creates an internal conflict for researchers. If they are reflexive about their emotional attachments and feelings toward their data, then their integrity is questioned, if they choose instead to exclude or edit these feelings, then they feel dishonest. Many ethnographers have written about the awkward position positivist traditions have put them in, describing it as a type of schizophrenia (Harper, 1992; Mies, 1996). An inherited tradition which relies on a tradition taken from the natural sciences has resulted in an uncomfortable binary system. Relying on an inherited and presumptuous treatment of the research process as objective, ethnographers are conditioned to instinctively write themselves out of their research (Harper, 1992). Due to the epistemology of ethnography which treats experience, of both the researcher and researched, as data, there emerges an unnecessary urge to hide, repress, or otherwise manage emotional data as it emerges. Sociologist Dennis Harper writes.

> In the field, we develop empathy or antipathy for our subjects; yet we observe and record with the cold dispassion of a physicist. It becomes necessary to live in both worlds, motivated and affected by the genuinely subjective feelings (meaning that they have meaning for the observer only) that grow up in all intimate human contact, yet able to draw back sufficiently to treat one's subject in sociological terms. It is never possible to maintain that dualism completely. (Harper, 1992, p.151.)

Not only is the dualism a detriment to the collection and analysis of rich data, but it also creates a binary separation of self and research which is impossible to maintain. Furthermore, attempts to maintain such a separation often result in a disguising of the inherent power-values embedded in research. Speaking to this, sociologist and developer of institutional ethnography Dorothy Smith has highlighted that "beneath the apparent gender neutrality of the impersonal or absent subject of an objective sociology is the reality of the masculine author of the texts of its tradition and his membership in the circle of men participating in the division of the labour of ruling" (Smith, 1987, p.109). For ethnography, to exclude oneself from research is to render invisible the relations of power and hierarchies which have gone into such research.

Ethnography has answered the need to account for emotions whilst maintaining academic rigor through a process known as reflexivity. Reflexivity means both having the capability and language necessary to justify the methodological, theoretical and practical/pragmatic steps undertaken during data collection and analysis (Mason, 2002), and also the awareness of the researcher's relationship to the field. For computer games research, this type of reflexivity requires acknowledgement of when the researcher is, and is not, an embedded member of the community being researched. For example, early on in Raising the stakes, TL Taylor (2012) is reflexive of the fact that although she uses methods associated with ethnography, she does not consider the research she conducted within the e-sports community to be ethnographic. She admits that she "was always fairly outside" what she was studying by virtue of her status as "a noncompetitor, a woman, and a bit older" than her research participants (Taylor, 2012, p.29).

Taylor's acknowledgement of her status as an outsider both justifies her omission of the term *ethnographic* to describe her research and importantly highlights the invisible boundaries, emotional strains, and breakdowns in communication which may impede research. Even if her research was designed to be an ethnographic account of e-sports, Taylor's own reflexivity on her methodological choices and relationship to the field and participants required her to recognise that it was not, in fact, ethnographic.

As Taylor's experience helps to illustrate, researchers studying communities of players are often faced head-on with power imbalances, such as those relating to apparent gender or age, and often these experiences are integral to the experience of playing within a given community. As Kathy Charmaz writes, "we interact with data and create theories about it, but we do not exist in a social vacuum" (Charmaz, 2006, p.127). The power relations in gaming communities are undoubtedly affected by the imbalance in who designs and creates the games available for play, and this is combined with the power structures inherent within the academic institution of the researcher. These relations of power, particularly as they relate to gender, undoubtedly affect the experience of researching as well as the results of research. To leave them unacknowledged is to misrepresent our process of knowing. Additionally, it is an opportunity to gain a greater understanding and appreciation for what it feels like, in the case of computer game research, to embody an avatar and live in a virtual world. As we shall see later in this chapter, very real emotions are experienced by real people even if the impetus for these emotions stems from virtual or imaginary situations. As Charmaz writes, "we can know a world by describing it from the outside. Yet to understand what living in this world means, we need to learn from the inside" (2004, p.980). For researchers focusing on computer game research, part of learning from the inside involves acknowledging the humanity which takes place there. Living, virtually or otherwise, amongst participants affords a unique insight and contextualisation for the norms, values, power relations and beliefs of a particular community. When researcher emotions and experiences are also taken into account, we step closer to gaining a full picture of the social reality of a particular community.

So far, the discussion of emotions in ethnographic research has largely been positive. Whilst it is the intention of this chapter to motivate researchers to include themselves and their emotions in their research whenever possible, there are occasional cases which merit exception—or at least discussion. Sex, when it occurs outside of the research environment, is an activity fraught with social, political, and even economic complications and power differentials. It should come as no surprise that sex as a research topic is complex, particularly when discussing the management of emotions. For this reason, the next section will use sex as an example of ethnographic research which requires special care and emotion management.

Studying sex

Sex as a research topic is controversial, emotionally charged, and provides an extreme example of the invocation of emotions in research. Sex is a particularly appropriate example when discussing emotion in ethnography as it has the potential to conflate most of our personal and professional beliefs. This is the case both in the sense of politics surrounding sex, which may persuade a researcher to choose a purposeful sampling when researching a controversial issue (Paasonen, 2010), but it is also the case in terms of the relationships which develop between researcher and participant (Sundén, 2012). As a key component of doing ethnographic research, "[...] participant observation entails a certain level of intimacy with informants, in the sense of closeness and deep rapport. Such closeness naturally has the potential, under certain circumstances, to eventuate in sexual activity" (Boellstorff, et al., 2012, p.144). Although most researchers agree, or at least understand, the natural social bonds and intimacies which arise from doing fieldwork, there is an understandable discomfort when this is applied to studying sexuality.

As in the above quote, there is always a concern that the intimacy between researcher and participant will develop into an emotional bond, romantic feelings or attractions. Even if these emotions do not manifest themselves into action, they are always present in subtext. John Campbell, an Internet researcher who wrote about his experience in gay men's chatrooms gave an example of how one particular interview participant often took a playful and flirtatious tone. He accounts for this in his research by writing,

> This instance is indicative of the sexual tensions underlying the negotiation of power between myself as both researcher and community member and those participating in this study. It became evident at points that there were unexpressed contentions over who dictates whether an online interaction will be a serious interview or flirtatious encounter. At other times, there were significantly deeper emotional (and erotic) tensions underlying interviews- tensions originating from the history I shared with a particular subject. (Campbell, 2004, p.40.)

Community membership for ethnographers studying sexuality comes at a high price. In order to be fully embedded in the community, and participate in defining activities, all ethnographers must be prepared to be open themselves. In Campbell's case, this involved being open about the history he shared with his research subjects. This is not only for reasons of reciprocity, but also due to the nature of social interactions. To provide an honest account of such interactions adds depth, context, and provides further insight into how a community operates. This personal and uncomfortable process is essential for both good ethnography and for telling sexual stories which accurately and compassionately consider the power researchers have to normalise and privilege certain types of sexual behaviour whilst damning others (Weeks, 1985; Plummer, 1995; Stanley, 1995). By being open, researchers are able to reassure participants that they have a vested interest in the public representation of the community under study, as well as provide context for readers of the invested nature of their involvement as researcher. Past objective, positivist research which shuns this acknowledgment has had the unfortunate, and perhaps unintended, consequence of othering and externalising the behaviours of research participants. Whether or not the intended goal of such research is to provide a descriptive account of normality by referencing the unusual, the externality which results from the abstraction of researcher from data conflicts with the heart of ethnography.

Whilst most researchers have an understanding that the power relationships between researcher and researched trouble notions of consent and render sex between the two complicated, if not outright wrong, there is little conversation about grey areas. If we take intercourse with research participants to be an extreme example of misconduct in the field, what about the less extreme, less direct expressions of affection and intimacy? Of course there is an obvious discrepancy between feeling good will toward a participant who is particularly humorous and feeling intimate desire for a participant, but where the line is drawn is a question which must be asked. Of course the opposite applies as well. What if we develop an antipathy for a particular participant based on their behaviour? What if this dislike stems from a conflict between their expression, treatment or views of sexuality and the researcher's own? Furthermore, conducting research in virtual, imaginary, and playful environments troubles attempts to control emotions in ethnography further. Certain research methods which would be unquestionably unethical in the real world, such as covertly observing sexual interactions, are discussed more flexibly when contextualised as virtual. To provide answers for these questions, as well as practical advice, the following section will focus on three key ways to account for emotions in ethnographic research.

How to account for emotions in ethnographic research

Now that this chapter has outlined and described what ethnography is, how emotions are involved in the process of doing ethnography, and the politics of studying sexuality, we can now progress to discuss practical ways to account for awkwardness in computer games research. As noted above, sex research in computer games will be used as an organising theme around which I will centre the discussion. Due to its controversial nature, examples of researching sex through ethnography in computer games provides an interesting, concrete way to think about how emotions are involved in research and possible methodological and ethical implications. To do this, I will use past research and my own personal experience researching sexuality to focus on three practical solutions. These solutions will focus on boundary management (Boellstorff, et al., 2012), autoethnography (Sundén, 2012), and case studies (Brown, 2013). After each solution has been outlined and described, a discussion will follow which discusses the advantages and drawbacks each presents to the management of emotions in ethnographic research.

BOUNDARY MANAGEMENT

The first solution I will discuss is boundary management. Boundary management is a term which I have synthesised out of the recently published Ethnography and Virtual Worlds by Tom Boellstorff, Bonnie Nardi, Celia Pearce, and TL Taylor (2012). Although used throughout the social sciences in other contexts, here I take boundary management to mean an active policing of communication and behaviour which is intentionally done to manage emotions. To some extent, everyone does this type of emotional labour every day. For traditional ethnographers conducting fieldwork in the physical world, boundary management might be otherwise termed professional behaviour. For example, ethnographers studying social interaction in night clubs might choose not to dance with participants because this might be construed as favouritism or flirtation and interfere with the research outcomes. Although there are clearly exceptions to this, and we can easily imagine a researcher dancing with participants for one reason or another, the fact there would need to be a reason to justify the behaviour is indicative that boundary maintenance is taking place.

In their book, Boellstorff, et al. (2012) caution ethnographers away from engaging in sexual activities with participants. They write this is because of two reasons: "first, we often do not know the meanings our informants attach to sex [...] Second, since sexual activity (especially when first initiated) is by nature unpredictable, it may be difficult to anticipate possible consequences to our research or careers, and to our informants' feelings and lives" (Boellstorff, et al., 2012, pp.144–145). They also point out the power relationships between researcher and participant, such as those discussed earlier in this chapter, further complicate matters. Unfortunately, they offer only vague advice about how to best manage emotions and relationships with participants. They note, "sex is pretty easily avoided if we so choose, but intimacy in some form is central to the very practice of ethnography" (Boellstorff, et al., 2012, p.145). So, whilst it is easy to avoid sex—although they never provide a definition for what sex is but presumably rely on the assumption of a physical act—it is not as easy to avoid feelings of intimacy. Although, as they rightly note, there are no generalisable rules as to how intimate is too intimate, they do encourage researchers to be conscious of the information they release in research and how this may affect their participants. They write,

Writing up the material gained through encounters seen to be intimate in some fashion requires extreme sensitivity and tact. Each case is different; there are no cookbook rules we can propose. In general, if we feel hesitation or pangs of guilt or concern as we write, it is probably wise to move to other topics [...] Ethnography in certain circumstances demands restraint, and judgements regarding the release of information are sometimes best rendered conservatively. (Boellstorff, et al., 2012, p.145.)

Rather than provide concrete suggestions or guidelines for setting boundaries for the types of interaction or data collection which should take place in the field, the authors instead suggest care is taken during the writing up process. To some extent, this advice makes sense. To advise ethnographers on practical ways to control for, or limit, behaviour in the field would be to advise them not to conduct an ethnography. By the very nature of the methodology, researchers lack control over the research environment, and participants. Although researchers can, to some extent, control their own behaviour and reactions, they cannot control for the behaviours or actions of others. Speaking from my own personal experience, it is difficult to predict and plan for uncomfortable situations.

In one example from my own fieldwork, a participant asked if I would be interested in viewing a transcript of one of her intimate role-play experiences. I was conducting ethnographic research in a community of *World of Warcraft* players who used the game to role-play with sexual content, also known as *erotic role-play*. As noted in the previous section, the location of the game and play in the virtual often troubles our sense of research ethics. If I had conducted this type of research in the real world and a participant had asked if I would have liked to view a video of themselves engaging in sex with their partner, it would have been very easy to say no. The idea of viewing such a video is immediately flagged as uncomfortable, wrong, and too intimate—in my mind anyway. However, being that the research was carried out in a fictional game world with fictional characters, and rather than a pornographic video this would be an erotic chat transcript, I said I would be interested. Greedy for data, I saw this as a once in a lifetime opportunity to see what really happens during an erotic role-play experience.

A few days after our conversation, the participant sent along a transcript of one of her erotic role-play sessions. I opened the attachment, skimmed through it, and immediately regretted what I had done. The transcript was copied and pasted from an in-game encounter between the participant and her erotic role-play partner. It included their character names, as well as what was said and done between their characters. Although I had agreed with the participant that I would not quote the transcript, but rather use it to gain a general flavour for how erotic encounters functioned in the game, I realised even that crossed an uncomfortable boundary. Not only did reading the document feel like an invasion of privacy for the participant, but also for her erotic role-play partner who may or may not have consented to this information being released. I closed the document, deleted it from my hard drive, and emailed the participant to thank her and explain I would not be using the transcript in any capacity.

In the following months of fieldwork, I had to control my emotions, thoughts, and feelings during every interaction with both the participant and her partner. I had glimpsed a very private, very intimate moment in their everyday lives, even if the act took place in a virtual environment. This was very difficult to reconcile with my otherwise friendly and professional relationship with the two of them. This particular example usefully illustrates not only how difficult it is to make general rules about intimacy in fieldwork, but also how carefully researchers need to manage their relationships—even in computer game worlds. Later, in the discussion and conclusions, this example will be reflected upon and some concrete tips will be given for the management of boundaries.

The second solution I will discuss is autoethnography. Autoethnography, as the name suggests, is a type of ethnography centred on the self. As a method, it acknowledges the subjective self as part of the process of doing ethnography and seeks to document the feelings, thoughts, and experiences generated by research and embodied by the researcher. Perhaps on the very opposite end of the spectrum to positivist methods, autoethnography seeks to not only acknowledge the place of the researcher, but also to situate the research within that position. Dennis Harper, a sociologist famous for his autoethnography of railroad drifters, writes, "researchers learn to eliminate editorial or subjective elements from their writing by writing in the third person or the passive voice and by using qualifiers. In the narrowest sense, the point of the research report is to describe 'objective social facts' [...]" (Harper, 1992, p.155). Harper's own work challenges the tradition of writing the researcher out of research by documenting not only his thoughts and feelings as he travelled across the United States with a group of homeless, seasonal labourers, but also by writing at length about the social bonds he made during the journey.

Harper's position on autoethnography conflicts with many methodological rules we have learned. Authoethnography often takes the form of what John VanMaanen (1988) has termed *confessional* and *impressionist* tales. Within scientific circles, the term *impressionist* is often used derogatorily to refer to a method which lacks sufficient rigour. Here, however, it is used to reference an experiment of presentation, which has come from the postmodern critique of ethnographic knowledge (Harper, 1992; Reed-Danahay, 1997). It is important to note that this method emerged out of postcolonial critiques of the generation of knowledge (Pratt, 1992), particularly as it concerns traditional ethnography's othering of non-white, non-European peoples. Through being confessional and impressionistic, autoethnography provides a critique of objectivism, realism, and the idea of a coherent and autonomous self (Reed-Danahay, 1997; Sundén, 2012). By placing the ethnographer at the centre of the research, autoethnography is able to provide a deep, rich account of social interactions and bonds in a community through first-hand knowledge.

A fantastic example of autoethnography used to study a computer game comes from past research by Jenny Sundén (2012). During her fieldwork for a study on representations of queerness in *World of Warcraft*, Sundén found herself confronted with her own desires. In her 2012 paper, *Desires at play: On closeness and epistemological uncertainty*, she discusses an unexpected experience in fieldwork. Whilst at a bar in the real world, she met and brought home a *World of Warcraft* player. The morning after, their conversations turned to the game and they exchanged in-game contact information. Due to their physical distance in the physical world, they began meeting in the game to spend time together. The rich description Sundén provides of this experience in her article is not only an example of how autoethnographies in virtual worlds should be written, but it is also moving. An excerpt has been reproduced below:

> She gave me a jump-start into the game. Slap protected Bricka [Sundén's character] with her playing body, introduced her to all sorts of in-game peculiarities, showed her places, and generally showed her a good time. Bricka had things to offer in return. Her good humour and wit, which made orc laughter blend with troll laughter as they ran together over the hills. Of relevance for a research project on emotion, sexuality, and games, I experienced first-hand the sensation of desiring someone through the game interface. An already enticing, immersive game experience was all the more charged through the ways in which desire and physical attraction came to circulate through the game. I would see 'her', the muscular orc woman, with her white tiger,

come running toward me (or Bricka) across the dunes, the sand spurting from under foot and paw. Bricka's heart would skip a beat. Or was it mine? Did it matter? (Sundén, 2012, p.168.)

This excerpt, like much of the article, demonstrates qualities which we might term both impressionistic and confessional. It is impressionistic in its detailing of the imprints the experience left, and confessional in its reveal of the physical symptoms of desire experienced by the researcher. Far from attempts to remain objective, Sundén provides an honest account of not only what happened in the game between two players, but also the effect it had on her and her body outside of the game. Sundén's article provides a concrete example of the benefit autoethnography has, in some situations, over traditional ethnographic methods. Traditional methods would limit the researcher to describing a second-hand account, or analysis of a participant's first-hand account, of such an experience for fear the research is accused of insufficient rigour and the researcher of malpractice. Through bravely detailing her and Bricka's experience, Sundén provides games research, and sexuality studies, with one of few first-hand accounts of the intersection between desire, play, and technology.

Details about the complex relationship between character and player, and the biological impulses experienced, are a great way to provide an intimate account of the emotions involved in both play and research. In Sundén's example, emotions are managed through an open account of what transpired between researcher and participant. The term 'participant' is used tenuously here as Sundén's partner did not actually take part in her larger study on queerness. Had Sundén met her participant through recruitment practices related to her study, the ethics of including the participant in a publication could foreseeably be called into question. Additionally, if this experience was included in a traditional ethnography which centred on the experience of participants, there would likewise be some cause for concern. Such an act might be construed as a type of social experiment in which sexual intimacy occurred for the purposes of measuring response. Due to the fact Sundén's experience happened organically, and we might say unexpectedly, and because her account of this experience centres on herself, it reads as an ethically viable way to account for emotions in fieldwork.

Of course this method has drawbacks, namely in that it requires a good deal of confidence and openness on behalf of the researcher. The researcher must be confident in the methodological soundness and the ethical viability of what they have done to publish their findings and leave themselves open for criticism and potential accusations of malpractice. Additionally, the researcher needs be prepared to open up a particular chapter of their lives to being researched. The type of self-reflexivity, especially as it concerns personal relationships, is demanding in a way which other methods are not. These drawbacks and potential issues will be discussed in greater depth later. For now, the discussion will turn to case studies.

CASE STUDIES

The third, and final, solution which I will discuss in this chapter is case studies. As a method I have personally used in the past, I would describe case studies as lying somewhere between boundary management and authoethnography. In many ways, a case study can be a tool for the management of boundaries, and they can also take on qualities and elements of an autoethnography. To be specific, "a case study is an empirical inquiry that: investigates a contemporary phenomenon within its real-life context; when the boundaries between phenomenon and context are not clearly evident; and in which multiple sources of evidence are used" (Yin, 1984, p.23). Practically, this means case studies can take multiple, diffuse forms. *World of Warcraft*, for example, can be taken as a case study of successful and popular fantasy massive multiplayer online role-playing games (MMORPGs) to make generalisations about the genre of games as a whole. Likewise, an individual case from a large data set can be pulled aside and individually analysed to provide context and description on which to situate the findings of a quantitative study. The type of case study I will reference in this chapter, however, deals specifically with ethnography.

The ethnographic case study is one which focuses not only on individual participants as cases, but also includes the researcher's relationship to the particular participant. As Dennis Harper has written, "[...]the ethnographic case study draws on both affective and rational sentiments enmeshed in many-dimensioned human relationships [...] to describe not only what happened 'out there', but also what happened 'in here'" (Harper, 1992, p.155). Taken in this way, case studies are a way to account for the multi-dimensioned relationships between researcher and participant, and can occasionally be used as a reflexive tool for the maintenance of boundaries, as well as a means to place the self in research. Practically, this means the researcher keeps a case file on individual participants which includes relevant field-notes, snippets of interactions, as well as impressionistic or confessional journal-style entries which reflect on the researcher's sentiments toward the participant. I will rely on my own fieldwork experience studying erotic role-players in *World of Warcraft* to provide practical examples as to how case studies can be effectively used for computer game ethnography.

As already mentioned elsewhere in this chapter, part of the research for my PhD thesis involved an ethnography in *World of Warcraft* with a community of players who engaged in a style of play popularly known as erotic role-play. Like other types of role-playing, erotic role-play involves temporarily taking on the identity, or playing the role, of a fictional character within a fictional world. Players develop an individual personality for their character, a set of likes and dislikes, and often will adapt an argot to separate character speech from their own. With limited animated actions available in game, the majority of all role-playing occurs through typed text. Players utilise the game's in-built chat system to not only speak as their characters through /say, but also to describe character actions and reactions through /emote. Typically, "/say" and "/emote" command outputs are viewable to other players. Due to the private nature of erotic role-play, as well as its existence outside the social rules of the game, players typically erotic role-played through private channels. For this reason, my fieldwork was limited to studying public interactions which, typically, did not go beyond flirtation or kissing. There were a few exceptions to this, such as the emailed chat transcript discussed above. Predominantly, participant observation involved observing public social interactions within the community which centred on in-game events relating to sexuality, such as hen nights (i.e., bachelorette parties, weddings, and Valentine's Day celebrations.

During these social events and interactions, I began to develop feelings towards participants, and these feelings were not always positive. Although this chapter has thus far focused on positive, erotic emotions, it is also important to consider less positive, but equally subjective, types of human emotion, such as antipathy. To be clear, I did not feel antipathy toward any participants, but rather towards one particular character. I want to caution against the temptation to suggest that because a player controls the character, a dislike of a character transfers to the player. From early in their career, role-players learn to separate in-character and out-of-character actions, thoughts and behaviours. This situation is no different. Whilst I took issue with this particular character, I actually grew close to the player and developed a friendship. Below is an excerpt from my thesis detailing my relationship with both participant and character:

> One of the first interviews I conducted was with [participant name] and I was shocked that she had volunteered. Her character and mine never agreed on anything and would often have public spats. Whilst we chatted out-of-character and became friends, I was still annoyed by her character's behaviour, and presumably she was annoyed by mine. She eventually decided to kill her character permanently... (Brown, 2013, p.197.)

Some role-players, such as the participant above, design their characters to be rude, argumentative, or otherwise ornery. This is usually done for the purposes of creating a richly developed and detailed fantasy world through realistic conflict, strife, and less-than-pleasant characters. Although I understood why someone would want to play an argumentative character, interactions between my own and the participant's character were still stressful. Dealing with the difficult character in role-play drained my emotional energy and I found it very difficult to participate whilst conducting observations. I quickly came to dread seeing the character's name pop up in chat, and grew to loath group interactions.

Throughout the course of fieldwork, the player eventually decided to kill this particularly difficult character. There were multiple reasons she decided to do so which focused on the character's background, storyline, and overall development. When I discovered the character's death when reading the community's forums, I felt a mixture of elation, relief, and guilt. Although characters may experience hundreds of deaths during their lives in *World of Warcraft*, role-players interpret these as knock outs or incapacitations. Killing a character means either deleting it or never playing it again. As a single character represents hundreds of hours of game time, and likely hundreds more hours of role-playing time, the decision to permanently kill a character is one which is not taken lightly. It is an emotional experience for the player, and sometimes for the community.

The mixture of emotions I felt when the player announced this character would die made me feel uncomfortable. Feeling happiness or relief over death, even of a game character, conjures up pangs of discomfort and disrespect. When I conducted an interview with the participant, I asked questions about the decision making process which resulted in the character's death, as this fell within the remit of the research design. During the interview, I felt nervous and awkward. I was unsure whether or not I should explain my feelings about the character to the participant, or if I should attempt to remain impassive during the interview. I decided to choose the latter option, believing it to be safer to manage my emotions than to expose my feelings. Weeks later, after reviewing the interview transcript and making an attempt at analysing it, I decided I needed to vent the troubling feelings I was experiencing and admitting those feelings felt even worse—as though I failed in my role as a researcher.

The uncomfortable mixture of emotions I experienced led me to initially consider withdrawing the participant from the study. Because I had experienced such strong feelings and emotions toward the character, I assumed my analysis of observations and interviews would likely be biased. After some discussion with my very helpful and insightful thesis committee, I decided to keep the participant in the study and use the experience as a case study. It was one of the best decisions I made. Not only has it allowed me to provide a first-hand, general account of the out-of-character emotions experienced during role-play, but it has also allowed me to reflect on how much social bonds influence research—whether we admit to them or not. As Dennis Harper (1992, p.149) wrote, we need to account for the subject in ethnography, as "it is extremely important in that the things we learn are deeply influenced by the nature of the social bonds we maintain with those we study". When committing to an ethnographic research design, researchers are committing themselves to see the world as their participants do. To ignore the bonds which develop, even negative ones, and the individual relationships between researcher and participant which assist in this way of seeing is to ignore the process of researching.

Discussion and conclusions

This chapter has provided an introduction to accounting for the presence of the researcher when studying communities of computer game players using ethnographic methods. After a general introduction to ethnography, the emotions involved in research, and the often troublesome and polarising nature of studying sexuality, this chapter provided three examples of methods which can be used to account for emotions in ethnographic research. Boundary management, autoethnography, and case studies were each discussed as providing a way for researchers to think about, document, and write about their involvement with communities of players and the research process. Although the practical application and drawbacks of each were briefly discussed in each section, the chapter will conclude by providing some final words of advice for the practical application of each.

Boundary management was discussed as being close to every day emotional labour. In other contexts, this method might be simply called professionalism. The key way in which this chapter has distinguished boundary management from professionalism lies within the acknowledgement that professionalism for researchers might take multiple forms depending on culture, context, and comfort. In the nightclub example, one researcher dancing with participants might be viewed as exhibiting unprofessional (ab)use of power, whereas another researcher dancing with participants might be undergoing the process of ethnography. As noted by Boellstorff, et al. (2012), it is difficult, if not impossible, to set rigid guidelines for conduct in fieldwork as each case is likely to be different. There is, however, some constructive advice for how individual researchers can set, and manage, their own boundaries.

Before entering the field, and perhaps during research design, ethnographers should reflect on personal levels of comfort. Thinking about, and perhaps making a list of possible scenarios which may be encountered, will help in increasing preparedness should any of the possible scenarios occur. In my experience, some institutional review boards even require this as part of the proposal review process. Even if none of the scenarios do happen, having a list will likely increase feelings of preparedness and efficacy before entering the field which might mean that if the unexpected arises researchers will feel better able to respond to the situation.

Researchers should also reflect on what is known, or what they believe is known, about the types of social interactions they will encounter once in the field. For example, going into my fieldwork I knew that playful language relating to sexuality and the body was used with limited significance in the community I planned to study. Because I knew this, when I asked a participant if they had read and understood the informed consent and they responded with a quip suggesting they wanted to try out some non-consensual interview methods, I knew this was a humorous reference to bondage, domination, sadomasochism (BDSM). The joke did not trigger my boundary maintenance because I was able to read and contextualise it as a part of the community's sense of humour.

Should a situation occur which crosses personal boundaries of comfort, the best advice I can give is to step away from the situation and reflect. This advice comes from my own experiences- particularly the situation which resulted in my adaptation of case study methods after fieldwork had already begun. In order to see the world as our participants do, occasionally some distance is needed to think about the context and situational circumstances which resulted in feelings of discomfort. Removing oneself from the field both immediately ends the situation, thus preventing further discomfort, and allows space for reflection on the types of data collected. In this way, maintaining boundaries may lead to the adaptation of other ethnographic methods, such as autoethnography and case studies, to explain the reason for the discomfort. It might be that the origin of the uncomfortable situation stems from a situation in which expected behaviour, norms, values, or the beliefs of the participants' clashes with the researcher's own, or it may be that it occurs because the researcher encountered the unexpected which conjures up awkward emotions. Recognising this emotion, and being honest about it, enables the researcher to not only re-enter the field, but also re-enter it with additional insight.

Authoethnography likewise requires the researcher to be honest about their process and it additionally requires researchers to open themselves to being researched. Authoethnographies are one of the most genuine, detailed, and richly descriptive ways to account for the social nature of doing research. As evidenced in Jenny Sundén's (2012) account of intimacy within *World of Warcraft*, autoethnography enables researchers to provide a first-hand account of not only "[...] what happened 'out there', but also what happened 'in here'" (Harper, 1992, p.155). As a methodology, autoethnography is usually a part of initial research design. It would be difficult, but not impossible, to switch mid-fieldwork to conducting an autoethnography from another methodology as the principles and premises on which autoethnography is founded conflict with many other research epistemologies. Researchers can, however, use autoethnography to account for an unexpected and tangential experience which arises from fieldwork. As evidenced by Jenny Sundén's use of autoethnography to account for romance which occurred during fieldwork, but tangentially to data collection, the methodology can be applied mid-project to account for an unexpected, and even awkward, experience during fieldwork.

Due to the ambiguity of the term and mixed method approach, case studies can be applied in multiple contexts. In this chapter, case studies were viewed as a practical way to bridge the gap between boundary management and autoethnography. Although case studies can be a part of the research design from the beginning, there is flexibility for implementation mid-fieldwork. In the example taken from my own research, I employed case studies when I felt my personal feelings toward a participant were interfering with the collection and interpretation of data. I employed case studies in my own research by stepping away from an awkward and uncomfortable situation, reflecting on my thoughts and emotions, and then documenting these thoughts and emotions about individual players alongside my field notes. Field notes can then be used later in the analysis and write up of data to not only be reflexive about the research process, but also to add context and richness to the presented data.

This chapter opened by providing an example of an uncomfortable encounter in a virtual world to highlight that awkward situations do occur during research. More than just awkward situations, this chapter discussed the intertwined relationship between emotions, ethnography, and researching computer games to make the point that emotions are always a part of research—whether researchers account for them when they write their results or not. For anyone undertaking an ethnographic project, accounting for emotions and adapting methodologies and methods to document them is integral to being an immersed member of the community being studied, but this is particularly the case for studying computer games. For a field of research which has been built on love and passion for the medium, we need to think critically about the ways in which we manage our emotions in games studies and employ adaptive research practices to allow the humanity in our research to shine through.

Recommended reading

- Boellstorff, T., Nardi, B. Pearce, C. and Taylor, TL., 2012. *Ethnography and virtual worlds: A handbook of method*. Princeton: Princeton University Press.
- Sundén, J., 2012. Desires at play: On closeness and epistemological uncertainty. *Games and Culture*, 7(2), pp.164-184.
- Kirkpatrick, G., 2009. Technology: Taylor's Play between worlds. In: F. Devine and S. Heath, eds., *Doing social science*. Hampshire: Palgrave, pp.13-32.

Acknowledgements

Special thanks go to Professors Sue Heath and Jennifer Mason for their support, insight, and encouragement.

References

Blizzard Entertainment, 2004. *World of Warcraft*, [game]. Irving: Activision Blizzard.

Boellstorff, T., 2008. *Coming of age in Second Life: An anthropologist explores the virtually human*. Oxford: Princeton University Press.

Boellstorff, T., Nardi, B. Pearce, C. and Taylor, TL., 2012. *Ethnography and virtual worlds: A handbook of method*. Princeton: Princeton University Press.

Brown, A., 2013. *Sex between frames: An exploration of online and tabletop erotic role play*. PhD. The University of Manchester.

Campbell, J.E., 2004. *Getting it on online: Cyberspace, gay male sexuality, and embodied identity*. London: Harrington Park Press.

Charmaz, K., 2004. Premises, principles, and practices in qualitative research: Revisiting the foundations. *Qualitative Health Research*, 14(7), pp.976–993.

Charmaz, K., 2006. *Constructing grounded theory: A practical guide through qualitative analysis*. London: Sage.

Fine, G. A., 1983. *Shared fantasy: Role-playing games as social worlds*. London: University of Chicago Press.

Harper, D., 1992. Small N's and community case studies. In: C. Ragin and B. Howard, eds., *What is a case?* Cambridge: Cambridge University Press, pp.139–158.

Hine, C., 2000. *Virtual ethnography*. London: Sage.

Kirkpatrick, G., 2009. Technology: Taylor's Play between worlds. In: Devine, F. and Heath, S. eds., *Doing social science*. Hampshire: Palgrave, pp.13–32.

Linden Research Inc, 2003. *Second Life* [game]. San Francisco: Linden Labs.

Mason, J. (2012). *Qualitative researching*. 2nd ed. London: Sage.

Mies, M., 1996.Towards a methodology for feminist research. In: M. Hammersley, ed., *Social research: Philosophy, politics, and practice*. London: Sage, pp.64–82.

Nardi, B., 2010. *My Life as a night elf priest: An anthropological account of World of Warcraft*. Ann Arbor: The University of Michigan Press.

O'Connell Davidson, J. and Layder, D., 1994. *Methods, sex and madness*. London: Routledge.

Paasonen, S., 2010. Online pornography: Ubiquitous and effaced. In: R. Burnett, M. Consalvo and C. Ess, eds., 2010. *The handbook of Internet studies*. Chichester: Wiley-Blackwell, pp.424–439.

Plummer, K., 1995. *Telling sexual stories: Power, change and social worlds*. London: Routledge.

Pratt, ML., 1992. *Imperial eyes: Travel writing and transculturation*. London: Routledge.

Reed-Danahay, D., 1997. Introduction. In: D. Reed-Danahay, ed., *Auto/ethnography: Rewriting the self and the social*. Oxford: Berg, pp.1–17.

Smith, D., 1987. *The everyday world as problematic: A feminist sociology*. Boston: Northeastern University Press.

Stanley, L., 1995. *Sex surveyed 1949–1994: From mass-observation's little Kinsey' to the national survey and the Hite reports*. London: Taylor & Francis.

Sundén, J., 2012. Desires at play: On closeness and epistemological uncertainty. *Games and Culture*, 7(2), pp.164–184.

Taylor, T.L., 2006. *Play between worlds: Exploring online game culture*. Cambridge: MIT Press.

Taylor, T.L., 2012. *Raising the stakes: E-sports and the professionalization of computer gaming*. Cambridge: MIT Press.

Turkle, S., 1995. *Life on the screen: Identity in the age of the Internet*. New York: Simon and Schuster Paperbacks.

VanMaanen, J., 1988. *Tales of the field: On writing ethnography*. Chicago: University of Chicago Press.

Weeks, J.,1985. *Sexuality and its discontents: Meanings, myths and modern sexualities*. New York: Routledge.

Yin, R.,1984. *Case study research: Design and methods*. London: Sage

7. In-depth interviews for games research

AMANDA COTE AND JULIA G. RAZ

Videogames are fundamentally interactive, relying on communication between the player and their character, the player and the content, and even players with one another. What this means is that while games are developed in a studio, at least part of their meaning and significance is created at the moment of play and through the people who play them. As researchers, therefore, we find that many of our questions can best be answered through our own interaction with gamers, generally in the form of experiments, surveys, participant observation, or the focus of this chapter—in-depth interviews.

In-depth interviews can be an excellent way to collect information about gamers' preferences, opinions, experiences, and more, but only provided they are approached carefully and systematically. As with any research method, it can be easy to conduct a bad interview, but it is not necessarily so easy to conduct a good interview—one that collects interesting and usable information. Researchers need to think through a number of steps before starting the interview process and as they proceed to collect data in this fashion. To help with this method, this chapter will draw on our experiences with in-person and online interviews, as well as interviews conducted by other contributors in the field. It will use these examples to outline best practices for planning and conducting an interview-based study, to ensure that data can be used to craft quality, original research.

When to choose in-depth interviews

The initial section of this chapter interrogates interviewing as a methodology for videogame scholars. Specifically, we discuss the importance and utility of this method within the field of game research. We begin with a discussion of the strengths and weaknesses of this particular method. In doing so, we draw from selected works in the corpus of game research scholarship that have employed interviews as a methodology.

When considering a research method, the first step of the investigator is to determine what approach fits their paradigmatic orientation and can best answer their particular research questions. Like all methods, interviews have strengths and weaknesses. For instance, when researchers seek to make generalizable conclusions, arguing how often people tend to do something or how likely an effect is, in-depth interviews are generally not useful because they tend to use non-random samples. In other words, they do not allow researchers to draw inferences about a population at large because the people they talk to are not representative of that broader group. Rather, in-depth interviews excel at achieving a detailed level of personal depth and describing a smaller, specific group.

Take, for instance, a researcher interested in learning about how teachers in the United States utilize videogames in the classroom for learning (e.g., Squire 2003; Blumberg, et al., 2004). Blumberg, et al. (2004), for instance, interviewed 2nd and 5th grade boys in order to determine what they learned from playing videogames. From this data, they determined the cognitive strategies employed by boys who play videogames. Using interview methodology, the investigator could conduct in-depth interviews with teachers at a particular school, county, and state. From the resulting data, the investigator could draw conclusions about the importance and utility of games in schools in that particular setting—learning about specific situations, anecdotes, and preferences—but the researcher could not apply those conclusions to other schools or districts. Thus, the specific context in which our data were collected matters to the results.

There is no simple test to decide whether in-depth interviews are the best methodology for a study; however, there are a number of factors one can use to determine which method to employ. In the following, we address some, but not all, of the considerations a qualitative videogame researcher can take into account when deciding whether to engage in-depth interviews or an alternative method. Each study will have unique elements that may affect the choice of data collection method, but we address each of the following issues as possible starting points: the paradigmatic orientation of the researcher, the depth of the information of the topic of interest, the amount of control in each setting, and ethical considerations.

EPISTEMOLOGICAL ORIENTATION

First, a researcher need take into consideration their paradigmatic orientation, or the underlying assumptions and structure around which they base their analysis and understanding of the world.

For example, a researcher who comes from the orientation of social constructivism believes that an individual's understanding of the world is developed through social and cultural processes, rather than being natural or inherent. Social constructivists then view the world as having no single truth, but rather multiple truths that are dependent on an individual's cultural context and experiences. They may prefer in-depth interviews over other methods due to their possibilities for co-construction (Lincoln and Guba, 2000). One-on-one interviews allow participants to help direct the flow of the conversation, constructing the interview's narrative together with the researcher (Lincoln and Guba, 2000). The researcher and the informant can gain a close relationship, rapport is maintained, and the co-constructed narrative can be confirmed via member checks, where the researcher verifies their explanations with the participant (Morgan, 1997). The constructivist may find that methods like the focus group, in contrast, may not fit within their epistemology, as the role of the researcher is a moderator in the focus group, rather than a co-constructor in the narrative (Lindlof and Taylor, 2002). As a moderator, the researcher's role is to observe group interactions and regulate conversation. For the constructivist, this could be viewed as too top down, with analysis built more by the researcher alone than as a joint project with the participant.

Researchers who are committed to some other epistemology, such as post-positivism, may find that interviews do not fit their goals adequately. Post-positivist work recognizes that people are changeable and varied but still looks for empirical, measurable characteristics or patterns that can be explained scientifically (Baran and Davis, 2011). For these goals, they require control and the ability to compare across groups in order to make predictions and develop explanations. The targeted nature of the in-depth interview and its generally unstructured format make it unlikely to be the first choice for a post-positivist researcher; however, if they frame their questions in more structured ways, it can still be a possibility. Indeed, both positivists and post-positivists can employ this methodology. For example, surveys are a form of interviewing, although they are far more structured than an in-person, open-ended interview. The technique of sampling in surveys ensures that the data is representative in the analysis process. Alternatively, open-ended interviews, when analysed using a strict codebook that focuses on certain topics, can also be useful to more quantitative designs.

DEPTH OF INFORMATION

The depth of information needed to address the research questions is another key consideration for a researcher. An advantage of individual interviews is that a researcher can gain in-depth information about the topic of interest (Morgan, 1997). When a researcher is interested in people's life histories, for instance, in-depth interviews would make more sense than some other methods, like focus groups. People have significantly more time to share about themselves in a one-on-one setting than in a group setting and may feel more comfortable sharing after having built rapport with the researcher (Morgan, 1997). Further, when a researcher is interested in learning about controversial or private topics that people would not feel comfortable discussing in a group setting, such as sexuality or issues regarding race, individual interviews would be a more suitable method (Lindlof and Taylor, 2002).

If the researcher is primarily interested in getting many people's opinions on the topic of interest, on the other hand, interviews may not be suitable. When seeking "concentrated amounts of data" (Morgan, 1997, p.13), focus groups are often preferred. Through the member interactions that occur in a focus group, the researcher is able to gather a large amount of data in one sitting. This is a main strength of focus groups and the reason for their reputation of being "quick and easy" (Morgan, 1997, p.13). There are instances where issues of depth can favour focus group methods as well, such as when discussing every day, mundane topics. Morgan (1997) provides the example of people discussing a particular brand of soap. In a one-on-one interview this topic could quite brief; however, in a focus group, discussions about an everyday household product can result in a meaningful dialogue. For more information on focus groups and when to use them, see Eklund (chapter 9).

Another consideration of interviews is that they are limited insofar as they require participants to have thought through and be able to verbalize an answer to any question. As such, they can be weak at exploring new topics. However, when it comes to more established research areas, past material can be used to develop new questions, pushing previously studied topics to new levels of depth. For instance, T.L. Taylor's (2003) work Multiple pleasures: Women and online gaming contributed greatly to the area of gender and games, as her interviews showed what earlier surveys often ignored: that while many women found violence in games off-putting, some enjoyed it, finding it to be an empowering experience or an outlet for anger that they struggled to express outside of games. While other work had focused on generalizable results, Taylor's interviews explained more specific phenomena, with very interesting results. An individual who intends to employ interviews as a methodology needs to think through his or her research questions carefully, considering what the interviews are likely to add and other pros and cons before settling on this method.

LEVEL OF CONTROL

Like all research methods, individual interviews have strengths and weaknesses in terms of the amount of control the researcher holds. In individual interviews, the researcher has a high level of control, as they are interviewing only one person with whom they have gained rapport over a period of time (Lindlof and Taylor, 2002). Further, the one-on-one nature of the individual interview setting allows the researcher to have more control over the direction of the conversation if it needs guidance (Morgan, 1997). Unclear questions can be rephrased, and off-topic tangents can be carefully redirected to bring the participant back to the topic of the research while avoiding making them feel unheard.

An important consideration for both general studies and those specifically about gaming is that it can take a substantial amount of time to gain rapport with the person you interview, and more is at stake in your personal relationship in this method (Lindlof and Taylor, 2002, p.181). The researcher must allocate time to explain the purposes of the study and make the participant feel at ease with their role in the research. Additionally, the investigator needs to consider that, even when they are carefully structured, interviews may reveal sensitive personal information. Because most in-depth interviews are largely unstructured, to allow the participant to reveal new and interesting avenues of thought, it is particularly crucial to ensure participant confidentiality. Specific strategies for establishing rapport and protecting a subject's identity and information will be explored throughout the remainder of this chapter.

ETHICS

Ethical considerations are an additional realm that researchers need to consider when deciding which method is appropriate for their study. Because an individual interview takes place only between the researcher and the interviewee, the researcher need not be as concerned with additional people learning or sharing the interviewee's personal information as with other methods like focus groups. In qualitative reports of an individual interview, typically the researcher refers to interviewees using a pseudonym and changes any personal information so as to maintain the individual's confidentiality. This protects the participant and can confirm that sensitive material they share will not be linked back to them. Researchers must ensure that they can complete these necessary steps before choosing interviews, or else employ a different method. They should also think through ethical considerations specific to games studies, some of which will be outlined more fully in the next section.

SECTION SUMMARY

Overall, there are a number of strengths and weaknesses of interviews as a methodology, and these need careful consideration when deciding which method to use in a study. This section has covered the following areas that need be assessed: paradigmatic orientation of inquiry, particular topic(s) of interest, depth of the topic of interest, issues over control of the group, as well as ethical issues that need to be taken into account when decided the method to engage with. Additionally, researchers can also consider the possibility of mixing methodologies, such as coupling survey, experimental, and interviewing methods simultaneously (Morgan, 1997).

Specific ethical considerations for games research

In any study, the researcher is responsible for protecting their informants. Ethical researchers must obtain the approval of their Institutional Review Board (IRB) or department prior to beginning a study, although specific guidelines vary by country and individual IRB. Overall, a researcher needs to be aware of the sensitivity of the information they gather and ensure this cannot be linked to their participants specifically. When using interviews, this usually includes employing pseudonyms and disguising personally identifiable information in the final report. Obtaining informed consent is essential as well. This involves sharing enough details of the study with the participant so that they can make an educated decision whether or not to be interviewed. Researchers also need to allow participants to leave the study and remove their contributed data at any time if they no longer want to participate (cf. chapter 9).

In addition to these basic guidelines, however, games research faces some particular challenges in the area of online studies. The Internet environment opens up a plethora of online worlds, fan websites, forums, and more, where games researchers can study people, games, and cultures. This is what Lotz and Ross (2004) call the "Pandora's box of Internet-based audience research" (p.502). The new media environment allows researchers to access participants in original and exciting ways, but it also introduces substantive challenges in conducting ethical research. For instance, there are new difficulties regarding informed consent procedures and informant anonymity. In the following, we address these two issues and some of the ways that researchers can navigate them, clarifying possible approaches using exemplars from Boellstorff's (2008) study of the online virtual world, *Second Life* (Linden Research, Inc., 2003) and Nardi's (2010) anthropological account of *World of Warcraft* (Blizzard Entertainment, 2004).

In order for a study to be approved by the IRB or relevant department, the institution need know that the study protects its human subjects. A challenge that qualitative researchers face in the online environment is that they have to obtain informed consent via the Internet (e.g., chat rooms, voice chat, Skype), rather than the traditional in person, face-to-face method (Lotz and Ross, 2004). Boellstorff faced this challenge in his ethnographic study of the online world of Second Life (Linden Research, Inc., 2003). To deal with potential problems, he opted to be open about his position as an anthropologist throughout his work and held interviews and focus groups in the online world under the group name, "Digital Cultures." Those who participated signed a virtual informed consent form using their avatar's screen name. Boellstorff used the same format of consent form that he employed in his non-digital fieldwork in Indonesia (which was approved by the IRB), and had his participants type the words, "I agree to participate in your study." By using identical consent forms as to everyday-life studies and being open about his positionality as a researcher and the nature of his study, Boellstorff successfully navigated the challenge of informed consent in the online world.

Another way the researcher can traverse the concerns of the people they interview online is through preparation and willingness to answer any questions that may arise from the participants (Lotz and Ross, 2004). Nardi (2010) was upfront about her positionality throughout her research in World of Warcraft (Blizzard Entertainment, 2004), as the guilds she joined knew who she was, what she was studying, and what she hoped to find out. This gave her informants clear pathways through which they could ask questions and learn more about the research or their role in it. They also knew how to remove themselves from the study if necessary.

A related challenge that qualitative researchers face online is maintaining the anonymity of participants (e.g., Boellstorff 2008; Pearce 2009; Shaw 2012). When conducting individual interviews in a face-to-face environment, information is generally collected privately. Once you change a participant's name and disguise identifying information, the informant is relatively well protected. In online contexts, identity is more complicated. Even when researchers may be unaware of the true identity of the person on the other side of the computer, they are still faced with additional challenges in protecting that identity, such as the permanence and searchability of online posts or screen names (Lotz and Ross, 2004). Information collected in many online contexts is inherently more public than that collected in a face-to-face conversation and can often be linked back to specific individuals more easily.

Regardless of the topic of interest the qualitative researcher brings to the online research, he or she needs to ensure the anonymity of those they interview. Methods for this include: changing direct quotations from online forums or emails, altering screen names, or choosing not to disclose the exact website where fieldwork occurred (Lotz and Ross, 2004). Pseudonyms should be distinct not only from the participant's given name but also from any screen names or character names they use online; these can often be connected to real identities through a simple Internet search and therefore need to be avoided. In Boellstorff's (2008) study of Second Life (Linden Research, Inc., 2003), he did not inquire about the real life information of the people he spoke with, and he had those who signed the informed consent do so with their avatar's name; using this approach, he could not possibly reveal personal information or identities in his final work, protecting them entirely

Finally, researchers may run into various difficulties when it comes to following up with participants. Identity persistence can be low online; participants may change avatars or screen names, leave a game environment or forum, or even lose access to the Internet. When this occurs, researchers may not be able to ask further questions or pursue new avenues of research with the same participants. Such a problem should be explained fully in the final report, but the researcher can still be confident using partial data provided it is clearly contextualized. In fact, the loss of participants may add to analysis in many circumstances, as losing track of fellow players is a problem faced by gamers on a daily basis. The same is true for possible technical issues, such as a lapse in Internet connectivity during an interview. Many gamers have experienced lagging out of an Internet-enabled game. Contextualizing the difficulties of online research in terms of their relevance to the lives of gamers can help make potential flaws into assets. Likewise, this can stave off potential methodological criticisms through transparent recognition of the strengths and weaknesses of this method.

Overall, despite the challenges and concerns in videogame research, interview methods, and in person and online settings, this need not impede qualitative researchers from conducting studies in online environments.

Participant selection and recruitment

To recruit effectively in the modern era, researchers must determine who to talk to and where they can be found. Many in-person events—professional competitions, industry conventions, or local game nights—can be useful. At other times, investigators will have to turn to online communities. With either approach, carefully selected participant characteristics and recruitment tactics can provide a strong foundation for data collection.

When it comes to interviews, the selection of participants involves a number of steps, as talking to every individual involved in a particular area is largely impossible. "An intelligent sampling strategy enables researchers to make systematic contact with communicative phenomena with a minimum of effort" (Lindlof and Taylor, 2002, p.120). Researchers who carefully think through the desired characteristics of their population will be able to collect better results with a smaller time investment, making their project both successful and efficient.

The process of choosing participants must start from a theoretical, rather than practical perspective. A prospective games researcher needs to consider the type of results they want to achieve before taking any other step. Generalizable results that can be used to describe a large population, for instance, are difficult to achieve via interviews, but could be obtained with a broad, randomly selected sample of participants. Specific, nuanced results regarding a particular phenomenon, on the other hand, require targeted sampling procedures, where participants share at least some basic characteristics. For example, when exploring practice habits developed by professional videogame players, it would be useless to talk to a person who has never played professionally and does not desire to play professionally. Interest in the arena of e-sports would be a required characteristic for study participants. The direction a researcher takes in choosing a sample must start with a consideration of the expected results, and then move into a deeper understanding of the characteristics needed for participants to contribute effectively to those results.

The characteristics needed in a sample will always be specific to the research questions or goals of a project. However, a beneficial place to start is by thinking through basic personal characteristics like gender, race, nationality, age or sexual orientation. In video gaming particularly, personal characteristics can mean the difference between welcome into the community and a life spent on its edges, between acceptance and discrimination. Being female or being non-white can result in insults and trash talk, or general treatment as an outsider (Schott and Horrell, 2000; Bryce and Rutter, 2002; Shaw, 2012; Nakamura, 2012). Therefore, researchers intending to explore aspects of community will need to determine how to explore these divides, perhaps through the use of a diverse pool of participants, or how to ask a research question that does not need to take them into account.

Researchers can also identify the desired characteristics of their interview population by drawing on previous research or statistics. For instance, a study on mobile games might want to focus on women, considering them to be the target audience for casual games (Juul, 2009). However, a 2013 analysis of in-game purchases demonstrated that men actually spend more money on mobile games (Ligman, 2013). Therefore, a study on spending habits of casual gamers may need to focus more closely on men, while interviews regarding reasons to play or frequency of play may want to include more women. In this way, new information or older theories can both influence the selection of participants.

Some researchers choose to target a group of participants based on specific games or genres they wish to explore. A number of studies have focused on massively-multiplayer role playing games (MMORPGs) such as *World of Warcraft* (Eklund, 2011; Nardi, 2010; Taylor, 2003). Their reasons for targeting in this fashion are varied, reaching from a desire to focus on games where women have been a bigger part of the audience to interest in the deeply social aspects of such games. However, each defended a targeted focus into a particular aspect of video gaming and recruited a sample of participants that reflected that focus.

Finally, researchers can define a sample according to the broad area of the medium they want to explore. A researcher interested in the inner workings of the industry will likely not receive useful information about this area from a normal game player, while exploring the audience is unlikely to be accomplished only by talking to game designers.

RECRUITMENT

In the modern gaming environment, researchers have an overwhelming variety of options for reaching out to gamers. Not only can they be found in person, at game stores, industry events or e-sports arenas, but many gamers turn to online options such as reddit.com, battle.net or other forums to discuss their preferences and play habits with others who share their interest. Interviews can even be conducted within games themselves, through networks like Xbox Live or through wholly online options like *World of Warcraft*, one of the most frequently studied games in existence. These options allow researchers to target their recruitment efforts very carefully or to aim more broadly in order to explore a wider range of opinions and experiences. Each recruitment method has its potential pros and cons.

As videogame researchers, we do have some small advantages when it comes to recruiting participants. We study a form of entertainment that large groups of people love and enjoy, but which has historically been seen as a lowbrow form of mass media and looked down on in society at large. Despite the fact that this is changing, our respect for the medium can be a powerful incentive for gamers to participate in our studies; we give them an opportunity to discuss one of their favourite activities and to be taken seriously in that discussion. This can be beneficial when it comes to both recruitment and to conducting interviews, as people's passion for a topic can lead them to join the study and to elaborate on answers without much prompting. Furthermore, the shared, social nature of many games makes reaching players easier; they are often used to cooperating and conversing with strangers. This helps the researcher transition from simple playing to more formal interviews.

At the same time, there are some potential pitfalls, such as the still common perception of many videogames as for boys. When reaching out to prospective participants, researchers must decide in advance how they are defining *gamer* and determine whether that definition will be shared by their intended targets. As researchers like Shaw (2012) and Thornham (2008) have demonstrated, the industrial and popular perceptions of gamers as anti-social, young, and male often lead people who do not share these characteristics to avoid defining themselves as such, even if they play video games frequently. If one is aiming for a specific, game-intensive population that matches up to the traditional perception of a video gamer, this language will be acceptable in recruitment and study materials. Male adolescents who play *Halo 4* (343 Industries, 2012) at least five hours a week, for instance, will probably respond to gamer-oriented calls for participation.

On the other hand, a researcher exploring the playing habits of middle-aged, female *Candy Crush Saga* (King, 2012) players will want to define their study in different terms. These women might play for many hours a day, and may be involved in a number of other casual games as well, but their age, gender, and interest in only a small subset of videogames will probably prevent their identifying as a gamer. Even researchers who are aiming for a broad swath of the videogame playing population—men and women, older and younger, various socio-economic groups, of a variety of races—should think carefully through the language they use. Recruiting participants using the term "gamer" may artificially limit the sample a researcher can collect.

ONLINE RECRUITMENT LOCATIONS

Given the modern connectedness of videogames, many researchers have turned to online means for collecting information from users. This approach allows researchers to avoid problems of geography and reach people from around the world. This broad reach can be particularly useful when looking for a very specific type of participant, one which may be difficult to find when limited to only a local area. However, like all recruitment methods, the online approach has its pros and cons.

Online recruitment can take place both within a specific game or via broader forums or online communities. Specific videogames are particularly good when the research questions only concern those games and when those games have a sustained social structure (Nardi, 2010; Boellstorff, 2008; Taylor, 2003). MMORPGs have guilds that tend to last for extended periods of time; it is almost impossible to complete the higher levels of the game without a group of people used to working together. Other games, where higher level play can be individual, may not be as useful for recruitment purposes.

General forums can overcome this problem and can also be used to gather information across a wide variety of games. However, forum participants generally represent the more involved, committed videogame players who consider games important enough to discuss outside of play; therefore, participants recruited in these places will likely not include more casual gamers who play for shorter periods of time or who are less involved. Online forums for gamers may also lack the wide variety of people, described earlier, who do not consider themselves gamers even if they play frequently.

Therefore, different recruitment areas are more effective for some questions than others, and online recruitment may not be the best choice for all projects.

OFF-LINE RECRUITMENT LOCATIONS

Some research questions are better addressed via offline recruitment. Off-line locations can include arcades, industry events, professional gaming tournaments, consumer events like the Penny Arcade Expo (PAX), local game nights, or even individual homes. Again, choosing between these will depend on what the research questions for the project are, and where people who can address those questions will be found. In researching casual games and their role in the videogame industry, Julia G. Raz found recruitment at events like the Electronic Entertainment Expo (E3), which is specifically tailored to industry workers, to be particularly useful (Raz, 2014). Audience research, on the other hand, would be better addressed at a consumer event. Researchers interested in the continued existence of arcades despite the thriving home game market would be well served by recruiting participants at arcades; those interested in PC gaming would gather better information from attendees at a Local Area Network (LAN) tournament focused on PC games.

The main benefit of offline recruitment is that potential participants can easily put a face to the project, which makes many people more comfortable volunteering. The interview itself can occur in person, often at the location of interest, allowing interviewees to reference specific environmental factors when talking. Interactions at a professional gaming event, for instance, could spark participants to talk more deeply about the spatial organization of players and how that affects spectators.

REACHING PARTICIPANTS

After choosing a location, there are a variety of ways in which to reach potential participants. If the sample does not need to be particularly targeted, a broad, scattershot approach may be easiest; posting flyers in relevant offline locations or calls for participation on online forums can result in the collection of an interested group of participants. When more specific results are needed, attending associated consumer or industry events, playing the relevant game as a means for meeting participants, or joining a more targeted forum may be more useful. Attending local game nights can also yield valuable results.

When recruiting, researchers may often find a snowball approach to be beneficial. In a snowball sample, the researcher finds one participant who fits the required criteria for involvement in the study, and then asks them to direct him or her to other people who also possess those characteristics. This can be particularly useful when trying to reach a small, hard to find community, or when the research question may be a sensitive one. "A referral from a well-respected community member or a friend of the informant can help provide a foundation for trust" (Boellstorff, et al., 2012, p.95), leading participants to be more open or honest. A personal introduction from a fellow industry member, for example, may help a researcher connect to other game developers and to obtain real information from them, rather than prepared, public-relations sound bites.

In terms of weaknesses, snowball sampling does not work well in situations where the desired participants may not know each other. For instance, Eklund (2011) found that this strategy was not the best procedure for reaching female gamers, as they tended to know very few other women who played. The snowball approach requires at least a loosely connected set of relationships in order to be effective. It is also possible that snowball sampling can result in perspectives being somewhat homogeneous, as people may tend to befriend others like themselves. If diversity of opinion is significant to the project's goals, researchers can request that their participants direct them to people whose opinions might differ from their own, in order to obtain more variety. They should also carefully consider whether snowball sampling is the best approach to finding participants in the first place; it may not be the ideal choice for all studies.

Finally, researchers should determine if there is a gatekeeper they would need to cooperate with in order to reach their desired population. A gatekeeper manages access to a particular set of people; when the gatekeeper is interested in the research, they can encourage participation among community members. When they disapprove of the research, they can entirely block progress. Gatekeepers are particularly common in industry research. Many companies will insist their PR department approve the topic of the research before allowing access to their employees. Being careful to protect the identity of the company and carefully explaining the goals of the research can help allay corporate fears that a researcher is seeking to do an exposé on the company.

Gatekeepers are less common in audience research, although they do still exist. Access to videogame guilds or clans may require the assistance of the guild leader or another group officer, while recruitment posts on online forums may be taken down if moderator approval is not gained first. For in-person locations, such as local game nights or professional tournaments, shop owners or tournament organizers can be invaluable; these individuals are familiar with the people a researcher would want to talk to and can provide personal introductions to establish rapport with participants. If they do not approve of the project, they can encourage potential interviewees not to participate, sabotaging the researcher's efforts before they even begin.

When asked for assistance, videogame gatekeepers are frequently excited to participate in research projects due to their own passion for games and desire to see them taken seriously. However, it is important to remember that gatekeepers generally see few personal or professional benefits from their assistance; therefore, clearly stating the potential risks and rewards of their participation can help assure them that their help will have positive results.

Conducting interviews

Finally, after thinking through all the preliminaries and finding participants, one can actually conduct the interview. While this might seem a straightforward process, interviewing well can be surprisingly difficult. Participants consistently provide surprising answers or bring up new topics that even the most prepared researcher will not have considered. A good interviewer needs to be primed for these; otherwise, the opportunity to dig deeply into surprising cases can be lost. In an interview with a female gamer about women's place in the videogame community, Cote, in her doctoral research, found herself more than a little shocked when the participant said she honestly felt men were better at videogames than women. Not expecting this from a committed and very talented gamer, Cote responded, "Wow, you really think that?" and then failed to press further, due to her surprise. This was a terrible missed opportunity, as the participant's opinion differed strongly from other interviewees' views. Preparing a quality interview guide in advance, choosing a good interview location and practicing active listening and feedback skills can help prevent gaffes like this.

WRITING AN INTERVIEW GUIDE

Prior to scheduling an interview, a researcher should create an interview guide, laying out the general structure of their topics and the specific questions they plan to use to start exploring these topics. As Lindlof and Taylor (2002) explain, "Questions are potent tactics for starting discourse along certain tracks or for switching tracks later. They can be used to open up a shy person or to persuade a talkative respondent to speak more economically" (p.194). Thus, interviews are meant to be similar to a conversation; however, like any conversation, they can easily go off track without at least some idea of the subjects to be covered. A guideline to the key questions the researcher hopes each interview will answer, can help remind them of their purpose and encourage the conversation back to those areas if necessary.

Table 1 displays typical components of an interview guide, as a starting point for new researchers. Interviews generally fall into one of three types—structured, semi-structured or unstructured—according to the specificity of the interview guide and how closely the researcher follows their prepared questions. In a structured interview, questions are the same across interviews and are generally asked in the same order. Researchers who have a specific topic to explore, or a strong idea of what they want to ask based on past research, may find this approach most useful. On the other side of the spectrum, unstructured interviews often start with broad prompts, rather than specific questions. These aim to bring up new ideas and make unique connections. Semi-structured interviews form a middle ground, providing some consistency while allowing for off-topic exploration. Researchers should consider the approach that best fits their goals while creating their guide, and be open to adjusting interview questions later as necessary.

Common Interview Guide Components	Purpose	Tips
Introductory Script	To open the interview and cover necessary information with the participantTo remind the researcher of the study goals	• Summarize the purpose/goals of the study • Discuss informed consent form and procedures • Overview the interview procedure
Warm-up Questions	Put the participant at ease and build rapport	• Focus on things the participant will be able to express easily, such as their positive experiences playing games • Ask simple but on-topic questions- ex. "How long have you been playing videogames for?", "What's one of your favourite gaming memories?"
Substantive Questions	Collect deeper data that answers the research questions	• Try to provoke more thought in participants • Make questions open-ended • Prepare potential follow-ups to prompt elaboration or help you respond to surprising answers (ex. "How interesting! Can you tell me more about that?")
Demographic Questions	Gather data needed to describe participants in the final research report	• Think critically about the participant characteristics that matter to your research question

Table 1. Parts of an interview guide.

Writing an interview guide can be a difficult process. Many researchers struggle to create properly open-ended questions, or questions that allow participants to answer in a variety of ways and which encourage elaboration. This leads interviews in ways that the researcher may not have anticipated, but which can be informative. Another struggle is knowing whether or not you have created good interview questions. As mentioned earlier, some questions are difficult to answer in interview format; in a one-on-one setting, asking someone about a topic they have not thought through can make them feel uncomfortable or pressured. This is where a researcher needs to draw on earlier works and to think logically through a question. If you were being interviewed, would you be able to answer this question? If not, it should be rephrased or dropped. Pre-testing interview guides on friends or colleagues can also be good practice; if those individuals, who are already familiar with the project, can't answer the question, it is unlikely that a regular participant will be able to do so. Researchers can also use early interviews to test for necessary changes, including adding more participants as needed.

Furthermore, it is important to consider how interview questions and corresponding responses operate among particular contexts. For instance, when conducting interviews with videogame industry professionals, the interviewer must keep in mind how the posed questions might warrant highly managed, corporate responses. In an interview with a marketing executive at a major videogame corporation, Raz, asked whether he would like to have his name and company name changed for the purposes of publication. The respondent claimed, "You can say my name and the company's name, as I would give this same sort of answer to anyone that interviewed me. This could be published in a newspaper or book." While some questions could be answered with such company-approved responses, others might require more personal answers. Researchers should plan for this as they write their questions, structuring the interview so that they are more likely to get the type of material they need.

One positive aspect of interview-based studies is many researchers who choose this method also choose an unstructured interview approach; therefore, interview guides can change as necessary. Cote once started a study intending to ask women how they felt about the hypersexualization of female characters and how it affected their playing habits. She quickly realized, however, that this topic could not be explored without attention to game narratives; participants were frustrated with character sexualization when it detracted from the storyline, but accepted such characterization when it made sense within the game's broader context. Upon realizing this, Cote adjusted her guide to attend to questions of narrative and entered later interviews more prepared.

In addition to writing the questions of an interview guide, the researcher should think through the perspective they wish to take within an interview and how they plan to communicate that position (Lindlof and Taylor, 2002). For instance, many videogame players are aware of the academic discourse surrounding videogame violence and its potential pitfalls. Because of this, they may avoid commenting on violence in games out of fear that they will further negative stereotypes, or they may take a defensive position on this matter in order to protect the games they enjoy. A researcher who is doing work on violent games such as first person shooters may therefore want to position themselves as a fan of that genre, so that participants do not fear sharing their perspective. At other times, particularly when investigating the mundane, day-to-day activities that occur within and around videogames, a researcher may be better served by ignorance, either real or feigned. For example, Eklund (2011) found via interviews with female *World of Warcraft* players that many women were directed to the priest or paladin classes by their gaming boyfriends (p.329). A researcher who took the position of a *WoW* expert might miss these gendered divisions; participants would assume the researcher understood the different characters, and would therefore not explain their class selection process as thoroughly as they would to an ignorant party. Researchers should consider whether an insider or outsider position will serve their purposes more effectively in interviews, depending on the topic at hand.

SCHEDULING AN INTERVIEW

Finally, the researcher can schedule a time to meet with the participant and conduct the interview. Where and when an interview will be conducted should reflect the schedules and pressures faced by the respondent, rather than those of the interviewer. For instance, when interviewing parents, a researcher needs to take into account the pressures of child care and avoid trying to schedule interviews for a time when parents are picking children up from day-care, or school, or taking care of meals, among other responsibilities.

Other than general schedule restrictions, however, "the qualitative interview is a remarkably adaptable method. Interviews can be done in a research lab, during a walk along a beach, at a corner table in a restaurant, or in a teenager's bedroom—anywhere two people can talk in relative privacy" (Lindlof and Taylor, 2002, pp.170–171). One strategy is allowing the participant to select a place where the interview can be conducted, or suggesting a place that is already in the respondent's environment. These considerations will ensure that the participant feels at ease throughout the interviewing process.

In terms of videogame research, questions are often not particularly sensitive, making coffee shops and other casual public places ideal locations for interviews, provided the volume is regulated and will not interfere with audio recording. If a topic requires more privacy, meeting in a research lab may be a better choice, to avoid any awkwardness on the part of the interviewee. When recruiting participants at an industry or other gaming event, such as E3, PAX or a Major League Gaming (MLG) tournament, private areas in which to conduct an interview may not be readily available. In these circumstances, researchers should focus on finding an area quiet enough to record a clear interview, or should use these spaces simply for recruitment, actually conducting interviews at a later date.

Any time interviews will be conducted in person, whether on the spot or planned in advance, researchers should bring relevant consent forms and information on the study, a means for taking notes while talking, and an audio recorder, so that the interview can be transcribed and analysed in depth at a later date. Because interviews are dynamic and involved, researchers are rarely able to take detailed enough notes to complete a whole project while conducting the interview; it is only later that patterns can be discovered and comparisons made.

For interviews where the participant has been recruited online, the researcher again has options regarding how to proceed. Perhaps the biggest decision in this situation is choosing the type of communication method to use. Generally speaking, the options are video, audio or text, with the benefits and limitations of each outlined in Table 2. Researchers should choose between these based on both the comfort of the participant and what they have available for use, as well as on the quality or type of data the researcher seeks.

Method	Strengths	Weaknesses
Video (ex. Skype, Google Hangout)	• Closest alternative to face-to-face conversation • Rich in terms of material • Easy to communicate tone and emotion	• Participants must have a camera and microphone • May require additional software to record audio • Requires transcription
Audio (ex. Skype, VoIP software like Ventrilo)	• Tone and emotion still clear • Frequently used by many online players while gaming	• Participants must have a microphone • May require additional software to record audio • Requires transcription
Text Chat (in-game)	• Already used by participants • Location within the game environment can lead to more detailed answers • Convenient for participants with speech or hearing difficulties • Does not require transcription	• Participants may be distracted by other factors in game • Many chat mechanisms are not permanent; researchers will need a strategy for recording the interview to a more permanent location (e.g. video capture software) • Takes longer to complete than a verbal interview • Loses vocal and emotional tone (although caps, emoticons and punctuation can sometimes act as stand-ins)
Text Chat (out-of-game, ex. Google Chat or MSN Messenger)	• Convenient for participants with speech or hearing difficulties • Does not require transcription	• Takes longer to complete than a verbal interview • Loses vocal and emotional tone (although caps, emoticons and punctuation can sometimes act as stand-ins)

Table 2. Online interview approaches

A GOOD INTERVIEW

Once the researcher is actually sitting down with the participant, ready to conduct their interview, there are some strategies that can yield better results. These include establishing a good rapport, listening clearly, and dynamically adapting according to how the interview proceeds.

By rapport, we mean a carefully cultivated sense of respect, where the participant knows that their opinions will be respected by a non-judgmental interviewer. Rapport is based on honesty and openness. At the start of the study, participants should be given a clear idea of the study goals and their role in it (Lindlof and Taylor, 2002). Reassurance that the researcher is looking to understand the participants' lived experiences and worldview can also encourage openness; participants are well-versed in their own histories and preferences. For example, asking the participant to talk about positive experiences and interests at the beginning of the interview can put them at ease. This can ensure that they are more comfortable answering deeper, more sensitive questions later in the conversation.

If a question is unusual or particularly delicate, it may be helpful to indicate that you, the researcher, have heard all manner of answers and will not be surprised by anything the participant says, so they feel their response will not be judged. An alternative strategy is to phrase the question in such a way as to ask about others (Boellstorff, et al., 2012). For instance, the question, "Why do you engage in gender-swapping in online games?" may get only a prepared joke answer, such as "If I have to stare at a character's butt all day, I'd rather it be a girl's", a common response from male online gamers. However, asking, "Why do you think people tend to gender-swap online?" could allow people to talk more broadly about the reason behind their own choices, phrased protectively as stories about others. The appropriate way to navigate difficult questions may change from interview to interview, but an awareness of overall strategies can help the researcher adjust as necessary.

A researcher must also be prepared to listen carefully to what the participant is saying. Positive feedback and encouragement can be key to getting deep, detailed information. Eye contact and subtle body language, like a nod or leaning forward, both indicate attention to the speaker and can push them to expand on a point more fully. A good listener also prompts for further details, but limits their own input. When listening back to an interview at a later date, the interviewer should be heard very little, while their participant speaks quite frequently. Another approach is to make connections to the participant's earlier answers. Instead of inquiring, "What characters do you like?" a more involved researcher might ask, "You mentioned that you love playing as Link from *The Legend of Zelda* games—are there other characters that you really like?" This demonstrates clear listening and will also help the participant connect earlier and later questions in a coherent manner. Particularly in the area of videogames, participants enjoy being able to share their knowledge and perspectives with someone who is actively listening.

Finally, the researcher needs to alter questions as necessary. If a participant brings up an interesting point that was not on the researcher's interview guide, it is still a good idea to pursue that avenue of thought, particularly if it is clearly related to the overall research questions. If a participant mentions something that the researcher had included at the very end of the interview, covering those questions sooner will help the conversation flow more effectively. Interview guides are key to ensuring that all relevant areas of the research are covered, but the researcher should not be shackled into a particular order of questions.

Analysing data

Following a series of interviews, the researcher arrives at arguably the most complicated step in interview research: deciding what to do with all the collected material or data and how to interpret it. Analysing interviews always involves transcription, coding data for patterns, and theorizing the results, but the ways in which one can go about this are extremely diverse and depend on the goals of the project.

TRANSCRIPTION

Transcription, put simply, is the process of writing down the content of an interview so that it can be looked at in depth and analysed for patterns. However, a number of elements need to be considered in order for the transcript to be useful for any given project. Before beginning transcription, researchers should consider the level of detail they require. Will pauses need to be indicated? If the participant fills gaps in speech with "um" or "like", should that be included? Will words like "gonna" be corrected to the more grammatical "going to", or does the abbreviated inflection matter to the results? Researchers need to represent what the participant is saying and who they are, while being careful to avoid communicating stereotypes that could affect readers' interpretations in a negative way. Possible language difficulties, such as accents, colloquialisms or complete translation, may affect the process of transcription as well, given that the final written copy needs to be usable and understandable by the researcher.

Who will transcribe is an important consideration. The most detailed data analysis occurs when the researcher completes transcription themselves; this allows them to evaluate both the words an interviewee says and the emotions attached to them. In terms of videogames, this also means that an experienced individual will be transcribing game titles, character names and player slang, leading to fewer issues in the final record. However, a practiced transcriber tends to take at least three hours to record one hour of high-quality tape, and longer if the audio is imperfect. For new transcribers, it is not unusual to take ten or more hours to copy over a single hour of audio. Transcription is especially slow when using standard computers; a researcher who has a large amount of material should invest in a foot pedal to control audio playback, in order to free both hands for typing and remove the need for switching between software programs. Even with a foot pedal, however, having a single individual complete all the interviews required for a project is an extremely time consuming process.

One alternative is to recruit research assistants who are familiar with videogames and are unlikely to make mistakes in transcribing game-specific terms. Not being seasoned transcriptionists, they will be slower than a well-trained individual. They also may miss some of the inflection contained within a given interview, but a small team will still be able to complete transcription in a shorter period of time than an individual.

The final option is to send interview recordings to a professional transcription company to have them turned to text. This option is likely to be fastest and easiest on the part of the researcher, who will not have to train student transcribers or do the work on his or her own. However, professional transcribers can be expensive, may also lose the emotional details of an interview, and may be unfamiliar with videogame terminology, potentially leading to mistakes in the final text. When time is of the essence, though, a good professional transcriber can be invaluable.

ANALYSIS

Once a few interviews are transcribed, the researcher can begin analysis. As with most other steps of research, how an individual chooses to perform analysis is deeply connected to their paradigmatic orientation. Overall, however, the process of analysis consists of breaking down patterns in the data and putting those patterns into a meaningful theoretical framework to draw conclusions.

Breaking data down is frequently referred to as "coding and categorization". In this process, researchers look for broad patterns and themes, ideas, or language that repeat across a number of interviews, or areas where different perspectives seem to conflict. When an analyst encounters these characteristics, they create a relevant category into which similar ideas can be grouped. As these categories build up, they become what is known as a "coding scheme" or a classification plan systematically applied across all the interviews in a study.

Table 3 shows a sample coding scheme, which breaks down some statements from an interview about different video game consoles and how they are perceived by gamers. The researcher (Cote, 2010) has marked each line with the specific thing the participant was talking about, a few of the themes the line seems to relate to, and the broadest category into which she feels the line should fall, at least at this time; coding is an iterative process, and individual lines frequently change location multiple times before the analysis is finalized. In this case, the broad categories represent sections of the potential research report, while themes are smaller ideas that will be discussed within the various areas of that framework; however, different researchers may choose to code in different ways, according to their preferences and particular approach to making sense of the world.

Line # from Transcript	Quote	Specific Topic	Themes	Broad category
217	Wii is the family console	Wii	• Family • Casual	Console characterisation
218	it's uh for casual gamers	Wii	• Casual	Console characterisation
218	you can come into it with no experience and still enjoy yourself	Wii	• Casual • No experience	Console characterisation
224	Xbox and PlayStation they really push sort of the hardcore gaming angle	• Xbox • Playstation	• Hardcore • Serious	Console characterisation
225	People that are willing to invest 40 hours at a stretch to, you know, play through a game	• Xbox • Playstation	• Hardcore • Serious • Invested	Console characterisation
227	a lot of the ads are really geared towards guys	• Xbox • Playstation	• Hardcore • Male • Advertising market	Console characterisation
229	In what ways would they possibly be geared towards women?	• Ads • Xbox • Playstation	• Advertising • Gender • Target Audience	Gender questions
230	Why does it necessarily have to be that playing Halo is a male thing?	Male games	• Advertising • Gender • Target Audience	Gender questions

Table 3. Sample coding scheme (Cote, 2010)

Coding schemes can come from two main places: the data itself or previous research. In a popular approach to theorizing interviews known as grounded theory (Glaser and Strauss, 1967; cf. chapter 18), researchers develop both their coding strategies and their overall interpretation of the data from the material contained within the interviews, with no initial reliance on outside theories or research. This approach prizes the input of the participants above all other potential sources. The resulting conclusions are firmly rooted in the data, although they can be compared to the results of other studies. The coding scheme in Table 3 employed grounded theory type of approach and developed from the data itself.

At other times, coding schemes can be developed based on earlier studies, rather than taking them into account at the end of the process. For instance, analyses of videogame content have consistently demonstrated a high proportion of sexual and violent content (Smith, B., 2006; Smith, S., 2006; Burgess, et al., 2007; Dill and Thill, 2007). Therefore, a researcher might expect these characteristics to resonate with audiences and prepare a coding scheme including different aspects of character sexualization and violent content. The particular approach a researcher should take depends on their paradigm and the extent to which they feel their results need to be linked to their specific data. For example, ethnographers and constructivists, who prize the lived experiences and individual worldviews of participants, tend to rely on grounded theory, while post-positivists, who are interested in generalizability, are more likely to develop coding schemes in advance.

Coding, as stated earlier, is an iterative process; researchers can start with just a few interviews and develop part of a coding scheme, but when new, interesting material arises, they will have to return to the original interviews and apply the newly developed categories to that material as well. This is not a flaw in the process; rather, it is an integral part of developing a deep familiarity with the data in order to extract to extract the most significant components. "The most fundamental approach to data analysis is to engage in a rigorous intellectual process of working deeply and intimately with ideas. Analysis is not primarily about tuning coding schemes or tweaking data analysis software. It is about finding, creating and bringing thoughtful, provocative ideas to acts of writing" (Boellstorff, et al., 2012, p.159).

Throughout this whole process, a researcher must keep track of where they are in analysis and what their data looks like. There are a variety of ways in which to do this, and the choice of which to use is fully dependent on the researcher's preferences. Traditionally, data is coded on paper, with different lines from the interviews written on notecards and sorted into piles or stuck to bulletin boards according to their category. Being able to engage with information visually is a key part of analysis for some researchers; others find this approach overwhelming or fear losing essential pieces of data in the shuffle of piles. These researchers may be better served by one of the many software packages where one highlights and tags different sections of data according to their category. Both proprietary packages like NVivo and open source software like Atlas.ti can be used for this purpose; a full comparison of the available options can be found at the ReStore Web Resource Database (see Koenig). Some researchers may even find a balance between paper and computer, doing some work on the computer, then printing it out to check the accuracy of the coding by hand. New researchers should experiment between these methods until they stumble upon their best approach.

VERIFICATION

The final step in interview analysis is an attempt to verify the researcher's interpretation of the data. Not all paradigmatic frameworks call for this step; some approaches consider the researcher's process of meaning-making to be significant in and of itself, without requiring verification from other sources. However, for approaches that are concerned with validity, there are two main processes that can be used.

The first is triangulation, in which data collected by other means is compared with the results of the interview analysis, to check for agreement (Lindlof and Taylor, 2002). Generally speaking, interview results that agree with other approaches are seen as more valid in this approach. To continue a recent example, interviews that focused on these prominence of sex and violence in games would triangulate well with the results of earlier content analysis. The potential problem with triangulation, however, is that it can result in researchers ignoring real differences between their participants and other sources, missing out on meaningful conflict.

Those more interested in a participant-centred validity check can engage in member validation, in which they bring a draft of their results to the community they gathered data from. If community members agree with the researcher's interpretations, the information is considered valid. However, member validation is only useful if the researcher checks with a variety of community members, to avoid privileging an individual's perspective over all the other members'. It can also be difficult to achieve agreement when the research is on a particularly controversial area, where individuals are inclined to disagree strongly.

As with most other steps in the interview process, deciding whether or not to validate and what approach to use is highly dependent on the research questions at hand and the overall goals of the project. Researchers should rely on their own assumptions and beliefs in order to navigate this process.

Summary

Interviews are an extremely useful method for collecting in-depth information on topics that require individual components, like personal opinions, preferences and experiences. They allow researchers and informants to discuss topics in a naturalistic, free-flowing way, yielding new ideas and interesting observations. At the same time, each step of preparing an interview-based study requires careful thought.

The researcher needs first to determine that interviews are likely to collect usable information that is better than that which could be gathered via a different method. Ethical considerations need to be taken into account, particularly if the research is being done online, and participants should be selected carefully and in line with the research questions. Even the act of conducting interviews requires preparation and practice, as does analysis.

The guidelines provided in this chapter may not guarantee an effective interview, especially as we cannot predict how videogames will change in the future or account for all the possible questions researchers may be asking. However, they do serve as a basic framework for a beginning scholar who aims to use interviews as a means for producing high-quality, original works, and will, of course, continue to develop as the field matures.

Recommended reading

- Boellstorff, T., 2008. *Coming of age in second life: An anthropologist explores the virtually human.* Princeton: Princeton University Press.
- Boellstorff, T., Nardi, B., Pearce, C. and Taylor, T. L., 2012. *Ethnography and virtual worlds: A handbook of method.* Princeton: Princeton University Press.

- Lindlof, T. R. and Taylor, B. C., 2002. *Qualitative communication research methods.* Thousand Oaks: Sage.
- Nardi, B. A., 2010. *My life as a night elf priest: An anthropological account of World of Warcraft.* Ann Arbor: University of Michigan Press.
- Shaw, A., 2012. Do you identify as a gamer? Gender, race, sexuality, and gamer identity. *New Media & Society,* 14(1), pp.28–44.

References

343 Industries, 2012. *Halo 4* [game]. Xbox 360. Microsoft Studios.

Baran, S. and Davis, D., 2011. *Mass communication theory: Foundations, ferment, and future.* Boston: Wadsworth Cengage Learning.

Blizzard Entertainment, 2004. *World of Warcraft* [game]. Blizzard Entertainment.

Blumberg, F. C., and Sokol, L. M., 2004. Boys' and girls' use of cognitive strategy when learning to play video games. *The Journal of General Psychology,* 131(2), pp.151–158.

Boellstorff, T., 2008. *Coming of age in second life: an anthropologist explores the virtually human.* Princeton: Princeton University Press.

Boellstorff, T., Nardi, B., Pearce, C. and Taylor, T. L., 2012. *Ethnography and virtual worlds: A handbook of method.* Princeton: Princeton University Press.

Bryce, J. and Rutter, J., 2002. Killing like a girl: Gendered gaming and girl gamer's visibility. In: F. Mäyrä, ed., *Proceedings of computer games and digital cultures conference.* Tampere: Tampere University Press, pp.243–255.

Burgess, M.C.R., Stermer, S.P. and Burgess, S. R., 2007. Sex, lies and video games: The portrayal of male and female characters on video game covers. *Sex Roles,* 57(5–6), pp.419–433.

Cote, A., 2010. *The gendering of video game consoles* [unpublished interview data]. University of Michigan.

Dill, K.E. and Thill, K.P., 2007. Video Game characters and the socialization of gender roles: Young people's perceptions mirror sexist media depictions. *Sex Roles,* 57(11–12), pp.851–864.

Eklund, L., 2011. Doing gender in cyberspace: The performance of gender by female World of Warcraft players. *Convergence,* 17(3), pp.323–342.

Glaser, B. G. and Strauss, A. L., 1967. *The discovery of grounded theory: Strategies for qualitative research.* Chicago: Aldine Publishing Company.

Juul, J., 2009. *A casual revolution: Reinventing video games and their players.* Cambridge: MIT Press.

King, 2012. *Candy Crush Saga* [game]. King.

Koenig, T., n.d. *CAQDAS Comparison*. Available at: <http://www.restore.ac.uk/lboro/research/software/caqdas_comparison.php>.

Ligman, K., 2013. The biggest spenders on mobile? Men who like console games. *Gamasutra*. Available at: <http://www.gamasutra.com/view/news/198971/The_biggest_spenders_on_mobile_Men_who_like_console_games.php>.

Lincoln, Y.S. and Guba, E.G., 2000. Paradigmatic controversies, contradictions, and emerging confluences. In N.K. Denzin and Y.S. Lincoln, eds., 2000. *Handbook of qualitative research*. Thousand Oaks: Sage, pp.163–188.

Linden Research, Inc., 2003. *Second Life* [game]. Linden Lab.

Lindlof, T.R. and Taylor, B.C., 2002. *Qualitative communication research methods*. Thousand Oaks: Sage.

Lotz, A.D. and Ross, S.M., 2004. Toward ethical cyberspace audience research: Strategies for using the Internet for television audience studies. *Journal of Broadcasting and Electronic Media*, 48(3), pp.501–512.

Morgan, D.L., 1997. *Focus groups as qualitative research*, 2nd ed. Thousand Oaks: Sage.

Nakamura, L., 2012. "It's a nigger in here! Kill the nigger!" User-generated media campaigns against racism, sexism, and homophobia in digital games. *The International Encyclopaedia of Media Studies*, 5, pp.2–15.

Nardi, B. A., 2010. *My life as a night elf priest: An anthropological account of World of Warcraft*. Ann Arbor: University of Michigan Press.

Pearce, C., 2009. *Communities of play: Emergent cultures in multiplayer games and virtual worlds*. Cambridge: MIT Press.

Raz, J.G., 2014. Casualness. In: M.J.P. Wolf and B. Perron, eds., *The Routledge companion to video game studies*. New York: Routledge, pp.134–142.

Schott, H.R. and Horrell, K.R., 2000. Girl gamers and their relationship with the gaming culture. *Convergence*, 6(4), pp.36–53.

Shaw, A., 2012. Do you identify as a gamer? Gender, race, sexuality, and gamer identity. *New Media & Society*, 14(1), pp.28–44.

Smith, B. P., 2006. The (computer) games people play: An overview of popular game content. In: P. Vorderer and J. Bryant, eds., 2006. *Playing video games: Motives, responses, and consequences*. Mahwah: Lawrence Erlbaum Associates, pp.43–56.

Smith, S., 2007. Perps, pimps and provocative clothing: Examining negative content patterns in video games. In: P. Vorderer and J. Bryant, eds., *Playing video games: Motives, responses, and consequences*. Mahwah: Lawrence Erlbaum Associates, pp.57–76.

Spradley, J., 1980. *Participant observation*. Minneapolis: University of Minnesota Press.

Squire, K., 2003. Video games in education. *Games & Simulation*, 2(1), pp.49–62.

Taylor, T. L., 2003. Multiple pleasures women and online gaming. *Convergence*, 9(1), pp.21–46.

Thornham, H., 2008 "It's a boy thing": Gaming, gender and geeks. *Feminist Media Studies*, 8(2), pp.127–142.

8. Studying thoughts

Stimulated recall as a game research method

JORI PITKÄNEN

Stimulated recall (SR) is a family of introspective research procedures through which cognitive processes can be investigated by inviting subjects to recall, when prompted by a video sequence, their concurrent thinking during that event. (Lyle, 2003, p.861.)

When choosing an appropriate method for a study, the researcher is faced with two simple questions: What is the study trying to find out? How does the study have the best chances of finding it out? When play experience, decision-making, play culture or interactions are the focus of the study, or if one is interested the thoughts of players during certain events, stimulated recall provides a very practical tool.

Although similar methods have been used in game research, stimulated recall is still fairly unused, but can be a valuable addition to the toolset of game researchers. In short, stimulated recall refers to post-participation interviews where the participant is supported in their recall of their thoughts during the event by being shown recorded media (e.g., audio, video, and still images) of their participation. The immersive nature of games may make recalling thought processes that occurred during gaming after-wards challenging. The use of stimulated recall offers a way to aid participants in recalling their thought processes during the experience and relating to the researcher.

Building a common understanding between the researcher and the research subject is important in acquiring new knowledge. A particular challenge in the domain of game research is that since many game researchers are game enthusiasts themselves (cf. Montola, 2012), researchers might interpret the participant's statements through the lens of their own experience as game players. Even if the researcher is not a game enthusiast (Sotamaa and Suominen, 2013; Mäyrä, van Looy and Quandt, 2013) building a common understanding between the researcher and the informant is important and stimulated recall can support this process.

This chapter will introduce stimulated recall as a research method, discuss its history, advantages and challenges and make suggestions how it could be used in game research.

History of stimulated recall

In the opening quote of this chapter, professor of coaching and coach education John Lyle gives an exact and self-explicatory definition of stimulated recall (Lyle, 2003, p.861), which was also very close to the professors' of linguistics Mackey and Gass' definition: stimulated recall is viewed as a subset of introspective research methods, in which the researcher accesses the informants' own interpretations of his or her mental processes. Its roots are in philosophy and psychology. (Mackey and Gass, 2005, cited in Fox-Turnbull, 2009, p.205.)

One of the first to use the stimulated recall method was the educational psychologist Benjamin Bloom who made use of sound tapes when researching the thought processes of university students. Bloom describes the method as follows: "The basic idea underlying the method of stimulated recall is that a subject may be enabled to relive an original situation with vividness and accuracy if he is presented with a large number of the cues and stimuli which occurred during the original situation." (Bloom, 1953 cited in Eskelinen, 1993, pp.69–70.)

Researchers coming from the tradition of action theory in cognitive psychology have used a technique similar to stimulated recall, called self-confrontation interviews. These interviews also use video material of certain actions by individuals or groups, but these actions are relatively short-stretched. Immediately after the recorded actions, the interviews take place. The interviews consist of watching the video material and asking the subjects at regular intervals (from 15 seconds to one minute) what they are thinking about their actions. The interviews try to find out whether the actions are intentional or goal-oriented. (Dempsey, 2010, p.352; von Cranach, et al., 1982; Valach, et al., 2002.) According to Dempsey, the difference between this research method and stimulated recall is that self-confrontation interviews emphasize a short time-lag between action and interview, privileging cognition about action, whereas stimulated recall in ethnography emphasizes broader cultural values and the participant's strategies for interaction, as emphasized in sociological ethnographies. (Dempsey, 2010, p.353.) The stimulated recall interviews are also planned according to the video material of the event, whereas self-confrontation interviews follow a certain structure applied to each interview.

There are examples of methods similar to stimulated recall being used in game research. The study by Bentley, et al. (2005) explored the use of the cued-recall debrief methodology, a form of situated recall, as a method to elicit information about user affect during system use. The results indicates that the cued-recall debrief can successfully elicit information about user affect while playing computer games. Cue recall used head-mounted cameras and like in self-confrontation interviews, the interviews were held immediately after the action. Jørgensen (2011) also used cued recall as part of her cross-methodological study of players as co-researchers.

Stimulated recall is not uncommon in analyzing classroom interactions (e.g., Beers, et al., 2006; Plaut, 2006; Sime, 2006; Stough, 2001), psychological studies, sport research (e.g., Mackenzie and Kerr, 2012) or ethnography (e.g., Dempsey, 2010). Svartsjö, et al. (2008) studied poker players with gambling problems using a similar method, but did not do not use the name stimulated recall.

Philosophy behind stimulated recall

Stimulated recall is an interview method in which the subject of research analyzes his or her own actions using stimuli such as an audio or video recording. The method aims to support the participant to rebuild the original situation in their mind as authentically as possible in order for him or her to be able to analyze their actions and thought processes during the actions. A stimulated recall interview can be structured or non-structured. Whether to use a structured or non-structured form depends on the research questions; if the researcher is interested in all thoughts arising at a certain event, a non-structured interview is more suitable. If the research questions have a definite focus (such as in the examples mentioned below in *Two cases of stimulated recall research*), some structure serves the researcher in focusing the interviews with relevant questions.

In qualitative research, the goal is to describe and understand a phenomenon in a specific context; the researcher and the subject are always subjective. The stimulated recall method gathers research material relating to the participant's experience in relatively natural circumstances. During the interview the researcher builds the understanding of the phenomenon together with the participant.

A stimulated recall interview gathers information about the thoughts, reasons and motivations behind actions. This information can be valuable for game researchers interested in topics such as game design, monetization, strategic thinking, educational aspects of gaming, social aspects of gaming or any other aspect where the player experience is central. The information is subjective, since the informant analyzes his or her own actions. The validity of the information is discussed in more detail in the next section.

Advantages and challenges

One of the definite advantages of stimulated recall compared to traditional interviews is that the informant is forced to confront their actions as they actually happened (within the limitations of recording and reproduction equipment). When informants are interviewed they discuss actions that they actually engaged in during ongoing interactions and not actions they falsely recall in error, reducing how hypothetic the interview is. The researcher can ask why the informant reacted in a certain manner shown on tape instead of how the informant claims they would react. When the researcher shows the informants their own reactions, the informants are in position to remember their exact outward responses and can attempt to retrace their thought process as it unfolded in real time. (Dempsey, 2010, pp.350–351.)

In stimulated recall, the participant is not relying solely on his or her memory during the interview, reducing the amount of forgotten thought processes. It is possible to research the participant's thought, motivation and orientation processes with very little disturbance compared to having an observer present.

The most obvious challenge is the presence of a camera and how it affects the participants' behavior. Participants may feel nervous in the presence of a video camera and behave as if they are performing rather than behaving naturally. Referring to other researchers (e.g., Engeström, et al., 1988, Loven, 1991), The presence of a camera seems to affect more the superficial behavior and not the more constant behavioral patterns. It is difficult for an individual to change such patterns, because usually they are not aware of them. Stimulated recall is also a revealing method. It helps the participants to give a truer image of them, since the action is on tape and it is more difficult to whitewash.

When discussing reliability, one of the critiques concerning the stimulated recall is the human need to explain things. Subjects may try to rationalize their actions and explain them without the actual knowledge of what took place in their thought processes (Gass and Mackey, 2000, pp.5–6). Stimulated recall has developed with the critique. Some of the critiqued aspects can also be seen as the strength of the method: if the interview contains rationalization and general principles given by the subject in addition to the thought processes revealed by the stimuli, it can also lead to a wider research material.

How to build a stimulated recall study

This section presents a step-by-step guide to stimulated recall research. First the steps made by Dempsey (2010, pp.345–346) are introduced, and based on those steps I have built the steps for the stimulated recall method in game research.

Dempsey conducted a study in sociology, and he studied jazz jam sessions in which he himself participated. He provides seven steps for a successful stimulated recall project in ethnography. These steps are

- conducting traditional participant-observer ethnography
- developing a general rubric describing activities in the field
- developing questions about processes in the social field being studied
- recording participants' activities
- developing a unique interview protocol for each interview
- interviewing the informant using the stimulated recall technique
- refining the rubric and subsequent protocols. (Dempsey, 2010, p.354–355.)

STIMULATED RESEARCH FOR GAME RESEARCHERS: 6 STEPS

Based on Dempsey's steps, the following steps are a good guideline for a game researcher using stimulated recall. Before doing the actual study, there is preparation activity to undertake; formulating the research questions, getting acquainted with existing research, selecting the most appropriate and practical methodology. Cote and Raz (chapter 7) discuss how to select, contact and recruit participants. The approaches mentioned in their chapter work very well with this kind of interviews as well.

Step 1: Understanding the game

Every game is its own specific system, consisting of rules, goals and the manner of acting inside a system. It is very important for the researcher to understand what choices are available to players before attempting to research the thoughts behind the player's actions. For example, a classic puzzle-based adventure game offers quite different options to a modern computer role-playing game, whereas (typically) in table-top and live actions role playing games the number of choices is only as limited as the player's imagination. Researching the reasons behind actions in a puzzle-based adventure game with a linear storyline would concentrate on puzzle-solving processes with strictly limited possible actions.

Step 2: Understanding the idioculture of the gamer's society

If the game is played in a group or has any social level at all, this is also a relevant step. The idioculture may have great effect on the decisions during the game. Online game communities and larper groups have their own cultures and social status systems which may affect the playing experience. The researcher needs to be mindful of this dimension when seeking to understand the player's choices and actions.

First, the researcher should try to understand the general culture associated with the game, and then go on to understand the culture of the informants in this particular research. The researcher should create questions about the aspects of the idioculture that might provide insight into the choices of the players.

Step 3: Recording the game

Since most games are strongly visual, this section will concentrate on video recordings. Before recording, it is important to inform the players that the game is being recorded. It is also important to decide on which players are the informants before recording. Deciding which to use as informants afterwards increases the potential for bias in the results; a researcher could choose (consciously or otherwise) data that fits their intended conclusions. When recording a live event, the participants may feel awkward at first, but the informants usually get comfortable with the cameras (cf. Svartsjö, 2009). Gameplay on a computer can be recorded without cameras, unless video of the player is also needed.

When recording, the researcher should also take notes of relevant actions that need further research during the interviews.

- *Recording video games:* When researching video games on different platforms (console, tablet, or computer), the researcher needs to decide whether only the recording of on-screen events is necessary or if footage of the player's reactions is also needed. This depends very much on the research questions. The recording requires video capture software capturing both audio and video on the player's playing device.
- *Recording table-top games:* When recording table-top games (e.g., roleplaying games such as *Dungeons & Dragons* (1974), traditional table-top board games such as chess, card games such as poker), play normally happens at one location. A static camera is sufficient, but multiple cameras to capture each player's reactions is desirable.
- *Recording location-based and live-action role-playing games:* When recording location-based and live-action role-playing games, the manner of recording depends whether the game happens in one room or more. In some location-based games the events on the screen can also be recorded. One-room games can be recorded with one or two cameras, if all action is visible and the there are few enough participants that speech is understandable. When games happen in wider spaces, the researcher needs to consider how to follow the participants. One option is additional static cameras, but this results in more material to go through and of the usefulness of the recording is erratic. Another option is to follow the players who are informants. As long as the researcher gets enough material from each player, this is a good option. The challenge is avoiding disrupting the participant's immersion in play. It helps to create an in-game reason or role for the cameras that it will affect the player's playing as little as possible. A third option is

using head-mounted cameras, which provide a recording of the whole game experience. This was used in adventure sport research by Mackenzie and Kerr (2012, p.60).

Step 4: Planning the interviews

The recorded material should be watched through very shortly after recording the event. When building the video material for each interview, the researcher must decide what recorded material is important and what is not, depending on the research questions. Ideally, clips for the interview can be extracted using video editing software; otherwise the researcher can mark the times of each clip manually. The chosen clips should contain only the actions of each informant that are needed for the research. For example, a moment in a larp where the player just sleeps, eats or is idle might be useless in terms of research.

After editing the video material for the interviews, the researcher plans out each individual interview. It is often useful at this phase to go back to the research questions and remind oneself what the research goals are. The work during the previous steps may also provide material. When building questions, the researcher should also leave room for free answers that are not only stimuli-related. Stimulated recall interviews often have surprising and unexpected moments (Dempsey, 2010, p.355).

A useful guideline on designing an interview script is presented in table1 in Cote and Raz (chapter 7), consisting of the introductory script, warm-up questions, substantive questions and demographic questions. The introductory script and warm-up questions should take place before the stimulated recall interview with the video recordings. The substantive questions often relate to the video material, but can also include other topics to get a deeper understanding of the informant's thoughts. The demographic questions concern the informant's characteristics: what characteristics of the matter to the research question? The characteristics that do not matter should be left out of the final rapport.

Step 5: Interviewing the informants using stimulated recall

The interviews should be carried out as shortly after the event as possible to enable better recall. Depending on both the research questions and the answers provided, the researcher has to decide when to give the informant space and when to follow the prepared structure. Most stimulated recall interviews are semi-structured: an interview which has been structured to accompany the video with questions referring to particular actions in the video. The research should plan questions to elicit information relevant to the research questions. The structure of the interview should have room for free expression and thought. When a video clip seems to have more importance during the interview than the researcher has anticipated, the researcher should stray from the intended interview structure.

Like the moderator discussed by Eklund (chapter 9), the interviewer should attempt to make the situation as comfortable for the informant as possible. In the beginning of the interview the researcher should give the informant more space and time to adjust to the awkwardness of facing oneself on video. When the informants are comfortable, they will be more confident to provide information.

Step 6: Analyzing the interviews

After the interviews are done and transcribed, the researcher has to choose, how to analyze the data. A good example method for this process is the EPP-method described below. However the best choice of method also depends on the research questions. Cote and Raz (chapter 7) also point out the importance of verifying the researcher's interpretation of the data.

Analyzing the results

The most appropriate way of analyzing the data depends on the original goals of the research. For example, if the research aim is to gain insight into what the player thinks he is thinking, qualitative analysis methods normally used for the interviews such as discourse analysis are most appropriate (cf. Gee, 2005).

Another commonly used analysis method in qualitative research is thematic analysis (see, Braun and Clarke, 2006). *Thematic analysis* is a method for identifying, analyzing, and reporting patterns (themes) within data, which minimally organizes and describes the data set in rich detail. (Braun and Clarke, 2006, p.6) Thematic analysis works quite well for stimulated recall studies. The pointers given by Cote and Raz (chapter 7) and Eklund (chapter 9) are applicable when analyzing stimulated recall interview analysis.

The section below gives a more detailed description of a particular method formerly used in analyzing the interview data gathered with visual stimuli, the EPP method. The EPP method is deriving from empirical phenomenal psychology, and shares many traits with thematic analysis. It is a good analyzing tool for a wide range of different phenomenon (Svartsjö, et al., 2009, p.41.)

EPP METHOD

Svartsjö, et al. (2009) used a method resembling stimulated recall to study poker players with a gambling problem. Svartsjö, et al. videotaped poker players playing *Texas Hold'em*, and afterwards let them explain their choices. In addition to a traditional stimulated recall interview, the poker players had sensors attached to them measuring heart functions and the electrical conductivity of the skin, which helped analyze also the results of the interview. Svartsjö, et al. used the EPP-method from empirical phenomenological psychology to analyze data.

The aim of the methodology is to understand the experience of the subject from their own point of view. A typical approach for gathering information is to ask the subjects about the phenomenon they experienced from a relevant point of view concerning the research questions. It is important to get a spontaneous and detailed report from the experience. (Svartsjö, et al., 2009, p.41.)

I have divided the phases of analysis are described in Svartsjö, et al.'s (2009, pp.41–42) research into eight phases that are explained below.

Phase 1: open-minded perceiving of research data and bracketing

The interviews are transcribed into text and read through multiple times. More details on transcribing data can be found, for example in Eklund (chapter 9) and Cote and Raz (chapter 7). The idea of this phase is to get deeply acquainted with the data and begin bracketing; bracketing refers to reading and interpreting the data without hypotheses or presumptions deriving from theoretical basis, thus avoiding the trap of interpreting the data too subjectively and receiving distorted results.

Theoretical basis and hypotheses are allowed. However, the analysis should not be affected by the theoretical basis or hypotheses. After analyzing the data, the pre-research hypotheses can be revised or even rejected.

Phase 2: Finding themes in and structuring the data

When analyzing the data and trying to find themes, the researcher should first try wider and more general themes before narrowing it down. This way all the useful data concerning the research questions should still be in the analyzed data. The themes can be altered and narrowed later.

Phase 3: Dividing the data

The data should be divided into units that form meanings. The dividing is a process where the researcher pays close attention to what the meaning of each unit is. The units can consist of one sentence, more sentences or even just one word. The aim of this phase is to create a structure for ease of managing the data; researchers should remain aware of how detailed analysis is needed to answer their research questions.

Phase 4: Translating into the researcher's language

When dividing the data, the researcher may find some patterns, where some meanings appear more frequently than others. The next phase is to translate patterns and units of meaning into the researcher's language. It is crucial for the researcher to express the core meaning of the unit in an unambiguous manner. When doing this, it is important to constantly reflect between the unit and researcher's summary of the unit. It is helpful to use expressions that different people will understand in the same manner.

Phase 5: Categorizing units into themes

The researcher categorizes the meaning-units into themes. One unit can be categorized into multiple themes if needed.

Phase 6: Finding connections

First the task is to find connections (meaning-relations) between units inside themes. These connections may be unique or repeated. The connections can also be between units from different themes.

Phase 7: Building a meaning map

The researcher finds connections between themes and builds a *meaning map* for each interviewed person trying to visualize each one's unique experience of the researched phenomenon.

Phase 8: The shared meaning map

After building personal meaning maps the researcher aims to find connections between them and build shared meaning maps where the unique, personal experience is not present anymore.

Stimulated recall as part of cross-methodological research

Aside, from being used in it's own right, stimulated recall is also useful as one of multiple methods in cross-methodological research. Working cross-methodology can bring more credibility and more valid data, since stimulated recall is a heavily informant-oriented method. There is always the option of receiving distorted data (see section *Advantages and challenges* below). Having a video analysis of the players' actions using ethnographical methods before the interview and comparing the results of the interview with the video analysis might bring the researcher to more valid conclusions about the players' thoughts. Further information about these steps can be found in Dempsey (2010, pp.345–356).

As mentioned before, Svartsjö, et al. (2008) conducted a study where they combined psychophysiological experiment with stimulated recall. They interviewed the subjects with the video recordings, and the subjects gave answers about their thoughts during the actions on tape. Afterwards they compared the psychophysiological data from the activity with the answers given during the interview, to evaluate the validity of the stimulated recall answers. (Svartsjö, et al., 2008, pp.38–42.)

Other cross-methodological options could also combine other electronic research equipment into the stimulated recall interview. For example, one could combine cognition sciences and brain scanners into stimulated recall and compare the results of the scanning equipment and the stimulated recall interview. This would benefit both the analysis of the scan results and the stimulated recall interview. The problem with scanners is that they could create an artificial environment and the feeling of being observed might influence the actions. When Svartsjö, et al. did their research, however, the informants claimed that the research equipment (electrodes measuring heart functions and skin censors) did not disturb them too much when playing (Svartsjö, et al., 2008, p.39). When researching computer, board or table-top role-playing games, this is a valid option, but such scanners seldom are wireless, which makes larp research very difficult. The scanning devices could also heavily influence both the play experience and the interaction of other players, if the equipment does not have an in-game meaning (e.g., some cyberpunk larp in a totalitarian world, where the equipment could be spying equipment of the government).

Avoiding pitfalls

When using the stimulated recall method, the researchers should be aware of issues of memory, retrieval, timing and instructions (Fox-Turnbull, 2009, p.205). Fox-Turnbull gathered several studies to build an excellent list of what to do to avoid pitfalls with stimulated recall interviews. The following list is synthesis of various sources (Schepens, et al., 2007; Seung and Schallert, 2004; Moreland and Cowie, 2007; Lyle, 2002; Fox-Turnbull, 2009, p.205–206).

- The protocols should include opening interviews with background questions and open-ended prompts to give the researcher information on participants' understanding.
- Each participant must be given clear guidelines.
- The stimulated recall interview should be very close to the actual action in order for the stimuli to awaken authentic thought processes. Many researchers suggest that the interviews should be right after the action, and some say they should be at the latest inside three days of the researched action, because of the nature of human short-term memory. If it is postponed too long, details of thought processes get lost.
- Each interview should be audio taped and transcribed. The recording device should be tested

during the interview to avoid technical problems. Some researchers even prefer to use two recording devices to ensure the success of recording.

- Participants should be given enough information about the interview in order to carry it out. They should, however, not receive extra and unnecessary knowledge.
- The stimulus should be strong. In game research, visual stimulus is strongly recommended.
- Involving the participants in the selection and control of the stimulus episodes may result in less researcher interference.

Many of the points of the list might also apply to other research methods than stimulated recall.

Ethical questions

Wiles, et al. (2008) summarized the core questions of visual research ethics as follows:

- "researchers should strive to protect the rights, privacy, dignity and well-being of those that they study"
- "research should (as far as possible) be based on voluntary informed consent"
- "personal information should be treated confidentially and participants anonymised unless they choose to be identified"
- "research participants should be informed of the extent to which anonymity and confidentiality can be assured in publication and dissemination and of the potential re-use of data". (Wiles, et al., 2008)

These core issues apply also stimulated recall research. The informants should be anonymous in the research should they not choose otherwise and they should be well aware of how the visual data is used afterwards. Anonymizing video data requires much work.

Usually it is enough anonymity for the informants, if the video is only used as a stimuli for the interview and not distributed or used otherwise afterwards. This usually gives the researcher permission to film even persons who do not normally want to be filmed. If, however, such persons are present during filming, it is crucial to discuss the filming process with them beforehand. Do they appear on the video and if they do, can the video be anonymized?

If the informants want to be identified in the research, the researcher should go through the interview data with the informants even after analyzing it. This helps avoid misunderstandings and showing informants in a less favorable light than they want to, although this may introduce a bias to the results. If the informants are minors, usually the parents or legal guardians should be contacted for permissions for the research. When asking for permissions, the researcher needs to be clear about the issues mentioned above: anonymity and the potential re-use of the data.

It helps the researcher if the research is well prepared and all the obligatory permissions are taken care of beforehand. Good preparation saves the researcher from a lot of post-research problems.

Two cases of stimulated recall research

This section describes two different examples in detail of game research using the stimulated recall method. The first took place 2007, described also in my master's thesis (Pitkänen, 2008). The second study is ongoing and has not yet been submitted to any paper. I present both projects, because they were quite different from each other. In the first, the informants were familiar with me and I participated in the game design, and in the second I only functioned as a researcher and lacked information about the game design. The second one works also as a cautionary example about the researcher's preparations not being sufficient.

VIIKIN NORMAALIKOULU: HISTORICAL EMPATHY RESEARCH

Viikin normaalikoulu is a school where trainee teachers do their practicum (five weeks of strongly guided teaching practice). The idea of the research was to find out whether a group of sixth graders (12–13 years old) showed signs of historical empathy while participating in an edularp.

In the first phase, I interviewed the teacher of the class in order to get perspective on the game, the class and the culture of the class. Both the teacher and the class were familiar to me, and I had a small part in planning the game.

In the next phase, four students were randomly chosen to participate as the main informants. The edularp took place in the Turku castle, and the students were playing the court of Duke John, once a resident in Turku castle. The video material for the interviews was filmed with several static video cameras and two moving cameras, one operated by the teacher of the class and the other by me. I went through the video material and cut the interviews for each student. After three days—a bit too long to be optimal for the stimulated recall interview—I interviewed the students watching their video material and afterwards analyzed the results using the content analysis method. In analysis I set apart action-oriented thinking ("I'm delivering this letter to the queen, because that guy told me to") and thinking that showed signs of historical analysis and empathy ("I'm wondering how my decision concerning this Polish princess will affect the Finnish-Swedish relationship").

The results of that study suggested that preparations for the game were central: the players with more beforehand knowledge of the era were able to participate in the learning process with much more depth. They showed signs of learning and historical empathy untypical for sixth graders, whereas the non-prepared did not seem to learn during the game. Whether that game motivated them to study afterwards, I did not research. (Pitkänen, 2008)

ØSTERSKOV EFTERSHOLE: THE RELATIONSHIP BETWEEN GAME DESIGN AND PLAYER'S THOUGHTS

- sterskov Efterskole is a Danish boarding school in Hobro for 9th and 10th graders (15–17 years old). In Østerskov Efterskole, games and especially educational live action role-playing games, edularps, are the main teaching method. The students learn in the games and when they study outside the games, they use the knowledge they acquire in the next phase of the game. In spring 2014 I conducted a study using stimulated recall at this school, with the intention of finding out how much game design affects the thinking of the players. Teachers of Østerskov

Efterskole were the game designers and the students were the players. I had help from a Danish assistant, Dennis Larsen. Because in stimulated recall interviews the informant has to describe his or her actual thoughts, it is crucial that the language used is very strong, preferably the informant's native tongue. Therefore it was essential for me to have a Danish assistant assisting with the interviews, transcribing and translating the transcribed text.

The first phase was to go to the school, making observations. I visited the school in Autumn 2013 and made basic observations about the school culture, strongly leaning on Hinde's (2004, p.1–2) questions about the school environment. I also had an interview with the principal Mads Lunau to understand the Østerskov environment and teaching philosophy. I met some pupils who led me around the school and had the opportunity to observe them as well. I developed an understanding of the idioculture, learning environment and games in Østerskov Efterskole.

The next phase of the research was interviews with the teachers. In Østerskov each week has a different game, with a different single teacher responsible for it. Other teachers run workshops which are tailored to fit the theme of the game. First, I did an email interview with the main teacher, followed by a Skype interview after he had the opportunity to ask his fellow teachers about their workshops. The idea of the interview was to get information about their game design: what would they want the students to think during the game? What kind of elements have they implanted into the game in order to provoke such thinking? How do they see the possibility to affect the player's thinking? When interviewing the teacher, the teacher was worrying whether his week would be optimal for the study. We still decided to go to the school to film and research.

With information about the schedule of the workshops on our filming day, my assistant and I developed a filming plan. The student informants were chosen randomly in the beginning of the research day. We followed their lessons and tried to deepen our understanding of the school culture and environment. We filmed material and while filming, we realized that the material was not suited for our original research questions and a stimulated recall interview. What we saw was more of a theatre practice than a game; the players had no free will or decision-making inside the action, making the stimulated recall interview of little value to the purpose of the research. We had to postpone our research and make new dates, ensuring this time that the game they would play at the school would suit our research. The video we recorded was still transcribed and translated for possible future reference.

We intend to repeat the first phases again and return to the school with a clearer understanding of the game and whether it will suit our purposes. We will choose new students and film their play. Using video editors, we will put together the interview material (video) for each individual interview. We will concentrate on finding clear actions on tape, where the informant had made decisions on how to act. Each interview will be designed separately, watching the interview tapes and deciding on questions for actions. The interviews will be designed together with Larsen performing them.

In the fourth phase we have the actual interviews. The interviews will consist of both structured questions and room for free expression. The interviews will take place the next day after the filming to help the informants remember their thoughts during the filmed action. The interviews are themselves recorded, which will later be transcribed and translated into English.

The last phase is analyzing the results. As an analysis method for the stimulated recall interviews I will use the EPP-method. When the interviews are analyzed, I will compare the results with the teacher interviews in order to find both connections and disconnections. The results and the full research will be then published.

Examples on simulated recall possibilities

In this section, I provide suggestions about where to use the stimulated recall in game research. One should not limit ones views on the suggestions in this chapter, but rather take them as examples on when stimulated recall is a relevant method.

When one needs in-depth analysis of the reasons behind the player's actions, stimulated recall will provide a handy tool. The gameplay is videotaped, and afterwards analyzed with the player and the researcher.

In real-time strategy games decisions need to be quick and intelligent. A potential research candidate would be how the best players in the world form their strategies. The research could gather data on each player including data on their background, their academic success in subjects that could be imagined to be helpful in the particular strategic game, their values, their player profiles, and temperaments. The actual research would be done with video takes of their games, very shortly after the game has been played. The interview would be more freeform, with just a few questions from the researcher. The idea would be for the players to go through the video material and tell about each decision; why did they choose each action they did during the game? The data gathered from the interview would be analyzed with the EPP-method and, if possible, the researcher could try to find connections with the data gathered before the interviews and connections between reasons for actions. What makes a top strategist?

Another interesting subject of research could be the emotional reactions of a player to the game. When the gameplay and the player are simultaneously videotaped, the player's reactions can be pointed to specific gameplay situations and afterwards analyzed with the stimulated recall method. If possible, this could be a cross-methodological study with means to measure brain activities as well.

The research could concentrate either on games with strong, emotional story lines or intensive and immersive games which need constant player reaction. When the player is shown recordings of both the game and his or her reactions, the analysis could provide the researcher (and the game designers, as well) with very interesting explanations, why the players were reacting the way they were.

I have used stimulated recall when researching educational larps (Pitkänen, 2008) as well as in an ongoing study at Østerskov. However, the method has not been used when studying traditional larps. Traditional larps would be a fruitful research ground with the stimulated recall ground, since many larpers aim for immersion, and immersion aims for the loss of self and making the game world even more real than the real world (Balzer, 2011, pp.33). One could imagine that seeing the in-game actions on video afterwards would the players to describe their reasons behind their actions better than an interview without any stimuli.

In interview of professor Lainema, Lainema explains that in his business simulation games, he has noticed that his students do in-game business deals with the persons they know off-game rather than with the persons the deal would be most profitable with (Lainema, 2011). However, Lainema's students sometimes are experiencing that sort of learning environment for the first time, and might not be totally comfortable with that way of learning. This provides an interesting subject for research: how do off-game relationships affect in-game decisions? Is there a difference between experienced larpers and non-experienced? In order to research these questions, I would suggest a cross-methodological study with quantitative methods combined to the stimulated recall method.

This research would require a game with clear in-game goals requiring player interaction (larps, business simulations, MMORPGs, pervasive games) and players having to interact with both players they know outside the game and players they do not know. The studied players should consist of both experienced and non-experienced players. The data acquired before the stimulated recall interviews would be central in understanding the results: the relationships of the subjects, their experience, their backgrounds. This study might need a game written especially for it, and the subjects should know as little as possible about the researcher's goals so it would not affect their gameplay.

Many multiplayer games have in-game goals for each character. Since the games are highly improvised events, it is up to the player how much those goals affect his playing. It would be interesting to research that via stimulated recall. When showing the players video material about their decisions and actions during the game, the researcher could make a freeform interview about their thoughts during the decisions and actions. Afterwards the data gathered in the interview would be compared with the played character's goals and connections and disconnections would be located. This research question could also be included in the previously mentioned research, the relationships between in-game and off-game relationships.

Table-top role-playing has many elements that are improvised storytelling. In table-top role-playing games the game master (GM) usually designs and facilitates all non-player character actions and facilitates role-playing. It could be seem as the GM is acting as the game designer of each role-playing session. He gives the player's characters circumstances to which the characters react, and then he decides on and relates the reaction of the world surrounding the characters. Before each session the game master can prepare the circumstances and try to predict some of the players' actions to prepare the surrounding fictional world's reaction to some alternatives, but since the players are in charge of their characters, there will always be surprises.

A very interesting research subject would be the game master's thinking. How does the GM react to different situations? Do off-game relationships matter to the GM's decisions? What does the GM base his decisions upon: the adequate challenge level, good story line, his preparations, or the interaction between the character's and the world? If this research had enough informants (game masters), the research could build game master profiles and possibly compare them with research about game designers.

Conclusion

The suggested examples made above are only a few of stimulated recall's possible research targets in game design, and they focus heavily on my own interests. Stimulated recall is a method researching the informant's personal, subjective experience of a phenomenon and whenever that is essential in the research, it is a valid method of acquiring data. It can be a valuable asset to cross-methodological research. Because of the video recordings and editing it requires a bit more work than unsupported interviews, but it also provides different insight into the informants' worlds. The informants may still distort the truth, describe their reasons in a more positive light and even lie. The best way to avoid these pitfalls is good preparation and being truly aware of the method's strengths and weaknesses. Strong analyzing methods and also cross-methodology may help the results become more reliable.

Recommended reading

- Dempsey, N.P., 2010. Stimulated recall interviews in ethnography. *Qualitative Sociology* 33(3), pp.349–367. DOI=10.1007%2Fs11133-010-9157-x
- Gass, S.M. and Mackey, A., 2000. *Stimulated recall methodology in second language research.* Mahwah: Lawrence Erlbaum Associates.
- Lyle, J., 2003. Stimulated recall: A report on its use in naturalistic research. *British Educational Research Journal*, 29(6), pp.861–878.
- Mackenzie, S.H. and Kerr, J.H., 2012. Head-mounted cameras and stimulated recall in qualitative sport research. *Qualitative research in Sport, Exercise and Health*, 4(1), pp.51-61.

References

Beers, P. J., Boshuizen, H.P.A., Kirschner, P.A., Gijselaers, W. and Westendorp, J., 2006. Cognitive load measurements and stimulated recall interviews for studying the effects of information and communication technology. *Education Technology Research Development*, 56, pp.309–328.

Bentley, T., Johnston, L. and von Braggo, K., 2005. Evaluation using cued-recall debrief to elicit information about user's affective experiences. In: H. Shen, eds., *OZCHI 2005 proceedings*. New York: ACM, pp.1–10.

Braun V. and Clarke V., 2006. Using thematic analysis in psychology. *Qualitative Research in Psychology*, 3(2), pp.77–101.

Dempsey, N.P., 2010. Stimulated recall interviews in ethnography. *Qualitative Sociology*, 33(3), pp.349–367. DOI=10.1007%2Fs11133-010-9157-x.

Eskelinen, T., 1993. *Opotunti. Opetusintentiot, mielekkyys ja vastavuoroisuuden kokemukset peruskoulun oppi-laanohjaustunnilla.* Joensuu: Joensuun yliopiston monistuskeskus.

Fox-Turnbull, W., 2009. Stimulated recall using autophotography: A method for Investigating technology education. In: *Pupils' Attitudes Toward Technology Conference (PATT-22)*. Delft, The Netherlands. 24-28 Aug 2009. Available at: <http://www.iteaconnect.org/Conference/PATT/PATT22/FoxTurnbull.pdf>.

Gass, S.M. and Mackey, A., 2000. *Stimulated recall methodology in second language research.* Mahwah: Lawrence Erlbaum Associates.

Gee, J. P., 2005. *An Introduction to Discourse Analysis: Theory and Method.* London: Routledge.

Gygax, G., Arneson, D., 1974. *Dungeons & Dragons.* Lake Geneva: TSR Inc.

Hinde. E. R., 2004. School culture and change: An examination of the effects of school culture on the process of change. *Essays in Education*. 12, pp.1–12.

Jørgensen, K., 2011. Players as co-researchers: Expert player perspective as an aid to understanding games. Simulation & Gaming, 43(3).

Lainemaa, T. 2011. *Timo Lainema's video interview*. Interviewed by M. Laakso. Available at: http://prezi.com/ez9pwujegfin/bisnespeli-real-gamen-avulla-yritysoppimista/.

Lyle, J.,2003. Stimulated recall: A report on its use in naturalistic research. *British Educational Research Journal*, 29(6), pp.861–878.

Mackenzie, S.H. and Kerr, J.H., 2012. Head-mounted cameras and stimulated recall in qualitative sport research. *Qualitative research in Sport, Exercise and Health*. 4(1), pp.51–61.

Montola, M., 2012. *On the edge of the magic circle*. Tampere: University of Tampere.

Mäyrä, F., van Looey, J. and Quandt, T., 2013. Disciplinary identity of game scholars: An outline. In: *DiGRA 2013: DeFragging Game Studies*. Atlanta. Aug 26–29. Available at: <http://www.digra.org/digital-library/publications/disciplinary-identity-of-game-scholars-an-outline/>.

Pitkänen, J., 2008. Pedagoginen liveroolipelaaminen historian opetusmetodina. MA. Univerity of Helsinki. Available at: <https://helda.helsinki.fi/bitstream/handle/10138/20093/peda-gogi.pdf?sequence=1>.

Plaut, S., 2006. "I just don't get it": teachers' and students' conceptions of confusion and implications for teaching and learning in the high school English classroom. *Curriculum Inquiry*, 36(4), pp.391–421.

Sime, D., 2006. What do learners make of teachers' gestures in the language classroom? *International Review of Applied Linguistics in Language Teaching*, 44(2), pp.211–230.

Slough, L., 2001. Using Stimulated Recall in classroom observation and professional development. In: *American Educational Research Association Conference*, Seattle.

Sotamaa, O. and Suominen, J., 2013. The long decade of game studies: Case of Finland. In: *DiGRA 2013: DeFragging Game Studies*. Atlanta. Aug. Available at: <http://www.digra.org/digital-library/publications/the-long-decade-of-game-studies-case-of-finland/>.

Svartsjö, M., Kinnunen, J., Paloheimo, E., Mäyrä, F., 2009.*Järjellä vai tunteella? Nettipokerin pelikokemus ja pelaamisen hallinta*. Helsinki: Stakes. Available at: <http://www.julkari.fi/bitstream/handle/10024/77919/R24-2008-VERKKO.pdf?sequence=1>.

Wiles, R., Prosser, J., Bagnoli, A., Clark, A., Davies, K., Holland, S. and Renold, E., 2008. *Visual ethics: Ethical issues in visual research*. Southampton: ESRC National Centre for Research Methods. Available at: <http://eprints.ncrm.ac.uk/421/1/MethodsReviewPaperNCRM-011.pdf>.

9

Focus group interviews as a way to evaluate and understand game play experiences

LINA EKLUND

This chapter deals with researching people's experiences and understandings of video gaming by the use of focus group interviewing. Focus group interviewing is a method where several participants are prompted to discuss a subject under the guidance of a moderator. There are many cases where players' experiences and their understanding of these are the primary concern. For instance, if the aim is to assess or evaluate a game or a game design feature, one might want to understand how this game or feature is experienced and understood by players in addition to how they use it. Or someone may be interested in how players themselves experience certain types of gameplay in order to understand gaming as an activity; for example, in exploring if and how players' experiences differ when playing face-to-face or online, or perhaps how players experience interaction with non-human NPCs? The range of questions and situations when someone wants to delve into gaming experiences and understanding of these is wide and focus groups interviewing is then a useful tool. This chapter will explore the practicalities as well as the methodological challenges of focus group interviewing, leaving the reader capable of setting up and carrying out their own focus groups. The methods and techniques presented here can of course be used to study anything, not only video games.

Focus groups

Focus group interviewing is a specific technique originating from the work of American sociologist Robert Merton. During the Second World War, Merton was part of a research group developing this style of interviewing—which he called *Focused Interviews*—with the aim of investigating the effectiveness of media communication in the form of morale boosting radio and TV shows (Merton, 1987). Keeping morale up during the war was a prime concern in the West at that time. Today focus groups are widely used in marketing, where the aim often is to assess people's reactions to certain products or brands, as well as in many areas of research such as phenomenological sociology, audience reception and media studies, and evaluation research, to mention a few examples (Stewart, Shamdasani and Rook, 2007).

Focus group interviews are here defined as *in-depth group discussions focusing on a particular topic of interest or relevance to the participants as well as the researcher*. Merton and Kendall (1946, p.541) state that in a focused interview participants have all been involved in a particular concrete situation; have listened to a radio show, say, or have read the same book or—one might add—played the same game. Many different issues can be the focus in this type of interview, from shared experiences to identities. In my own work I have performed focus group interviews with participants who were all playing the same game, but also with participants sharing an identity as 'video gameplayers or gamers' rather than a concrete experience.

FOCUS GROUPS AND GAMES

While focus groups have been used extensively in media research and other sciences the method has not yet found its place in game research, although there are a few examples of focus group studies. Miller, Chaika and Groppe (1996) compared how young American girls with little or no computer experience and others with extensive computer experience interacted with computer software such as games. They used six focus groups, each with five girls of similar age and computer experience (10 participants each from grades 6–7, 8–9 and 10–12). All groups met three times and participants received a small payment. Another study exploring the nature of game experiences (Poels, de Kort and Ijsselsteijn, 2007) argues that focus groups is an underused, although advantageous method in game research. The authors organized four focus groups, two groups with frequent players and two with infrequent gamers. Of the groups with frequent gamers one consisted of university students and one of working individuals. The groups met once for around 90 minutes to discuss both in-game and post-game experiences. Participants received a small payment (Poels, de Kort and Ijsselsteijn, 2007). A third example is my own work on social video gaming. In Eklund and Johansson (2013), focus groups where used as a complement to other data to gain understanding of how a specific design change to the 'grouping tool' in the online game *World of Warcraft* (Blizzard, 2004) impacted on social play. Initially interaction data was gathered by filming interactions between gamers using the game tool. After these videos were analysed, a mixed gender focus group was conducted with six gamers where this tool was discussed. The focus group data provided in-depth understanding of the observed behaviour that had become observed in the interaction data. In another, larger study, focus groups were used to investigate social gaming (Eklund, 2012). I will draw extensively on this latter study to give examples in the text and will therefore not discuss it more here.

Video games are in one sense different from other media, for unlike radio or TV shows each gaming session is distinct. Even in highly scripted games, any two different gamers' experiences can differ in pace, solutions, interpretation and so on. Focus groups allow individuals to compare these experiences and the researcher to observe gamers discussing these and so uncover certain similarities and differences. Due to the social interaction between participants, focus groups not only show us what people think, but also how and why they think in that way (Kitzinger, 1995).

Lunt and Livingstone (1996) argue that in contemporary research on media, focus is often on people's interpretations of media rather than, for example, on how media affects users. In studies on how people interact with technology, here video games, usage as well as how users make sense of their activities need to be taken into consideration. We know that how users make sense of media is dependent on the social environment that users reside in. In other words, gamers do not understand gaming in a social vacuum, but do so in relation to previous experiences and knowledge, along with the values and norms of the game community. Reading reviews and talking to other gamers in different forums make users part of a gaming culture with certain values and ways of understanding games and gaming (Consalvo, 2007). Considering this, focus group interviewing is a particularly useful method as focus groups do not reduce individuals to separated nodes, but rather sees the social nature of interaction and communication as an important feature of data gathering.

UNDERSTANDING FOCUS GROUPS

Focus group interviewing is a data collecting method by controlled group discussions. However, choosing a method is seldom enough; one also needs to have a clear methodology: a theoretical understanding of the method. All methods have different theoretical backgrounds, which impose certain perspectives on reality (Berg, 2009, p.5). Each method therefore gives a slightly different insight into the things studied. Denzin (1978) describes methods as a kaleidoscope, that tube with mirrors and coloured glass which, as you turn it, changes its colourful patterns. Depending on what method is chosen, or how the kaleidoscope is turned, different things will be shown. A theoretical understanding of a method can therefore answer why some data is better suited to answer some research questions or study some fields. In regard to focus group interviews a certain type of data is received where the social interaction between participants is part of the data gathering process. For further reading on how different qualitative methods can be understood, refer to Creswell (2007).

In focus groups, a moderator asks participants to discuss their experiences and their understanding of them; focus groups thus bring the social construction of meaning into the data gathering process. The social construction of reality is a way to describe how the social world works based on phenomenological thinking. What this means is that reality, or the knowledge about how things work, is created by ordinary members of society as they act out this knowledge. Berger and Luckmann (1967) explain this process by showing how our everyday routines and understanding of them, for example, how to behave at a wedding or a funeral, is ultimately decided by how people act and behave at weddings and funerals. This knowledge is taught to individuals by their parents or other significant adults in their childhood and is reinforced as individuals take part in social interaction where these norms are enacted. We know knowledge is social in this sense, as different cultures have different norms about how individuals are supposed to act in these situations. Even in western culture, how to act at, for example, a funeral has varied immensely through history or across local cultures. This everyday knowledge about how to act in the world is ordered and organized around the here and now, and it is shared. Yet in everyday lives individuals experience this knowledge as objective structures which they have no part in creating. Norms and values on how to act and who can act in what way simply become part of 'how things are' (Berger and Luckmann, 1967). Understanding these social norms and values is in one sense to see how they are reinforced, and here focus groups are helpful.

In the same sense, what games a culture appreciates and how they should be played varies both between and within groups. Thus, the basic idea of focus group interviews is that meaning is created in the interaction between the participants in the same way that meaning is created in society, by people expressing and comparing their knowledge. Gibbs (1997) defines focus groups as giving "[I]nsight and data produced by the interaction between participants". Focus groups and interviews share in a way this social aspect of data gathering. Yet, in a focus group the researcher takes a less active position and allows the participants' social interaction to determine the outcome to a large degree, similar to unstructured interviews (Kvale, 2007).

Focus group interviewing has a broad range of application; for example, evaluating how participants experience and perceive a product, such as a consumer item or a software program. When studying games, group discussion can allow the researcher to understand how players experience certain features, games or play styles. Groups can play a game or test a specific design feature and then discuss their experience and interaction with it. Moreover, players can discuss the meaning they attribute to gaming as a cultural phenomenon or their own experiences of gaming. The opportunities are endless; focus group interviews are inherently good at capturing people's everyday knowledge and how they interpret and make sense of their experiences in a social context. In this sense focus group interviews "[...] afford that social world [to play] a key role in the data collection process" (Wilkinson, 1998, p.121).

STRENGTHS AND DRAWBACKS OF FOCUS GROUPS

As Cote and Raz (chapter 7) discuss in their chapter on interviews, all methods have different strengths and drawbacks. Interviews, both individual and in groups, are good at eliciting in-depth information about perceived motivations behind actions, why people think they do what they do. Note, however, that interviews look at expressed motivations. In reality people tend not to consider or to question their motives and actions; asking informants to give concrete examples can therefore be good for figuring out what they do. In my study of social gameplay, informants often discussed making friends through online gaming. Yet, when pressed for examples from their own lives it became apparent that they repeated second hand stories. Only one participant had personal experience of making lasting friendships online. The ideology surrounding what and how online gaming should be was so strong that the players repeated this knowledge without reflecting upon its relevance for themselves. This is why people engaging in game research should be careful and question their own preconceptions about video gaming so that it does not shape the direction of the research unduly; although this of course is not unique or even specific for game research but relevant for all studies.

A strength of focus groups is their flexibility, that they can be carried out in many ways and accommodate varying numbers of participants, different topics, sampling strategies, budgets and so on. Focus groups can, due to the active role of the participants, be very good at exploring topics about which little is known or understood; the participants become experts that the researcher can learn from. The open structure of focus groups and the more equal power relations between participants and researcher allow this. Focus group interviews can be empowering as well, allowing participants to discuss common experiences and to understand that they are not alone (Kitzinger, 1995). One should, however, keep in mind that focus group studies normally are performed with a small number of participants who are not random representatives of the larger population and thus are limited in their ability to give generalizable results. Another significant drawback is that focus groups can be difficult to assemble; researchers may struggle to find enough participants of the right kind to fill the groups. Berg (2009, p.165) has a more comprehensive list of the benefits and drawbacks of this method.

How to plan and conduct your own focus group interview

Once focus groups have been decided on as the method to be used, several practical questions are raised regarding how to proceed in order to obtain as useful data as possible. This section will give concrete tips and recommendations using practical examples; from how many participants you need in a focus group to how to analyse the data. In each section a short checklist with the most important points to think about is given. Students should use this checklist to guide their work as well as their writing.

PLANNING YOUR STUDY

The planning stage is of great importance for any successful study. This section will give practical advice on what to consider and the pitfalls to avoid. Examples from my own research will be used to illustrate and explain the reasoning behind different methodological questions.

There are many ways of gathering people to take part in a focus group. How to sample participants is of course of great importance in any study, as our results are dependent on who is being studied. Focus groups mostly use a *qualitative sampling strategy*. The aim is to gain in-depth understanding of a phenomenon, not to generalize, but samples should reflect the diversity of the studied group. For studies of players it is important to balance your sample by studying different types of players, or at least be very clear about your reasoning when limiting yourself to a specific demographic of game users. A sample for a focus group in itself presupposes some of the analysis as the sample will determine the results (Barbour, 2007); depending on whom one asks one will receive different answers. This is why a well-balanced or well-argued sampling strategy is necessary. Studying what still sometimes is a specific interest, like gaming, often requires gathering people by word of mouth, advertising, and spreading the word in one's social network. There are several ways of thinking on this issue and for further discussion about sampling strategies, refer to Barbour (2007).

Focus groups, unlike other methods, must also try to sample participants that will work well together in order to create functioning group discussions. In general, focus group interviews can consist either of naturally occurring clusters of people or of groups put together by the researcher. The difference is that in the first, all group members are connected prior to the focus group—for example they could be friends or part of the same online game guild—while in the latter random people are brought together. Lunt and Livingstone (1996) argue for using naturally existing groups, something I support. One argument for this, as Blumer (1970) writes, is that the empirical social world should be studied as it is, not in categories or through experiments artificially defined by the researcher, and this requires natural groups. Of course, the discussion in a focus group is artificial in that the researcher has created the social situation, but drawing on pre-existing relationships can help emulate the actual social world more closely. It is recommend choosing participants who are at least in some way similar to each other as this will facilitate the discussion. If, for example, researching how players experience harassment behaviour in online gaming, it makes sense to divide men and women into different groups to allow for better discussions as it is likely that the types of harassment performed and exposed to varies for these groups. Different types of participants in the same group can, however, also be fruitful, yet the moderator needs to be careful and attentive to how hierarchies might structure the data. A person with a strong personality or position compared to the others might shape the views taken by the rest (Kitzinger, 1995). One reason is that participants may lack the courage to express their true opinions in a group situation where they are surrounded by strangers, although research has questioned this assumption, showing that strangers sharing a strong experience and feeling safe can create valuable and ethical focus group discussions (Wilkinson, 1998).

Previous research has shown that players are both men and women, come in different age groups, have different preferences, and vary in how they play and want to play games depending on their life situation (Eklund, 2012; Juul, 2010). One strategy is to take advantage of this when designing a focus group study and contrast different demographics against each other (e.g., Miller, et al., 1996). A common design is to compare two different types of groups; for example, adult players with full-time jobs and little free time with young players still in school with ample free time. These groups will have very different gaming patterns and see their gaming in different lights. Another common sampling choice when testing game design is to compare veteran gamers with new players; both games and game features are interpreted differently by these groups. If testing a design feature, one strategy is to have these two groups try the specific feature and then discuss it in separate focus groups. Yet, one should be careful when comparing the results, often new gamers have not yet made the everyday knowledge and norms of the gaming community their own and putting too much emphasis on differences between these two groups might only capture this difference in knowledge. Also worth keeping in mind is that when comparing two groups, differences will always be found. Thus researchers should ask; how similar are these groups and are any differences relevant or even accidental?

Be careful not to construct groups with people you found unless they match your research purpose. It takes time and effort to gather people for a focus group, plan for this. Skipping corners and filling up empty positions with people who do not fit the research aim will cost time and quality in the end and results will suffer. Also make sure when comparing different demographics to motivate the number of groups used and how they are constructed in order to fulfil the research aims. That way a reader can better judge the quality of your results. A general rule on how many groups one needs is to continue to run groups until nothing new is learned; the so-called saturation point. "A useful rule of thumb holds that for any given category of people discussing a particular topic there are only so many stories to be told." (Lunt and Livingstone, 1996, p.7). As knowledge is social and shared, sooner or later a researcher will have heard most stories before. However, one should not forget that there could be a difference between majority groups' and marginalized groups' stories. For example, if studying romance options in digital games one might consider that straight and queer gamers could have very different experiences from mainstream games that still mostly enact heterosexual stories. This makes it difficult to know in advance how many groups will be needed. I know studies where ten informants have been enough and studies where 40 or 50 informants have participated before saturation has been reached. This will of course depend on the research question; for example, any study comparing different demographics will need more groups than one without a comparative element.

In my experience each focus group should ideally contain somewhere around 4–6 participants, enough to create a group but not too many so that speaking time is limited. Others recommend as many as 8 participants in one group (e.g., Berg, 2009), which can work well, just ensure that there is enough time for everyone to have the opportunity to speak their mind. With more participants the moderator has to make sure that all participants can be heard; this might on occasion mean asking certain participants directly for their opinions.

When I first studied social video gameplay, how and the different ways gamers played with others, I designed a focus group study. I was interested in the social situation, of gamers engaging in games together. I had also decided on an explorative approach: I wanted to know how gamers themselves experienced games and how they reasoned, as there was not much previous research on this subject at the time. Simply put, I wanted to keep an open mind towards my data. For this approach a focus group study was deemed the best method as focus groups come into their own when you allow the participants to guide the discussion.

In my study of social gameplay I wanted to make sure that I took into account different play practices and experiences. The sample was constructed with previous research in mind, especially the increasingly diverse player base. The aim was to gain contested views as well as to be able to validate the results by widening the range of informants, and in this sense my sample helped shape analytical focus later on. Groups were constructed based on this focus: one group of young female gamers and another with young male gamers; one group of older gamers; two groups of online gamers, one with older gamers from one guild and one with younger participants from another guild; and two small groups, one with a romantically involved couple playing together and one with a parent and teenager playing together. In the younger groups men and women were separated, as norms about proper behaviour are strong in this age group, and some still, links gaming linked to masculinity. Had the groups been mixed it is possible that neither the young men nor the women would have been able to speak as freely. From previous research it was clear that online games are very social and so two focus groups were conducted, one older and one younger. Moreover, to be sure that some specific categories were covered two small groups with a parent and child playing together and a romantically involved couple playing together were included.

The aim was not to compare different groups; if that had been the case then more than one focus group from each category would have been needed. Instead, focus was on exploring new topics and areas. The study was a long term, open-ended project and thus quite different from most student projects which will by necessity be smaller in scale. Yet the methodological reasoning can be used to consider all sorts and sizes of samples. The final sample consisted of 26 participants, 14 men and 12 women which was complemented with five individual interviews for maximum coverage and to double check that saturation had been reached. The focus groups were all made up of participants who knew one another in some way; for example, from school, from an MMO, or being friends. Additionally, as this research focused on gamers the focus group participants all shared a hobby, video gaming, as well. The fact that a group has an interest in the subject in focus is essential and will help to create a good and engaged discussion.

Questions to consider:

- How are focus group interviews the best way to collect data to answer your research question?
- How are you going to structure your groups to answer your research aim?
- Who should be in your groups, and why?

Carrying out a focus group interview

THE MODERATOR

The moderator role is specific to the focus group method and differs from how researchers act in an individual interview. The moderator is absolutely crucial to the outcome of a focus group and has to create a good discussion climate where participants feel at ease and are given the opportunity to speak. It is also important to provide clear instructions so that the group discussions match the research focus.

In a focus group, in contrast to an individual interview, the moderator plays a more passive role. The aim, as described above, is for the participants to discuss the focus among themselves in their own words. Therefore, the moderator starts the focus group by explaining how the group discussion should proceed. The moderator needs to tell the participants what is expected of them and be clear that the participants should talk to each other, not address themselves to the moderator. Otherwise there is the risk that counter-productive social behaviour is established where participants wait for questions from the moderator and direct their answers to her. Once this has happened it is often impossible to break the pattern; therefore, a clear explanation of how the group's discussion is to proceed must introduce every focus group setting. Clear instructions will ensure that the quality of the results is as high as possible.

To further the aim of group discussion, open-ended questions are necessary. They allow the participants to explore the issue in their own vocabulary; open-ended questions may even take the research in new and unexpected directions (Kitzinger, 1995). The very nature of focus groups are open ended as the moderator allows the participants to talk to each other, ask questions from each other, and question each other's statements (Gibbs, 1997). Therefore, the moderator gives up some control of the social situation and places it in the hands of the participants, which is precisely what can yield the greatest benefits—when the participants' discussions give the moderator new and previously unconsidered ideas. The moderator should be aware of this beforehand, leaving pre-conceptions behind in the interview situation and avoiding controlling the discussion too much or asking too specific questions. If specific questions need to be asked they should be saved to the very last; this allows the discussion to flow unhindered, with only some guidance on the topic by the moderator.

It is difficult to be a good moderator. The moderator role foremost places great demands on interpersonal skills as well as being a good listener who does not judge or play favourites (Gibbs, 1997). A good moderator has to be adaptable and allow control over the discussion to be in the hands of the participants, while not letting the situation get out of hand or drift too far away from the topic. Interfering, offering personal opinions and other signs of unprofessionalism should be avoided. The more trust the participants have in the capabilities and personal qualities of the moderator, the better the results of the focus group will be.

If there is more than one researcher present at the focus group it is common practice that one takes notes while the other acts as moderator. It is less confusing if only one person steers the discussion, and this divide also makes sure that the participants can gain some control over the direction of the discussion. Just ensure that the participants are aware of who is in what role.

THE INTERVIEW

When the participants have been invited and a time and date set, preparations can begin. A moderator or *topic guide* should be created and an appropriate setting should be prepared. A quiet, calm room is necessary both for a good discussion and to make sure the discussion can be recorded properly. The interview setting should be free from distractions. Make sure mobile phones are switched off. Seating is important as the participants must be able to face each other properly for a good discussion. If they are seated next to each other, then they will talk to the moderator and not to each other. Set out chairs before people arrive (in a circle or around a table are good options). Focus groups normally last between one and two hours so it is generally good to offer some refreshments to the participants. This also helps create a relaxed and safe atmosphere. Test your recording device and place it in a central location where all of the participants' voices will be clear. It may be wise to use a backup recorder. Some researchers recommend filming focus groups, and a visual recording will of course retain more information, which can be especially useful if there is more than one researcher involved who might want to study the focus group. However, if the research question does not specifically concern such things as body language, soundless interaction or how meaning is created in the specific situation then a voice recording is often adequate. A transcribed (see below) recording combined with detailed notes from the discussion can suit many game research questions.

I prefer to keep my focus groups face-to-face, as there is so much extra information to be had when seeing your participants interact with each other. This is also true for the participants, of course. Many social cues are lost in mediated communication. Yet, researchers are exploring online focus groups and there are some instances, such as online gaming, when this type of data could be considered. Groups could take place in the game world in question and participants could be present with their avatars. The groups can still be recorded with either video capturing software or a text logging program and if the group uses audio chat the sound can be recorded easily on a computer. It is important, however, to choose participants who are comfortable with this type of interaction and to ensure that participants have equal opportunity to take part. Online focus groups are easier to organize as each participant can be in their respective homes. However, it becomes easier for the moderator to lose control over the situation, and you will miss out on wordless social cues. For more tips on online focus groups, refer to Berg (2009).

Before the interview, make sure that a *topic guide*, also called interview or moderator guide is prepared. The *topic guide* should contain information for the moderator and act as a memory aid. Put down notes about what to say initially so you do not forget and so that all groups receive the same information. A *topic guide* for a focus group normally contains a few, open ended themes or perhaps questions for discussion. For more information on how to create and structure a *topic guide* look at Barbour (2007). I normally use a broad, open interview structure in the style of open structure interviewing (Hayes, 2000, p.122–127). I select broad themes that I want my participants to discuss. These themes are often asked as questions which sometimes lead to follow-up questions constructed *ad hoc* in response to the discussions. I prefer simple *topic guides* with plenty of space in which to take notes. Along with each theme I often write a few keywords which summarise some of the subjects I hope the group will discuss; these I can tick off as the discussion proceeds or bring up as questions if the group has not touched on them. I always take extra care when choosing the first question or theme for discussion; it has to be clear and invite discussion from all participants. If the discussion is initially slow, try supportive prompts of the type "Please talk more about this [...]" Just make sure the interview is open at the start; more structure can be added later. The first question sets the stage and if badly formulated might hinder rather than facilitate a good discussion. In Cote and Raz (chapter 7) there is more on how to formulate interview questions.

It is beneficial to take notes during the interview and jot down things that you need to remember to ask the group at an appropriate moment. Notes are also useful in the analytical process as they can help clarify moods in the group and add additional information. Just make sure your attention is not fixed on your notes but on the person speaking. Nodding repeatedly and smiling should not be underestimated; this can have a significant effect on maintaining a good discussion. Most participants look to the moderator for confirmation that they are doing it right.

During the interview the moderator should draw on the social interaction within the group. Ask them to compare their experiences or to clarify for each other when they disagree. The interaction during the discussion is a main feature of focus groups because it highlights participants' views of the world and beliefs about a situation in their own words (Kitzinger, 1995). They can also ask questions of each other or reconsider their own opinions and experiences. The following short quote from a focus group comes from my study on social gaming; two of the participants are twins and are discussing non-social gaming.

> Twin1: When I sit and play with my IPhone touch [...] It's not like I tell someone of my new high score for gathering cheese doodles with the jumping mouse–[Twin2: but you did]–yeah, ok I do.

> Twin2: 23 or something

The example shows how participants who know each other can add or refute information or question what is said and through that enrich the knowledge gained.

In a good focus group where the participants trust each other the group might develop and explore solutions to particular problems as a unit (Kitzinger, 1995). Yet focus group situations can be difficult for shy people or those who are not used to expressing themselves or reflecting on their own experiences. Here the aim of the group discussion can make a significant difference. As Gibbs expressed it: "[...]if participants are actively involved in something which they feel will make a difference, and focus group research is often of an applied nature, empowerment can realistically be achieved." (Gibbs, 1997).

EXTRA MATERIAL, VISUAL AIDS, AND QUESTIONNAIRES

Sometimes in interviews, visual aids are used to prompt discussion, for example, what Pitkänen (chapter 8) calls stimulated recall. In game research there are several possibilities, for example using pictures or short video clips from games to prompt discussion on everything from graphics, narrative to gameplay as shown by Pitkänen (chapter 8). Game scenarios can also be used. Two students of mine compared ethical responses to moral dilemmas in games such as *Dragon Age: Origins* (Bioware, 2009) by allowing groups of avid gamers and more casual players to read game scenarios and then discuss them from a moral standpoint. When evaluating a design it can be valid to remind group participants about it by showing pictures or video clips, perhaps from gaming sessions with the participants, and then asking about their gameplay and reasoning.

Another way of gathering extra material is to use a questionnaire before or after the group discussion; this is often called extended focus groups (Berg, 2009). For example, a short questionnaire after a group discussion allows each participant to leave comments on the discussion or add things they wish they had said (Kitzinger, 1995). Another option is to have a questionnaire before the focus group to suss out opinions about the subject before the focus group session. A questionnaire could gather information about the participants and their life situation, something that rarely is discussed in the actual focus group but which is useful to know for any results presentation.

In my study on social gaming a short questionnaire was handed out in conjunction with all groups to gather additional information and ask about gaming habits. This gave the opportunity to access background information in an unobtrusive way and save time for all participants during the interviews. Also, as stated, these were used later to compare how much time people spent on gaming or for how many years informants had engaged in video games. On these I also asked the participants to fill in their e-mail address if they felt comfortable with me contacting them again. This way I could contact them to ask questions should something turn up while transcribing that I needed more information on.

Questions to consider:

- Are you prepared for your role as a moderator, do you have a clear notion about the focus for the group discussion so that you can explain this to the participants?
- Have you prepared a suitable location and checked that your recording device works?
- Is the topic guide finished and do the topics match the research question?
- Will you be using any visual aids or do you intend to use a questionnaire. If so, what is the aim of these aids?

AFTERWARDS: TRANSCRIBING AND ANALYSIS

After the focus group has been conducted it is time for data processing and analysis. The first stage is transcription. Transcribing is the act of writing down the full text of the interviews. Through this the researcher also learns the data intimately, which is a great aid in the analysis. Transcribing requires listening to the recording and writing down what is said. This can be difficult and time consuming; transcribing is a skill that needs practice. In contrast to individual interviews, transcribing focus group data is more complex as there are more participants. When people are engaged in a subject, they will interject, interrupt and talk at the same time. This makes it hard to transcribe recordings. To minimize frustration it is advisable to transcribe interviews as quickly as possible after the interview. This way the discussion will be fresh in memory and so what was said, how and, very important in focus groups, which voice belongs to whom remembered.

Depending on the research focus, different transcribing techniques can be used but there are some guidelines that should be adhered to:

- 1) be rigorous, shortcuts gain you nothing and reduce quality
- 2) use the same transcription technique all the way through
- 3) ask yourself what information you need to answer the research question and adapt your transcription technique to that.

For more information on transcribing in general refer to Cote and Raz (chapter 7). However, a brief example will be presented here to highlight some solutions to challenges that focus group transcribing present. The aim is a transcript rich in information that will facilitate later analyses but that uses a simple, easy-to-master technique.

The following transcript is a slightly altered example from a focus group interview on social gaming. The transcript contains more information than what is said and will therefore keep the original meaning more effectively. Yet, one should not forget that transcriptions always lose detail as you translate from oral to written language. When you transcribe you change and make decisions and what you end up with is always somewhat artificial (Kvale, 2007). Therefore, be clear in any results presentation on how you transcribed your data.

Moderator2: Talk more about gaming.

Jenny2: Yes, it's not like watching a film either because a film—[Anna2: I don't feel that way either]—because you can't be part of a film— [several voices shout: exactly!]—I'm allowed to be part of and do everything, it makes me so engaged as well *laughter*

The numbers after the names indicate how far progressed the interview is. The first discussion topic is number one; as the participants change topic or the moderator asks a new question, the following discussion will get number two and so on. The number allows researchers to remember where in the discussion a quote comes from during the cut-and-paste process that often takes place during analysis and is seldom left in at the final written presentation of the material. The—[ ]—brackets mark out interjections and overlapping speech and aim to capture some of the pace of the conversation. Moreover, these show when participants strongly agree or disagree during discussion. Asterisks (*), on the other hand, are inserted to catch the mood or wordless information such as extended pauses or hesitations, sighs, laughter, disapproving 'tuts' and other noises people make in everyday conversations that carry meaning. I also use them to mark out modes of speech that change intended meaning, such as irony. Irony seldom translates well in written transcripts and so special care must be taken, as it often reverses the meaning of a sentence.

Analysing focus group data is in many ways similar to the analysis of any interview data. In Cote and Raz (chapter 7) as well as Pitkänen (chapter 8) you can read more on analysis. Often content analysis is performed on the raw data, that is, the transcripts and notes from the group discussion. The researcher looks for patterns, words, themes and so on in the text and uses some sort of system for indexing these (Berg, 2009). Themes for analysis can of course also come from theory or previous research. These themes make up a coding scheme used to structure the material. For small studies colouring is often a good way of marking different themes in the transcripts. Once different themes are identified it is important to go through your data once for each theme; in this way you can guide your search for one theme at a time which will make it easier to identify that theme and make sure you do not miss anything. This will also allow you to see when your themes overlap or are too wide. Sometimes themes might need to be split and sometimes two themes joined together. Analysis, like transcription, takes time if it is to be done well. Remember that it is not enough to see what the group is discussing; for proper analysis one must genuinely understand what each thing means in the context of the research. In light of this, never use a quote in a text without explaining its meaning to the reader, and one quote per analytical point is often enough.

Kitzinger (1995) suggests some points that should be taken into consideration when analysing focus groups. First, deviant cases should be addressed in the result description. Who disagreed with the group and why? Deviant cases can lay bare information-rich strains. On the same theme, it can be beneficial to pay special attention to what is allowed and what is not. What are the group norms? Are some opinions lifted up as better? Are some opinions silenced or dismissed by the group? Exploring cases like this will lay bare norms and values carried by the group. Furthermore, in focus groups you have to be careful to distinguish between individual and group opinions (Kitzinger, 1995). If something was agreed upon by the entire group or only advocated by one member against the others it gains a different meaning and should be separated in the analysis. Make sure the language in the analysis makes clear who says and argues what.

Also be careful *not to quantify your results*. I often see students presenting results saying 50% of participants agreed or "three in the group agreed and two were against". In a small focus group study it can be difficult to generalize results, in the sense that good control over the sample is needed to be able to say anything about the applicability of the results to other people or groups. Using percentages and numbers is therefore seldom valid or interesting when using this type of data and is often a consequence of weak analysis. What a reader wants to know is what the groups discussed, what they agreed on and what they did not, as explained above.

Questions to consider:

- Have you transcribed your data in a way so you can analyse it in order to answer your research question(s)?
- Which method(s) of analysis are you using and why?
- Have you paid special attention to deviant cases and cases when certain opinions have been silenced or heralded by the group?
- Are you explaining your quotes, not just leaving it up to the readers' interpretations?

How to deal with ethics in focus group research

Focus groups have some specific ethical issues connected with them. This section will discuss some points that need consideration when dealing with focus groups before, during and after the interview.

First, you can never be sure that members of the group will keep what is said to themselves (Berg, 2009). This is important to consider when discussing sensitive issues; is this something that might hinder a good discussion? This is also why Morgan (1996) suggests that focus group interviewing is unsuitable for such studies. Gibbs (1997) emphasises that participants need to be encouraged to keep in confidence what is said and, moreover, that you should never pressure participants to speak. Informants should know beforehand what is expected of them and the purpose of the research (Gibbs, 1997). This demands some special attention from the moderator.

The moderator must state some ground rules at the start of every focus group. Best is to have these as notes on the topic guide; this way there is no risk of forgetting them. Rules should ask the participants not to spread what individuals say in the group afterwards, even if you cannot, of course, guarantee that this is adhered to. However, as focus groups often consist of people who in some way know each other this is important. The participants must feel safe in the group or the discussion will suffer. Secondly, the moderator should ask participants to show respect towards each other and conflicting opinions. While this should be taken seriously, a moderator should not frighten the participants into silence. Rather, the aim is to lay out directions so that the discussion can be as informative and respectful as possible.

During the focus group make sure that uncomfortable situations are dealt with. The moderator is responsible for the social situation, and this responsibility must be taken seriously. If, for example, a participant is not treating another respectfully the moderator must step in and repeat that everyone's opinions matter and that disrespectful behaviour is not acceptable. If unsure whether to intervene remember that it is always better to do so and not risk a situation getting out of hand. In a group discussion on games, one example of a situation that requires intervention is if a participant is mocking or questioning the validity of another member's identity as 'a proper gamer', a common power struggle seen in gaming culture. A second example is if a participant starts talking about something highly sensitive or personal. In this case the moderator must judge how closely connected to the research it is and whether 1) to lift it up and discuss it or 2) acknowledge that this is interesting or relevant, but that perhaps the informant would like to discuss it after the group discussion is over; although the interviewer is *not* a therapist and must never slip into playing that role. The main idea is to never sweep things under the carpet; if an informant brings up a sensitive issue then it must be acknowledged. It is important that the informant feels heard and that the moderator shows the group how to handle the situation. Even in cases where the moderator deems it unlikely that the subject for the interviews is sensitive these issues should be kept in mind. It is inadvisable in any interview situation to take things for granted; one can never know what will be raised. I am often surprised at the stories people tell and how open people can be even in group situations.

To insure a good interview climate *informed consent* should be strived for (Kvale, 2007). Informed consent can be achieved if the participants have enough information about the research and their role in it to make an informed decision to take part or decline. Before all interviews you should inform participants how confidentiality will be handled. It should also be clear what the interviews are going to be used for. Participants should be informed beforehand on the topic for the discussion and the fact that the focus group will be recorded and transcribed. Usually, to ensure confidentiality, none of the interviewee's names are used in final products.

Finally, respect your informants. It is a great opportunity to take part in and listen to their discussions. For their effort and their willingness to share their own experiences participants should have our full respect, and the moderator should finish by acknowledging their contribution and thanking the informants properly. As long as the moderator shows respect, this generally spreads to the participants and lays the ground for a successful group discussion.

Questions to consider:

- Have you clearly explained the ground rules for the discussion?
- Have you prepared different strategies to handle difficulties during the interviews?
- Are you keeping the confidentiality of your informants in the written text; are names and other identifiable information removed?

Summary

Focus group interviewing allows researchers to investigate how participants understand and interpret experiences in a social context. A focus group interview is a group discussion where a moderator presents one or a few topics that a group of participants then proceeds to discuss. Focus groups are in one sense unique in that they allow us to observe everyday talk such as jokes and banter, arguments and discussion (Kitzinger, 1995), offering us an insight into everyday life and the production of knowledge that emerges. In game research one can use focus groups both in evaluative processes as well as in studies of playing and game culture. On the other hand, focus groups are less suited to answer questions related to internal psychology. Focus groups have been relatively little used in game research even though, as is clear from the text above, this method has many advantages. The attention to the social context and levels of knowledge construction makes focus group interviews distinct tools in the methodological toolbox for game research.

Further reading

- Barbour, R., 2007. *Doing focus groups*. London: SAGE Publications Ltd.
- Kitzinger, J., 1995. Qualitative research. Introducing focus groups. *BMJ: British medical journal*, 311(7000), pp.299–302. DOI= 10.1136/bmj.311.7000.299.
- Morgan, D.L., 1996. Focus groups. *Annual Review of Sociology*, 22, pp.129–152.
- Wilkinson, S., 1998. Focus groups in Feminist research: Power, Interaction, and the Co-construction of Meaning. *Women's Studies International Forum*, 21(1), pp.111–125.

References

Barbour, R., 2007. *Doing focus groups*. London: SAGE Publications Ltd.

Berg, B.L., 2009. *Qualitative research methods for the social sciences*. 6th ed. Boston: Pearson Education.

Berger, P.L. and Luckmann, T., 1967. *The social construction of reality: A treatise in the sociology of knowledge*. Imprint 1991. London: Penguin Books Ltd.

Bioware, 2009. *Dragon Age: Origins*, PC. [game] Electronic Arts.

Blizzard, 2004. *World of Warcraft*. [game] Blizzard Entertainment.

Blumer, H., 1970. Methodological principles of empirical science, In: N. K. Denzin, ed., 1972. *Sociological methods: A sourcebook*. Chicago: Aldine. pp.20–39.

Consalvo, M., 2007. *Cheating: Gaining advantage in video games*. Cambridge: MIT Press.

Creswell, J.W., 2007. *Qualitative inquiry and research design: Choosing among five approaches*. London: Sage Publications.

Denzin, N.K., 1978. *The research act: a theoretical introduction to sociological methods*. 2nd ed. New York: McGraw-Hill Book Company.

Eklund, L., 2012. *The sociality of gaming: A mixed methods approach to understanding digital gaming as a social leisure activity*. PhD. Stockholm University.

Eklund, L. and Johansson, M., 2013. Played and designed sociality in a massive multiplayer Online Game. *Eludamos*, 7(1), pp.35–54. Available at: <http://www.eludamos.org/index.php/eludamos/article/viewArticle/vol7no1-2>.

Gibbs, A., 1997 *Focus groups, social research update, winter 1997*. Surrey: Department of Sociology, University of Surrey. Available at: <http://sru.soc.surrey.ac.uk/SRU19.html>.

Hayes, N., 2000. *Doing psychological research*. Maidenhead: Open University Press.

Juul, J., 2010. A casual revolution: Reinventing video games and their players. London: The MIT Press.

Kitzinger, J., 1995. Qualitative research. Introducing focus groups. *BMJ: British medical journal*, 311(7000), pp.299.

Kvale, S., 2007. *Doing interviews.* London: Sage.

Lunt, P. and Livingstone, S., 1996. Rethinking the focus group in media and communication research. *Journal of Communication, 46* (2), pp.79–98.

Merton, R.K., 1987. The focussed interview and focus groups: Continuities and discontinuities, *The Public Opinion Quarterly*, 51(4), pp.550–566.

Merton, R.K. and Kendall, P.L., 1946. The focused interview. *American Journal of Sociology*, 51(6), pp.541–557.

Miller, L., Chaika, M. and Groppe, L., 1996. Female participants' preferences in software design: Insights from a focus group. *Interpersonal Computing and Technology*, 4(2), pp.27–36.

Morgan, D.L., 1996. Focus groups. *Annual Review of Sociology*, 22, pp.129–152.

Poels, K., de Kort, Y. and Ijsselsteijn, W., 2007. It is always a lot of fun! Exploring dimensions of digital game experience using focus group methodology. In *Proceedings of the 2007 conference on future play*. New York: ACM, pp.83-89. DOI=10.1145/1328202.1328218.

Stewart, D. W., Shamdasani, P. N. and Rook. D. W., 2007. *Focus groups*. Thousand Oaks: SAGE Publications, Ltd.

Wilkinson, S., 1998. Focus groups in feminist research: Power, interaction, and the co-construction of meaning. *Women's Studies International Forum*, 21(1), pp.111–125.

PART III

QUANTITATIVE APPROACHES

10

Quantitative methods and analyses for the study of players and their behaviour

RICHARD N. LANDERS AND KRISTINA N. BAUER

O ften, when studying games, researchers need to describe, explain, or predict human behaviour. The behaviour we're interested in may occur outside of a game—for example, does violent videogame play cause aggression in children? But the behaviour we're interested in may instead occur inside of a game—for example, does tweaking a particular game element increase player satisfaction?

In both of these cases, we want to know the answer to what appears on its surface to be a straight-forward question: given a particular situation of interest, what do people do? Unfortunately, people's behaviour is difficult to predict well because people vary to a high degree both interpersonally and across contexts. They have different hopes, dreams, ideas, experiences, skills, attitudes, abilities, and so on, all of which come together to influence their reactions to any particular situation. So how do we develop general rules for how people behave?

An introduction to research

The key to understanding human behaviour is research, but there are many different approaches. First, we can split such efforts into *empirical* and *non-empirical* research. Non-empirical research relies on human intuition and reasoning. In the study of games, this is typically the approach of philosophers and other humanists. To answer the question of a tie between violent video games and aggression, a digital humanist might look at the history of games, evaluating the portrayal of violence as it has evolved with games, trying to rationally link (or separate) the two through well-constructed argument. The downside to non-empirical approaches is that such efforts are completely through the lens of human reasoning. Thus, non-empirical approaches only describe reality insofar as human beings are rational creatures. Unfortunately, we are often irrational.

Empirical approaches provide a potential solution to this problem by relying on the collection of *data*. The processes used to collect data are intended to be as objective as possible, in order to minimize the impact of faulty human judgment. Although complete objectivity is impossible to achieve, empirical approaches aim to minimize the subjective aspects of observation as much as possible through the application of the carefully constructed and refined rules of the scientific method. In doing so, researchers can minimize the number of alternative explanations for those observations. Thus, empiricists collect data and then make conclusions based upon their interpretation of what patterns those data reveal.

Within empirical research, two major data analytic strategies have developed. The first of these is *qualitative* data analysis. Qualitative researchers embrace the idea that humans are subjective, complex creatures, concluding from this that the complexity of human thought and behaviour is exactly what research should aim to explore. These approaches use data collection techniques like focus groups or open-ended survey questions, and it extracts broad themes or trends among respondents. *Quantitative* research is the second approach, and its approach to understanding people is quite different. Because humans are subjective, complex creatures, quantitative researchers aim to measure them in as precise and replicable a way as possible. If there is fault in measurement, it is left to future researchers to continuously improve, over years or decades, until firm conclusions can be made, reaching what is referred to as *scientific consensus*.

Many modern researchers utilize a mix of these two approaches, depending upon their specific research questions (see also chapter 16). One common approach is to take a qualitative approach when studying a phenomenon that is ill-defined and ambiguous, and then following up with quantitative research to verify the trends identified in the qualitative research. For example, when studying computer games, researchers might first conduct a qualitative study of how players experience stress as they play a competitive first-person shooter. After compiling the results of that study, the researchers might next create a scale to quantify that stress numerically and test if stress (as represented by numbers) can be used to predict outcomes of interest. Another common approach is to take a quantitative approach when studying a phenomenon initially, following up with a qualitative approach to provide additional context. For example, researchers might first conduct a quantitative study estimating the impact of violent video game play on aggressive behaviour. After identifying an effect, the researcher might next conduct follow-up interviews to identify the cause of the change in aggressive behaviour as perceived by the participants.

Either of these approaches is potentially valid within a particular field of study, but the choice of approach brings with it a variety of advantages and disadvantages in terms of feasibility and interpretation for the researcher. The primary advantage to qualitative approaches is the richness of information obtained. The primary advantages to quantitative approaches are the ability for future researchers to replicate your approach and results (a key component of the scientific method) and improved objectivity in the research process. The remainder of this chapter will be devoted to exploring the broad issues faced when considering a quantitative approach.

RECOMMENDED READING

- Popper, K., 2005. *The logic of scientific discovery*. New York: Routledge.

Psychometrics

When considering quantitative approaches, the first major problem faced is how to capture numerically the ideas and processes you want to capture. Sometimes *objective measures* are available, which makes this easy. If you want to predict the "number of times the players open the game on their smartphones," this number can be collected, without human error influencing its value, directly from game databases. More often, however, researchers need to use *subjective measures,* because whatever they are interested in measuring is not directly observable. For example, if you want to understand whether or not a player experienced a sense of meaning by playing your game, there is no way to capture sense of meaning from a database. You must either ask questions of the player directly or infer this meaning from their behaviour. The study of this process, how best to represent ambiguous psychological states and traits as numbers, is called *psychometrics*.

CONSTRUCTS AND THEIR OPERATIONALIZATION

When delving into psychometrics, we must first identify a *construct* of interest. A construct can be any unmeasurable characteristic of a player or a game. For example, a player's preference for role-playing games is a construct, but so is a game's effectiveness at convincing people to change their attitude on homelessness (and attitude is yet another construct!).

Since constructs are unmeasurable, we must *operationalize* constructs, and the goal of operationalization is to ensure the way that the construct is measured is as accurate a representation of the construct as possible. *Operational definitions* are precise, objective ways that we try to measure constructs. Figure 1 displays an example of a construct-operationalization pair.

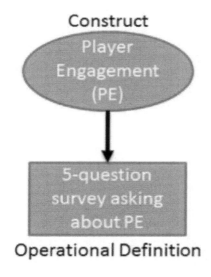

Figure 1. Operationalization.

Figure 1 is also an example of a *path diagram,* and the specific shapes chosen and arrow directions in such diagrams are important. Ovals are used to represent constructs, whereas rectangles are used to represent operational definitions. Arrows are used to represent the direction of causality. In general, we theorize that *constructs cause operational definitions*. In other words, the construct is the real attribute of the person; the operationalization is just one way (of potentially many ways) to measure that construct (for more discussion on causal order in this context, see Edwards and Bagozzi, 2000).

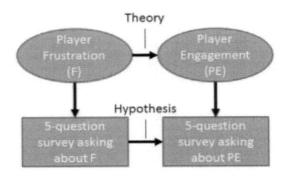

Figure 2. A theory and a hypothesis testing that theory.

Relationships between constructs are generally referred to as *theory*, whereas relationships between operational definitions are referred to as *hypotheses*. In the example theory depicted in figure 2, we are proposing that player frustration causes changes in player engagement. Most likely, we are proposing that increased frustration leads to decreased engagement, but this isn't indicated in the path diagram – only the direction of causality is shown. Because constructs are unmeasurable, it is *impossible* for us to test this theory directly. Instead, we must test the relationship between operational definitions. In this case, we provide five survey questions on each construct and see if there is a relationship between the means of each set of survey questions. If we find a statistical relationship between our operational definitions, we can then conclude that the results of our *hypothesis test* are consistent with our theory, which increases our belief that our theory is true.

THE CORE QUESTIONS

All of the techniques and strategies developed for quantitative data analysis were thus developed to solve only a few major problems:

1. How do we ensure our operational definitions measure the same thing every time we use them?
2. How do we ensure our operational definitions actually represent the constructs they are intended to represent?
3. How do we test hypotheses so that they are reasonable tests of theory?

To illustrate the importance of these issues, consider the words of Korman (1974, p.194): "The point is not that adequate measurement is 'nice'. It is necessary, crucial, etc. Without it we have nothing."

Classical test theory

Classical test theory (CTT) is the basis for addressing all three of these questions. Classical test theory states that all *observed scores* are composed of two elements: a *true score* plus *error*. It is commonly stated as

$$X = T + e$$

where X = an observed score, T = true score, and e = error. In the case of operationalization, we could re-write this formula as

Operational definition score = Construct score + Mis-measurement of construct

By looking at measurement through the lens of CTT, we can conclude that the best way to measure a construct is to minimize error, which in this case would be referred to more specifically as *measurement error*.

But we can apply CTT more broadly than this. For example, let's consider the problem of *sampling*. Sampling refers to how well the particular group of people you conduct your study on, called a *sample*, represents the group that you drew them from, called a *population*. We might want to make conclusions about "game players in general" (our population), but we can only get 100 particular game players at our local university or in our online community to respond to our survey (our sample). We can restate the CTT formula as

Population score = Sample score + Mis-measurement of the population

The formula is still the same, but some of the details have changed. In this case, the best way to measure a population is to minimize error, and in this case, we would refer to that error as *sampling error*.

There are numerous techniques for assessing and minimizing both measurement error and sampling error, the most common of which we'll discuss later in this chapter.

Figure 3. Normally distributed population.

ASSUMPTIONS OF CTT

CTT makes three major assumptions:

1. In the population, errors must average to zero. Sometimes this is referred to as *unsystematic* error. For example, if we wanted to measure player enjoyment with a particular game, we would need to assume that if every player we ever wanted to know about played that game, their scores on our survey would revolve around a single true score. Some might have enjoyed the game more, and others might have enjoyed it less. But those deviations from the mean must be random, higher or lower from the mean in an unpredictable fashion. A depiction of

what such a population might look like appears in figure 3. Errors average to zero because there are an equal number of people both below and above the population mean.

2. Second, in the population, true scores and error scores must be independent. If people who tend to be low in the distribution are measured with greater error than those high in the distribution, the middle of that distribution becomes uninterpretable.

3. Third, errors must themselves be independent. This assumption is most often violated when multiple items are used on a survey to assess a particular construct, but when two or more of those questions unintentionally tap onto an unknown, second construct.

When one or more of these assumptions are violated, researchers must either alter their approach so that the assumption is no longer violated (e.g., by using different measurement or sampling techniques) or adopt a *nonparametric* approach that does not require the assumptions of CTT. Because the assumptions of CTT enable a wide variety of powerful quantitative analyses (most of which are *parametric*), most researchers take the first approach.

AN APPLICATION OF CTT: SCALE DEVELOPMENT

To examine the value of CTT as an explanatory framework, let's consider an example of a common problem faced by computer games researchers.

For his dissertation, Joe needs to know how much people play videogames each week. Thus, we have a construct: weekly videogame play. A common approach at this point is to ask a single question, for example:

- How many hours each week do you play videogames?

The problem with asking a single question is that we do not know how much error it contains. If X = T + e, any answers to this single question will contain both T and e. The most likely cause of error in this case is the word "videogame." How do we know that every participant will interpret the word "videogame" the same way? We do not. So to minimize error, we should ask multiple questions that all get at the same basic idea, for example:

- How many hours each week do you play videogames?
- How many hours each week do you play cell phone games?
- How many hours each week do you play console games?
- How many hours each week do you play handheld games?

By asking multiple questions and calculating the average response across these four questions, we should minimize the effects of e. Some people will report playing many hours of cell phone games and few hours of console games, and others will report the reverse; but these errors in measuring overall *weekly videogame play* should average out to zero. Thus we can be more confident that our survey actually measures the true score, which we can in turn be more confident really is *weekly videogame play*.

In this case, there may be more cause for concern, however. After running this study, Joe might find that the relationship between responses to the *cell phone games* question and responses to the *handheld games* question are stronger than between the other items. This is potentially a violation of the third assumption of CTT; the error of these two items may not be independent because they both ask about mobile device play (unlike the other two items). In this case, Joe would probably need to eliminate one of the items to obtain better measurement.

This iterative process of measure refinement is why rigorous quantitative studies adapt pre-existing multi-item measures where possible. Where such measures are not available, pilot studies are sometimes used to test out a new measure's psychometric properties before using it in a broader study. Single-item measures of constructs are generally inappropriate for quantitative research unless those constructs can be defined objectively and without error.

Recommended reading

- Nunnally, J. C., 1978. *Psychometric theory.* 2nd ed. New York: McGraw-Hill.

Reliability

Reliability assesses the first of our core questions: How do we ensure our operational definitions measure the same thing every time we use them?

Reliability, broadly, is defined as consistency of measurement. Assessing it involves first identifying what aspects of the underlying true score *should* stay consistent, and from that, identifying what aspects of an observed score should be considered error. For example, persistent lifelong psychological traits, like general cognitive ability, should not change over time. Thus, if a general cognitive ability measure was given to a group of people twice, with a two-year-gap between administrations, we would not expect scores to change very much. If the scores do not change, we generally conclude that the measure is reliable given the sample with which it was tested. If the scores do change, we generally conclude that it is unreliable.

This decision is critical because misidentifying the source of error could lead you to erroneous conclusions. For example, imagine that you develop a survey to assess the construct *fun* and then ask people to play the same game twice, on two different days. You find that the scores do not agree very well, but does that mean your *fun* measure is unreliable? Not necessarily. Because the experience of *fun* is so context-dependent, you wouldn't expect it to stay the same over time—one play session might be much more (or less!) fun than the last.

Once the most appropriate source(s) of error has been identified, you can choose which type of reliability is most appropriate to assess your developed measure. Although there are many ways to assess reliability, we will discuss the most commonly needed here.

As a rule of thumb, Nunnelly (1978) suggests that a reliability coefficient of 0.70 is adequate for research. In practice, this means that only 70% of the variance in observed scores can be explained by variance between true scores, which is not very high. The lower the reliability of your measurement, the larger a sample you will need to find statistical significance, so it is in your best interests to identify measures with maximum reliability. Generally, one wants above 0.90 if possible, but 0.80 or higher is a reasonable middle ground.

TEST-RETEST RELIABILITY

Test-retest reliability is an appropriate way to assess reliability when you expect consistency of a single operational definition over time. Typically, test-retest reliability is used when construct measurement involves correct answers (e.g., knowledge tests, cognitive ability tests). To calculate it, use your measure at two different time points (could be minutes, days, or years apart, depending upon how long you expect scores to be consistent), and then calculate the *correlation* between the two (in most cases, a *Pearson's product-moment correlation coefficient*, also called a *Pearson's r*). The value you obtain for this correlation is your reliability coefficient (e.g., if you calculated the correlation between Time 1 and Time 2 such that $r = 0.85$, you would expect that 85% of the observed variance in the Time 1 measurement is due to true score variance).

INTER-RATER RELIABILITY

Inter-rater reliability is used to assess reliability between multiple independent operational definitions of the same construct. However, it is a little more flexible in that more than two sources can be compared. It is most commonly used when multiple people make numerical ratings of the same behaviour. For example, you may want to assess how much a child engages in antisocial behaviour during a group play session. To assess that, you might ask three people to watch each child and rate on a 1-to-5 scale how antisocially they were behaving. You would not want a single rater to make this judgment, because a single rater can be biased (no way to control error, in the CTT sense). To calculate reliability in this context, you will need to calculate an intra-class correlation (ICC, see Shrout and Fleiss, 1979 for more information).

INTERNAL CONSISTENCY RELIABILITY

Internal consistency reliability is the most commonly assessed form of reliability. It is most appropriate when you have survey-type measures (i.e., when multiple survey items are written as operationalizations of the same construct). Like inter-rater reliability, it does not include variation over time in what it considers to be error. There are many ways to calculate internal consistency reliability, but the most common is a statistic called *Cronbach's alpha* (α). Although an oversimplification, it is easiest to understand alpha as the mean correlation between all scale items. For example, if you had a 10-item scale, it is similar to the value you would obtain by averaging the 45 possible correlations one could calculate between those 10 items. For more on alpha, see Cortina (1993).

Recommened reading

- Pedhazur, E.J., and Schmelkin, L.P., 1991. *Measurement, design, and analysis: An integrated approach*. New York: Taylor & Francis Group.

Construct validity

Once reliability is established, we can safely conclude that our operational definition measures *something*. But it is not yet clear what that *something* actually is. This is an important distinction. To illustrate why, consider graphology, the study of handwriting. Handwriting is highly reliable. If you ask a person to write a particular sentence today and then again in a year, the two versions will be quite similar to one another. However, it is not quite clear what handwriting actually tells us about a person. Even a few years ago, many people believed that you could discover a wide range of human characteristics from handwriting alone; for example, that by examining someone's handwriting, it could be determined the career for which they were best suited, or if they had violent tendencies. However, upon empirical scrutiny, none of these claims were supported. This is an example of a measure that has reliability (it measures *something* consistency) but not *construct validity*.

Construct validity assesses the second core question: how do we ensure our operational definitions actually represent the constructs they are intended to represent?

Reliability can be tested statistically, since it is a question solely about operational definitions. Construct validity cannot. Because we can never measure constructs directly, the validity of a measure is supported by inference from evidence, not specific statistical tests.

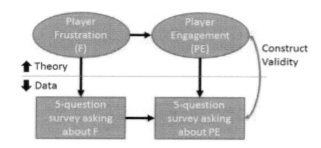

Figure 4. An illustration of construct validity.

Figure 4 expands our previous diagram to include more explicit consideration of these relationships. Constructs (above the horizontal line) can never be measured, whereas operational definitions (below the horizontal line) can. Thus, any analysis that occurs below the line, like reliability, can be done statistically. Validity addresses the question of "how well does my operational definition capture my construct?" When you assess construct validity, you have already decided that measurement is reliable, because without reliability, a measure cannot be valid. Thus, you should always remember this distinction: *A valid measure is always reliable, but a reliable measure is not always valid.*

Because validity is not a statistical concept, there are many more ways to obtain (or fail to obtain) evidence of validity in comparison to reliability. In this section, we will describe some of the most common and most useful.

ESTABLISHING CONSTRUCT VALIDITY

Evidence for construct validity can be collected using a variety of methods. Historically, these came under three different headings: construct validity, *content validity*, and *criterion validity*. However, after the work of Messick (1995) and the American Educational Research Association (1999), these concepts were simplified into the one overall concept of *construct validity*, with several types of evidence to support it. Critically, there is never a particular point where a specific measure is named valid. Instead, validity evidence is built over time, increasing our confidence in that measure as new evidence is added. Each of the major types of evidence most relevant to videogames research will be explained next.

EVIDENCE FROM TEST CONTENT

What used to be called *content validity*, evidence from test content is evidence built from our trust in the experts that formed the basis for a test. For example, one common approach to developing a new measure is to poll a variety of experts for their opinions about the content, create the measure, and then present the measure to those experts again to ensure that their understanding of the construct is appropriately represented in the items developed. Test content evidence is one of the weakest forms of construct validity evidence because even experts are humans—and thus biased. But nevertheless, it is a common first step.

EVIDENCE FROM RESPONSE PROCESSES

When a measure is created for the explicit purposes of measuring a particular human characteristic, processes related to that characteristic should be invoked when reading about the item. For example, when attempting to establish the construct validity of videogame play observers making assessments of antisocial behaviour, a secondary study might be conducted asking the assessors what types of behaviours they were identifying when making their ratings. By matching the specific processes engaged in by the raters with processes intended to be captured in the intended construct, researchers can provide some evidence that those raters are indeed capturing antisocial behaviours.

EVIDENCE FROM THE INTERNAL STRUCTURE OF MEASURES

Although reliability can be assessed quite simply (e.g., by calculating correlations or Cronbach's α), more complex approaches are available that provide some evidence of construct validity. The most common approaches involve the use of exploratory and confirmatory factor analyses, which are powerful statistical tools for identifying the underlying influence of constructs that may not have been obvious when surveys were originally written. For example, imagine the researcher that theorizes that engagement with videogames is really composed of three facets: physical engagement, emotional engagement, and cognitive engagement. Confirmatory factor analysis could be used to verify that this three-factor structure actually emerged from the data collected. Such an approach would still be limited, though, in that it could not verify that those three factors were the only three factors.

EVIDENCE FROM EXPLORATION OF THE NOMOLOGICAL NET

The *nomological net* refers to the web of other constructs, including antecedents, component processes, and outcomes, surrounding a particular construct of interest. For example, it is now generally accepted that the personality trait Conscientiousness is one of five major traits describing personality (alongside Openness, Extraversion, Agreeableness, and Neuroticism), each of which is made up of numerous facets (although the specific nature of these facets is less agreed-upon). Conscientiousness is also known to predict several outcomes—such as job performance, academic performance, and life satisfaction. Thus, if researchers were to create a new measure of conscientiousness, we would expect that measure to fit in the nomological net in the same way—it should predict the other four personality traits at the level other conscientiousness measures do, and it should predict the outcomes named similarly. If so, we can add to the body of validity evidence that our new measure is indeed a measure of conscientiousness. This type of evidence is probably the most rigorous of all types, and as a result, there is a substantial body of work exploring how such evidence can be obtained (see, for example, *concurrent validation* and *predictive validation* approaches).

Recommended reading

- Pedhazur, E.J., and Schmelkin, L.P., 1991. *Measurement, design, and analysis: An integrated approach*. New York: Taylor & Francis Group.

Research designs

After establishing the reliability and validity of a measure, you are able to use it as part of a *research design*. Quantitative research designs address the third core question: How do we test hypotheses so that they are reasonable tests of theory?

A research design is like a blueprint—it is the plan for studying a scientific question. The plan includes how data will be measured, collected, and analysed. When we put our operational definitions into a particular study, we refer to them as *variables*. Numerous types of research designs exist to examine variables, and the remainder of this chapter describes three broad classes of design for this purpose: correlational, experimental, and quasi-experimental. We also highlight appropriate statistical approaches for analysing data from each type of design and present examples from the published games literature of each approach.

One important distinction between research designs is the researcher's ability to make a *causal claim*. Often, researchers are interested in concluding that one construct causes changes in another construct. For example, a videogame researcher might be interested in concluding that increasing frustration from a videogame causes decreases in player engagement. However, to make such a claim, three rules must be satisfied:

1. covariation
2. temporal precedence
3. no alternative explanation.

The first rule requires that the two variables are related to each other. The second rule means that the cause must precede the effect in time. The third rule, which is the most difficult to satisfy, requires the elimination of all plausible alternative explanations, called *confounds*, for the observed relationship. The most powerful way to satisfy the third rule is to implement an *experimental design*. In the example above, the videogame researcher would need to show that

1. frustration and engagement are correlated
2. the increase in frustration occurs before the decrease in player engagement
3. there are no other reasons that the increase in frustration and the decrease in engagement might be related.

In this case, the researcher may need to rule out challenge as a possible alternative cause—something that is challenging may be both frustrating and engaging.

An important distinction applicable to research design in general is whether a *between-subjects* or *within-subjects* strategy is chosen. When using a between-subjects strategy, participants are compared to each other. When using a within-subjects strategy, participants are compared to themselves. The choice of strategy is driven by your research question. For example, if you wanted to know if people improve at playing a particular game (e.g., *chess*) as they practice, you would be interested in a within-subjects design. If you wanted to know if differences between people in experience with a game predict their comfort with a similar, new game, you would be interested in a between-subjects design. The use of both strategies simultaneously is referred to as a *mixed model*. Any of these three strategies can be used in the specific designs that follow, especially when multiple research designs are integrated into a single study.

Regardless of the type of design utilized, there are some preliminary issues to be considered. For example, a researcher must decide on a minimum number of participants to sample. This is determined using a *power analysis*, which is a function of how strongly variables are related to each other and how comfortable the researcher is falsely concluding there is not a relationship even when one really exists. There is freely available computer software (e.g., G*Power) to aid researchers in conducting a power analysis.

When deciding how many participants to sample, an exceptionally large number of participants can cause interpretative problems too. When a researcher finds *statistical significance*, the only valid conclusion is that if no effect really existed in the population, the effect found in the sample would be unlikely. But improbability alone is not enough to conclude that a research finding is meaningful. It is critical to also interpret *practical significance*, which refers to how large an effect one variable has on another. For example, a correlation of .02 may be statistically significant (unlikely to have occurred by chance if the population correlation was .00), but lack practical significance (the first variable only explains 0.04% of the other variable).

Another important decision is what analyses will be completed. Researchers should decide on their intended analyses before data collection begins. When analyses are decided on after data collection, it is more likely that the researcher will go fishing for significant results. This unfortunately common practice increases the likelihood that a researcher will make inaccurate conclusions. Statistical corrections can be made to analyses determined after data collection to reduce the risk of such errors (see Maxwell and Delaney, 2004).

Recommended reading:

- Bruin, J., 2006. *G*Power data analysis examples*. UCLA: Statistical Consulting Group. Available at: <http://www.ats.ucla.edu/stat/stata/ado/analysis/>.

CORRELATIONAL RESEARCH DESIGNS

Correlational designs are used to answer questions about the association between variables. Among research designs, they provide the weakest evidence for causal questions. In a correlational design, one or more variables are used to predict one or more other variables. When the researcher is trying to support a causal relationship in such a design, a causal variable is called a *predictor*, whereas an outcome is called a *criterion* or *response variable*.

There are two categories of correlational designs. In a *cross-sectional design*, all variables are measured simultaneously. In a *longitudinal design* (also called a *repeated-measures design*), multiple measurements of predictors and/or criteria are conducted over time. The strength of a longitudinal design is that it increases support for both the second and third rule when making casual claims. Within both cross-sectional and longitudinal designs, there are three common strategies for data collection: *naturalistic observation, survey research,* and *archival research*.

Types of correlational designs

In naturalistic observation, researchers collect data by examining the natural environment of behaviour. For example, a researcher interested in support behaviours after a losing a game could observe sports teams post-game behaviours. In this type of research, measures are most commonly amounts of time or counts of specific behaviours. One advantage of this type of design is that the researcher can view the behaviour as it occurs in everyday life. Researchers may also use their observation to generate new research ideas. On the other hand, naturalistic observation can be time consuming and costly, and the researcher is unable to control extraneous variables.

Survey research is the most common data collection strategy when studying people and their behaviour. In a cross-sectional design, surveys contain all variables of interest, whereas in longitudinal data collection, some variables may be included at each time point or in all time points. There are several advantages to survey research, including time and cost efficiency, as well as flexibility. A researcher can quickly and cheaply collect a large amount of data. However, the quality of survey research is dependent on the quality of the survey itself. Each measure must be validated prior to use. Another drawback to surveys is that participants may try to present themselves in a positive light or to answer questions based upon what they believe the researcher wants to know.

Archival research involves accessing some type of previously stored data. The data may take the form of public records, previously published empirical studies, or other historical data. A special type of archival research, called *meta-analysis*, is used to summarize all prior empirical evidence about the relationships between variables. To illustrate, a researcher who wants to draw conclusions about the relationship between game play and attention span could gather all of the quantitative studies that examined this relationship and summarize that relationship with a single number. The quality of archival research is limited by the quality of the original data collection strategy that produced the archival data.

Recommended reading

- Bordens, K.S., and Abbott, B.B., 2011. *Research design and methods: A process approach.* 8th ed. Boston: McGraw Hill.

Statistics to analyse correlational designs

A *correlation coefficient* is used to assess the degree of association between two variables. Several types of correlations can be used depending on the type of data being analysed. The *Pearson product-moment correlation coefficient* (more commonly referred to as *r* or *Pearson's r*) assesses the relationship between two continuously measured variables (e.g., the correlation between player frustration and player engagement in a videogame as measured with survey questions) and is the most commonly used correlation. Other correlations include *Spearman's rank-order correlation*, which is used with two rank-order variables, the *point-biserial correlation*, which is used with one dichotomous variable (only 0 or 1) and one continuous variable, and the *phi coefficient*, which is used with two dichotomous variables.

In general, correlations range from -1 to +1. The sign of the correlation indicates the *direction* of the relationship. When both variables increase (or decrease) together, a correlation is *positive*. When one variable increases as the other decreases, a correlation is *negative*. Correlations close to zero indicate *no relationship*. Figure 5 depicts a positive and negative correlation as well as no relationship. The *magnitude* of the correlation is a sign of the strength of the relationship between the two variables. Cohen (1992) provided the convention for small, medium, and large effect sizes of 0.10, 0.30, and 0.50, respectively, regardless of direction.

 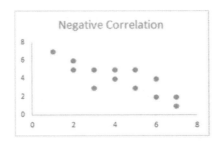 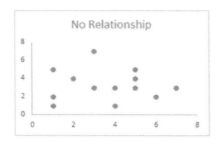

Figure 5. Scatterplots showing various correlations.

A simple correlation is only useful if a researcher is interested in the relationship between *two* variables. Often, researchers ask questions about how several predictor variables are simultaneously related to an outcome, which requires *multiple regression*. For example, a researcher might ask how both player frustration and skill relate to engagement in a videogame. Regression enables researchers to draw much more precise estimates of relationships than possible with correlation alone. *Regression weights* (*b* and *β*) are used to describe the strength of each relationship, whereas a *multiple correlation* (*R*) is used to describe the strength of all predictors as a group.

More advanced statistical approaches to correlational designs include *hierarchical linear modelling* for research involving people nested within larger groups, and *structural equation modelling* (see chapter 15) for research examining more complex variable interrelationships.

Recommended reading

- Cohen, J., Cohen, P., West, S.G., and Aiken, L. S., 2003. *Applied multiple regression/correlation analysis for the behavioral sciences*. 3rd ed. Mahwah: Lawrence Erlbaum Associates.

Example of correlational research

Domahidi, Festl, and Quandt (2014) examined the relationship between social online game use and gaming-related friendships. For simplicity, we focus on the results that pertain to the authors' subsample of social online players—people who reported playing online social games with other players at least occasionally. Data on 849 social players were obtained using a telephone administered survey, which assessed game use and number of friendships as well as other variables of interest. Figure 6 illustrates Domahidi and colleagues' design; each box is a variable of interest and the sample represents a single population of social online players. The double-headed arrow represents the correlation between the two variables.

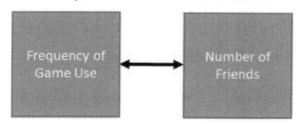

Figure 6. Illustration of Domahidi, et al.'s (2014) design.

This example from research is a cross-sectional correlational design using a survey strategy. This type of design is appropriate to determine the relationship between the game use predictor and the friendship criterion, but is not a strong enough design to allow us to make a causal conclusion. Domahidi and colleagues (2014) utilized some of the advantages of survey research (easy and cheap data collection), but use of a telephone interview increased the amount of time required to collect data. The survey contained measures utilized in previous research, which enhances generalizability of the measured variables to the constructs of interest, but self-reported frequency of time spent gaming may not reflect actual time spent gaming. Additionally, using a longitudinal design where number of friendships was measured later in time would have strengthened the study design.

The researchers used regression to examine how well frequency of online social game use predicted the number of friends a person had (Domahidi, et al., 2014). They found that social gaming frequency was unrelated to the number of friends a person has, and instead, being younger and male was associated with having more friends. You may have noticed that the language above does not include statements about cause and effect. Causal language cannot be used with a correlational design.

EXPERIMENTAL RESEARCH DESIGNS

Experimental designs are used to test causal questions and have two major features: a *manipulation* and *random assignment.*

The first feature is the manipulation of an *independent variable (IV)*. The IV is the causal variable and is under the researcher's control. To manipulate the IV, the researcher must create at least two levels or groups. The simplest experimental design is a two-group post-test design. The first group is an *experimental group* receiving a *treatment*, and the second group is a *control group* not receiving a treatment. Treatment broadly refers to any experimental manipulation. For example, patients recovering from stroke might be assigned to a game-based virtual reality rehabilitation system (treatment) or to a typical rehabilitation program (control). The manipulation of the IV is followed by the measurement of a *dependent variable (DV)*. The DV is the outcome of an experiment and is observed or measured by the researcher.

The second feature of an experiment is the use of random assignment. Because of what we know about classical test theory, collecting one large sample of people and randomly splitting them into two smaller groups creates two groups that are roughly identical in terms of their scores on all potentially measureable variables (regardless of whether any of those variables are actually measured). Thus, after the manipulation, the only variables that are different between the two groups should be ones changed as a causal result of the manipulation. This is the power of experiments.

Types of experimental designs

In practice, experimental designs are rarely as simple as randomly assigning participants to one of two groups. One of the benefits of an experimental design is the flexibility to accommodate more complex designs. Consider a researcher comparing a videogame with adaptive difficulty to a videogame without adaptive difficulty. This is an example of a *one-way design* because one IV was manipulated (adaptive difficulty). However, researchers are able to manipulate multiple IVs. In a *two-way design*, two IVs are manipulated. The number of experimental conditions depends on the number of levels of each IV. If this researcher also manipulates the difficulty of the videogame by making easy, medium, and difficult versions, the second IV has three levels. The researcher now has six conditions (2 levels of the first IV crossed with 3 levels of the second IV) and has created what's called a 2 X 3 factorial design.

Researchers can choose to manipulate more than two IVs, but very rarely manipulate more than three. The number of conditions grows multiplicatively based on the number of levels of each IV, and study design should be as simple as possible given a particular research question. In most cases, if more than three IVs are needed, there is a better way to ask your question.

Recommended reading

- Bordens, K.S., and Abbott, B.B., 2011. *Research design and methods: A process approach.* 8th ed. Boston, MA: McGraw Hill.
- Shadish, W.R., Cook, T.D., and Campbell, D.T., 2002. *Experimental and quasi-experimental designs for generalized causal inference.* Boston: Houghton, Mifflin and Company.

Statistics to analyse experimental designs

Several statistical tests are available to analyse experimental data. We will discuss two major types: *t-tests* and *analysis of variance (ANOVA)*. The appropriate statistic depends on the complexity of the experimental design. For a simple experiment with only two groups, the *independent samples t-test* is used to compare the means of the groups. When an independent-samples t-test is statistically significant, it means that if we were to assume there was no true difference between the experimental groups, it is highly improbable that the difference we found in our study would have occurred. To illustrate, the researcher comparing adaptive difficulty to non-adaptive difficulty obtains a significant independent samples *t*-test. If the DV is higher in the adaptive game condition, then the researcher can conclude that adaptive difficulty caused the change in the DV.

ANOVAs are used to analyse experiments with more than two groups. When a researcher only manipulates one IV with three or more groups, a *one-way ANOVA* is used. The output of a one-way ANOVA is an *F-test* that indicates whether there is a difference between at least two group means. The *F*-test is like a gateway; a significant value opens the door to follow-up with additional tests that determine where the significant differences lie. If two IVs are manipulated, a *two-way ANOVA* is used. When examining the results of a two-way ANOVA, there are three *F*-tests. Two of the *F*-tests are for the *main effect* of each IV. A main effect describes the differences between groups on each IV averaging across the other IV. The third *F*-test is for the *interaction effect*, which tests whether group differences in one IV depend on differences in the other IV. If the interaction effect is statistically significant, the main effects are no longer interpretable. Instead, the researcher must follow-up the interaction with additional tests or by graphing the interaction to help visualize it.

Recommended literature

- Maxwell, S.E., and Delaney, H.D., 2004. *Designing experiments and analyzing data: A model comparison perspective*. New York: Psychology Press.

Example of experimental research

Erhel and Jamet (2013) examined how game instruction type and feedback impacts learning and motivation in an educational game. For simplicity we focus on instruction type and learning in this example. The researchers wanted to know whether two different but common types of instructions – entertainment or learning – differ in their effect on how much students learn. Entertainment instructions focus on the fun aspects of game play, whereas learning instructions focus on the educational aspects of game play. Erhel and Jamet created two groups, one receiving entertainment instructions and the other receiving learning instructions. Undergraduate students were randomly assigned to one of the two groups. These students completed a knowledge measure after playing an educational game designed to cover four aging-related health issues. Figure 7 illustrates Erhel and Jamet's design; each box is a variable of interest with the box on the left representing the manipulation of type of instruction. Figure 7 also shows how the use of random assignment created two equivalent groups within the population of undergraduate students.

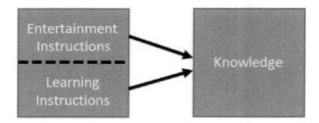

Figure 7. Illustration of Erhel and Jamet's (2013) design.

The example from current research illustrates the simplest experimental design discussed earlier, the two group post-test design. Erhel and Jamet (2013) manipulated an independent variable (game instruction) and created two groups, illustrating the first feature of an experiment. The researchers also randomly assigned participants to one of the two groups, satisfying the second feature of an experiment. In this example, the study does not have a control group (a group playing the game with no instructions). Instead, the authors chose to have two treatments. One drawback of this choice is that we don't know how participants would have performed without instructions. At the same time, it seems unlikely that students would play an educational game in school without any form of instruction. The authors used ANOVA to analyse the data and found that participants receiving learning instructions scored higher on the knowledge test than participants receiving entertainment instructions.

QUASI-EXPERIMENTAL RESEARCH DESIGNS

The final type of design is a quasi-experimental design, which is used when the researcher wants to compare groups but is unable to conduct a controlled experiment for either logistical or ethical reasons. Quasi-experimental designs are very similar to experimental designs. In fact, on the surface, they often look identical. The distinction is that quasi-experimental designs lack random assignment to conditions.

Non-random assignment may occur for a variety of reasons. One common reason is the study of intact groups. For example, a researcher may want to implement a new videogame into a college class to determine its effect on student learning, comparing this group to another class without that videogame. Students in each class were not randomly assigned to their class; they picked it themselves. Perhaps more conscientious students sign up for classes early in the day and less conscientious students sign up for later classes. This *external variable*, conscientious, is now an alternative explanation for the causal effect.

Another reason that random assignment may not occur is because a researcher is interested in a non-manipulable IV. A variable might be non-manipulable because it has pre-existing levels. The variable is referred to as a *quasi-independent variable*. Gender and ethnicity are common examples. Alternatively, a variable might be non-manipulable because it would be unethical or unrealistic to manipulate it. The impact of long-term violent videogame play in adolescence on adult delinquency is a principal example. To conduct a true experiment, a researcher would need to randomly assign adolescents to either play violent videogames or not to play violent videogames for years and then measure their delinquent behaviour years later as adults. However, knowingly manipulating a variable thought to contribute to crime rates is unethical. Furthermore, it is not realistic to impose that sort of control over adolescent behaviour over several years.

Types of quasi-experimental designs

There are as many types of quasi-experimental designs as there are experimental designs. Two characteristics of quasi-experimental designs are important to discuss: 1) the presence of one or more comparison groups, and 2) the presence of *control variables*. Quasi-experimental designs that lack both of these are generally uninterpretable, because they lack the control required to rule out alternative explanations for any observed differences.

Arguably, control variables are more desirable than comparison groups. The inclusion of controls allows the researcher to statistically adjust for pre-existing differences between groups. In contrast, experimental designs do not require control variables because there are no pre-existing differences between groups for which to control.

When choosing control variables, the best variables are identical to the post-test and collected before the manipulation. These are called *pre-test variables*. If a pre-test is not possible, a variable should be chosen that would correlate strongly with the pre-test, if the pre-test had been collected. For example, in a study comparing students who volunteer to play learning games versus others who choose not to, researchers might also collect measures of prior gaming experience and prior academic performance as controls.

In quasi-experiments without controls, the only remaining approach to improve confidence in causal conclusions is to add additional comparison groups. For example, in the above study comparing students who volunteer to play learning games versus others who choose not to, researchers might add a third group of students who were not given the choice to play games at all.

Even with controls and/or comparison groups, it is still difficult to rule out all possible alternatives to the cause-effect relationship. Experimental designs, if feasible, are preferable to both correlational and quasi-experimental designs.

Recommended reading

- Shadish, W.R., Cook, T.D., and Campbell, D.T., 2002. *Experimental and quasi-experimental designs for generalized causal inference*. Boston: Houghton, Mifflin and Company.

Statistics to analyse quasi-experimental designs

As with experimental designs, t-tests and ANOVAs can be used to analyse quasi-experimental designs. Commonly, however, *analysis of covariance (ANCOVA)* or *regression* is more appropriate as an analytic strategy. In quasi-experimental designs, control variables are commonly used to rule out potential alternative explanations for observed results. In the context of regression and ANCOVA, these control variables are called *covariates*. In the previous study comparing students who volunteer to play learning games versus others who choose not to, a researcher might add a control variable measuring prior gaming experience. Because prior gaming experience might drive the relationship between game choice and outcomes, the researcher could include prior gaming experience as a covariate to improve the credibility of causal conclusions drawn from ANCOVA or regression.

Recommended reading

- Maxwell, S.E., and Delaney, H.D., 2004. *Designing experiments and analyzing data: A model comparison perspective*. New York, NY: Psychology Press.
- Cohen, J., Cohen, P., West, S.G., and Aiken, L. S., 2003. *Applied multiple regression/correlation analysis for the behavioral sciences*. 3rd ed. Mahwah: Lawrence Erlbaum Associates.

Example of quasi-experimental research

Hess and Gunter (2013) conducted a study examining the difference between game-based and nongame-based online courses for high school students. The authors were interested in whether students in a game-based online American History course would finish the course faster than students in a nongame-based version of the same course. Students were chosen from pre-existing online courses, and data were provided by the school, including demographics, control variables, and time to completion. Figure 8 depicts Hess and Gunter's design. Unlike with the example of an experiment, there are two boxes to represent the manipulation of type of course. Two boxes are used to illustrate the manipulation because the use of existing classes created non-random assignment and potentially two different populations of students.

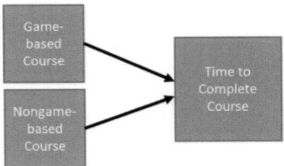

Figure 8. Illustration of Hess and Gunter's (2013) design.

The example quasi-experiment illustrates a two-group post-test only quasi-experimental design. No covariates were identified. In the case of time to completion, a pre-test is not feasible. Students would only have a pre-test time to completion if they were taking the course a second time. Instead, another control variable, like time to complete from another course, would have been more appropriate. The proxy pre-test would have strengthened Hess and Gunter's (2013) design and helped them rule out more possible alternative explanations for the hypothesized cause-effect relationship (e.g., type of online course causes completion speed).

The use of intact classes is the reason this design is not considered experimental. Students self-selected into either the game-based or nongame-based American History course. The demographic information across the two courses highlights the problem with self-selection. Students in the game-based course had previously completed more courses and were concurrently enrolled in more courses than students in the nongame-based course. Both of these differences are alternative explanations for the speed of course completion and could have been used as covariates themselves.

The authors used a *t*-test to analyse the data and found that students in the game-based course took longer to finish than students in the nongame-based course. Their intent was to explore the causal effect of game-based instruction on the length of time to completion. However, an alternative explanation is that students in the game-based instruction took longer solely because they were taking more courses and had less time to devote to American History than students in the nongame-based instruction. This possibility could be tested by using course load as a covariate in an ANCOVA.

Validity of research designs

Broadly, validity refers to the accuracy of an inference made from research (Shadish, et al., 2002). Construct validity, covered at the beginning of this chapter, allows researchers to make inferences about the constructs being studied. When conducting any research study, the underlying goal is to make assertions about the relationship between variables and to generalize the results from the study sample to the larger population of interest. Thus, construct validity is just one component of the broader validity question. In terms of the research design itself, assertions of validity can be examined from three perspectives.

INTERNAL VALIDITY

Internal validity refers to how safely a study's statistical conclusions can be used to make a causal statement. In other words, establishing the internal validity of study is necessary to satisfy the third rule of causation (i.e., ruling out all possible alternatives). In an experimental design, manipulating an IV and randomly assigning participants to conditions supports the internal validity of the study. In correlational and quasi-experimental designs, researchers must painstakingly rule out all threats to internal validity either through measurement of control variables or through solid theoretical evidence. Construct validity is thus one component of a study's internal validity.

EXTERNAL VALIDITY

External validity refers to the degree to which researchers believe results will generalize to a broader group of people. Two factors impact the external validity of a study. First, the type of people sampled and the way people were sampled impacts external validity. For a sample to be externally valid, it should be *randomly selected* from a population of interest. For example, if researchers want to draw conclusions about "all game players," the sample should consist of people randomly identified from "all game players." If a researcher chooses a sample that is not representative of the population, then the study will not generalize. For example, a researcher interested in the use of games to improve working memory among older adults decides to sample college students; this sample would not represent the population. Another issue is how participants are obtained. Researchers often use a convenience sample or non-random sample. For example, Domahidi and colleagues (2014) used a non-random sample, because they oversampled (chose extra) online social players, which was also their population of interest. In this case, the authors used an elaborate recruitment strategy and justified each choice they made with respect to sampling, making generalization to the population more likely. Unfortunately, such thoughtful recruitment and sampling is relatively uncommon.

True random sampling is generally impossible because researchers rarely have access to the entire population of interest (e.g., all players, all those self-identifying as gamers) in order to randomly select people from it. Instead, most researchers rely on some sort of *convenience sampling*, in which a sample is chosen because it is available to the researcher and not due to any favourable statistical properties. In addition, even when a random sample is available, participants will choose not to participate or may drop out before completing the study. If the reason participants do not complete the study is systematic, non-responders differ from responders on some variable, then the results will not generalize (e.g., a survey of problem players might collect fewer answers from problem players than non-problem players because problem players are less likely to respond to a survey). In the end, it is up to the researcher to argue that a particular sample's convenience does not harm the conclusions of research drawn from it (for examples of such arguments, see Landers and Behrend, 2015).

Ecological validity refers to how well a study appears to generalize across contexts. For example, in studies of the effects of violent videogames on aggression in children, aggression is typically operationalized as the extent to which children engage in aggressive play with other children immediately after playing a violent videogame. To the extent that such studies are internally and externally valid, they validly predict the behaviour of children in precisely the same situation—after playing a violent video game for an hour and immediately being required to interact with other children. However, such studies are sometimes used to draw conclusions about the behaviour of children *in general* as a result of violent videogames. Such claims lack ecological validity, because there is little evidence to suggest that studies examining short-term effects in a narrowly defined situation can be used to make claims about societal problems.

Ecological validity differs from internal and external validity in that it is not a property of the research design or of measurement; instead, it is a property of the claims made when drawing conclusions from the results of a research study. It is similar to internal and external validity in that it can never be a purely statistical argument.

VALIDITY TRADE-OFFS

Validity is not an either–or question; although it can be absent, it is never definitive. That gradient applies to each of these three types of validity individually. For example, a study can have high internal validity but low external validity. When researchers design an experiment, they have to make choices about the way to measure each variable, the way to collect data, and the type of control they have over the topics under study. In the real world, these choices translate into trade-offs, because the choices made to enhance one type of validity often detract from another type of validity. Most commonly, increases in internal validity tend to lead to decreases in external validity and vice versa.

For example, greater control is available in a research laboratory, enabling experimentation and increasing internal validity, but moving research to the laboratory may decrease its resemblance to real-world processes, potentially decreasing external validity. Correlational designs often have strong external validity, but weak internal validity because they do not have the same level of control over the IV, making it more difficult to rule out alternative reasons for the observed relationship. It is up to the researcher to create the strongest design—to maximize internal and external validity to the greatest extent possible—based on the research question and the resources available.

Recommended reading

- Shadish, W.R., Cook, T.D., and Campbell, D.T., 2002. *Experimental and quasi-experimental designs for generalized causal inference*. Boston, MA: Houghton, Mifflin and Company.

References

American Educational Research Association, 1999. *Standards for educational and psychological testing*. Washington: American Educational Research Association.

Bordens, K.S., and Abbott, B.B., 2011. *Research design and methods: A process approach.* 8th ed. Boston: McGraw Hill.

Cohen, J., 1992. A power primer. *Psychological Bulletin, 112,* pp.155–159.

Cohen, J., Cohen, P., West, S.G., and Aiken, L.S., 2003. *Applied multiple regression/correlation analysis for the behavioral sciences.* 3rd ed. Mahwah, NJ: Lawrence Erlbaum Associates.

Cortina, J.M., 1993. What is coefficient alpha? *Journal of Applied Psychology, 78,* pp.98–104.

Domahidi, E., Festl, R., and Quandt, T., 2014. To dwell among gamers: Investigating the relationship between social online game use and gaming-related friendships. *Computers in Human Behavior, 35,* pp.107–115.

Edwards, J.R., and Bagozzi, R.P., 2000. On the nature and direction of relationships between constructs and measures. *Psychological Methods, 5,* pp.155–174.

Erhel, S., and Jamet, E., 2013. Digital game-based learning: Impact of instructions and feedback on motivation and learning effectiveness. *Computers & Education, 67,* pp.156–167.

Hess, T., and Gunter, G., 2013. Serious game-based and nongame-based online courses: Learning experiences and outcomes. *British Journal of Educational Technology, 44,* pp.372–385.

Korman, A.K., 1974. Contingency approaches to leadership. In: J.G. Hunt and L.L. Larson, eds., *Contingency approaches to leadership.* Carbondale: Southern Illinois University Press.

Landers, R.N. and Behrend, T.S., 2015. An inconvenient truth: Arbitrary distinctions between organizations, Mechanical Turk, and other convenience samples. *Industrial and Organizational Psychology, 8*(2).

Maxwell, S.E., and Delaney, H.D., 2004. *Designing experiments and analyzing data: A model comparison perspective.* New York: Psychology Press.

Messick, S., 1995. Validity of psychological assessment: Validation of inferences from persons' responses and performances as scientific inquiry into score meaning. *American Psychologist, 50,* pp.741–749.

Nunnally, J.C., 1978. *Psychometric theory,* 2nd ed. New York: McGraw-Hill.

Pedhazur, E.J., and Schmelkin, L.P., 1991. *Measurement, design, and analysis: An integrated approach.* New York: Taylor & Francis Group.

Popper, K., 2005. *The logic of scientific discovery.* New York: Routledge.

Shadish, W.R., Cook, T.D., and Campbell, D.T., 2002. *Experimental and quasi-experimental designs for generalized causal inference.* Boston: Houghton, Mifflin and Company.

Shrout, P., and Fleiss, J., 1979. Intraclass correlations: Uses in assessing rater reliability. *Psychological Bulletin, 86,* pp.420–428.

11. Sex, violence and learning

Assessing game effects

ANDREAS LIEBEROTH, KAARE BRO WELLNITZ, AND JESPER AAGAARD

Sometimes stories about games make their way into the media. Around the year 2000 they were usually about how games turns mild-mannered suburban kids into desensitized high school-shooters. But things have changed. Warnings about aggressive emotions, caricatured gender images, and detrimental effects of time spent in front of a screen now compete with claims about gamification as a magic key to business success and utopist visions of a better game-based tomorrow for education, citizenship, and science participation. The claims are many—but they all seem to agree on one thing: games affect us. And we all want to prove our claims, but how do we test the impact of games?

In this chapter, we discuss empirical logics and approaches known from large- to small-scale effect studies traditionally found in educational, political, and biological sciences. There are two premises in this approach: We assume that causal effects of games can be specified and measured (often by proxy) in a statistically valid way, and that findings from studies allow us (at least with a few caveats) to generalize cause and effect to other players at other times. The balance between control and real-world relevance varies a great deal across methods; this we will return to repeatedly.

The ideal of evidence-based practice emerged in the world of medicine (Evidence-based medicine working group, 1992; Sackett, et al., 1996) and means striving for a world where professional decisions are informed by the most recent and nuanced standards of empirical evidence. For instance, The National Television Violence Study classified frequencies and types of media violence, finding that a staggering 61% of all television programming had a violent content, which would increase to 81% for prime time and the Saturday morning pro-wrestling and cartoon time slot watched by a lot of children (Gentile, et al., 2007; Gentile, 2009). This finding naturally led to parental and public concern. But, for regulation and 18+ labels to make sense, such interventions should also rest on evidence-based understandings about the extent to which media violence actually has an effect on viewers—including which groups, which behaviors (if any) actually emerge from the cognitive and emotional influences, and under which circumstances? With increasingly immersive video games reaching larger and larger populations, such concerns have high priority for legislators as well as morally alarmed citizens, and consequently scientists and designers must work together to create a realistic image of the psychological effect of games. Hence the many references to studies of violence and video games in this chapter. However, effect studies have much more practical implications to designers who hope to sell or otherwise monetize good or addictive game experiences. The industry works faster than academia, but methods for collecting metrics like *daily and monthly active users* (DAU and MAU) or in-app purchases before-and-after implementation of new updates or banner campaigns (Fields, 2014) follow the logics used in experiments and *in vivo* effect studies. Knowing how professional scientists go about measuring effects, and what can be considered evidence rather than statistical flukes, can make a great difference in terms of both time and money.

As you will see, we do not claim that quantitative studies are the only legitimate way to investigate the impact of games on people's lives, but we do believe that anyone venturing into conversations about the dangers or benefits of gaming should be aware of the scientific standards for measuring effects. Ignoring the state of affairs in scientific culture is counterproductive and will halt conversations about games across disciplines.

This chapter provides an overview of methods as well as a discussion of the dilemmas and limitations inherent to measuring anything in the lives of diverse groups such as students or gamers. The chapter ends with a discussion of the inherent problems of causal and probabilistic claims in media psychology and argues that it is necessary to keep in mind that humans are interpretative beings. But first, a few words about evidence and (unfortunately) math.

Beyond pie charts and percentages

In general, *evidence* relates to knowledge that makes it possible to predict an outcome based on a measurable variable. In applied science, this can mean whether or not the national weather service should send out a storm warning based on aggregated meteorological data. In schools, this may mean policy recommendations regarding the use of games in class. However, unlike gauging pressure with a barometer or counting the number of apples growing on a particular tree, theoretical constructs such as trait aggression, academic ability, and gender stereotypes can be hard to operationalize and may require proxy measures like surveys or how participants react in a staged conflict situation (Segovia, et al., 2009). As the less-than-perfect record attests, television meteorology is inherently probabilistic and overly general, and so is policy recommendation—even when based on rigorous science. This is the name of the game and the reason why media psychologists get very hung up on statistical probabilities and the magnitude of a predicted effect of gaming.

Since effect studies usually rely on quantitative research, we will have to discuss the logics of effect size, significance in the face of randomness, and causality and prediction as they are expressed in typical statistical tests. Some techniques are used to check for co-occurrence of things in the world (like gun ownership and the risk of getting shot), others allow researchers to see the difference between two groups of people (A/B-tests of a banner campaign) or the same group of people at two points in time (like students before and after a game-based learning program). Many other techniques could be mentioned like tracking a graph over time or building complex multi-causal models, but we try to only go into "statistics mode" to convey a sense of how scientific methods typically work. We are painfully aware that some concepts may be very hard to grasp, especially for someone instilled with a healthy fear of math in school, but we recommend friendly books like Huff's (1973) classic *How to lie with statistics* and Wheelan's (2013) *Naked statistics* to get in the habit of critical statistical thinking in everyday life—without delving deep into the mathematics.

However, when defining something as evidence, the most important thing is first and foremost to establish and retain a scientific mindset where research questions, measures, and conclusions are specific and valid. Marx (1963 cited in Shaughnessy, Zechmeister and Zechmeister, 2010, p.28) suggested the following criteria (table 1) to distinguish everyday knowledge from scientific knowledge.

	Everyday (non-scientific)	Critical (scientific)
General approach	Intuitive	Empirical
Attitude	Uncritical, accepting	Critical, skeptical
Observation	Casual, uncontrolled	Systematic, controlled
Reporting	Biased, subjective	Unbiased, objective
Concepts	Ambiguous	Clear definitions
Instruments	Inaccurate, imprecise	Accurate, precise
Measurement	Not valid or reliable	Valid and reliable
Hypotheses	Untestable	Testable

Table 1. General distinction between scientific and non-scientific knowledge as suggested by Marx (1963).

This is where method becomes very important indeed. How confident are you that you can actually say anything about the effect of gaming on variable *x*, be it aggression (Uhlmann and Swanson, 2004; Gentile and Stone, 2005; Anderson, et al., 2010), gender profiling (Dill, et al., 2008), or educational benefits (Hattie, 2009; Burgess, et al., 2012; Granic, et al., 2014)? Can other variables explain the difference that you see just as well (Buckley and Anderson, 2006; Pfister, 2011)? And is *gaming* and *effect x* even specified clearly enough to make a study meaningful?

Although qualitative methods such as ethnography and interviews may fulfill these requirements quite well (Stevens, et al., 2008; Iacovides, et al., 2011), the expectations of evidence-based practice fundamentally rest on quantitative approaches (Sackett, et al., 1996; Gilgun, 2006), where techniques used to describe data can be divided into two broad types: descriptive statistics and inferential statistics. Descriptive statistics involve counting the values measured in your research population and summarizing the results in numbers or graphs. However, statements like "the students answered 64% of the questions correctly" are uninformative; there is no way of knowing if this is a good result or not. This is where inferential statistics enter the picture: They tell us if the data allow us to confidently infer anything from the research population to the general population

Many people are unfamiliar with inferential statistics and therefore assume that graphs, pie charts, and percentages are acceptable documentation for scientific findings. However, one needs to know whether differences shown in children's behaviors between two time points are the result of chance, naturally occurring development, or an introduced intervention (e.g., gaming). One also needs to know if the difference is big enough to be important. And finally, one needs to know whether the result can validly be inferred to the general population (e.g., all gamers). Does the instrument one used actually measures the construct it is suggesting to address, and how does it fare in different contexts across different individuals (i.e., validity and reliability, see chapter 10)? So, let us look at the most common quantitative data gathering approaches and return to this later.

In vivo effect studies

Effect studies for games center on finding the impact of playing games; from how much a medical exercise game reduces symptoms (Elliott, de Bruin and Dumoulin, 2014), over the effect of a new recruitment strategy on a game's DAU and MAU (Fields, 2014), to whether witnessing morally abhorrent events in virtual reality rubs off on people's moral actions (Segovia, et al., 2009).

The two classic types you should know about are *between-group* (independent measures or cohort) and *within-group* (repeated measures) designs (or between- and within subject, if you are, e.g., dealing with intrapersonal factors like personality dimensions and particular behavioral outcomes (see chapter 10). Between-group setups are often used in real-world effect measurements and are based on the logic of cohort studies where two (or more) groups of people are selected based on differences in their exposure to a particular thing (such as media exposure, game availability, a drug, or an environmental toxin) and followed up to see how many in each group develop a particular outcome such as a disease (Greenhalgh, 1997). For a game study one may, for example, follow neighborhood youths in an after-school program that allows them to play PEGI-18 games rich in violent content and see if they become more aggressive toward a confederate at the time of measurement than *another group* across town, which has played prosocial games during the same period (Gentile, 2009). It must be specified how the conditions differ. For example, will the PEGI-18 gaming group be required to play at least two hours a day, or will they be asked to report how much time they have spent gaming in general? If these factors are not clearly defined, there is no way of knowing what a found effect is indicating. Fortunately, well-tested instruments for measuring complex psychological phenomena are available, for instance, different dimensions of aggression are suggested to result from video games (see Anderson, Gentile and Dill, 2012). Established tools usually include clear definitions of the variables they measure and are preferable to building scales from scratch. However, working with new phenomena in the quickly evolving world of games may require researchers to break new ground to develop variables such as player preference profiles (Sherry and Lucas, 2006; Yee, et al., 2012).

Within-group designs compare just *one group* of players at two or more time points. The logic of this design is to get a baseline and then see what will happen when the *exact same people* are exposed to something. For instance, a repeated measures study investigated the effects of using a dance game that incorporated pelvic floor muscle contractions to treat incontinence (Elliott, de Bruin and Dumoulin, 2014). Researchers measured symptoms of mixed urinary incontinence in 24 elderly women averaging 70 years of age before inviting them to take part in an exercise class that incorporated the dance game. After 12 weeks of one-hour sessions, the researchers again measured symptoms using a self-reported 72-hour urinary diary as well as several tests used by doctors to assess related problems including impact on quality of life. The women were very content with the program, and 92% of them even continued to do the exercise regimen at home. Improvement from before (baseline) to after was statistically significant.

Between-group designs often suffer from a shortcoming: Two independent groups with different people in each are used, but baseline levels are not measured. Suppose a difference in aggression between the two groups is found, what would one be able to conclude? Would the conclusion be that the game influenced the participants' level of antisocial behavior? It would not if the development in antisocial behavior during one month is actually what can be expected during a month through natural variation in people. Differing groups do not pose a problem to within-group designs. Measuring people three times and creating two intervals where changes can ensue freely (one before and one after game-intervention) will provide baseline knowledge of naturally occurring changes over one month, hence the baseline problem will disappear. Will it then, with reasonable confidence, be possible to conclude that a difference in antisocial tendencies between time points two and three results from the introduction of the game? If we assume that the game was introduced in September 2001, would it then be possible to rule out that a difference between the intervals was not caused by fear induced by the September 11 attack? Probably not. An elegant change can solve the problem: Instead of letting all participants play the game during the second month, the participants are distributed to two groups: One plays the game, while the other continues to live their ordinary lives. Both groups would experience and react to the tragedy, while only one group had been playing the violent game. So, if a difference is not only seen between interval one and two, but also between two groups in interval two, it would, finally, be possible to establish that the game would actually lead to violent behavior. A design mixing repeated measures with the creation of different groups is called a *mixed design* (not to be confused with *mixed methods*, Chapter 16), and is, if practically possible, the way to go when conducting real-world effect studies.

Even though in vivo effect studies use the same logics as lab experiments, they are much closer to everyday reality. They pragmatically aim at testing the effect of something that is already happening. This makes most in vivo studies ecologically valid, but relinquishes a lot of the control scientists usually have over research environments, and thus the ability to pinpoint exactly what caused the changes seen. The dance game study cannot, for instance, be considered an adequate experiment for inferring systematic effects generalizable to all old women because of an insufficient N (number of participants), lack of blinding, and no control group. As a feasibility effect study, however, the results were interesting and even garnered mention in *Nature* (Payton, 2014). In the world of medical or education research it will often be reasonable to run smaller 'studies of convenience' as a pilot study before larger interventions. Indeed, many research committees and funding bodies require statistically sound proof of concept before approving large-scale studies and expensive experiments.

Randomized controlled trials

Researchers testing hypotheses about effects of games on human beings can employ experiments resembling the ones used in biological and behavioral labs (Dill, et al., 2008; Fischer, et al., 2009) known as *randomized controlled trials* (RCTs). A move toward RCTs may increase the standard of game research by allowing control over independent variables (IV). In an experimental logic, measuring effects on a dependent variable (DV) usually involve exposing one group to a predetermined independent predictor (e.g., a drug treatment or a particular game experience), and then comparing them to a control group (see also Chapter 10).

RCTs are seen as the gold standard of evidence-based practice (Evidence based medicine working group, 1992; Sackett, et al., 1996) based on a positivistic knowledge paradigm from medicine, assuming that it is possible to reach objective knowledge free of any kind of interpretation. Psychiatrists have, for instance, called for more stringent analyses of confounders in game effects (Porter and Starcevic, 2007).

A strength compared to in vivo effects studies is the ability to randomly assign people to either treatment or control groups and to set up treatments and measurements where ideally neither the participants (single blind) nor the assistant administering the treatment (double blind) know which condition they are assigned to. Hence, no pre-treatment recruitment bias from studying real-world interventions in different neighborhoods can *systematically* interfere, and no *psychological biases* will influence the effect systematically. Researchers doing statistics or biological analyses can also be blinded as to what they are working with (triple blind) to remove researcher bias (for a discussion, see Pannucci and Wilkins, 2010). All of this is done to ensure a better basis for concluding causality than ecological settings can provide. In essence, if an experimental scientist was asked "what caused *effect x?*", he would want to be able state "exposure to *game y* did—*because I put it there!*" (Brewer and Hunter, 2006). If asked "but how can we know that *game y* is the real cause?", he would want to be able to follow up with "because I *did not* put *game y* in my otherwise identical control group, and *effect z* did not occur for those people!".

For instance, Dill, Brown and Collins (2008) tested the hypothesis that exposure to images of sex-typed video game characters (aggressive males and objectified females) result in greater tolerance of sexual harassment by exposing college students to a PowerPoint presentation with images of either sex-typed video game characters or press photos of current US senators. Participants then read a real-life story of a male professor putting his hand on a female student's thigh. Afterwards, they were asked to respond to seven questions about the episode on a 0–9 scale, for instance, *"If the student's story is true, would you personally believe that Prof. Bloom is guilty of sexual harassment?"* with 0 being *"not at all guilty"* and 9 being *"definitely guilty"*. These items were scored on an overall sexual harassment judgment scale. Results showed that tolerance for sexual harassment was the greatest for males in the group exposed to the PowerPoint with sexual content, followed by males in the control group, and females in the control group.

Factors introducing unexplained variance to a study are called confounders, noise of experimental nuisances, depending on their effect on the internal validity of the setup. To address this, confounds ranging from gender, over individual psychological differences to everyday play patterns, can be gauged as part of the study and entered into the equation—for instance, by controlling for them statistically or adding their explanatory power to mathematical models of combined effects (Pfister, 2011). Truly thorough experimentalists, however, make sure that treatment group(s) and controls are equally matched on predictable confounders (e.g., gender, age, handedness, prior game exposure) beforehand, which makes the experiment a *blocked design*. This is especially important for studies in relation to which treatment effects may take days or weeks to set in, and participants have to be let loose into the wild before measuring effects.

A closed lab setting is often a good place to introduce treatment and measure interesting DVs (for instance, changes in cerebral blood flow, or staging a situation where players can either help or thwart a schoolmate within ten minutes of playing), sealed off from outside influences. Ideally, this allows the scientist to control everyday factors that may skew the outcome, but it also means that experiments often lack ecological validity and may not generalize beyond the artificial situation created in the lab. Lab settings and heavily controlled experiments lose some of the richness that real-world effect studies accept into their center. Despite their methodological qualities, generalizing effects from labs to the real world thus always require some leaps of faith (or bridging, see chapter 16), and must be treated with some care when extended into practice (Howard-jones, 2007). Field experiments avoid this by trying to introduce manipulations such as images or marketing messages, in natural settings and by assessing people's real actions such as littering behavior (Ernest-Jones, et al., 2011), but this often means loss of randomization and control and introduces a lot of external noise. Thus, the defining factor is not necessarily the lab setting, but the degree of randomization and control enforced by researchers.

Cross-sectional studies

The merits of a robustly designed RCT is often overshadowed by its limited scope and ecological validity (see Chapter 10), and sometimes researchers want to gauge the relationships between games and real-life outcomes such as later school achievements or jail sentences served (Almeida, 2012; Katsiyannis, et al., 2012). In addition, not all RCTs are possible because of ethical reasons. This calls for a different approach. *Cross-sectional studies* trade control for a one-time snapshot of potentially related variables gathered from real life. This may entail studying patterns of co-occurrence within existing data from, for instance, national health databases, school records, or other non-obtrusive measures. If the necessary information is not readily available, scientists often resolve to send out surveys (e.g., Meriläinen, 2011; Yee, et al., 2012). For instance, a negative correlation between heavy gaming and school achievement has been found when using this technique (Burgess, et al., 2012). Compared to experiments and ethnographic observation, cross-sectional studies cannot deal well with influences present in the environment at the time of data collection, but, if measured, they can be sifted out statistically, often with enlightening results. It may, for instance, be possible to control for effects of sociodemographical status in schools that happen to use a particular learning game, and thereby achieve a clearer picture of gaming versus achievement across the board.

Cross-sectional studies are usually correlational, which means that scientists make probabilistic predictions based on observed co-occurrences. For instance, if 60% of people in a sufficiently large sample of prosocial gamers display a tendency toward prosocial behavior, we could predict with 60% confidence that a person would be inclined to help a person who dropped his or her groceries, *if* this person were known to be playing prosocial games. Effects of this kind are, however, rarely unidirectional or based on just one variable, so if a researcher collected more data by, for example, looking through someone's window, hacking someone's emails, and going through the same person's garbage, his or her ability to predict helpfulness would increase (although this would obviously be an ethically unacceptable research strategy). In this hypothetical case, the dubious researcher might use *multiple regression* or even *Bayesian algorithms* like the ones employed by *Netflix* or *Amazon.com* rather than simple correlations to infer the relative predictive power of each bit of information. Things obviously become a bit more complicated, but the predictive model would improve with each theoretically well-motivated variable entered into it.

Selecting representative samples from a general population is especially central to cross-sectional studies. The logic is simple: If we want to know the relationship between heavy gaming and achievement in college, we document both variables in a representative random sample of the population and check for correlation. Normally, this will entail a numerically specific chunk of the general populace or a specific subgroup (e.g., *World of Warcraft* players), but sampling often has to be a matter of convenience (such as players who decide to help out with a questionnaire and allow their provider to share login-data). The number of people needed to make statistically valid predictions is related to the so called *statistical power* and can be calculated using a priori power analysis with an eye for representativeness (does the number of females who responded to the survey match the proportion of females playing?). There are online tools as well as plugins for statistical software available for this. Depending on the population and the statistical techniques one intends to use, and the effect size you are hoping to achieve (see below), good cross-sectional studies include data on hundreds of people to represent the population adequately. If the sample is too small or does not match the population, it will be hard to generalize. Good researchers make sure to mention such shortcomings when smaller studies are published.

Standardized scales are often accessible for public use, although some require prior approval, non-disclosure of content, specific training (e.g., in psychiatry to administer diagnostic tests), or payment, but far too many researchers, especially students, create their own surveys. Coming up with questions is easy, but validating and shaping a questionnaire is hard work, and requires validation, to make sure that the questions are balanced to jointly measure the supposed underlying psychological construct with the right balance between variability and redundancy (Rust and Golombok, 1999). This is why psychologists use scales with hundreds of questions about the same things. Homebrewed surveys rarely live up to these standards and, what is worse, will not compare readily with other studies, this makes meta-analysis difficult and creates a mess of small pockets containing incomparable findings.

The main weakness of cross-sectional studies is that they are correlational: Correlation implies neither causation nor non-causation, just a statistical relationship (Prot and Anderson, 2013). Further, self-reported measures (if used) can be unreliable and subject to bias such as the tendency to cast oneself in a positive light (Podsakoff, et al., 2003; Wheelan, 2013). For instance, Meriläinen (2011) set out to study the effects of role-playing on a series of factors like social competences and creativity, but replies to his surveys could just as easily reflect people's views of themselves within the frame of the hobby. He therefore ended up rephrasing his results as measures of the *self-perceived* benefits among players. A solution to the problem of causality is triangulation with other methods like interviews, ethnography, or experiments, where indications of causality may be more visible (Collier, 2011; chapter 16).

Longitudinal research

In principle, any study measuring effects over a period of time is longitudinal (again, see also Chapter 10). As seen in the previous sections, many studies on games have been conducted, but most are limited to controlled lab- or auditorium-situations, snapshots in time, or follow up on effects within maximum a few months (Telner, et al., 2010). Attempts at assessing the long-term impact of digital learning tools such as games have had limited success and been criticized for lacking both design and content to assess how psychological effects remain in people's lives and learning trajectories (Henderson, 2007). For instance, we know too little about differences between one-off experiences with game-based learning and repeated exposure to the same and/or varying game technologies across school years. Prospective cohort studies are conducted by following up on participants over the years, which can be difficult and resource demanding since studies over time require large participant pools, are vulnerable to dropout, and often lack sensitivity to contextual variables.

Sometimes big longitudinal data banks exist. Alison Parkes and colleagues (2013) used data from the British Millennium Survey, a multifaceted prospective study based on data fromchildren born between September 2000 and January 2002. Children's media use habits were recorded at age five, while the *strengths and difficulties questionnaire* measuring conduct problems, emotional symptoms, inattention and hyperactivity, peer relationship problems, and prosocial behavior was administered at ages five and seven. Few young children played hours of electronic games, but most watched 1–3 hours of TV on a daily basis. The researchers built several statistical models to check for effects of, for example, age differences, gender, and familial background, and ended up concluding that more than three hours of daily TV at age five predicted increased problems with psychosocial adjustment at age seven, but no similar effects were found for video games. Times have changed, though, and maybe children play more electronic games today. If so, a replication of the study would probably have more gaming habit variety to work with, which would give even more informative statistical results.

The technique known as *case-control studies* retrospectively relies on a mix of current information plus data available from past time points (Mann, 2003). Here, researchers choose a population that has already displayed a symptom. In evidence-based medicine, this usually means looking through a patient database, but school dropouts or membership of religious or political organizations with highly misogynic opinions may fit the needs if these data are stored somewhere. Researchers then look backward at time-points to gauge if subjects have been exposed to certain influences for extended periods of time (contaminants in the underground being a salient example), and compare the outcome variable (symptoms from the toxins) to an otherwise identical sample of people who did not get exposed (lived in a similar neighboring town). If inferential statistical tests reveal that the exposed group scores significantly higher on symptoms than the control group, we can venture an informed guess about causality. In this sense, the case-control approach mixes experiment with cross-sectional data. The problem, of course, being researchers' inability to measure things that already happened, forcing reliance on prior data.

A tricky part of longitudinal research is that studies are only as valid as their data-collection and analysis methods (see chapter 10). If an effect study with biyearly follow-up measurements is executed, numerous intervening factors may slip into the design as participants' life situations change (Wheelan, 2013). If a cross-sectional design is replicated with the same population over the years, one will have the opportunity to control for many factors statistically, but inferring causality between data snapshots will still be problematic. Another problem is dropout. People move away, lose interest, or quit the assigned treatment. For this reason, longitudinal projects need large numbers of loyal participants *or* robust ways of gathering (sometimes retrospective) data such as medical records, college grades, or metadata from online gaming accounts like *Battle.net,* for example, to monitor how oscillating gaming habits predict variability in other factors across the lifespan.

Longitudinal approaches add to the strength of effect studies by following up over time. They introduce a stronger connection to lifelong changes, but also include many additional sources of noise. Given the lack of good long-term evidence and pervasive presence of gaming in all walks of life, more prospective longitudinal studies would be a worthwhile endeavor for the next generation of game scholars. Especially since players now leave many traces in the cloud, which means embedded learning assessment and predictive algorithms for pools of big data will more or less intentionally automate longitudinal data storage in the near future.

What can be considered evidence?

Generally, the scientific community requires a certainty of *at least* 95% that a given result is not just obtained by chance. If *at most* a *p-value* of $< .05$ is gleaned via statistical tests (meaning that you are 95% certain that the result is not a chance result, i.e., a false positive), convention states that the effect is *significant*, and the effect can be reported with confidence. Some fields use 95%+ *confidence intervals* instead of p-values because they reveal otherwise invisible information about the data and its qualities. However, the principle is the same: If the two groups of CIs do not cross, they are significantly different. The larger the group of participants, the easier it will be to achieve reliable result on either statistics. This means that large medical studies or *big data* analyses with samples of +10.000 people can predict to the general population with quite a bit of confidence. But significance is only half the story. A tricky problem, no matter how statistically savvy a researcher might be, is determining if an effect is actually important in the big picture. Quantitative effect studies try to establish *the magnitude* of a statistical relationship—for example, correlation or difference across time points—between variables. Depending on research field, if a difference is only very small, one may say that the *practical significance* of the result is trivial. Sometimes effects of violent video games are therefore dismissed as negligible in the big picture, while critical media psychologists such as Anderson find the idea of neglecting repeatedly proven effects abhorrent, no matter how small they are (DeLisi, et al., 2012; Prot and Anderson, 2013;). For changes over time, which most effect studies measure, the appropriate statistical test is a comparison of means (such as a t-test), where the effect measured in Cohen's d. $d=0.5$ means that the trait measured is one half of a standard deviation above a previous measuring point. In broad strokes, Cohen suggested (1988; 1992) that an effect of 0.2 is small (explaining only about 1% of the variance), 0.5 is medium (6%), and above 0.8 is a large effect (16%). Cohen's d is just one effect size tied to particular statistical tests. Different methods express effect sizes with other terms, meaning that the field as a whole can be very confusing. To make things easier, Cohen (1988, 1992) suggested a series of benchmarks to separate small, medium and large effect sizes (Table 2).

Test	Effect size index	Small	Medium	Large
t-test	Cohen's d.	0.20	0.50	0.80
f-test (ANOVA)	Partial Eta squared ($\eta p2$)	0.10	0.25	0.40
f-test (Pearson correlation, multiple regression)	R2 / Adjusted R2	0.02	0.15	0.35
Chi-squared	Cramer's V	0.10	0.30	0.50

Table 2. Suggested effect sizes by Cohen (1988; 1992).

However, within any domain from crime statistics to education, it is hard to tell if a medium effect size is actually important. What if a vast array of other factors also have a medium or large effect? This is why effect studies must rely on a thorough review of previous findings and ideally be compared to overviews of effects from meta-analyses. For examples of effect meta-analyses about games, see Anderson, et al. (2010), Wouters (2013), and Greitemeyer and Mügge (2014). Indeed, even though a prevalent publication bias means that a lot of null-findings are rejected by journals and end up in the grey literature of conference presentations, dissertations and office drawers, reviews and meta-analyses are perceived as having more weight than individual studies, as the pool of scientific evidence is always a work in progress (see figure 1).

Acclaimed education researcher John Hattie (2009) devised a "barometer of influence" (figure 2) for effects of interventions like video games on academic achievement (Hattie, 2009). By compiling more than 800 meta-analyses of educational effects, Hattie was able to critically assess not only what works, but more importantly what works *better* than that which an average teacher will achieve on a good day. Hattie's massive work illustrates that difference in itself is not necessarily interesting. In fact, children tend to learn *something* even without teachers, games, or textbooks. Over one year, student maturation alone accounts for an effect-size of $d=0.15$ (Cahan and Davis, 1987 cited in Hattie, 2009, p.20). Hence, if

Figure 1. Hierarchy of evidence in medicine (adapted from Greenhalgh 1997).

a year-long educational game curriculum (e.g., Hyltoft, 2008) was implemented, and researchers found that students had only improved, e.g. $d=0.08$, on a measurement of general academic standards over a year, the intervention would actually seem to have been harmful to students' learning. On average, teaching improves student achievement by $d=0.15–0.40$ (Hattie, 2009), so a teacher improving his or her students achievement by $d=0.25$ with game-based teaching should *not* necessarily be rated as more effective than his colleagues. In Hattie's estimation, only new initiatives increasing achievement above $d=0.60$ should be considered truly excellent (2009, p.17). Therefore, put simply: if we want to know the effect of a school-intervention and look at the same students over time, Hattie would prefer yearly improvements above $d=0.40$. Important to note is the fact that meta-analyses pool studies with subtle differences. This means that all meta-analyses are based on assumptions that all the studies selected are measuring the same underlying construct even if the instruments used to do so differ. Hattie (2009) focused strictly on performance, even though the summarized studies may have also discussed multiple other factors or even looked at moderating variables. Ultimately, this means that the pooling of different studies might blur effects (see, Snook, O'Neill, Clark and Openshaw 2009 for comment on Hattie, 2009).

A recent meta-analysis focused solely on serious games in schools, included game interventions with a *negative d* for skill- or knowledge-domains (compared to other teaching) and very high effects for others. (Wouters, et al., 2013). Since everything works (Hattie, 2009, p.16), Hattie's barometer helps us critically evaluate the costs of developing and implementing a whole new educational game relative to its benefits, compared to other possible teaching interventions, or going about business as usual. To sum up: Just seeing a significant difference ($p<0.05$ or lower) between groups or over time is not necessarily of

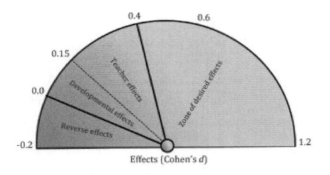

Figure 2. Barometer of influence (adapted from Hattie, 2009).

practical relevance. Effect sizes for games must be compared to literature and industry knowledge in the field of study. For instance, aggression and sensation seeking increases significantly as children enter adolescence (Cairns, et al., 1989); this naturally points back to issues discussed above and to the importance of keeping a critical scientific mindset toward design and results.

Discussion and reasons to remain critical

We have concluded each section in this chapter with brief discussions of the limits inherent to each approach, especially when it comes to generalizing findings into the real world. There are, however, more and deeper reasons to be cautious when inferring causality.

Evidence-based practice is not a neutral framework, but originates from economics and medical science (Biesta, 2007), The medical search for effective interventions is based on a *causal model* of professional action: Professional subjects (e.g., doctors) do something to physiological bodies in order to bring about certain effects. When a doctor taps the ligament just below the knee and a patient's leg shoots up, this process is explainable in terms of a causal relation between two entities: The knee-jerk response is *caused* by the tap. This just happens. There is no reason, no interpretation, no right or wrong. This causal model has been immensely successful, but a problem occurs when the model is extrapolated inappropriately to other domains. Only a very limited number of human behaviors can legitimately be considered physiological reactions, and sneezes, yawns, and other reflexes seem to exhaust this category (Packer, 1985, p.1085). The rest of our everyday lives consist of purposeful practices that cannot be explained in terms of cause and effect (or stimulus and response). There is, basically, an essential difference between a *causal* account of physical objects and an *interpretive* account of human practices (Dreyfus, 2011). According to a hermeneutic approach to social science (the term "hermeneutic" comes from the Greek word for interpretation), human beings are separated from other objects in that we *care* (Heidegger, 2008). Natural objects are indifferent, but human beings are not. Things matter to us and we act accordingly.

This insight means that the medical cause and effect model is not necessarily transferable to game studies. Consider the difference between crying when cutting onions and when watching a sad movie. When one cuts onions, chemical processes produce syn-propanethial S-oxide (C_3H_6OS), a volatile sulphur compound that reacts with the sensory fibers of the eyes and causes the lachrymal glands to release tears to wash away the irritant. Like the knee-jerk example, this physiological reaction just happens. There is a stimulus and there is a response. It is "the action of a defined physical or chemical agent on a locally defined receptor which evokes a defined response by means of a defined pathway" (Merleau-Ponty, 1942, p.9). Compare this process to the experience of watching a sad movie and starting to cry. These tears are not the *effect* of the movie in any mechanical way. An existentially tragic theme such as the loss of a significant other (Bambi's mother, Simba's father) may compel a human being to shed tears, but only if the movie is *interpreted* accordingly, only if the movie somehow speaks to the viewer. This is an important point to keep in mind when studying games.

We could take the findings from the Dill and colleagues (2008) "sex case" presented in the RCT-section to mean that "media images of demeaned women *cause* men to advocate keeping women "in their place," while they *cause* women to advocate for social justice" (p.1406, our emphasis). But ask yourself this: Did the male researchers become sexists after viewing the slideshow? As Gauntlett (1998) points out, there is a tendency among media researchers to state that media *cause* certain behaviors in specific groups while remaining unconcerned for their own well-being as these effects only seem to apply to "other people". If you are male, how would you react after reading this article? But, most importantly, would males in the experiment have reacted similarly had they known about the research hypothesis? All this is to problematize a simplistic notion of "causality". When social psychological theories are distributed societally, humans have an ability to react against and thus contradict the theories (Gergen, 1973). Knowing that games can influence one's attitude toward sexual harassment, one may be more prone to reject sexual harassment or at least make more cautious judgments about questionable scenarios. No matter how hard one tries to emulate the natural sciences, social scientific research cannot be purified from interpretation. Social science is in other words never objective understood as independent of human interests.

Should we then give up the search for effects? Should we admit that any effect of a specific game is ultimately up to human interpretation? This equally deficient instrumentalist view considers the game as a neutral instrument that cannot change the internal compulsions of its user. As if a game is a passive intermediary merely serving the purpose of whoever uses it. The media theorist Marshall McLuhan (2010) likened this instrumentalist view to sleepwalking and argued that this response to media "is the numb stance of the technological idiot" (p.19). Just because we relinquish talk of cause and *effect* does not follow that we are not *affected* by games. We must try to navigate between the Scylla of causal determinism and the Charybdis of naïve instrumentalism. *How* games influence our behavior becomes the frustratingly difficult question. At the very least, bridging studies may be needed to validate quantitative data in the real-life fields they probe—especially if causal processes are inferred (Chapter 16).

Conclusions

We have discussed how effects of games can be measured in a number of ways such as in vivo effect studies, RCTs, cross-sectional, and longitudinal studies. There are actually many more terms and approaches than we have covered here. Most disciplines have developed their own vocabularies and standards, and use different statistical measures, so making sense of effects can be very confusing. We have focused on the kind of tests that we find useful and meaningful in the context of games. We have also tried to illustrate how there are always tradeoffs in accuracy and ecological validity, as well as several new risks of introducing new biases into a study, when moving on the continuum from very controlled randomized trials to in vivo research and snapshots of real people's real lives.

Doing experimental instead of real world studies makes it possible to control for a large host of confounding variables, but then new challenges arise, such as how well the experimental manipulation corresponds to the real world. The problems never end. This is why science is a continually evolving process, which often tests the same hypotheses over and over again with slight variations in setups. Always stay critical and keep considering alternative explanations to the results you find. If you succeed in being critical, you will never go all wrong.

Recommended reading

- Evidence-based medicine working group, 1992. Evidence-based medicine: A new approach to teaching the practice of medicine. *JAMA*, 268(17), pp.2420–2425.
- Prot, S. and Anderson, C.A., 2013. Research methods, design, and statistics in media psychology. In: *The Oxford handbook of media psychology*. New York: Oxford University Press, pp.109–136.
- Wheelan, C., 2013. *Naked statistics: Stripping the dread from the data*. New York: W.W. Norton. Wouters, P. et al., 2013. A meta-analysis of the cognitive and motivational effects of serious games. *Journal of Educational Psychology*, 105(2), pp.249–265.

References

Almeida, L.C., 2012. The effect of an educational computer game for the achievement of factual and simple conceptual knowledge acquisition. *Education Research International*, 2012, pp.1–5.

Anderson, C. a et al., 2010. Violent video game effects on aggression, empathy, and prosocial behavior in eastern and western countries: a meta-analytic review. *Psychological bulletin*, 136(2), pp.151–73.

Biesta, G., 2007. Why "what works" won't work: Evidence-based practice and the democratic deficit in educational research. *Educational Theory*, 57(1), pp.1–22.

Brewer, J. and Hunter, A., 2006. *Multimethod research: A synthesis of styles*. 2 ed., Thousand Oaks: Sage.

Buckley, K. and Anderson, C., 2006. A theoretical model of the effects and consequences of playing video games. In: P. Vorderer and J. Bryant, eds., *Playing video games*, Mahwah: Lawrence Erlbaum Associates, pp.363–378.

Burgess, S.R., Stermer, S.P. and Burgess, M.C.R., 2012. Video game playing and academic performance in college students. *College Student Journal*, 46(2), pp.376–388.

Cairns, R.B. et al., 1989. Growth and aggression: I. Childhood to early adolescence. *Developmental Psychology*, 25, pp.320–330.

Cohen, J., 1992. A power primer. *Psychological Bulletin*, 112(1), pp.155–159.

Cohen, J., 1988. *Statistical power analysis for the behavioral sciences*, Hillsdale: Laurence Erlbaum Associates.

Collier, D., 2011. Understanding process tracing. *PS: Political Science & Politics*, 44, pp.823–830.

DeLisi, M. et al., 2012. Violent video games, delinquency, and youth violence: New evidence. *Youth Violence and Juvenile Justice*, 11(2), pp.132–142.

Dill, K.E., Brown, B.P. & Collins, M. a., 2008. Effects of exposure to sex-stereotyped video game characters on tolerance of sexual harassment. *Journal of Experimental Social Psychology*, 44(5), pp.1402–1408.

Dreyfus, H., 2011. Medicine as combining natural and human science. *The Journal of Medicine and Philosophy*, 36(4), pp.335–341.

Elliott, V., de Bruin, E.D. and Dumoulin, C., 2014. Virtual reality rehabilitation as a treatment approach for older women with mixed urinary incontinence: A feasibility study. *Neurourol. Urodyn*, ahead of print. DOI= 10.1002/nau.22553.

Ernest-Jones, M., Nettle, D. & Bateson, M., 2011. Effects of eye images on everyday cooperative behavior: a field experiment. *Evolution and Human Behavior*, 32(3), pp.172–178.

Evidence-based medicine working group, 1992. Evidence-based medicine: A new approach to teaching the practice of medicine. *JAMA*, 268(17), pp.2420–2425.

Fields, T., 2014. *Mobile & social game design: Monetization methods and mechanics*. 2nd ed. Boca Ranton: CRC press.

Fischer, P. Greitemeyer, T., Morton, T., Kastenmüller, A., Postmes, T., Frey, D., Kubitzki, J. and Odenwälder, J., 2009. The racing-game effect: why do video racing games increase risk-taking inclinations? *Personality & social psychology bulletin*, 35(10), pp.1395–409.

Gauntlett, D., 1998. Ten things wrong with the "effects" model. In: R. Dickinson, R. Harindranath and O. Linné, eds., *Approaches to audiences: A reader*. London: Arnold.

Gentile, D.A., 2009. Media violence and public policy: Cutting through the hype. *Pediatrics and Parents*, 8, pp.20–23.

Gentile, D.A., Saleem, M. and Anderson, C.A., 2007. Public policy and the effects of media violence on children. *Social Issues and Policy Review*, 1(1), pp.15–61.

Gentile, D.A. and Stone, W., 2005. Violent video game effects on children and adolescents: a review of the literature. *Minerva Pediatr*, 57(57), pp.337–358.

Gergen, K., 1973. Social psychology as history. *Journal of Personality and Social Psychology*, 26(2), pp.309–320.

Gilgun, J.F., 2006. The four cornerstones of qualitative research. *Qualitative Health Research*, 16(3), pp.436–43.

Granic, I., Lobel, A. and Engels, R.C.M.E., 2014. The benefits of playing video games. *The American Psychologist*, 69(1), pp.66–78.

Greenhalgh, T., 1997. How to read a paper: getting your bearings (deciding what the paper is about). *BMJ*, 315(7102), pp.243–246.

Greitemeyer, T. and Mügge, D.O., 2014. Video games do affect social outcomes: A meta-analytic review of the effects of violent and prosocial video game play. *Personality & Social Psychology Bulletin*, 40(5), pp.578–589.

Hattie, J., 2009. *Visible learning: A synthesis of over 800 meta-analyses relating to achievement*, London: Routledge.

Heidegger, M., 2008. *Being and time*. New York: Harper Perennials.

Howard-jones, P., 2007. *Perceptions of the role of neuroscience in education*. University of Bristol.

Huff, D., 1973. *How to lie with statistics*. New York: Norton.

Hyltoft, M., 2008. The role-players' school: Østerskov efterskole Malik Hyltoft. In: M. Montola & J. Stenros, eds. *Playground worlds – creating and evaluating experiences of role-playing games*. Helsinki: Ropecon.ry, pp.12–25.

Iacovides, I., Aczel, J., Scanlon, E., and Woods, W., 2011. What can breakdowns and breakthroughs tell us about learning and involvement experienced during game-play? In: *5th European Conference on Games Based Learning*. Athens. October.

Katsiyannis, A., Thompson, M.P., Barrett, D.E., and Kingree, J.B., 2012. School predictors of violent criminality in adulthood: Findings from a nationally representative longitudinal study. *Remedial and Special Education*, 34(4), pp.205–214.

Mann, C., 2003. Observational research methods. Research design II: Cohort, cross sectional, and case-control studie. *Emergency Medicine Journal*, 20, pp.54–61.

McLuhan, M., 2010. *Understanding media: The extensions of man*. New York: Routledge Classics.

Meriläinen, M., 2011. The self-perceived effects of the role-playing hobby on personal development: A survey report. *International Journal of Role Playing*, (3), pp.49–68.

Merleau-Ponty, M., 1942. *The structure of behavior*. Translated from French, 1984. Pittsburgh: Duquesne University Press.

Packer, M., 1985. Hermeneutic inquiry in the study of human conduct. *American Psychologist*, 40(10), pp.1081–1093.

Pannucci, C. and Wilkins, E., 2010. Identifying and avoiding bias in research. *Plastic and Reconstructive Surgery*, 126(2), pp.619–625.

Parkes, A., Sweeting, H., Wight, D., and Henderson, M., 2013. Do television and electronic games predict children's psychosocial adjustment? Longitudinal research using the UK millennium cohort study. *Archives of Disease in Childhood*, 98(5), pp.341–8.

Payton, S., 2014. Incontinence: Using a virtual reality dance game to improve mixed incontinence. *Nature Reviews Urology*,11(3), p.128.

Pfister, R., 2011. Gender effects in gaming research: a case for regression residuals? *Cyberpsychology, Behavior and Social Networking*, 14(10), pp.603–6.

Podsakoff, P.M., MacKenzie, S.B., Lee, J.Y., and Podsakoff, N.P., 2003. Common method biases in behavioral research: a critical review of the literature and recommended remedies. *The Journal of Applied Psychology*, 88, pp.879–903.

Porter, G. and Starcevic, V., 2007. Are violent video games harmful? *Australasian Psychiatry: Bulletin of Royal Australian and New Zealand College of Psychiatrists*, 15(5), pp.422–6.

Prot, S. and Anderson, C.A., 2013. Research methods, design, and statistics in media psychology. In: *The Oxford handbook of media psychology*. New York: Oxford University Press, pp.109–136.

Rust, J. & Golombok, S., 1999. *Modern psychometrics: The science of psychological assessment*. 2nd ed., London: Routledge.

Sackett, D.L., Rosenberg, W., Gray, J.A., Haynes, R.B., and Richardson, W.S., 1996. Evidence based medicine: what it is and what it isn't. *BJM*, 312, pp.71–72.

Segovia, K., Bailenson, J. and Monin, B., 2009. Morality in tele-immersive environments. In: *Proceedings of the 2nd international conference on immersive telecommunications*.

Sherry, J., Lucas, K., Greenberg, B.S. and Lachlin, K.. 2006. Video game uses and gratifications as predictors of use and game preference. In: P. Vorderer and J. Bruyant, eds., *Playing video games. motives, Responses Consequences*. Mahwah: Lawrence Erlbaum Associates, pp.248–263

Shaughnessy, J.J., Zechmeister, E.B., and Zechmeister, J.S., 2010. *Research methods in psychology*. 8th ed. Boston: McGraw-Hill

Snook, I., O'Neill, J., Clark, J., O'Neill, A. and Openshaw, R., 2009. Invisible learnings? A commentary on John Hattie's book—'Visible learning: A synthesis of over 800 meta-analyses relating to achievement'. *New Zealand Journal of Educational Studies*, 44(1), pp.93–106.

Stevens, R., Satwicz, T. and McCarthy, L., 2008. In-game, in-room, in-world: Reconnecting video game play to the rest of kids' lives. In K. Salen, ed., *The ecology of games*. Cambridge: MIT Press, pp.41–66.

Telner, D., Bujas-Bobanovic, M. Chan, D., Chester, B., Marlow, B., Meuser, J., Rothman, A. and Harvey

B., 2010. Game-based versus traditional case-based learning: Comparing effectiveness in stroke continuing medical education. *Canadian Family Physician*, 56, pp.e345–e351.

Uhlmann, E. and Swanson, J., 2004. Exposure to violent video games increases automatic aggressiveness. *Journal of Adolescence*, 27(1), pp.41–52.

Wheelan, C., 2013. *Naked statistics: Stripping the dread from the data*. New York: W. W. Norton.

Wouters, P., van Nimwegen, C., van Oostendorp, H., and van der Spek, E.D., 2013. A meta-analysis of the cognitive and motivational effects of serious games. *Journal of Educational Psychology*, 105(2), pp.249–265.

Yee, N., Ducheneaut, N. and Nelson, L., 2012. Online gaming motivations scale: development and validation. In: *Proceedings of the SIGCHI Conference on Human Factors in Computing Systems.*

New York: ACM, 2803–2806. DOI=10.1145/2207676.2208681.

12. Stimulus games

SIMO JÄRVELÄ, INGER EKMAN, J. MATIAS KIVIKANGAS AND NIKLAS RAVAJA

Computer games have already proved useful beyond their function as entertainment. Among others, they serve as a great resource for research by providing realistic, familiar, and yet relatively complex and diverse stimuli for experiments. However, the same features that make them potentially useful also make them particularly challenging to use in controlled experiments. Many of these challenges can be overcome by taking into account the special nature of computer games when designing the test setup, procedure and data analysis. Nevertheless, the use of games calls for weighing several factors, such as making complex decisions regarding benefits and tradeoffs of practical decisions, and anticipating the effects of potential confounding factors. This added complexity to the experimental settings call for particular care whenever games are used as stimulus. High attention to detail is also recommended when analyzing, communicating and interpreting study results.

Computer games engage the player in complex behavior, which—depending on the game design—can call upon various types of cognitive and emotional processes. As such, games provide an excellent vessel for examining a multitude of abilities and skills from memory encoding, to social skills, and decision-making. In a summary on the use of games in psychological research, Washburn (2003) distinguishes four distinct manners of using computer games in experiment setups: utilizing games as stimulus to study other forms of behavior; involving games to manipulate variables; using games to provide education and instruction; and employing gaming as a performance metric. In addition to psychological studies, games are central stimuli to any research striving to understand games and gaming as a phenomenon, evaluating design decisions and measuring the effects of playing or the playing experience itself.

Different research methods place different demands on how computer games are best utilized, and also on what has to be taken into account when designing the experiment and analyzing the data. In this chapter we consider motives for game choice, use of metrics and approaches to controlling relevant experimental variables. We also describe the practical issues involved in setting up an experiment utilizing a commercially available game title. While the focus is on computer games, various virtual environments provide similar possibilities and challenges when used as a stimulus in experiments. The following chapter mainly considers uses of games in very strictly controlled studies and will be valuable both to researchers who wish to utilize games in such studies, but also to those working with more forgiving setups. In addition, readers interested in the results of game-related research may find this chapter useful when evaluating published studies, considering the possible pitfalls in experimental setups, reconciling conflicting data and assessing the generalizability and relevance of individual results.

General considerations for choosing computer games as stimuli

Computer games are a natural choice for a stimulus, not only when studying gaming and gaming experience, but also for other research questions calling for an engaging, yet challenging activity. Computer games, and contemporary games especially, are very complex stimuli and they are in many ways a unique form of media. A large number of readily available commercial games exist that could potentially be used in an experiment, but the choice has to be made carefully.

ADVANTAGES OF USING COMPUTER GAMES IN EXPERIMENTS

The extraordinary high-levels of popularity of computer games these days confers three specific benefits.

1. The high penetration in the population serves to make games more approachable than abstract psychological tasks, which helps in recruiting participants.
2. The high familiarity with games allow the use of more complex tasks in experiments, and engage subjects in ways that would be very difficult to grasp if framed as abstract psychological assignments.
3. With proper screening, test procedures can rely on previously gathered exposure, which allows addressing, for example, accumulated skills and domain expertise. With experienced players detailed instructions are not needed unless it is desirable that the participants play the game in a specific manner.

As computer games are designed to address a range of emotions and with specific intent to cause certain reactions within the player, successful titles can be considered highly ecologically valid[1] instruments for eliciting emotions for various purposes. Different game genres typically address different emotions, for example, horror games aim for quite different emotional reactions and mood than racing games or educational games. Meta-genres such as casual games or social games introduce yet further dimensions to the emotional spectrum of playing. With the proper selection of games, a broad scale of emotions can be elicited in a relatively targeted fashion. However, as games most often do not focus on a single emotion, genres and styles are not guaranteed to provide any specific experience.

Furthermore, computer games provide safe virtual environment to conduct studies on topics and situations which might present either practical or ethical challenges in a non-digital environment. Yet the level of realism in games and virtual environments is high enough that they can potentially be used to simulate and draw conclusions about real-world events. For example Milgram's (1963) classic study is considered unethical by today's standards, but Slater and colleagues (2006) were able to replicate the study using a virtual game-like activity. In addition, as McMahan and colleagues (2011) state, using off-the-shelf games provides benefits of quick implementation, avoids some researcher bias and enhances study reproducibility.

---

1. Ecological validity refers to how closely various aspects of an experimental setup such as stimulus, task, setting etc. correspond to real life context. Ecological validity is discussed more in the sections *Advantages of using computer games in experiments*, and *Matching and regulating task type* as well as in Landers and Bauer (chapters 10) and Lieberoth, Wellnizt and Aagaard (chapter 11).

The distinctive qualities of games have to be well acknowledged if they are to be used in an experiment. Particularly the variation inherent in gaming will call for extra care in choosing the game title(s) for the experiment and defining experiment procedure. Furthermore, adequate data collection might prove challenging when using commercial games due to limited logging capabilities.

Similarity of stimulus

The actual content of games are defined and shaped by various factors. This creates a challenge for experimental research, where it would often be preferable to use as identical stimulus across the participants as possible. Instead, with games the interactive stimulus is never exactly the same, but changes according to participant actions. In virtual environments and MMOGs (massively multiplayer online games) this is even more prevalent as they are influenced by a large number of players at the same time. In addition, game settings, random elements within the game, and AI operation all affect how the game proceeds. While the fact that games are widely played ensures target group familiarity, the disparate skill levels of players can also considerably affect how they play and experience a game. Since games are interactive, this skill difference tends to cause not only different experiences, but often leads to changes in the actual content of the game. For example, a skilled player will likely progress further in a given time, use more diverse and effective playing styles, or have an access to more advanced game items than a less experienced player.

Therefore it is of utmost importance that the researcher is well aware of the dependent variables and how they might be influenced by the stimulus properties that vary between participants. The choice of what game is used must be done so that the stimulus is sufficiently identical between participants in the aspects relevant to the dependent variable. After that, other variance in the game can be considered irrelevant for the experiment, but it is good to note that they still contribute to the attractiveness of the game for the participant. It would be a mistake on part of the researcher to seek to strip a game from all irrelevant variance, as this makes the game just another psychological task without the positive qualities games can offer.

Furthermore, it is important to acknowledge that since game research is still a young field, there is little agreed upon theory on precisely which are the relevant aspects for a particular effect or game quality, or how to systematically describe them. Thus, even seemingly simple decisions will likely be based on assumptions about aspects that are not yet fully understood. As is common in debates around new media forms, the discussion on computer games has its dystopian and utopian visions, which introduce a number of personal and political agendas into research. Particularly for researchers who are personally less familiar with games there is a significant risk of overlooking how seemingly separate game features combine and influence the playing experience, that is, failing to identify game-specific features that confound the main effect. An agreement on desirable procedure can help mitigate these issues and make work more accessible and comparable across discipline borders.

Off-the-shelf vs. custom games

In general, the closed code of commercial games limits the possibility of modifying the game to suit the experiment. Developer tools and mod kits make some adjustments possible (Elson and Quandt, 2014).

However, it is worth noticing that any major changes come with a risk of compromising game quality. The closed system of most commercial games can also make it difficult to ensure what the program actually does. Adaptive difficulty adjustments, randomly spawning adversaries and minute modifications to auditory and visual stimuli can be hard to spot without extensive game analysis prior to the experiment, but still affect the results. Mohseni, Pietschmann and Liebold (chapter 19) discuss the use of mods for research.

> In a study examining the effects of violent computer games on desensitization and arousal, Staude-Müller, Bliesener and Luthman (2008) compared a high and a low violence game. They used mod kits for *Unreal Tournament 2003* (Epic Games and Digital Extremes, 2002) to create a low violence version of the same game that could be compared to the regular high violence version. The enemies were frozen instead of killed, no guns were in sight and also the sound effects were changed for less violent. Yet the core game remained the same thus providing a solid ground for comparing the conditions. In addition to controlling the stimulus in exemplary manner they also discussed how they modified the game in a rare level of detail.

A common disadvantage with commercial games is also the lack of logging capabilities (i.e., saving the data about what exactly happens in the game on code level). In some cases open source alternatives are practical for this particular reason. If available, log files are immensely useful, as they can be used in, for example, event-based analysis, segmentation, and performance appraisals and to spot game manipulations not evident from video recordings.

It is not uncommon for researchers to develop their own games to ensure that they target the desired effects and have a full control over the stimulus. With custom-made games the researchers have an opportunity to modify every detail of the stimulus and tailor the task to suit whatever the experiment might need. However, in addition to requiring considerable amount of work and time, custom-developed games may introduce experimenter bias. Games developed by small-budget research teams also are less likely to be as well-balanced, rich in content and engaging as commercial titles designed and developed by professionals. Employing less engaging games for research undermines one of the biggest advantages of using games as stimulus: when the games are engaging, the participants focus deeply on the task at hand and are more likely to act as they would outside an experiment and feel less distracted by the experimental setup. Thus, more engaging stimulus can produce better data.

Practical and methodological considerations

Besides general considerations on why to use computer games as a stimulus in the first place, several more practical and study specific issues that are relevant when designing an experiment should be solved. In this chapter we will discuss questions that are tightly connected to the methodology used. The four main considerations when preparing a study using games as a stimulus are:

1. matching and regulating task type
2. determining data segmentation and event coding
3. ensuring compatibility between participants
4. planning and conducting data collection.

Finding a suitable game is one of the first steps in designing a study. Gameplay consists of various tasks that define what type of a stimulus the game actually is. One way of approaching the question is to examine the kinds of cognitive tasks that are necessary to overcome the challenges presented in the game. Concentration, problem solving, using memory, quickly focusing attention, fast reflexes, planning ahead, spatial awareness are all tasks that are common in games, but disparate game genres generally weigh the importance of various cognitive tasks differently. Furthermore, all game tasks need to be considered in relation to the context they are presented in—the same task, but for example, with different time limitations will produce vastly different reactions. Intense repetition and extended task times can also significantly change the nature of a task compared to less taxing options. For example, both *Tetris* (Pajitnov, 1985) and a modern first-person shooter game might be an appropriate stimulus for a performance-based stressor task, but while the first is designed to be constant and increasing stress, the second might have wildly varying arousal levels (depending on the game, level and play style), not to mention the added efforts of 3D spatial processing, emotional content from the narrative, and so on.

Correll, Park, Judd and Wittenbrink (2002) developed a simple computer game to test whether White or African American racial profiles had an effect on reaction times in a shoot / no-shoot scenario. This manipulation of target ethnicity was implemented with game graphics and otherwise the tasks remained identical. Their study is a good example how games can be utilized in studying more general phenomena and not just the games themselves or their effects. It also displays simple and effective stimulus control and experimental manipulation.

Naturally the game should be chosen according to what type of a stimulus is preferable. There are no general rules applicable for how to make this selection. Games differ widely even within the same genre, and yet—depending on the research questions—comparable effects may be found in games of very different styles. In fact, choosing a game title is only part of the task of determining the experiment stimulus. The choice of stimulus goes down into choosing levels, playing modes and narrowing down tasks that are conducive to the intended research. For example, a study examining the effects of violent computer games might be based on General Aggression Model, which posits that violence in games elicits arousal and that contributes to resulting aggressive behavior (cf. Bushman and Anderson, 2002). In order to make such claims, it would be of utmost importance to make sure that the compared games would not differ in quality, that the pace of the game is similar in both cases and that the overall gaming experience is equally engaging in both cases, as all these factors might affect arousal levels (cf. Adachi and Willoughby, 2011).

When available, game taxonomies provide helpful sources for making informed game choices. Lindley (2003) slightly modifies Caillois' (1961) classical four elements (*competition*, *chance*, *simulation*, and *vertigo*) identifying three primary descriptors (*narrative*, *ludology*, and *simulation*), upon which operate additional dimensions differentiating the level of *chance vs. skill*, *fiction vs. non-fiction* and *physical vs. virtual*. Elverdam and Aarseth (2007) provide a higher level of detail with their 17-dimension taxonomy. Their taxonomy bears a strong link to game design, indeed, they specifically point out the relation to the component framework in Björk and Holopainen's (2004) *Patterns in game design*. Finally, Whitton (2009) provides a breakdown of game choice for education, in which she details the expected cognitive and emotional engagement within certain genres. Beyond these, less general taxonomies abound, for example differentiating games particularly based on interaction style (Lundgren and Björk, 2003; Mueller, Gibbs and Vetere, 2008), or the forms of social interaction they provide (Manninen, 2004).

Reviews and ratings can also be helpful in choosing the game. The ratings give an overall assessment on the quality of the game, which—while not objective—is not influenced by researchers' own views and preferences. Ratings are especially helpful when selecting multiple games to be used in the same experiment, as similar ratings lessen the risk that observed differences are simply due to comparing games of diverse quality.

Commercial games commonly have large number of adjustable features which can be utilized in the experiment setup. Visual settings, sounds, game preferences, difficulty levels, number of opponents, play time, controls etc. can all be used in controlling the stimulus and creating the necessary manipulations. Finally, task choice (the game actions) involves considering the length of task (can the task be extended, how long does it take, how much does the length vary between participants, is there enough or too much repetition?), how static the action is (is the difficulty level static or does it vary?). For any extended play scenarios it is necessary to consider how well the intended playing time matches the game in question, so as not to create untypical scenarios which would undermine the ecological validity of the gaming scenario.

- Define your tasks, find out what can be expected to affect it, to get an understanding what kind of games could be suitable and which could not.
- Play the potential game to get a feel for the tasks involved and to spot factors that might influence your task inadvertently.
- Use available reviews to pinpoint effects, challenges and possible shortfalls in the game design, and compare those with your understanding of relevant aspects of the task.
- Use available ratings to ensure the quality level of the game meets the study requirements.
- Utilize game levels and game control features in creating desired variation.

DETERMINING DATA QUANTIFICATION AND EVENT CODING

To be able to analyze effects associated with gaming, researchers typically need a strategy to quantify the gaming data. One possibility is of course to use a block design, for example to compare different games, levels, or game modes against each other. However, sometimes block designs are inadequate. For example, the focus of interest may be smaller events, such as particular actions (e.g., finishing the race, killing an opponent in a first-person shooter [FPS] or picking up a mushroom). For these cases, event-based analysis allows researchers to gain data on the events of interest, and minimize the confounding data from actions occurring before and after the moment of interest.

Event-based designs, however, introduce some additional considerations for the researcher. The choice of event coding is based not only on the game's available actions, but also on how isolated these actions occur during game-play. Often there are many over-lapping events that are hard to differentiate from each other. With many different elements affecting the subject at the same time, it can be impossible to say which of the elements caused a certain reaction or behavior (e.g., in combat in FPS game whether the reactions were due to shooting at the enemy or being shot at, or both). On the other hand, if events are too unique, the sample size might not be adequate for statistical analysis unless it is compensated with a high number of participants. The easiest events to study are those that appear frequently, and in sufficient isolation from everything else.

The same repeating event can occur in different contexts within the game thus framing it differently and so having a different meaning. Whereas some of this diversity can be controlled by fixing game parameters, the level of control varies greatly between games. The common solution is to have large enough sample of the same event so that the effect of random noise (e.g., slightly varying framing of the same event) is balanced out. Naturally these considerations should also affect game choice, as games where the same type of event takes place several times are more suitable stimuli as it is easier to have a satisfying sample size of events under scrutiny.

The optimal time scale needed for events has to be balanced in relation to the metrics used in the experiment. Various methods have different time resolution which often limits the size of events that can be examined. The necessary resolution influences the temporal accuracy needed for timestamps and also for data synchronization; these should all be in accordance with the research method used. The aim is to select a resolution for event coding that does not limit what can be analyzed from the data. Therefore, even longer duration events should preferably be coded with very accurate starting and ending times. The nature of the effect under scrutiny also determines the necessary duration of events and how event response times are matched to metrics.

The choice of method for analyzing the data can to some extent mitigate the challenge provided by concurrent and overlapping events. For example, the *linear mixed model* (hierarchical linear models) incorporates both fixed effects and random effects, and is particularly suitable to repeated measurements, where the effect is simultaneously influenced by many factors. This statistical method is necessary if the data is hierarchical (e.g., events within conditions within participants) or the number of samples varies within the unit of analysis (e.g., if a particular event occurs a different number of times for diverse players). Simpler data structures may offer the possibility to use other analysis methods.

While typical events in computer games are quite clearly separable from others, in some cases it is not self-evident how events should be defined. They might take over a longer undefined period of time (e.g., in a horror game, how long exactly does the suspense before release last?), or larger events may consist of a number of smaller events in ways that are difficult to precisely define for coding purposes. In these cases data driven approaches may be utilized to explore what clusters of events occur in the material, for example applying machine learning algorithms to find repeating patterns and connections in the event data (e.g., Kosunen, 2012). Data driven approaches may also be applied in order to provide complementary perspective to, or even to test the validity of, coding strategies done by other means.

When deciding on the event coding, it is useful to remember that one can always go from specific to general, but rarely the other way around without recoding the data. Finally, event coding is closely related to data acquisition and how you plan your experiment. It is advisable to have a clear idea what events will be used in analysis and how they are to be processed and plan the experiment accordingly. Options are often quite limited afterwards if enough data was not collected in the first place.

- Choose a game where the desired events occur often enough, preferably in isolation.
- Critically consider the various contexts in which events occur. In case of suspected effect, keep track of the context (log it) for each event occurrence.

- Ensure that the event of interest and metrics operate on similar time scales.
- Mitigate overlap and simultaneity by choice of statistical method. Take care that the hierarchical nature of data is accounted for.
- Consider data driven approaches if applicable.
- Code too much rather than too little detail. Extra coding can always be disregarded later, but accessing uncoded material is much more difficult.

ENSURING COMPATIBILITY BETWEEN PARTICIPANTS

Fundamental to a successful experiment is ensuring compatible test conditions between multiple participants. Since the game as stimulus changes depending on the participants' choices, skill level and preferences, this requires a balance between stimulus design (see *Matching and regulating task type* section above) and careful participant selection.

RECRUITING PARTICIPANTS

Unless the research specifically addresses learning, some experience with computer games is usually preferable, as learning basic skills can take up significant time and effort and any time spent on training sessions are away from the actual experiment tasks. Choosing only subjects that are experienced enough with the task at hand can ensure deeper skill levels during the experiment than what could be achieved by including a practice session or by giving instructions prior to the test session. In contrast, if novices are given too little time to get acquainted with the game, the lack of basic gaming skills is likely to influence the quality of the data. Importantly, gaming skills do not necessarily transfer across genre borders, and even within a certain genre small changes in, for example, controller behavior can have a major impact on play performance.

Theoretically, a large enough random sample of males and females provides the best basis for generalizing results over the general population and avoiding a gender bias. However, in practice this goal is often problematic to achieve. Although many women play computer games, gaming is still much more common among the male population (ESA, 2011), and therefore acquiring comparable numbers of experiment participants of both genders with good sample size can sometimes be difficult—particularly so if comparable gaming experience is a prerequisite. It is essential to have a clear idea of the population you are sampling from, and to which you are generalizing the results, as some gaming subcultures can be heavily male/female dominated and the risk that the sample is not representative of the population is significant. Similarly, it is virtually impossible to conduct an experimental study that would have enough participants in each age group to provide statistically significant results without limiting the amount of relevant variables through participant selection. Instead, these factors have to be taken into account when analyzing the data, interpreting the results and generalizing them.

COMPARABLE STIMULI

It is impossible to create gaming stimuli that is identical for all participants. Instead of aiming for similarity, the researcher should focus on what makes or breaks the experience of interest, and devise strategies for handling variation within this perspective. To ensure stimuli are comparable, and to minimize the impact of variation on results, the imperative is to identify the critical factors that affect the dependent variable(s), and control those as well as possible. Indeed, some variations may be necessary to ensure the overall gaming experience is compatible between participants. Moreover, in some cases individual variation in actual game content is not a problem, for example if measurement concerns general-level experiences such as overall performance and stress levels. Also, if both events and measurements can be narrowed down to a shorter time frame, these shorter spans of gameplay can be comparable between participants even when the whole game sessions are not.

One common aspect which requires consideration is game difficulty. Some games have built-in difficulty adjustments that automatically balance and change the difficulty of the game according to player's performance and choices within the game. Depending on the context and what is being studied, self-adjusting difficulty levels may either escalate or counterbalance the challenges of using a stimulus with inherent variability. When the aim is to ensure similar experiences across players, automatic adjustment can be useful in creating relatively equally challenging gaming experience to players of varying skill levels. In contrast, if using the same content for all participants is critical for the experiment, automatic difficulty adjustments can be detrimental to the process. Furthermore, automatic difficulty adjustment is often difficult to detect. In the absence of reliable information (e.g., from the developer) to confirm or rule out automatic difficulty adjustment, identifying it generally requires considerable familiarity with computer games. Moreover, even knowing that a game has difficulty adjustment, a researcher may struggle to determine precisely how the system works and how it impacts content.

If performance, and processes related to it (such as general arousal and feelings of frustration), are not relevant for the dependent variable, the difficulty of the game might not be relevant either. In such cases, difficulty level could even be left to participants to choose for themselves. However, this might necessitate using other ways to ensure comparability between trials, for example, by assessing subjective difficulty by a post questionnaire.

- Be selective with your participants, but cautious about generalizing results.
- Pay special attention to gaming experience already when recruiting participants.
- Evaluate gaming experience for the specific genre, game type and title used in the experiment.
- Decide if it is more important to ensure identical tasks and events, or identical difficulty level—if not possible to control both. If possible, include a metric to capture the dimension you do not control (subjective difficulty, counting the number of adversaries, etc.).
- Pay special attention to gaming experience already when recruiting participants.
- Evaluate gaming experience for the specific genre, game type and title used in the experiment.

PLANNING AND CONDUCTING DATA COLLECTION

Depending on the research method used a varying amount of data is needed but all data segmentation and event based analysis require information on what happened in the game. When available, automatically logging game-play provides a superior method for segmenting system data with sufficient temporal accuracy. Most games do not employ sufficient logging of game events, or logs are not available for the researcher. In this case, events have to be marked afterwards by reviewing recorded game-play (e.g., from video recordings), which can be very laborious. Furthermore, it is often the case that not all player actions can be identified and differentiated from mere recordings—in modern games with lots of different objects on the screen, it is not clear from the game video alone where the attention of the player is focused at a given moment, for example (though eye trackers can be used for that). Mod kits often provide extended logging capabilities, if available (cf. chapter 19).

If a built-in logging system is not feasible, some logs can be collected externally. Keyloggers, screen capture videos, and mouse-click recorders can provide helpful material both for analysis and preprocessing data before manual coding. At least a screen capture video of the game play should be recorded. Be sure to include good quality sound, as audio cues may be used to differentiate between visually similar-looking actions or inform about off-screen events. Most games have one or more innate performance metrics in them. High scores, achievements, goals, kills, repetitions, accuracy, lap times, duration, rewards, new items, levels, and so on, can be used as dependent variables or as covariates, complementing and validating external performance metrics.

It is imperative to calibrate the timestamps of different data sources. This is especially important if the analysis will operate on event data instead of whole blocks. Whereas some game events can be matched manually afterwards, other data sets contain no unambiguous handles for time-synchronizing data post hoc, and data will be practically useless to the analysis if the timestamps do not correspond. Depending on the setup several methods exists for anchoring timestamps across devices, for example, sending markers across devices, synchronizing device clocks or using video cameras. The precision of synchronization needed is naturally dependent on the research question, the measurements and choice of method.

- Utilize game logs whenever available.
- Consider using external logging to capture game data.
- Take advantage of the game's performance metrics when possible.
- Use the game's internal performance metrics to check external performance metrics.
- Be extra careful to calibrate and synchronize timestamps across data sources.

Checklist of Questions

The following is a checklist of elements that call for special attention when using a computer game as a stimulus. It is not exhaustive but considers the key questions typically addressed in the beginning of an experiment. For each question, respectively, we address the part(s) of the experiment workflow that is most influenced by the decision. This does not imply there is no influence to other parts of the work as well, instead it points out the work tasks calling for extra critical attention.

Checklist question	Why is this important?	Main influence on				
		Game choice	Event coding	Participant selection	Procedure	Analysis
What tasks does the game play require?	Match research questions and tasks required by the game.	x	x		x	
Is the task represented as game action that is separate from other task types?	Very complex and overlapping events may not allow distinguishing one event from another.	x	x		x	
How does task difficulty influence play? Can task difficulty be balanced?	The difficulty level should be suitable for all participants whether by choosing it properly for the target group, selective recruitment of participants, or by adjusting it case by case.	x		x	x	
What game events repeat themselves?	Frequently repeating game events provide larger sample size for event-based analysis and is necessary for within-subject methods.		x	x	x	x
Do repeating events occur in a similar context, or does context change?	Adding poorly comparable events only introduces more noise, which blurs results.		x			x
How similar as a stimulus is the game across participants?	Identical stimulus across participants is often desirable, but not always necessary.	x		x		x
How much does the player's skill level influence gameplay?	Different backgrounds can result in both factually and subjectively disparate experiences across participants.	x		x		x
What methods of data collection are available?	The research question may be addressed through various different combinations of event coding and data collection.	x	x		x	x
Does the game provide logs or is external recording needed? Are there developer tools or mod kits that can be customized for data acquisition?	Game logs are extremely useful, if available. The smaller events you want to examine, the more extensive data logging is required and the higher are demands for temporal acuity.	x	x		x	
How reliably can events be decoded from e.g. video recordings, keylogs, etc.?	Manually coding can be laborious, but may also affect data precision.		x		x	

Table 1. Checklist.

- American Psychological Association, 2010. *Publication manual of the American Psychological Association*. 6th ed. American Psychological Association.
- Cozby, P.C. and Bates, S.C., 2012. *Methods in behavioral research*. 11th ed. McGraw-Hill.
- Field, A., Miles, J. and Field, Z. 2012. *Discovering statistics using R*. London: SAGE.

References

Adachi, P. and Willoughby, T., 2011. The effect of video game competition and violence on aggressive behavior: Which characteristic has the greatest influence? *Psychology of Violence*, 1(4), pp.259–274. DOI=10.1037/a0024908.

Entertainment Software Association, 2011. *Essential facts about the computer and video game industry*.

Björk, S. and Holopainen, J., 2005. *Patterns in game design*. Hingham: Charles River Media.

Caillois, R., 2001. *Man, play, and games*. Urbana: University of Illinois Press.

Correll, J., Park, B., Judd, C.M. and Wittenbrink, B., 2002. The police officer's dilemma: using ethnicity to disambiguate potentially threatening individuals. *Journal of Personality and Social Psychology*, 83(6), pp.1314–1329. DOI=10.1037/0022-3514.83.6.1314.

Elson, M. and Quandt, T., 2014. Digital games in laboratory experiments: Controlling a complex stimulus through modding. *Psychology of Popular Media Culture*, ahead of print. DOI=10.1037/ppm0000033.

Elverdam, C. and Aarseth, E., 2007. Game classification and game design construction through critical Analysis. *Games and Culture*, 2(1). DOI= 10.1177/1555412006286892.

Epic Games and Digital Extremes, 2002. *Unreal Tournament 2003* [game]. Atari Inc.

Kosunen, I., 2012. *Clustering psychophysiological data with mixtures of generalized linear models*. MS. Aalto University.

Lindley, C., 2003. Game taxonomies: A high level framework for game analysis and design. *Gamasutra*. Available at: <http://homepage.ttu.edu.tw/jmchen/gameprog/slides/game taxonomy.pdf>.

Lundgren, S. and Björk, S., 2003. Game mechanics: Describing computer-augmented games in terms of interaction. In: S.Göbel et al., eds.,*Proceedings of TIDSE*. Stuttgart: Fraunhofer IRB Verlag. Available at: <http://www.itu.dk/stud/speciale/worlddomination/files/rikke/rh/speciale/staffan_docs/mechanics.pdf>.

Manninen, T., 2004. Rich interaction model for game and virtual environment design. PhD. University of Oulu.

McMahan, R., Ragan, E. and Leal, A., 2011. Considerations for the use of commercial video games in controlled experiments. *Entertainment Computing*, 2(1). DOI= 10.1016/j.entcom.2011.03.002.

Milgram, S., 1963. Behavioral study of obedience. *The Journal of Abnormal and Social Psychology*, 67(4), pp.371–378. DOI=10.1037/h0040525.

Mueller, F. "Floyd," Gibbs, M.R. and Vetere, F., 2008. Taxonomy of exertion games. In: *Proceedings of the 20th australasian conference on computer-human interaction designing for habitus and habitat (OZCHI '08)*. New York: ACM Press, p.263–266. DOI=10.1145/1517744.1517772.

Pajitnov, A., 1985. *Tetris* [game]. Spectrum Holobyte.

Slater, M., Antley, A., Davison, A. and Swapp, D., 2006. A virtual reprise of the Stanley Milgram obedience experiments. *PloS one*. DOI=10.1371/journal.pone.0000039.

Staude-Müller, F., Bliesener, T. and Luthman, S., 2008. Hostile and hardened? An experimental study on (de-) sensitization to violence and suffering through playing video games. *Swiss Journal of Psychology*, 67(1), pp.41–50. DOI=10.1024/1421-0185.67.1.41.

Washburn, D., 2003. The games psychologists play (and the data they provide). *Behavior Research Methods, Instruments & Computers*, 35(2). DOI=10.3758/BF03202541.

Whitton, N., 2009. Learning with digital games: A practical guide to engaging students in higher education. New York: Routledge.

13. Audio visual analysis of player experience

Feedback-based gameplay metrics

RAPHAËL MARCZAK AND GARETH R. SCHOTT

This chapter introduces readers to an innovative method designed specifically to meet game researchers' need to be able to analyse and explore players' experiences with any off-the-shelf PC game. We introduce how insights into players' experiences are achieved from automatically processing significant elements of the audio-visual feedback (i.e., moving image and sound) produced by the game.

Videogames contain a wealth of significant and (behaviourally) influential information that is conveyed to the player to facilitate advancement through a game. Such information can relate to virtual progress (e.g., maps, mission logs), player reserves (e.g., acquisitions) or vitality (e.g., health or stamina levels), to name but a few. By exploiting and analysing what is transmitted to the player during play, feedback-based gameplay metrics utilise the same content that the player comes into contact with during gameplay, therefore tying the method directly to individual *player experiences*. A distinguishing feature of this approach, when compared to existing methods available for gathering gameplay metrics relates to the way a feedback-based gameplay metric approach operates as a post-processing method that works with gameplay once it has been captured and saved as an audio-visual file. We aim to highlight the advantages of this approach in terms of the way it allows the researcher to revisit and deconstruct a gameplay session from a number of different angles, combining various different audio-visual processing techniques to answer either pre-defined or supplementary research questions. Examples of the different means of extracting information from the audio and visual content of videogames are presented to provide a strong sense of the capabilities of this particular method. The aim is to outline its contribution and value as a stand-alone method, although the method is also designed to work effectively within a mixed methods approach (see Schott, et al., 2013).

When confronted with data in the form of an audio-visual file that contains footage documenting hours of gameplay completed with a commercially available off-the-shelf game title, that is also the outcome of a player's distinct approach or playing style and determined by individual differences in learning style, comprehension and perception to name but a few variables, the task of understanding player experience constitutes a highly complex task. In order to be able to address this complex task, we approach gameplay as a predominantly *configurative practice* (Vught, et al., 2012), in that we acknowledge the way gameplay requires the player to "work with the materiality of a text, [that is,] the need to participate in the construction of its material structure" (Klevjer, 2002). In other words, we understand gameplay as an encounter between a player and a game system. In adopting this perspective, our approach to understanding player experience is guided, firstly, by the need to be able to break down a game's core structural features (Zagal, et al., 2008; chapters 3–4) before, secondly, mapping a player's relationship with those structures. The object of our analysis is the *result* of specific behavioural choices and action selections during the course of play that carry *implications* spatially (e.g. pathways taken, navigational choices and progression) and temporally (e.g., pace and the difference between voluntary versus an imposed suspension of forward momentum). In order to operationalize this process during research and achieve a method capable of identifying the relationship between player input and a game's structure, we have found it necessary to 1) characterise the structure of a game as a multimedia document (segmentation) before 2) generating a description of its content (indexing). The first task is a conceptual exercise that demands that the structure of specific games is identified, while the second requires a means of extracting desired information from game content. This process demands conceptual knowledge derived from game studies combined with the capacity to extract the required information from the game system, derived from the computer sciences. The process outlined briefly here in combination with the different scholarly traditions that it draws upon, reflects how this variety of game metrics is conceived as a game research tool rather than a tool for evaluating usability with the aim of contributing to game development processes.

Expanding game metrics

The potential connected with the appropriation of conventional methods of gathering game metrics for player experience research (as distinct from user experience research) has been both compelling (Nacke, et al., 2009) and well received by the wider game studies research community. It is safe to say that the current value of game metrics to player research is not that dissimilar however to its initial value to user research, in that its appeal can be traced to its standing as a quantitative method. Within user research, game metrics represented advancement in accuracy and process on the qualitative methods that were more typically employed to articulate user-experiences with game systems under development (Hilbert and Redmiles, 2000). A similar appeal has seen game metrics extend beyond computer sciences and enter the humanities inaugurated discipline of game studies. Game metrics have come to represent a potentially powerful technique that holds the ability to transform what has been conceptualized or theorized to-date in relation to player experience. Here we refer specifically to the value of game metrics for explaining the exact nature and function of player-system relations during play (Choi, 2000; Drachen, 2008; Waern, 2012). Typically, gameplay metrics are capable of providing researchers with information on player activity in relation to specific areas such as: "navigation, item- and ability use, jumping, trading, running and whatever else players actually do inside the virtual environment" (Drachen, et al., 2013, p.10). In addition, they are capable of covering the wider conditions of managing play that absorbs "all interaction the player performs with the game interface and menu" (p.11) termed interface metrics.

With the exception of recording player input, such as pressing keys on a keyboard (or keystrokes) that can be recorded using any type of key logger software system, the gathering of gameplay metrics typically prescribes a certain level of access to gaming software that is authorized or sanctioned by game developers. This can take the form of access to the game source code, through agreements, modding provision (Sasse, 2008) or if a release takes the form of an open source game (Pedersen, et al., 2010). The approach outlined in this paper seeks to circumvent these conditions by instead utilizing and translating video and sound feedback experienced by the player during play. To this effect, Fagerholt's (2009) research provided a strong indicator of the potential that exists for focusing on the audio-visual feedback provided to the player during play. From a review of First Person Shooter (FPS) games he was able to identify a number of game elements and outline the way information is broadcast to the player (see figure 1). Focusing on the *heads up display* (HUD) Fagerholt was able to draw attention to the manner in which videogames compensate for the player's physical disconnection from the game world requiring the game system to construct a sense of presence.

Table 1 (upper left):

	2D overlay (Permanent)	2D overlay (Pop-in)	2D Overlay (Dynamic)	Image Filter	Projected on Environment	Character Model	Camera Possession	Dynamic Audio Tracks	Audio Queues	Rumble
Aim Accuracy	4									
Ammo count	12	3				1			1	
Availabe objects/weapons	7	7								
Health Level	5	2		10					3	
Centre of View	16				1					
Taking hit / Hit Direction			11	5			1		17	13
Current Stance	4	3				1				
Special State		3		6		3			1	6
Picked up item		6		1						
Using weapon/Combat						17		5	17	9
Total nr of uses:	48	24	11	22	1	22	1	5	39	28

Table 2 (upper right):

	2D overlay (Permanent)	2D overlay (Pop-in)	2D Overlay (Dynamic)	In Pause Menu	Character Model	Informational Objects	Object/NPC Effects	Audio Queues	Dialogue	Rumble
Is target hostile or friendly	14									
Position of team mates	4		5	2		1				
State of team mates	3	2	2			1	1		1	
Proximity of Enemies	4		2	3				2	3	2
Enemy Health		1					3			
Object is interactive		13	2			1	6			
Object is "Pickupable"		5	2		1		5			
Object of interest (Danger)			2						1	
Total nr of uses:	25	21	15	5	1	3	15	2	5	2

Table 3 (lower left):

	2D overlay (Permanent)	2D overlay (Pop-in)	2D Overlay (Dynamic)	In Pause Menu	Informational Objects	Camera Possession	Dialogue
What is the current objective		6		11			1
Direction of Current Objective	5		4	2	3	1	
Total nr of uses:	5	6	4	13	3	1	1

Table 4 (lower right):

	2D overlay (Permanent)	2D overlay (Pop-in)	2D Overlay (Dynamic)	In Pause Menu
Instructions to player		13		
Information to Player	1	5	1	5
Total nr of uses	1	18	1	5

Figure 1. Erik Fagerholt and Lorentzon's (2009) summary of information broadcast using HUD elements within 19 FPS games.

All of the elements identified in Fagerholt's research refer to graphical and sound streams, which led us to consider the possibilities of capturing and measuring this information automatically. Here we refer to the potential application of algorithms that have been created to detect the presence of specific objects within moving-image (Bay, et al., 2008), automatically segment moving-image into sub-scenes (Huang and Liao, 2001; Saraceno and Leonardi, 1997) or extract symbolic information such as annotations (Chen, et al., 2001) and numbers (Ye, et al., 2005).

Additionally, signal processing of audio streams constitutes an established and active research field within the computer sciences. Algorithms have been created to detect speech and music in radiophonic streams (Richard, et al., 2007), music recognition (Orio, 2006) or to indicate moments of intensity in movies via audio tempo analysis (Yeh, et al., 2009). In processing digital games we have found it possible to adapt such algorithms as they display large amounts of information in abstract and schematic ways (e.g., via life-bar representation, icons of obtained objects, on-screen blur, screen desaturation, heartbeat sfx). Our method is based on the idea that different audio and visual design elements can be extracted accurately from output streams and analyzed to create a picture of the nature and developmental changes in players' interaction and experience with a particular game.

Segmentation and indexing gameplay performance

Gameplay *segmentation* has already formed the focus of research by Zagal, et al. (2008) as part of the *Game Ontology Project*. In this context we share the same understanding of segmentation as a process in which "a game is broken down into smaller elements of gameplay" (Zagal, et al., 2008, p.176). In their work, Zagal, et al., were clear to define the role of segmentation as an exploration of the structure of gameplay that supports an analysis of the role of design elements. We, however, seek to extend this process to encompass gameplay as both representative of *a* game system and *a* performance (Laurel, 1993). That is, we seek to segment games based on how players engage with the game structure and the possibilities offered by it rather than analyse a game for its structure and how it is likely to create specific gameplay experiences. In this context, performance becomes critical as it emphasizes the unfolding nature of games and relevance of player input to that process. The role of the player then becomes something more than just a necessary component to activate the game system (Aarseth, 2007).

Zagal, et al. (2008) have segmented *gameplay* on the basis of their temporal, spatial and challenge characteristics (see also, chapter 4). Yet, in illustrating their approach they apply their framework to vintage arcade games, games that foreground the rule system by virtue of their simplicity. This inevitably leads them to concede that contemporary games are likely to include "multiple forms of segmentation, that are interrelated, or even co-occur," (p.178) with novel game design also likely to require further ways of segmenting gameplay that may in turn call for a re-examination of existing segmentation principles. In this way, Zagal et al. acknowledge how such processes are required to evolve, or demand a more open-ended approach. By using a player performance determined segmentation process we aim to achieve this, in doing so, utilizing structure to achieve a segmentation that isolates relevant player experience.

When tailored to the experience of playing a game, segmentation needs to be based on portions of play that can be clearly identified by the homogeneity of the way breaks in the play experience present themselves to the player. Games are sub-divided in many different ways, the most basic being a new level or mission (e.g., *Battlefield 3* [Electronic Arts, 2011]) that can be accompanied by a pause whilst the next section of the game is loading. In doing so, a splash screen is often presented to players that can then be detected and time-stamped and used to illustrate the pace at which a player has progressed through the game. We use the term indexing to distinguish the identification and location of information that denotes a) where in the structure of the system the player is active, for example, in-game verses menus, b) the nature of the player's involvement, for example, Calleja's (2011) distinction between narrative and ludic involvement, or c) the degree of interactivity, for example, fully, semi or non-interactive. To summarise, segmentation is therefore the determination of the boundaries of a coherent section of play that is also comprised of a set of indexical properties. For example, the presence of a cut-scene can often represent the end of a large section of play and beginning of a new one, with the content of a cut-scene often containing a significant plot points that drive the change (segment). This event also denotes a distinction between the ludic and narrative involvement of the player and degree of interactivity of the player (index). Given our focus on player interaction, as indicative of player experience, this required that the algorithms employed to automatically segment game footage were capable of detecting indexical differences between interactivity and non-interactivity of different sequences. This was necessary in order to avoid incorrectly detecting actions on-screen like fighting, looting, walking as play when they occur in a sequence such as a non-interactive cut-scene.

In order to be able to reach more fine-grained aspects of a play experience, we conceptualize and divide the segmentation process into a multi-layered process. The layers, listed below, are employed in two different ways, the first, relating to the *process* of segmentation in which audio-visual footage of a gameplay session is processed or deconstructed as part of a method. Secondly, once this is completed, aspects of player experience can then be reconstructed using the layers to discern the meaning of a section of gameplay as part of the process of analysis. The five layers are:

- game system
- game world
- spatial-temporal
- degree of freedom
- interaction

The first step in our process is to acknowledge and treat the game system as a whole. That is, the initiation of gameplay, as the diegetic experience of playing in a fiction world, only occurs once players move from splash screens (e.g., copyright, production credits) to eventually reach a higher order main menu where players are able to activate play and enter the game world. Only when play is initiated does the player move from the *game system* layer to the *game world* layer, the 3D space in which the game is situated and play is realized. From that point onward, play is either broken or paused by the player, typically exiting play through higher order menus. The game world layer contains what we term *instances* of gameplay. During post-processing audio-visual analysis of such instances the player is present only as the entity behind, and responsible for generating and triggering the game footage under examination. The first key task in this process is to distinguish between in–out game and active–inactive as well as what this entails in terms of coherence between two consecutive frames. After this we begin to distinguish the *spatial-temporal* information contained within the game world layer as we identify deliberate pausing or detachments from the game world by the player, or information that is indicative of player progress relating to terrain traversed or activities completed that might trigger cut-scenes or new missions via a loading screen. These elements constitute identifiable nodes that map the progress and journey of the player and also the timing of when players experience core events in the game (useful for cross-player comparisons). Related to player progression through a game are the *degrees of freedom* and *interactivity* layers that constitute the manner in which the logic and rule system of the game is conveyed to the player and the degree to which the player is required to engage with the information provided by the game, or is permitted to ignore cues provided by the system.

EXAMPLE 1: LOOTING IN *BIOSHOCK 2*

To begin defining the contribution and function of each layer we present the example of the act of *looting* in *Bioshock 2* (2K Games, 2010) and examine its relevance as a source of information in terms of its meaning within each of our five layers. In this process the layers do not function in a hierarchical top-down manner, meaning that we arrive at the act of looting as an end result of a process of refinement, but instead, the act of looting can be understood in terms of its relationship to each of the layers. In this way the layers function is transversal, allowing for movement, meaning and implication to be derived from each one.

Looting a corpse in FPS body-horror game *Bioshock 2*, allows the player to gather resources, such as money, from deceased non-player characters. The player's attention is drawn to the possibility of looting by the appearance of a looting panel that overlays the game world and signals that there are items available to be looted. The appearance of a looting panel on-screen can be identified using the audio and video feedback streams. Additionally, a money logo accompanied by a sound file validates that money has been acquired if such an action is selected by the player. The presence of the looting panel, the money logo and the acquisition sound indicate an action has been performed in line with the cue provided. Whereas a looting panel and no money logo or acquisition sound indicates a player has not opted to loot in that instance (*interaction*).

The option to loot is built into the game system, providing a mechanism for the player to collect and store items and money that can be applied (at the player's discretion) in playing the game. The player is afforded the freedom of choice to loot or not loot. However, this option is also conditional on the game system allowing the player to explore the game space. That is, in interacting with the game space, player movement combined with first person perspective will lead the player to pass corpses on the ground. Proximity and gaze cues the game system to invite the player to loot by presenting the contents held by the corpse. Additionally, opting to not loot (in the here and now) may impact on players' *degree of freedom* further into the game world, giving meaning to the extent to which a player loots or not throughout the game.

Corpses are only found when the player moves through and acts inside the fictional space of the game (the city of Rapture in the case of *Bioshock 2*). It is not available to players in other spaces, like the help menu, loading screen or pause menu. As an act completed during gameplay, it is possible to map the instances of looting as a value of *spatial and temporal* movement. That is, how quickly or slowly a player progresses through the game and how they navigate the game.

Engagement with objects and structures within the city of Rapture is not offered to players until they decide to actually start the game and remain available only in the diegetic space of the game world (as distinct from higher order menus). It is possible to therefore identify when a player is in or out of the game world with reference to such acts such as looting.

Looting interactions are clearly part of the game system and the outcome of which are represented, collated, viewed and managed in higher order menus, representing actions that have been made in the context of 'game world' 'interactions' that can be related to 'degrees of freedom' afforded by the system but also are conditional on the degrees of freedom that a player possesses in future actions.

EXAMPLE 2: QUICK TIME EVENT IN BATTLEFIELD 3

In this second example, using *Battlefield 3* (Electronic Arts, 2011) we work back through the layers in the opposite direction. The game contains Quick Time Events (QTEs) that force the player to complete a series of rote-based actions (e.g., press E, left click mouse, then right click mouse). These prompts from the system are not presented to the player in a diegetic or narrative form, but remain procedural only really acknowledging the need for player input. In the context of QTEs the player temporarily loses all other agency possibilities (i.e. they are unable to move freely or use strategy or weapons of choice). The degree of freedom becomes highly prescriptive, as the system (which is always in control of such conditions) is much more explicit in its treatment of the player requiring the necessary input to activate content and progress gameplay. Each interaction is preceded by an on-screen prompt (or video feedback stream from the perspective of our metric method), that indicates the action required (e.g., a blue icon matching the expected player input, E, mouse icon with left or right highlighted). Should the player follow this prompt with the correct input, the icon will then blink in blue in response as means of validating the player's action. Failure to follow the prompt will lead to a red icon, indicating that a response was either incorrect or absent.

The *interactions* defined by their *degrees of freedom*, are built into the game system as a form of mini-game (a task outside what one might expect in an FPS game environment) that is defined by success or failure, upon which progression is conditional and non-negotiable. As a marker of player progression, when a QTE occurs for the player it is also indicative of space and time. That is, specific QTEs (like missions or levels) are conditional on players' ability to reach specific locations on a game map, but also indicative of how long it takes a player to reach these nodes within the game. A QTE will therefore be triggered only once a player has reached a pre-defined point in the game, and should the player succeed, the same QTE will not reappear in that version of the game again. To this degree, the time taken to activate different QTEs provide a marker of pace and rate of progression attributable to the levels of mastery possessed by the player, or nature and style of game-playing (e.g. exploratory and thorough verses action and goal oriented). Lastly, whilst an obvious statement, QTEs are part of the game world and therefore cannot appear should a player activate a pause or opt to manage the conditions of play through engaging in higher order menus. This provides a clear indicator for automatic processing of a game's audio-visual feedback as to when QTEs materialize for the player and the nature and degree of player activity that the player experiencing when QTEs occur.

Automatic processing

The chapter now moves on to demonstrate examples of audio and video processing algorithms that are being appropriated and used to gather information on player experience. The aim of automatic processing is obviously to reduce the complexity and time-demanding task of segmenting a *gameplay performance* manually. The algorithms introduced in this chapter cover the detection of both static and moving information sources, assessing bar progressions (e.g. health bars) and identifying specific sounds. It is worth noting that when algorithms are applied, they are done so with knowledge of the value of symbolic information in terms of what it signifies in relation to player activity and involvement. For example, when a logo-detection algorithm is applied to footage of gameplay, in order to confirm the presence of a logo the intent is not to learn about the morphological properties of the logo (for instance colour, size, shape, potential text content) but the meaning of its presence or absence. For instance, the presence of a HUD on-screen signifies gameplay is in session, whereas its absence can signify other events are in progress (e.g., a cut-scene). Similarly with sound detection, the intent is not to analyse the sound itself (in terms of frequency, amplitude or tonality) but the function of the sound (e.g., it might signify successful object acquisition). The researcher is therefore required to engage with the game under consideration in advance of processing in order to elicit the key gameplay concepts and match them to their various audio-visual representations.

The implementation of audio-visual processing algorithms, as described in this chapter, is an accessible process that one can repeat using the open source library *OpenCV* (Intel Corporation, Willow Garage and Itseez, 2014) for computer vision processing, or *libsndfile* (de Castro Lopo, 2011) for audio processing.

TREATING AUDIO-VISUAL PRESENTATION AS DATA

An *image* can be represented as a *matrix* or two-dimensional array of values matrix (Gonzales and Woods, 2007, chapter 2). In this case the value is represented by a *pixel* that represents both a colour value and assumes a specific location inside the *matrix*. The process of partitioning and translating an image into a set of values for processing is termed *discretization* (representing a transformation from continuous representation to discrete representation), or *sampling*. This process is also applied to moving image and sound (Roads, 1996, chapter 1) in order to create a database of elements that are accessible, readable and measureable.

In the case of an image, there is no immediate link between the physical dimensions of an image (width and height in cm) and the digital dimensions that are assigned to it (number of columns and rows). Indeed, the number of pixels can vary for the same image depending on the quality and detail of processing and level of access required. The image as a *matrix* of pixels allows for the position of each pixel to be plotted. In addition to the locality of a particular pixel, information on the colour represented by each pixel becomes significant in image processing.

Quantization represents the process of assigning a value to a pixel. For colour images, a pixel will be assigned three values (generally ranging between 0–255) that provide information on the ratio of red, green and blue (or RGB) within any colour. For instance, <255, 0, 0> represents red, <0, 255, 0> represents green, <0, 0, 255> represents blue, while <255, 255, 0> represents yellow. Alternatively, values can be assigned based on hue, saturation and value (or HSV). The key advantage of HSV in comparison to RGB, is that the former comes closest to human perception of colour, meaning that two close pixel values are more likely to look and be categorised as the same colour. By contrast, RBG contains much more variation, as it distinguishes minor changes in the ratio, whereas shades of the same colour will invariably contain the same hue value, allowing the presence or absence of a colour on-screen to be identified more easily.

Moving-images can be converted and conceptualised as a sequence of images that are temporally organized. In a similar manner to the way that the number of pixels used to define a physical area depends on the desired detailed required for the *discretization* process, there is no standard for how many images are needed to represent one second of video. While 25 to 30 images per second is usually used, this will vary depending on the function and intended usage of the video-image. For example, surveillance cameras can function effectively operating at 15 images per second, or cinematic presentation can rise to 48 images per second, while videogames that sometimes needs to run at 60 images per second. Each image is termed a *frame* that can be assigned a frame number. So, in a 30 frames per second (FPS) video, frame 90 represent the frame initiating the third second of the video. Once translated in this manner, a frame can be processed as a regular image, using *matrix* and *colour* representation as described above.

Finally, the notion of a *mask image* probably requires some introduction, as all the video-based algorithms presented bellow require a *mask image* as one of their key inputs. A *mask image* describes a means of specifying a sub-area of interest in an image or a video for processing. A *mask image* represents a binary image comprised of black and white (without grey nuances). White matches the video pixel positions that the researcher wishes to take into account, while black functions to identify areas that should be disregarded.

DETECTION OF STATIC INFORMATION

The first algorithm introduced in this chapter represents the most straightforward processing technique which is also highly accurate and generic enough to be applicable at any layer of *segmentation* process. Beginning with the objective of differentiating moments of play from other experiences that games also offer as a hybrid medium, it is useful to determine experiences categorized by reduced levels of interactivity. The algorithm that has proved extremely useful for discerning player activity is derived from research that pursues the automatic detection of logos enclosed in TV-streams (Mikhail and Vatolin, 2011; dos Santos and Kim, 2006). Typically, this strand of research seeks to automatically evaluate the presence, or absence of specific TV-channel logos that are indicative of normal stream (standard logo), live transmission (modification of logo) or commercial breaks (disappearance of logo). The application of logo detection to gameplay footage extends its application to TV-streams significantly due to the high number of symbolic elements broadcast via the video stream to the player (Fagerholt, 2009; Ruch, 2010). Indeed, detecting logos in the context of game analysis can mean:

- The detection of the presence of the Head-Up Display (HUD) that is indicative of the sequence being fully interactive (walking, running, crouching, crawling, collecting, fighting etc.), while its absence typically indicates cut-scenes, menu activation.
- The detection of the appearance or disappearance of a pop-up panel, informing or warning the player about a change in the game world, for example, when a new goal is created for the player to fulfill, when an NPC is trying to communicate with the player (e.g. radio icon) or when the nature of the challenge faced by the player intensifies (enemy wave icons, Zagal, et al., 2008) or increases in levels of difficulty (e.g., timed tasks).
- The detection of cues that relate to *player choices* (e.g., skip a cut-scene) or affordances available to the player, for more effective or strategic play (e.g. loot a corpse or container, spend money). When a player opts to follow a cue, this too is often visually represented (illustrating compliance or adherence to the cues presented), for example, the presence of an audio-diary icon in *Bioshock 2* is triggered when a player opts to listen to an audio-tape.
- The detection of specific graphical or design features illustrative of a distinct space, for example, in *Bioshock 2* where a neon logo is indicative of the vending machines which are accessible to the player.

Any kind of static information on screen can indeed be abstracted as a logo including any static text or static portion of screen (typically non-diegetic information that is superimposed over the game world). This processing method can be executed using either edge or colour recognition, depending on the design of the game under evaluation. In the case of *Max Payne 3* (Rockstar Games, 2012) the game employs a semi-transparent logo that updates the player on the status of avatar health. The transparency of the logo combined with player movement permits colours from the bottom layer (game world) to alter the colour of that logo. In this instance edge detection, focusing on logo shape, is preferable to colour detection as a means of recognizing the logo.

To conduct logo detection, the algorithm employed requires the following inputs:

1. A *reference image*, sourced from a screen capture containing the desired logo of interest that matches the size of the video frame.
2. A *mask image* indicating the area in which the logo is present and should be found.
3. An *error tolerance value*, specifying how much error is tolerated during the logo detection process between the reference image and the screen image.
4. A *time tolerance value*, specifying the minimum period of time that the logo should remain on-screen.
5. A *frame step* that reduces the processing process by not requiring each individual frame to be processed, but instead every 2nd or 10th frame.

Because the algorithm is based on edge detection and comparison, the first step is to transform the input reference image from a full colour image to a binary edge representation. A mask image is then employed to erase areas outside the mask. Figure 2 illustrates these steps with *Max Payne 3* from the reference image containing the HUD (lower-right corner) though to its conversion into grey scale then edge representation. Finally, the edged version is masked to determine that only the HUD area is assessed (see figure 3).

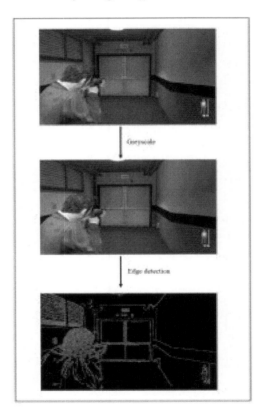

Figure 2. Image conversion to greyscale to edge detection.

Once the inputs are ready to be processed the algorithm is executed. This works in a similar fashion by automatically converting each video frame into grey scale and generating an edge image following the same process that produced the reference image. The frame and the reference image are then compared

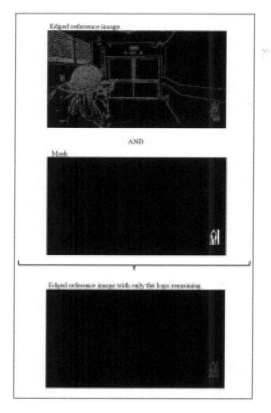

Figure 3. Achieving a masked edge image.

using a method for computing relative distance. For each white pixel (1) in the reference image, the distance between the pixel value and the matching pixel (i.e., pixel at the same position) value in the frame image is computed, resulting in a 0 if the two pixels are identical (i.e., both white), or a 1 if the two pixels fail to match. The distances are summed, and then divided by the total numbers of white pixels (1) in the reference image. The closer the result is to 0, the stronger the two images match, and the logo has been detected successfully. The relative distance is actually representative of an error value with 0 indicating no errors and 1 no match. Values between 0 and 1 represent a difference ratio. This is where the error tolerance value is employed. When the relative distance result is below the error tolerance value, the detection is accepted. If the value is above, the detection is rejected (see figure 4).

The following illustrations outline different results using a *static information detection* algorithm. Each result shown is linked to a different segmentation layer. Figure 5 illustrates the detection of the main menu of *Bioshock 2*, through the detection of the title logo. This demonstrates how the *static information detection* approach can indicate the instigation of the *game world instance* layer. This can be seen occurring in the beginning of the play session as shown in the timeline:

Figure 6 illustrates the detection of mission screens in *Battlefield 3*, using text as image and the word "mission" as a reference image. A mission-loading screen appears between each mission, signifying progression and also immediately after screen-death, reloading and sending the player back for a re-try. This result is linked to the *spatial temporal* segmentation layer. Here the timeline shows loading screens that occur as a result of level completion or as a result of screen-death (resetting the game). To distinguish between these two instances of the loading screen we would examine the results of this automatic

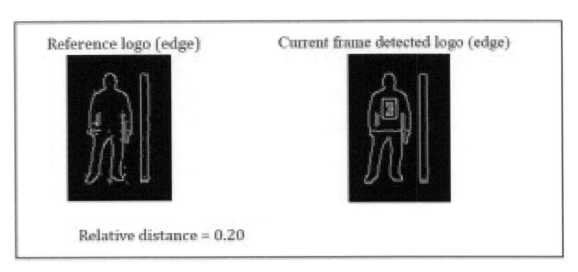

Figure 4. Relative distance result.

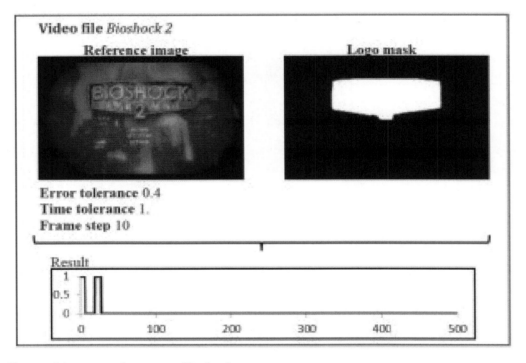

Figure 5. Main menu detection in Bioshock 2.

detection with the results of sound detection (discussed further on) to examine whether the sound indicating screen-death occurs prior to the loading screen. Its occurrence plus loading screen would indicate screen death and rule out mission completion.

Finally, figure 7 shows a moment in the game *Dead Island* (Deep Silver, 2011) when the player restores avatar health via the application of a first aid kit. Activating this process results in a first aid icon appearing in the upper-right corner of the screen. This represents feedback of player interaction. It is important to note that within the degree of freedom and the interaction layers, some static information can appear fleetingly (e.g., feedback icons, possible action cues), effecting the results of detection. For exam-

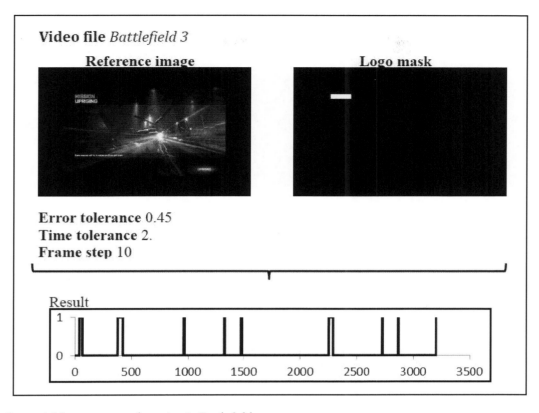

Figure 6. Mission screen detection in Battlefield 3.

ple, the detection of a logo prompting looting possibilities, discussed earlier in *Bioshock 2,* revealed how the automatic processing method missed a small number of logos when compared with a manual-coded process. These instances were missed due to a combination of the brief screen-time and because the logo colour blended with the background colour. However, such detection failures are negligible and do not compromise the overall validity of the results. The timeline demonstrates the frequency with which the player activated a health kit. Again these results will typically be contextualised with other results, such as measurement of health bar progression (discussed further on), to illustrate whether health kits are used in response to sudden health drops as the most likely outcome of intense conflict.

MOVING INFORMATION DETECTION

When an element of interest is not static or fails to appear in the same screen position, it is necessary to execute an algorithm capable of dealing with the localization and detection of objects that change position on screen. Here, a strand of research termed *image registration* (Pratt, 1978, chapter 19; Fitzpatrick, Hill and Maurer, Jr., 2000, chapter 8) can be employed. This research executes algorithms that are efficient in identifying commonalities between two images thus highlighting how they relate to each other. Thus, a smaller object can be located with a larger image when its position is not guaranteed. One method employed within this strand of research is *cross-correlation* (Pratt, 1978, p.553; Fitzpatrick, et al., 2000, p.489; Dos Santos, et al., 2006). This works by taking a *discretized* image, and scanning the reference image over each section of the larger image to seek a match. For each scanned position a correlation value is calculated (using a cross-correlation formula) with a value of 1 representing a perfect match.

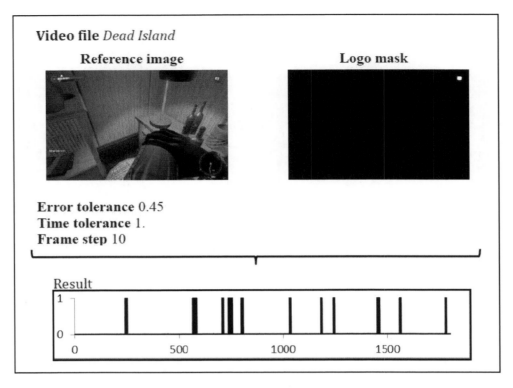

Figure 7. First aid kit used in Dead Island.

To execute detection of a non-static object, the algorithm employed requires the following inputs:

1. An *object reference*, representing the object that will be cross-correlated.
2. A *mask image* can be used to restrict the search area for an object in cases where the object only occupies a smaller area on screen. If no *mask image* is specified then the whole screen is scanned.
3. Once the scanned image locates likely matches, then an *error tolerance value*, will be employed to determine whether the object identified is a correct match.
4. A *time tolerance value*, specifying the minimum period of time that the object should appear on-screen.
5. A *frame step* that reduces the processing process by not requiring each individual frame to be processed, but instead every 2nd or 10th frame.

The algorithm functions similarly to the static object algorithm outlined above with the addition of several processing functions that account for the challenges of having to locate an object (or several objects) that may be repositioning. Once the object image has been converted into a binary edge representation it is shifted sequentially through every possible position over the video frame (beginning in the upper left corner of the frame and ending in the bottom right corner).

The correlation process (as shown in figure 8) illustrates the process of locating a "cross" logo that appears in the game *Battlefield* 3 and functions to indicate the positions of enemies at a distance (enemies that are also hidden behind objects). The cross logo has been sequentially shifted across the image, in doing so, correlation scores have been generated and stored in the image matrix (the whiter the pixel, the better the correlation score). Figure 8 shows an instance which display two perfect correlations in the upper right hand corner. These logos inform the research about the nature of the space (the player is in an environment where enemies are present), it informs the researcher as to the number of enemies (number of logos) and also provides information on the player's reaction (i.e., if the logo is in the centre of the image, then the player is typically attempting to aim at those enemies).

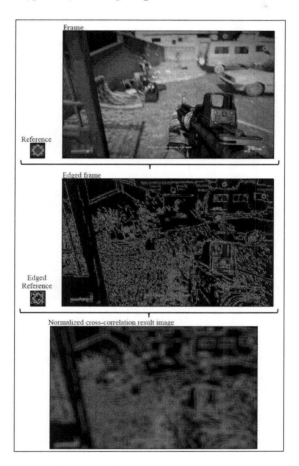

Figure 8. Cross correlation image.

As the above example demonstrates, several identical logos can be present on the same frame. In order to be able to achieve multiple detections, once an object has been detected for the first time, the correlation value of that position (where the object was detected) is reset to 0 in order to be able to repeat the process and initiate a new detection cycle (discounting objects that have already been found). The process is repeated until the logo detection algorithm is no longer able to locate the desired object. At the end of the process the results will convey the number of objects found and their position (in this case 1585, 121 and 1267, 21). Figure 9 illustrates this process.

Figure 10 illustrates the result of the example discussed above (from *Battlefield 3*) in which the logo representing enemy position can appear anywhere on-screen. The graphs included in figure 10 demonstrate the value of the logo position for the player. While the top graph demonstrates the appearance of logos on-screen, the lower graph indicates how the player has then responded to this information by adjusting their position, thus centring the logo position on-screen presumably to take aim and fire at the enemy (an action that can be further confirmed by keystroke measurement).

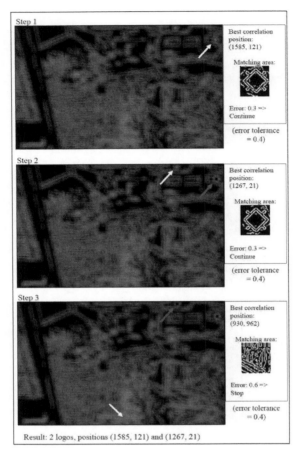

Figure 9. Multi logo detection on real example.

BAR PROGRESSION ASSESSMENT

The detection algorithms employed on graphical information presented thus far essentially produce discrete values, that is, being able to say whether a logo is detected or not and how many logos are detected and where. The information presented to the researcher utilizing these methods is therefore limited to information that confirms an action or presents the player with information that can cue behaviours (e.g., looting). However, there are other forms of information that are constantly present on-screen (whilst in play) that provide continuous updates on player's standing in the game, for example, health, power or stamina bars. *Bar progression assessment* addresses these informational sources that present continuous data. That is, a value can increase or decrease between minimum and maximum values. Such information allows the player to adapt their strategy appropriately in response to the current standing of their avatar. In the game *Dead Island*, for instance, a low health reading during a fight may trigger a desire in the player to run away, however, if stamina the levels required for running are low this may not be possible.

In order to execute an assessment of continuous values a *colour ratio algorithm* is employed. In this instance, a *colour ratio algorithm* is used to summarize and visualize the constant movement of a bar progression throughout play. Such a result can then be analysed to pinpoint moments in which key attributes related to avatar performance such as health or stamina drop. Conversely, when a player's standing increases suddenly, for instance when health is fully replenished after discovering a health kit.

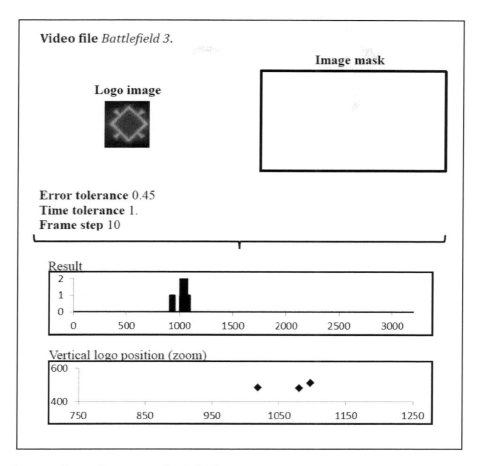

Figure 10. Enemy locations in Battlefield 3.

Bar progression activity serves as a key signifier of the intensity of action, as increases or decreases tend to occur in active moments that stand in contrast to more passive moments during gameplay where bar progression does not fluctuate so drastically. Such information is nearly impossible to extract accurately when done manually, due to its continuous nature.

A *colour ratio algorithm* functions to study each pixel colour in a given area (utilizing a mask image to pinpoint bar location and shape) comparing the background or vessel pixel colour with pixel colour that is employed to signify progression. The ratio between matching pixels and the maximum number of pixels in the area is calculated, with 1 representative of all the pixels matching the colour being searched, 0 in the case of no match. For this algorithm, the method of representation used for colour detection is HSV (rather than RBG). As discussed earlier in the chapter, HSV domain value is able to compensate for levels of transparency when a HUD overlays the game world. The required inputs to execute a colour ratio algorithm for a bar progression analysis are:

1. A *mask image* indicating the bar position, or at least a meaningful portion of it.
2. A *reference colour image* containing the colour (or colours) utilised in the bar to be processed.
3. The *tolerance values* for Hue, Saturation and Value of the colour domain that controls how much a pixel value can divert from the colour of interest and still be considered a match.
4. A frame step.

The algorithm functions by processing the reference colour image by extracting the HSV values from each pixel. Then, the number of white pixels in the mask image is calculated to represent the number of pixels indicative of the size and range of the bar (maximum number of pixels). For each video frame, the area defined by the mask is considered. Each pixel included in the bar is first converted into its HSV values, before comparing those to the reference colour. If the differences are lower than the tolerance values stipulated then the pixel is considered a match. A result of 1 is returned for a full bar, 0 for an empty bar with intermediate results between 0 and 1 indicating how full or empty the bar is at any given point. Figure 11 illustrates the application of the *colour ratio algorithm* to a gameplay frame taken from the game *Dead Island*. In this example, the health bar is processed. The figure shows how the bar is extracted from the frame using the mask image. When the ratio between the matched pixels and the total number of bar pixels was computed the frame revealed that 65% of the bar is complete. Figure 12 extends this example, to include the variance and changes in a health bar over a period of 30 minutes. As discussed, there are a number of moments in which health drops orrises dramatically amongst more stable moments. It is interesting to note that we can combine the output from the colour ratio algorithm with the findings shown for static logo detection (illustrated in figure 7), that displays the presence or absence of the health kit logo (indicating its use). We can therefore confirm whether health restoration is the result of a player acquiring a health kit.

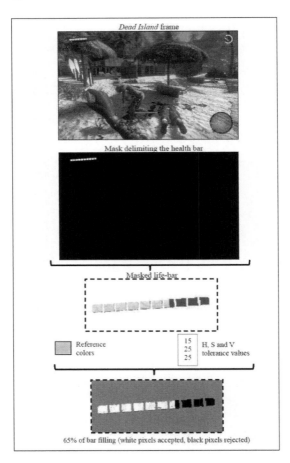

Figure 11. Life bar progression assessment in Dead Island.

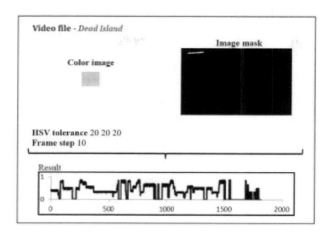

Figure 12. Health processed in Dead Island through life bar analysis.

SOUND

We would like to conclude this outline of feedback-based gameplay metrics with an example of the value of sound and how it is processed. The algorithm introduced in this final section of the chapter utilises *sound correlation* (Roads, 1996, p.509; Yarlagadda, 2010, chapter 2) techniques to identify key and significant sounds enclosed within the multi-layered audio-stream of the *gameplay performance* footage. The sonic atmosphere of most videogames carries a considerable amount of information. Some sounds extend beyond the graphic information directly presented to the player as objects in the diegetic world of the game can generate sounds even when out of the player sight. Furthermore, most of the graphical elements experienced within games are also paired with audio feedback that confirms actions. For example, a loss of health is accompanied by avatar screams in *Bioshock 2*, the use of slow motion in *Max Payne 3* possesses its own sound motif and even the most basic functions such as menu activation is also accompanied by specific sounds (e.g., *Dead Island*).

Similar to *cross-correlation* for image processing, a *sound cross-correlation* approach is employed to identify specific sounds within a multi-layered soundtrack. A similarity score is calculated to indicate when a comparison is located for a particular sound within a larger soundtrack. Again, the higher the score, the more likely the two segments are a match. The required inputs to execute a cross correlation for sound processing are:

1. A *reference sound* file representing the sound to find. This can be extracted either from footage taken from the game, selecting a clear articulation of the sound desired, or alternatively, the game can be played with soundtrack off in order to be able to go back and extract specific sounds using a sound editing application.
2. A *threshold value* is used in order to determine that only highest values are identified, for example, above 0.5.

The algorithm works by scanning the reference sound over the soundtrack, and comparing their amplitude (i.e., visualisation as a sound wave). For each scanned position a cross-correlation value is then generated. The closer the results are to 1, the better the match. Figure 13 demonstrates an example of the use of a sound cross-correlation using a 35-second extract from the game *Battlefield 3* in which the sound that accompanies screen-death is searched for. The figure shows how the correlation curve reaches its maximum at around 15 seconds. A time stamp is generated at the point of the highest value (above a provided threshold).

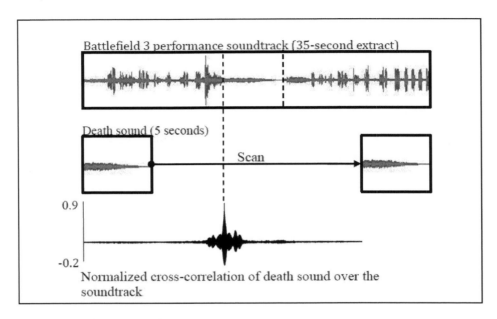

Figure 13. Sound cross-correlation.

Figure 14, illustrates the results of the process discussed above across a full session of gameplay. In this result we can see that the player died five times during the session. The validity of this result that can be confirmed by the detection of the loading screen that appears once a player dies as the game reloads (see figure 6).

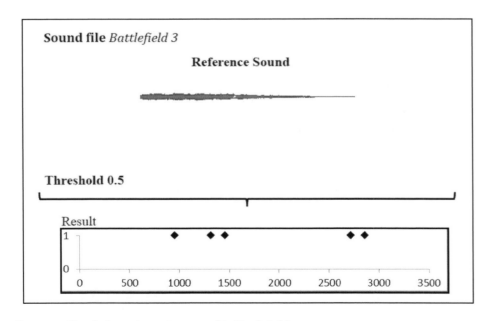

Figure 14. Death detection using sound in Battlefield 3.

Summary

This chapter has introduced a novel approach for the generation of game metrics that exploits the audio and visual feedback experienced by the player during play. Whilst it may appear a cumbersome method at this stage of its development, the application of algorithms are combined and tailored to the specific visual and sound design of the game under examination providing flexibility in its application. The method also has the advantage of allowing game researchers to accurately process footage from any PC-based game, reducing the demands and error associated with a manual analysis and permitting an examination of gameplay across a sample of players. Underpinning this method is also a framework for the segmentation and analysis of a gameplay performance to which the specific tools of the method can be contextualized and the value of specific informational sources can be assessed in relation to player experience. For an example of the application of this method readers are pointed to Schott, et al.'s (2013) use of the method in order to process play with *Max Payne 3* and assess the game's use of slow motion in terms of its impact on player experience. This research assessed whether the use of slow motion functions to glorify or aestheticize violence, or works strategically as part of the degrees of freedom afforded players.

This chapter has served to outline just a small number of examples of the algorithms that can be appropriated and adapted from computer sciences in order to automatically detect key graphical and sound streams in games. All the examples provided function with a high degree of accuracy, and contribute to the construction of an automatically generated summary of a play performance. Such summaries can then be employed in an interpretation of a player's experience of play from a behavioral perspective. The algorithms represent a straightforward method in terms of implementation, providing meaningful results that can contribute to the wider endeavors of player experience research.

References

2K Marin, 2010. *Bioshock 2* [game]. Microsoft Windows. 2K Games.

Aarseth, E., 2007. I Fought the Law: Transgressive play and the implied player. In: *Proceedings of DiGRA 2007: Situated Play*. Tokyo. September. pp.130–133.

Bay, H., Ess, A., Tuytelaars, T., and van Gool, L., 2008. SURF: Speeded up robust features. *Computer Vision and Image Understanding (CVIU)*, 110(3), pp.346–359.

Calleja, G., 2011. *In-game: From immersion to incorporation*. Cambridge: The MIT Press.

Chen, D. and Bourlard, H., 2001. Video OCR for sport video annotation and retrieval. In: *Proceedings of the 8th International Conference on Mechatronics and Machine Vision in Practice*. pp.57–62.

Choi, F.Y.Y., 2000. Advances in domain independent linear text segmentation. In: *NAACL 2000 Proceedings of the 1st North American chapter of the Association for Computational Linguistics conference*. pp.26–33.

Drachen, A. and Canossa, A., 2008. Defining personas in games using metrics. In: *Proceedings of the 2008 Conference on Future Play: Research, Play, Share*, New York: ACM, pp.73–80. DOI=10.1145/1496984.1496997.

Drachen, A., Seif El-Nasr, M. and Canossa, A., 2013. Game analytics—The basics. In: M.Seif El-Nasr et al., eds., *Game analytics*. London: Springer, pp.13–40.

Electronic Arts, 2011. *Battlefield 3* [game]. Microsoft Windows. PUBLISHER.

Erik de Castro Lopo, 2011. *libsndfile*. V1.0.25 [computer program]. Availabe at: <https://github.com/erikd/libsndfile/>.

Fagerholt, E. and Lorentzon, M., 2009. *Beyond the HUD: User interfaces for increased player immersion in FPS Games*. MS. Chalmers University of Technology. Available at <http://publications.lib.chalmers.se/records/fulltext/111921.pdf>.

Fitzpatrick, J.M., Hill, D.L.G. and Maurer, Jr., C.R., 2000. *Handbook of medical imaging*. Bellingham: SPIE PRESS.

Gonzales, R.C. and Woods, R.E., 2007. *Digital image processing*. 3rd ed. New Jersey: Prentice Hall.

Hilbert, D. M. and Redmiles, D.F., 2000. Extracting usability information from user interface events. *ACM Computing Surveys (CSUR)*, 32(4), pp.384–421. DOI=10.1145/371578.371593.

Huang, C.-L. and Liao, B.-Y., 2001. A robust scene-change detection method for video segmentation. *IEEE Transactions on Circuits and Systems for Video Technology*, 11(12), pp.1281–1288.

Intel Corporation, Willow Garage and Itseez, 2014. *OpenCV*. V2.4.9 [computer program]. Available at: <http://opencv.org/>.

Klevjer, R., 2002. In Defense of cutscenes. In: F. Mäyrä, ed., *Proceedings of computer games and digital cultures conference*. Tampere: Tampere University Press, pp.191–202.

Laurel, B., 1993. *Computers as theatre*. Reading: Addison-Wesley.

Mikhail, E. and Vatolin, D., 2011. Automatic logo removal for semitransparent and animated logos. In: *Proceedings of GraphiCon 2011*. Moscow. September 26–30. GraphicCon.

Nacke, L. E., Drachen, A., Kuikkaniemi, K., Niesenhaus, J., Korhonen, H.J., Hoogen, V.D.W., Poels, K., IJsselsteijn, W. and Kort, Y. 2009. *Playability and player experience research*. London, September. Available at: < http://www.digra.org/wp-content/uploads/digital-library/09287.44170.pdf >.

Orio, N. 2006. Music retrieval: A tutorial and review. *Foundations and Trends in Information Retrieval*, 1(1), pp.1–90.

Pedersen, C., Togelius, J. and Yannakakis, G.N., 2010. Modeling player experience for content creation. *IEEE Transactions on Computational Intelligence and AI in Games*, 2(1), pp.54–67. DOI=10.1109/TCIAIG.2010.2043950.

Pratt, W.K., 1978. *Digital image processing*. New York: Wiley-Interscience Publication.

Richard, G., Ramona, M. and Essid, S., 2007. Combined supervised and unsupervised approaches for automatic segmentation of radiophonic audio streams. In: *Proceedings – ICASSP*. PLACE. DATE, pp.461–464.

Roads, C., 1996. *The computer music tutorial*. Cambridge: MIT Press.

Ruch, A.W., 2010. Videogame interface: Artefacts and tropes. In: *Videogame Cultures and the Future of Interactive Entertainment Global Conference*. Oxford. DATE.

Santos, A.R. and Kim, H.Y., 2006. Real-time opaque and semi-transparent TV logos detection. In: *Proceedings of the 5th International Information and Telecommunication Technologies Symposium (I2TS)*.

Rockstar Studios, 2012. *Max Payne 3* [game]. Microsoft Windows. Rockstar Games.

Saraceno, C. and Leonardi, R., 1997. Audio as a support to scene change detection and characterization of video sequences. In: *Proceedings of 1997 IEEE international conference on acoustics, speech, and signal processing*. IEEE, pp.2597–2600.

Sasse, D., 2008. *A framework for psychophysiological data acquisition in digital games*. MS. Otto-von-Guericke-University Magdeburg. Available at: <http://www.gamecareerguide.com/thesis/080520_sasse.pdf>.

Schott, G., Vught, J.V. and Marczak, R., 2012. The "dominant effect" of games: content vs. medium. *CoLab: Journal of Creative Technologies*, Available at: <https://colab.aut.ac.nz/journal/the-dominant-effect-of-games-content-vs-medium/>.

Schott, G., Marczak, R., Mäyrä, F. and Vught, J., 2013. DeFragging regulation: From putative effects to 'researched' accounts of player experience. In: *Proceedings of DiGRA 2013: Defragging game studies*. Atlanta, Georgia. August. Available at: <http://www.digra.org/wp-content/uploads/digital-library/paper_29.pdf>.

Techland, 2011. *Dead Island* [game]. Microsoft Windows. Deep Silver.

Vught, J.V., Schott, G. and Marczak, R. 2012. Age-restriction: Re-examining the interactive experience of "harmful" game content. In: Nordic DiGRA. Tampere: June. Available at: <http://www.digra.org/wp-content/uploads/digital-library/12168.32309.pdf>.

Waern, A., 2012. Framing games. In: *Proceedings of Nordic DiGRA 2012*. Tampere. June. Available at: <http://www.digra.org/wp-content/uploads/digital-library/12168.20295.pdf>.

Yarlagadda, R.K.R., 2010. *Analog and digital signals and systems*. London: Springer.

Ye, Q., Huang, Q., Jiang, S., Liu, Y. and Gao, W., 2006. Jersey number detection in sports video for athlete identification. In *Proc. SPIE 5960, Visual Communications and Image Processing*. International Society for Optics and Photonics, pp.59604P-59604P.

Yeh, C.-H., Kuo, C.-H. and Liou, R.-W., 2009. Movie story intensity representation through audio-visual tempo analysis. *Multimedia Tools and Applications*, 44(2), pp.205–228. DOI=10.1007/s11042-009-0278-8

Zagal, J. P., Fernandez-Vara, C. and Mateas, M., 2008. Rounds, levels, and waves: The early evolution of gameplay segmentation. *Games and Culture*, 3(2), pp.175–198.

Zagal, J.P., Mateas, M., Fernández-Vara, C., Hochhalter, B., and Lichti, N., 2005. *Towards an ontological language for game analysis*. In: Proceeding of DiGRA 2005 Conference. Vacouver. June. Available at: <http://www.digra.org/dl/db/06276.09313.pdf>.

14. An Introduction to Gameplay Data Visualization

GÜNTER WALLNER AND SIMONE KRIGLSTEIN

The prevalence of internet-enabled gaming devices enables game developers nowadays to remotely and unobtrusively monitor every aspect of a game, allowing them to accumulate large amounts of data of the player-game interaction over extended time periods. This data has become a viable source for developers to guide decision-making throughout the game design process and even after the game has been released, for example, to identify balancing issues (Kim, et al., 2008; Zoeller, 2010), to understand player movement (Moura, El-Nasr and Shaw, 2011), to reduce production costs (Hullett, et al., 2011), or to uncover bugs (Zoeller, 2010), to name but a few. At the same time, the increasing popularity of online multiplayer gaming has attached great importance to in-game statistics to allow players to recap their performance and to compare it with others. This growing interest in game telemetry data is reflected by the emergence of the new field of game analytics—concerned with the discovery and communication of meaningful patterns in data as applied in the context of game development and game research (cf. El-Nasr, Drachen and Canossa, 2013). Game analytics heavily relies on visualization techniques to assist developers and players alike to understand, analyze, and explore the data (cf. Wallner and Kriglstein, 2013). Visualizations in game research can be helpful to discover unexpected paths which have been taken by the players, to identify possible design and balancing problems, or to find common patterns in the behavior of the players. Moreover, since the rich interaction possibilities provided by a game can give rise to emergent behavior which is hard to anticipate, visualizations can assist in exploratory data analysis helping the analyst to discover potentially interesting structures, trends, and anomalies not thought of beforehand.

Game Analytics

Analytics, in a broad sense, is the process of identifying and communicating meaningful patterns to inform decision-making. Analytics is multidisciplinary in its approach, encompassing fields such as statistics, artificial intelligence or machine learning. *Game analytics* can thus be understood as *the application of analytics to game development and research* (El-Nasr, Drachen and Canossa, 2013, p.5). From a technological point of view, the widespread availability of internet-enabled gaming devices can be seen as an important factor for the increased applicability of game analytics because it enables developers to remotely collect large amounts of game data, so called *game telemetry data*. Telemetry data as a source for game analytics can provide valuable information for various areas of game development, like game design, marketing and business, or programming. For example, it can be used to analyze how players play the game, to identify bugs in the game, or to monitor downloadable content or in-game purchases.

However, since the number of information which can be tracked via telemetry is enormous, the resulting data volumes can become very large and complex. For example, Zoeller (2010) mentioned that they recorded 250GB of data from *Dragon Age: Origins* (BioWare, 2009) and Williams, Yee and Caplan (2008) were confronted with 60TB of logged data from *Everquest 2* (Sony Online Entertainment, 2004). Beside data volumes, other factors, like bandwidth and latency also have to be taken into consideration. For example, Marselas (2000) noted that during test sessions for *Age of Empires II* (Ensemble Studios, 1999) more powerful computers were necessary to compensate for performance issues caused by unoptimized code and the enabled logging functions.

Because of the large data volumes involved, game analytics also heavily makes use of data visualizations to make sense of the data and to support exploratory data analysis. However, for a visualization to be effective it has to be appropriate for the specific tasks and goals of the user. In the remainder of this chapter we will discuss different types of visualizations and their applications to gameplay analysis. An in-depth description and discussion of game analytics and game telemetry itself can be found in the book by El-Nasr, Drachen and Canossa (2013).

Visualization

Visualizations are visual representations of data to perceive, use, and communicate information (cf. Andrienko and Andrienko, 2005; Card, Mackinlay and Shneiderman, 1999; McCormick, DeFanti and Brown, 1987; Ware, 2004). In many cases, it is often easier to use the visual representation than the textual or spoken representations, because visualizations can amplify human cognition and hence can help, for example, to represent, simplify as well as organize large amounts of information in a quickly accessible form (cf. Card, Mackinlay and Shneiderman, 1999). As a *valuable assistance for data analysis and decision making tasks* (Tory and Möller, 2004, p.1), visualizations support users to explore and learn more about the data and can help them to make new discoveries, to gain insights and build valuable knowledge that they were not aware of before (e.g., to detect patterns, anomalies or dependencies between data) (cf. Andrienko and Andrienko, 2005; Fekete, et al., 2008; van Wijk, 2005). Visualizations are also useful for quality control of the data itself and about the way how the data is collected, because visualizations make problems immediately visible (Ware, 2004).

In context of gameplay data analysis, the interest to use and develop visualization techniques increased in the last years among industry professionals and researchers. Visual representations of gameplay can support game developers and designers to analyze recorded player behavior to, for example, identify interaction or design problems or to understand the effects of design decisions (see, e.g., Moura, El-Nasr and Shaw, 2011). Medler, John and Lane (2011), for instance, developed a visual game analytics tool—called *Data Cracker*—to support game developers to monitor the behavior of players for the game *Dead Space 2* (Visceral Games, 2011). Another example is the visual analytics tool *SkyNet* (Zoeller, 2010) from game developer *BioWare*. *SkyNet* makes use of different visualization methods (e.g., charts) to not only support the analysis of the recorded in-game data for the purpose of improving the player experience but also to track bugs that have been found (Medler and Magerko, 2011).

However, game developers are not the only target group that can benefit from visualizations of in-game data. For example, in recent years a tendency to offer visualizations to players themselves could be observed. Visualizations can help players to analyze their personal gaming history or to compare their play behavior with other players. For example, the work of Medler (2012) gives an extensive analysis of different games that provide game-related data to players. Especially for multiplayer games, visualizations of gameplay data can be from interest for the players to help them to optimize their strategies or to improve their teamwork.

Visualization Techniques in Game Analytics

In this section we will discuss some of the most widely used visualizations in gameplay analytics, in particular: charts, heatmaps, movement visualizations, and node-link representations. For each visualization type we will give a short general description and discuss a range of examples—drawn from the literature—to give an overview of how the different visualizations can be used in the context of gameplay analysis.

CHARTS

Charts are pictorial representations of information. Charts exist in a variety of forms, like bar charts, pie charts, or scatter plots to name but a few with each of them having different advantages and disadvantages. Due to space limitations we will not cover all different forms of charts and their strengths and weaknesses in detail but instead refer to works such as Kosslyn (2006), Wainer (1984), and Macdonald-Ross (1977).

Charts can be used, among other things, to show the relationships between variables, to convey relative proportions, to show the distribution of values, or to visualize trends over time. Due to the large amount of different types of charts available and their versatility they are also widely used for visualizing gameplay related data. In the following we will shortly review works from industry and academia to give the reader an impression for what purposes different charts can be used with respect to gameplay analysis.

To begin with, bar charts are, for instance, appropriate if the size of different categories should be compared. For example, DeRosa (2007) used bar charts to visualize how much time players of *Mass Effect* (BioWare, 2007) spent on different activities, like character creation or optional mini-games. Charts can also be used to visualize data at different levels of detail. As an example, Kim, et al. (2008) used bar-charts to plot the average number of deaths players experienced in a mission to get a high-level overview of player performance in *Halo 2* (Bungie, 2004). By breaking down each mission into several smaller encounters and again plotting the average number of deaths per encounter, a more detailed view on the data was obtained in order to better isolate difficult areas of a mission.

Dankoff (2014) plotted money earned against money spent over time using a line chart in order to validate if the economic system in *Assassins Creed Brotherhood* (Ubisoft Montreal, 2010) was well balanced or not. Schoenblum (2010) used line charts to depict how often the different game modes of *Gears of War 2* (Epic Games, 2008) are played in order to see trends over time. Chong (2011) in turn used line charts to visualize player drop-off rates per level. Steep drop-off rates indicate some sort of problem, for instance, in the level design, which causes a high number of players to stop playing at that point. However, identifying the cause is not always straightforward. To get a sense what could be the source of the problem it can be helpful to relate the drop-off rate with other variables. Chong (2011) therefore also plotted the number of deaths per level in addition to the drop-off rate and could see—in his particular case—that the dropout could be caused due to some levels being too difficult. Hazan (2013), on the other hand, related the drop-off rate with the number of save-game loads to gauge the difficulty of levels.

Phillips (2010) used a scatter plot to show the relationship between the percentage of players getting an achievement in a game and the average time it took players to obtain it. Each dot in the scatter plot therefore represents a specific achievement, helping the designers to get a sense of player progression.

Lewis and Wardrip-Fruin (2010) used so-called box-and-whisker plots to depict how long it takes to level characters of different classes from level 1 to level 80 in *World of Warcraft* (Blizzard Entertainment, 2004) to see if the leveling times of classes are balanced or not. Box-and-whisker plots are useful for large data sets as they do not show the actual data values but rather certain summary statistics. In particular, the median, the first and third quartiles, and usually (but not necessarily) the minimum and maximum values. Box-and-whisker plots therefore provide a way to graphically compare these descriptive statistics among two or more variables. Lewis and Wardrip-Fruin (2010) also used box-and-whisker plots to depict the number of deaths of the different classes on the way toward level 80.

Charts can also be used in conjunction with other visualizations. For example, Moura, El-Nasr and Shaw (2011) used multiple views to display different bar charts, corresponding to different metrics (e.g., time spent in an area, time spent talking to non-player characters) next to a map of the game environment. Labels were used to show the connection between an area on the map and the associated bar in the chart. In addition, color was used to distinguish between different metrics. As a further example, Kriglstein, Wallner and Pohl (2014) used pie-charts superimposed over an aerial map of the game environment to convey the percentage distribution of different variables in certain regions of the map. This way the charts are directly placed at the source of the data. Figure 1, for example, uses such a visualization to depict which types of towers have been built at different building lots in a tower defense game (cf. Kayali, et al., 2014).

Heatmaps are two-dimensional maps which use colors to indicate the frequency of occurrence of a variable across the map (e.g., number of mouse-clicks superimposed over a website). Mostly a temperature color gradient, going from shades of blue (low rates of occurrence) to shades of red (high levels of occurrence), is used. Heatmaps have the advantages that they are easy to create, well-suited to recognize patterns of behavior, and that they provide a good overview of the relative data densities in a single image. However, heatmaps also have the disadvantage *to smooth over differences in individual behaviors* (Nielsen and Pernice, 2010, p.12). Results of a recent user study (Kriglstein, Wallner and Pohl, 2014) also suggest that the continuous color representation makes it difficult to judge the actual amounts and to compare areas of similar density. As heatmaps are often created from a top-down perspective, they can also lead to incorrect or false impressions if used for 3D games with multi-level architectural environments.

HEATMAPS

With respect to games, perhaps the most prominent use of heatmaps is to depict player deaths in first and third person shooters. To give a few examples: Valve Corporation (2006) published aggregated death maps of *Half-Life 2: Episode Two* (Valve Corporation, 2007a) based on data collected during a 12-month period. Valve Corporation (2012a) also released a heatmap showing firing locations of bullets based on data from beta-testers of *Counter Strike: Global Offensive* (Valve Corporation, 2012b). The

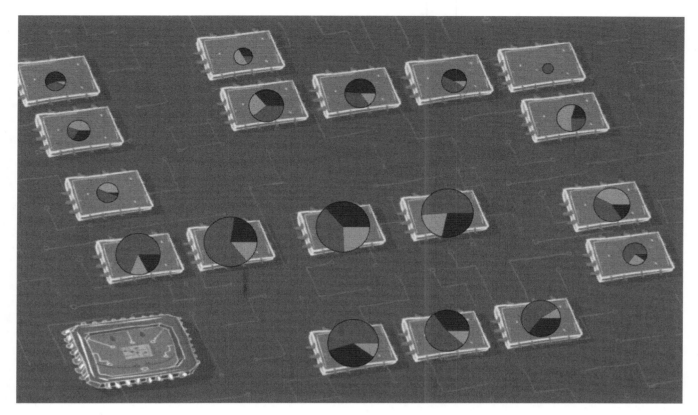

Figure 1. Pie-charts show which types of towers have been built on the different building lots. The radius of the pie-chart is proportional to the number of towers built (Kayali, et al., 2014).

heatmap can be filtered based on team and weapon type. Dankoff (2014) published a heatmap showing locations where playtesters of *Assassin's Creed Brotherhood* have failed.

Figure 2 shows a heatmap of death locations based on data from 16 matches played on the *Team Fortress 2* (Valve Corporation, 2007b) map *Goldrush*. The most lethal area for this particular dataset is located on the lower right corner of the map, where players have to pass through a narrow tunnel. Figure 3 shows a heatmap depicting where players of a tower defense game—part of an educational game called *Internet Hero* (University of Vienna, 2013; Kayali, et al., 2014)—collected coins that are dropped by defeated enemies. In both cases a temperature gradient has been used.

However, heatmaps cannot only be used to visualize aggregated data from huge data sets but can also be used to provide players with individualized visual feedback for the purpose of post-gameplay analysis. For example, the recently discontinued *Call of Duty: Elite* service—an online service for the *Call of Duty* franchise—allowed players to view heatmaps of their own recent matches (cf. Shamoon, 2012).

While heatmaps have traditionally been used to visualize the spatial distribution of a single variable, extensions to include further information have since been proposed. Drachen and Canossa (2009), by the way of example, superimposed multiple heatmaps, each one using a different color gradient and corresponding to a different cause of death (e.g., death by falling, death by drowning). Houghton (2011) combined two heatmaps, one based on the locations of the victims and one based on the locations of the killers, by subtracting the values of the death heatmap from the values of the kill heatmap. By using

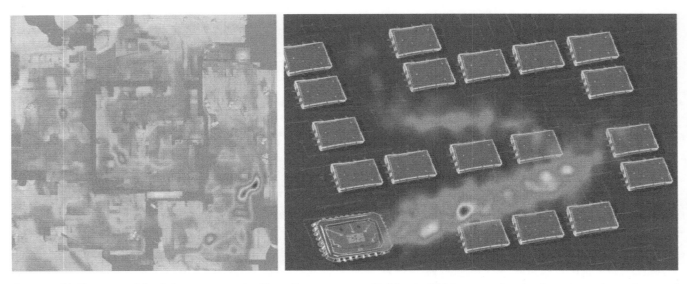

Figure 2. (a) Heatmap of death locations on the Team Fortress 2 map Goldrush. (b) Heatmap showing locations where players of a tower defense game collected coins dropped by defeated enemies (Kayali, et al., 2014).

a different color for positive values and for negative values, the resulting heatmap gives a good overview about highly lethal areas and effective killing spots in a single image. This concept is illustrated in figure 3 with data from the *Team Fortress 2 Goldrush* example presented earlier. Figure 3(left) shows the kill heatmap of the bottom right corner of figure 2 using a blue gradient and figure 3(middle) shows the death heatmap using a red gradient. Subtracting (middle) from (left) yields the heatmap shown in figure 3(right).

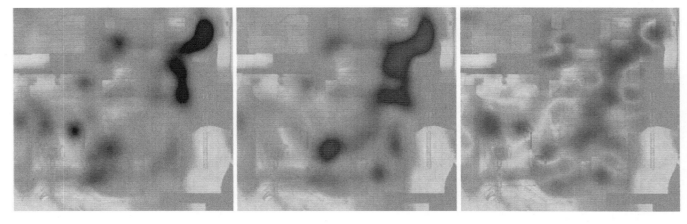

Figure 3. Two heatmaps can be combined into a single heatmap (right) by subtracting the values of one heatmap (middle) from the values of the other heatmap (left). (Based on Houghton, 2011)

As pointed out above, one of the biggest limitations of heatmaps for analyzing 3D games may be the loss of information when projecting the 3D data onto a two-dimensional plane. For example, if a building in a shooter game consists of multiple floors the flattened data may provide a false impression on how lethal the individual floors actually are. Therefore, extensions to 3D have been recently proposed. For example, the *GameAnalytics SDK* (GameAnalytics, 2013) provides the possibility to visualize 3D heatmaps directly in the scene view of the *Unity 3D Game Engine* (Unity Technologies, 2014). Not directly related to games, but still relevant in this context—particularly in view of new input devices like the *Oculus Rift* virtual reality headset—is the work of Pfeiffer (2010; 2012) on visual attention in 3D spaces. Pfeiffer proposed on extension of 2D attention heatmaps to 3D, called 3D attention volumes which model the 3D points of interest as a Gaussian distribution in space using volume-based rendering techniques.

MOVEMENT VISUALIZATIONS

Many games require the player to navigate a character (or multiple characters) through the game's environment. Understanding how players actually move around in a game can thus provide valuable information for level design. Especially if players behave differently than expected, it is from interest to find out what is actually happening. To track player movements it is necessary to record at least their position at regular time intervals. In addition, further variables like orientation or player health can be logged as well in order to provide contextual information. However, tracking the movement of a greater number of players can quickly lead to large data volumes. Visualizations can therefore be helpful to analyze and extract meaningful information from the accumulated data. For example, visualizations of player movement can be helpful to spot unintended paths taken by players (see Dankoff, 2014).

On a most basic level, sampled player locations can be represented as point clouds. Although such a representation does not provide information on how the data points are connected it still can offer valuable insights. For instance, Thompson (2007) describes an example from *Halo 3* (Bungie, 2007) where colored dots have been used to visualize player positions, sampled at five-second intervals, with the coloring reflecting the time-stamp when the position was recorded. In an early version of a map these colored points were scattered randomly across the map, indicating that people were wandering around aimlessly. Based on this information the designers changed the design of the map to hinder players from backtracking.

Another possibility to visualize player paths is to connect the tracked positions with straight line segments. Visual properties like color or size can be used to augment the paths with contextual information. Color, for instance, can be used to reflect a wide variety of parameters. To give a few examples: For a case study concerned with spatial analysis of player behavior in the third-person shooter *Kane & Lynch 2* (IO Interactive, 2010), Drachen and Canossa (2011) used color-coding to reflect the health of the player. Kang, et al. (2013) proposed a technique to automatically extract behavioral meaning (e.g., combat or social behavior) from trajectory data of *World of Warcraft* (Blizzard Entertainment, 2004) players. To visualize the results color-coding has been used to color the trajectories according to the identified behavior. This way, game developers are, for example, able to compare the actual player behavior with the expected behavior in certain areas of a map. Dixit and Youngblood (2008) utilized color-cycling to represent the flow of time, allowing the analyst to infer the direction of movement.

Figure 4 shows three examples of how path visualizations can be coupled with color-coding to augment the spatial data with additional data obtained from different data sources (from top to bottom: survey data, in-game data, and physiological measurements). The data for these examples was obtained by instrumenting the source code of *Infinite Mario* (Persson, 2008), a public domain clone of the classic 2D platform game *Super Mario Bros.* (Nintendo, 1985). In all three examples, coins scattered throughout the levels are depicted by yellow circles whose size reflect how often they have been collected by players. The top image couples the movement data of players with their expertise, which participants had to rate on a scale from 1 (beginner) to 5 (expert) prior to playing, with turquoise = 1, blue = 2, purple =

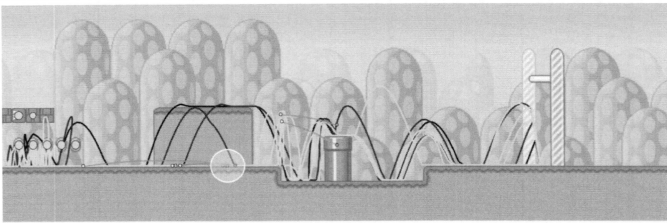

Figure 4. Examples of path visualizations coupled with color-coding to communicate additional information. Top: color coding reflects the reported expertise of players obtained through a pre-game survey. Middle: colors depict the state in which the player's character currently resides in. Bottom: the color-gradient reflects physiological data measured in the form of galvanic skin response (Mirza-Babaei, et al., 2014).

3 and red = 4. This can provide insights if players of varying levels of expertise behave differently in a game. In this particular instance, a player who considered himself almost an expert player (the red path) was not concerned about collecting coins but rather was constantly running—evident by the distance of jumps—whereas players with lower expertise were keen on collecting lots of coins. The middle

image uses color coding to reflect the state of Mario, the player-character, which can take on three different forms: normal Mario (black), Super Mario (blue) or Fire Mario (yellow)—allowing Mario to throw fireballs (visualized as orange arrows). Depending on the state, players exhibited a different behavior. For example, while players being in Fire Mario state threw fireballs at an enemy (marked with a white circle in figure 4), other players which could not take advantage of the shooting ability either evaded the enemy by jumping onto the platform above or killed the enemy by jumping onto it. Lastly, in the image at the bottom movement data was synchronized with physiological data, obtained in the form of galvanic skin response (GSR) to measure the player's arousal state (cf. Mirza-Babaei, et al., 2014). The recorded GSR values have been normalized and then mapped to a color gradient from yellow (low arousal) to red (high arousal). The overall hue of the paths therefore provides an impression of the arousal level of players in different parts of the level. In the left part of the visualization the arousal level was lower compared to the right part where players had to cross multiple gaps and at the same time be aware of an enemy located on a platform between those gaps.

However, as pointed out above, other visual cues other than color can be used as well or used in conjunction with color. Hoobler, Humphreys and Agrawala (2004), focusing on the team-based first-person shooter *Return to Castle Wolfenstein: Enemy Territory* (Splash Damage, 2003), used color-coding to depict team membership. In addition, thickness was used to indicate the direction of time with thicker lines depicting more recent movements. Understanding time based-movement can provide valuable information, for example, on how tactical positions have come about, as pointed out by Hoobler, Humphreys and Agrawala (2004).

Glyphs are another possibility to annotate movement data with further information. Glyphs can be defined as *graphical entities that convey one or more data values via attributes such as shape, size, color, and position* (Ward, 2002, p.194). However, if glyphs are used one should be aware that some visual attributes are easier to perceive or compare than others (cf. Ward, 2002). Ward (2002) also points out that the context can influence the perception of a glyph (e.g., background color can influence how the color of the glyph itself is perceived) and that mapping too many data attributes to a glyph can hinder interpretation of individual attributes.

Continuing with the example above, Hoobler, Humphreys and Agrawala (2004) further annotated the visualization with glyphs to indicate the different classes (e.g., medic, engineer) of the players. In team-based shooters different classes usually have different tasks and understanding their relative position to each other can often be of interest. The *Infinite Mario* visualizations presented earlier also used glyphs (the yellow circles) of varying size to highlight how often a specific coin was collected by the players.

Displaying the traces of each player individually permits an in-depth analysis of the behavior of individual players (cf. Drachen and Canossa, 2011). However, once the number of individual paths increases the resulting visualization can easily become visually cluttered and illegible. Also, displaying large amounts of individual paths makes it difficult *to gain an overall view of the spatial and temporal distribution of multiple movements* (Andrienko and Andrienko, 2013, p.11). In such cases, appropriate techniques are necessary to provide a more abstract view on the data. One such possibility is aggregation—the grouping of several data items into a single item. An overview of different aggregation techniques for movement data in general can be found in Andrienko and Andrienko (2010; 2013). In the following, however, we would like to shortly mention two examples dealing with movement in virtual environments.

The *VU-Flow* tool of Chittaro, Ranon and Ieronutti (2006), for example, provides five types of aggregated visualizations to identify, for instance, more or less traveled areas, the intensity of traffic congestions or the flow of movement. For the latter purpose they used flow visualizations where the vector direction in an area is the sum of all movement directions in that particular area. Tremblay, et al. (2013) used a probabilistic path-finding approach to predict how a particular level design facilitates the possibilities for stealthy movement. Instead of drawing all found paths on top of each other, paths were summarized in a heatmap to provide an aggregated view of all paths. The system has been integrated into the *Unity 3D Game Engine* (Unity Technologies, 2014), allowing the designer to interactively explore how changes to the level environment affect the predicted player movement.

It should also be emphasized that understanding movement data is an important aspect in many other application fields as well (see, e.g., Gudmundsson, Laube and Wolle (2012) for an overview). Thus, visualization methods developed in other areas of research, like traffic analysis (e.g., Lampe, Kehrer and Hauser, 2010) or analysis of animal movements (e.g., Shamoun-Baranes, et al., 2012) may therefore be of interest for game research as well. For example, the statistical software *R* (R Development Core Team, 2014) has open source packages for analyzing animal movement, such as *move* (Kranstauber and Smolla, 2014) or *adehabitatLT* (Calenge, 2104), which could be modified to work with games.

Up to this point we have considered movement to be a spatial property. However, movement in games could be defined in a more abstract manner as well. For example, Osborn and Mateas (2014) used polylines to visualize abstract play traces, in other words, sequence of decisions made by players, in order to help designers to understand which strategies were used by players to achieve an in-game goal (e.g., finding a solution to a puzzle). Similar traces are placed nearer to each other than dissimilar traces, yielding a tree like structure with paths converging and diverging if they become more similar or dissimilar respectively. Glyphs of varying color and shape were used to distinguish between different types of decisions.

NODE-LINK REPRESENTATION

Node-link approaches provide an intuitive way to visualize the relational structure of data items. Nodes represent the data objects themselves and links show the relationships between them. For that matter, nodes can be visualized with different shapes (e.g., circles or rectangles) and links can be drawn, for example, as lines, arcs, orthogonal polylines, or curves. Node-link approaches can also be used to visualize abstract or high-dimensional data.

The layout of a node-link diagram can be obtained using different techniques. In case the data set to be visualized contains spatial data (and this information is from actual interest) then this information can be used directly to derive a placement of the nodes. As a first introductory example, figure 5(left) visualizes player movement on the *World of Warcraft* continent *Outland* on a single day using data from the *World of Warcraft Avatar History Dataset* (Chen, Cheng and Lei, 2011). In *World of Warcraft* continents are broken down into different areas, which are represented by the nodes. Nodes have further been colored to differentiate between different types of areas, with regions being green, cities being blue, and battlegrounds being red. Arrows show movements between these areas. However, instead of drawing individual arrows for each player who moved from one area to another, aggregation has been used to reduce the visual complexity with the thickness of an arrow corresponding to the number of players

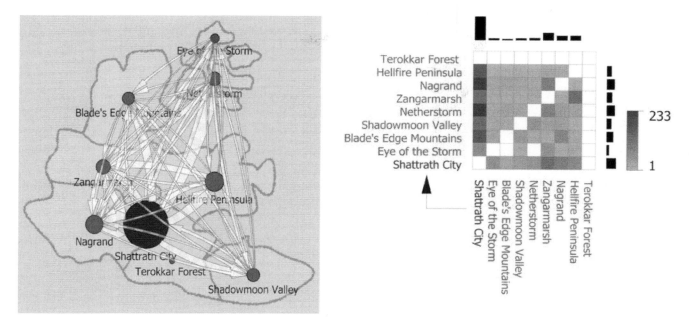

Figure 5. Left: Player movement between regions, cities, and battlegrounds on the World of Warcraft continent Outland. Right: Corresponding matrix view with cells colored according to the number of players moving from one area to another.

who moved from one area to another. In addition, arrows have been drawn on top of nodes such that they are not accidentally regarded to end at a node when in fact just crossing it.

As a side note, it should be pointed out that if the amount of data and the number of edge crossings increase, node-link diagrams tend to become visually cluttered and therefore hard to interpret. Especially for displaying densely connected graphs, adjacency matrix visualization techniques may be superior. In such a visualization the row and columns of the matrix represent the nodes and a cell [i,j] represents a link between node i and node j. Adjacency matrix visualizations are always free of occlusions (Ghoniem, Fekete and Castagliola, 2005) and scale well to very large graphs (Mueller, Martin and Lumsdaine, 2007). If the rows and columns are reordered appropriately, matrix visualizations can also reveal structural patterns in the data (Mueller, Martin and Lumsdaine, 2007). As an example, figure 5(right) shows the matrix visualization corresponding to the node-link diagram in figure 5(left). The different areas are placed along the rows and columns of the matrix. Labels are colored according to the type of the area and cells are colored according to the number of transitions from one area to another. In addition, the matrix visualization has been augmented with bars to the right and above the rows and columns to visualize the row and column sums. In this particular case, these sums reflect the total number of players leaving or coming into an area.

Another example of how spatial information can be leveraged for graph drawing can be found in the work of Bauer and Popovic (2012). Bauer and Popovic—being interested in deriving a graph structure from levels of a platform game to visualize the reachability of areas within a level—also used a node-link representation to visualize the generated graph structure. The visualization itself was overlaid on top of a level-editor and recomputated according to the changes made to a level. This way the visualization provided the designer with immediate feedback on how the changes affected the reachability of different parts of the level. From a visualization point-of-view, color-coding, instead of arrow-heads, was used to indicate the direction of edges.

If no inherent spatial location can be exploited then, for example, graph drawing algorithms (e.g., force-directed algorithms) or statistical techniques like multidimensional scaling can be used to find an embedding of the nodes. Graph drawing algorithms consider different aesthetic principles—like minimization of edge crossings, node overlappings, or link lengths—to provide a better readability (Chen, 2004; North, 2005; Ware, 2004). White-space also often plays an important role to organize the nodes and the relationships between them (cf. Card, Mackinlay and Shneiderman, 1999). A bibliography of different graph drawing algorithms (including a discussion of different aesthetic criteria) can be found in (Battista, et al., 1994). For example, Thawonmas, Kurashige and Chen (2007) used a force-directed graph drawing algorithm to derive a graph where nodes represent players and where the length of a link is proportional to the similarity of the two player's movement patterns. This way, players exhibiting similar movement patterns will form clusters in the node-link diagram.

To improve the readability of large graphs, edge aggregation (e.g., Holten, 2006; Holten and Van Wijk, 2009) or elimination of weak links to focus on the strong ties (cf. Chen, 2004) can be helpful as well. However, by removing links the visualization also loses information. Another possibility is the usage of navigation techniques, like zooming or filtering to handle the large number of nodes and their relationships.

Multidimensional scaling also received some attention in the game research literature. Generally speaking, given a set of objects and a matrix defining the (dis)similarity between each pair of objects, multidimensional scaling aims to find an embedding of the objects such that the distance between the objects in the embedding reflects the (dis)similarity. A comprehensive discussion of multidimensional scaling can be found in Kruskal and Wish (1978) or in the more recent book of Borg and Groenen (2007). Andersen, et al. (2010), for instance, used multidimensional scaling to derive the layout of node-link diagrams that describe the progress of players through games where gameplay cannot be described in relation to the game's environment (e.g., because the player does not control a character, like in some puzzle games). The nodes depict the various game states (e.g., in chess the game state could be expressed as the arrangement of the pieces on the chess board) visited by players while playing the game. Directed edges between the nodes, visualized as straight lines with arrow-heads to indicate the direction, represent player actions.

As final example in this chapter, figure 6 shows an aggregated node-link visualization (which also makes use of multidimensional scaling) of gameplay data from 34 players of the educational game DOGeometry (Wallner and Kriglstein, 2010). DOGeometry is an abstract puzzle game for young children where the player does not directly control a character. Instead the game requires the player to place and arrange road pieces on a given game board in order to build a path for a dog to a veterinarian's house. Hence, progress in the game cannot be expressed by means of avatar position but rather through the particular arrangement of the road pieces. Each node in the visualization corresponds to a particular arrangement. The layout of the graph has been obtained with multidimensional scaling such that nodes corresponding to similar arrangements are placed in proximity to each other while nodes with different arrangements are positioned farther away. In this particular example, cluttered areas of the graph can therefore hint at player confusion since such areas imply that players were experimenting with similar arrangements but were not necessarily sure which one was the right one to proceed. Arrows show transitions (triggered by the player by performing certain interactions within the game, for example, placing a road tile) from one state to another. To provide context, screenshots reflecting the arrangement are associ-

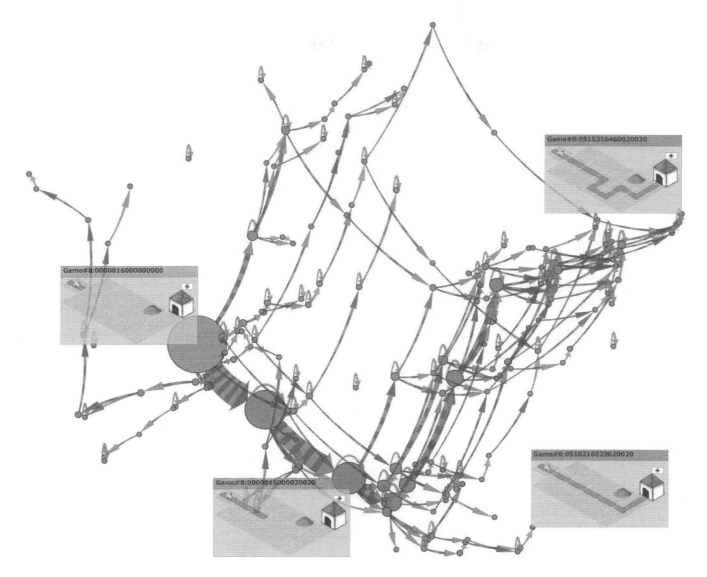

Figure 6. Node-link visualization of player behavior in an abstract puzzle game (Wallner and Kriglstein, 2012b).

ated with each node (four of them are visible in figure 6). Color-coding is used to distinguish between different types of nodes (e.g., the orange node depicts the initial state and purple nodes indicate solution states) and interactions. The size of the nodes and the thickness of arrows reflect how many players reached a particular arrangement at some point or performed a move, respectively. This way popular paths may easily be identified. To further accentuate those paths, weak links (in this case transitions performed by less than three players) have been removed. For example, the visualization shows that the first two to three moves (starting from the orange node) were rather straightforward but afterward the graph starts to branch out with different players proceeding in different ways. A more in-depth discussion of the evaluation of DOG*eometry* and these types of node-link diagrams can be found in Wallner and Kriglstein (2012a; 2012b).

Conclusions

In this chapter we provided an introduction to gameplay data visualization. We first briefly discussed the benefits of employing visualizations in game research and then gave an overview of different visualization techniques including charts, heatmaps, different kinds of movement visualizations, and lastly node-link representations.

A general description of each technique was provided. Table 1 summarizes shortly different advantages and disadvantages of the visualizations covered in this chapter. Of course, this enumeration should not be seen as comprehensive, but rather as a rough guide because the effectiveness of a visualization strongly depends on the specific tasks and goals to be achieved.

Representation	Advantages	Disadvantages
Charts	can be used to summarize and compare variables of a dataset or to display trends in the data over time, useful if specific questions are asked	choosing an inappropriate chart type can lead to false impressions and conclusions
Heatmaps	can be used for any variable that can be mapped to a specific location, spatial patterns in the data are easily perceivable	in general only a single variable is visualized at a time, information about the third dimension is lost, limited for analyzing temporal progression
Movement Visualizations	can be used to retrace players' visits, serve the exploration of movement patterns, help to identify areas of disorientation or problems with wayfinding	displaying a large number of individual paths will result in overlapping and visual clutter, can be quite costly to compute, simultaneous depiction of temporal and spatial data is challenging
Node-Link Representations	suitable for multidimensional or abstract data, succession of actions can be observed	dense graphs generally suffer from visual clutter, layout can look confusing without something to orient the data

Table 1. Different strengths and weaknesses of the discussed visualization methods.

In addition, a range of examples, drawn from the literature, was given to show how these techniques can be used for analyzing game telemetry data. As shown in this chapter, visualizations can be helpful, among other things, to depict trends over time, to identify areas with high or low player activity, to analyze the balancing of the in-game economy or of character classes, or to understand player movement, including recognition of backtracking or unintended paths. However, while game telemetry data can provide important insights about how players are behaving in a game it does not necessarily reveal the reasons why players behave the way they do. Qualitative methods like interviews or thinking aloud, on the other hand, can provide explanations for the recorded behavior. In this sense, both approaches complement each other and results from qualitative approaches may be integrated into visualizations of quantitative data sets to provide a more complete understanding of player behavior. Conversely, as qualitative playtesting can be costly and time consuming, visualizations of automatically logged gameplay data can provide pointers to crucial areas on which qualitative evaluations should focus.

Further reading

- El-Nasr, M.S., Drachen, A. and Canossa, A. eds., 2013. *Game analytics: Maximizing the value of player data.* New York: Springer.

- Isbister, K. and Schaffer, N., 2008. *Game usability: Advancing the player experience.* Burlington: Morgan Kaufmann
- Ward, M.O., Grinstein. and Keim, D., 2010. *Interactive data visualization: Foundations, techniques, and applications.* Natick: AK Peters, Ltd.
- Ware, C., 2012. *Information visualization: Perception for design.* 3rd ed. San Francisco: Morgan Kaufmann.

References

Andersen, E., Liu, Y.E., Apter, E., Boucher-Genesse, F. and Popović, Z., 2010. Gameplay analysis through state projection. In: *5th international conference on the foundations of digital games.* Monterey, Californi. 19–21 June. New York: ACM.

Andrienko, N. and Andrienko, G., 2005. *Exploratory analysis of spatial and temporal data: A systematic approach.* New York: Springer.

Andrienko, G. and Andrienko, N., 2010. A general framework for using aggregation in visual exploration of movement data. *The Cartographic Journal,* 47(1), pp.22–40.

Andrienko, N. and Andrienko, G., 2013. Visual analytics of movement: An overview of methods, tools and procedures. *Information Visualization,* 12(1), pp.3–24.

Battista, G.D., Eades, P., Tamassia, R. and Tollis, I. G., 1994. Algorithms for drawing graphs: An annotated bibliography. *Computational Geometry,* 4(5), pp.235–282.

Bauer, A.W. and Popovic, Z., 2012. RRT-based game level analysis, visualization, and visual refinement. In: *Eighth artificial intelligence and interactive digital entertainment conference.* Stanford. 8–12 October 2012. Palo Alto: AAAI Press.

BioWare, 2007. *Mass Effect* [game]. Xbox 360. Microsoft Game Studios.

BioWare, 2009. *Dragon Age: Origins* [game]. MS Windows. Electronic Arts.

Blizzard Entertainment, 2004. *World of Warcraft* [game]. MS Windows. [computer game] Blizzard Entertainment.

Borg, I. and Groenen, P.J., 2007. *Modern multidimensional scaling: Theory and applications.* 2nd ed. New York: Springer.

Bungie, 2004. *Halo 2* [game]. Microsoft Game Studios.

Bungie, 2007. *Halo 3* [game]. Microsoft Game Studios.

Calenge, C., 2014. adehabitatLT: Analysis of animal movements (0.3.16) [computer program]. Available at: <http://cran.r-project.org/web/packages/adehabitatLT/index.html>.

Card, S.K., Mackinlay, J.D. and Shneiderman, B. eds., 1999. *Readings in information visualization: Using vision to think.* San Francisco: Morgan Kaufmann.

Chen, C., 2004. *Information visualization: Beyond the horizon.* 2nd ed. London: Springer.

Chen, K.T., Cheng, Y.M. and Lei, C.L., 2011. World of Warcraft avatar history dataset. In: *ACM Multimedia systems conference*, San Jose. 23–25 February. New York: ACM.

Chittaro, L., Ranon, R. and Ieronutti, L., 2006. VU-Flow: a visualization tool for analyzing navigation in virtual environments. *IEEE Transactions on Visualization and Computer Graphics*, 12(6), pp.1475–1485.

Chong, B., 2011. *Indie game analytics 101.* Available at: <http://www.gamasutra.com/blogs/BenChong/20111121/90651/Indie_Game_Analytics_101.php>.

Dankoff, J., 2014. *Game telemetry with DNA tracking on Assassin's Creed.* Gamasutra. Available at: <http://www.gamasutra.com/blogs/JonathanDankoff/20140320/213624/Game_Telemetry_with_DNA_Tracking_on_Assassins_Creed.php>.

DeRosa, P., 2007. *Tracking player feedback to improve game design.* Gamasutra. Available at: <http://www.gamasutra.com/view/feature/1546/> [Accessed 31 March 2014].

Dixit, P.N., and Youngblood, G.M., 2008. Understanding information observation in interactive 3D environments. In: *ACM SIGGRAPH symposium on Video games.* Los Angeles. August. New York: ACM.

Drachen, A. and Canossa, A., 2009. Analyzing spatial user behavior in computer games using geographic information systems, In: *MindTrek 2009.* Tampere. September–October. New York: ACM.

Drachen, A. and Canossa, A., 2011. Evaluating motion: Spatial user behaviour in virtual environments. *International Journal of Arts and Technology*, 4(3), pp.294–314.

El-Nasr, M.S., Drachen, A. and Canossa, A. eds., 2013. *Game analytics: Maximizing the value of player data.* New York: Springer.

Ensemble Studios, 1999. *Age of Empires II: The Age of Kings* [game]. MS Windows. Microsoft

Epic Games, 2008. Gears of War 2 (Xbox 360). [computer game] Microsoft Game Studios

Fekete, J.-D., Wijk, J.J., Stasko, J.T. and North, C., 2008. The value of information visualization. In: A. Kerren, J.T. Stasko, J.-D. Fekete and C. North, eds., *Information visualization: Human-centered issues and perspectives.* Berlin, Heidelberg: Springer, pp.1–18.

GameAnalytics, 2013. *GameAnalytics wrapper for Unity 3D heatmaps and easy integration.* Available at: <http://www.gameanalytics.com/unity_integration.html>.

Ghoniem, M., Fekete, J.D. and Castagliola, P., 2005. On the readability of graphs using node-link and matrix-based representations: a controlled experiment and statistical analysis. *Information Visualization*, 4(2), pp.114–135.

Gudmundsson, J., Laube, P. and Wolle, T., 2012. Computational movement analysis. In: W. Kresse and D.M. Danko, eds., 2012. *Springer handbook of geographic information.* Berlin Heidelberg: Springer. pp.423–438.

Hazan, E., 2013. Contextualizing data. In: M. S. El-Nasr, A. Drachen and A. Canossa, eds. 2013. *Game analytics: Maximizing the value of player data*, New York: Springer. pp.477–496.

Holten, D., 2006. Hierarchical edge bundles: Visualization of adjacency relations in hierarchical data. *IEEE Transactions on Visualization and Computer Graphics*, 12(5), pp.741–748.

Holten, D. and Van Wijk, J. J., 2009. Force-Directed Edge Bundling for Graph Visualization. In *Computer Graphics Forum*, 28(3), pp.983-990.

Hoobler, N., Humphreys, G. and Agrawala, M., 2004. Visualizing competitive behaviors in multi-user virtual environments. In: *IEEE Visualization*. Austin, Texas, USA, 10-15 October 2004. Washington, DC: IEEE Computer Society.

Houghton, S., 2011. *Balance and Flow Maps*. [online] Available at: <http://www.altdevblogaday.com/2011/06/01/balance-and-flow-maps-2/> [Accessed 31 March 2014].

Hullett, K., Nagappan, N., Schuh, E. and Hopson, J., 2011. Data analytics for game development (NIER Track). IN: *33rd International Conference on Software Engineering*. Waikiki, Honolulu, USA, 21-28 May 2011. New York: ACM.

IO Interactive, 2010. *Kane & Lynch 2: Dog Days* [game]. MS Windows. Eidos Interactive

Kang, S.J., Kim, Y.B., Park, T. and Kim, C.H., 2013. Automatic player behavior analysis system using trajectory data in a massive multiplayer online game. *Multimedia tools and applications*, 66(3), pp.383–404.

Kayali, F., Wallner, G., Kriglstein, S., Bauer, G., Martinek, D., Hlavacs, H., Purgathofer, P. and Wölfle, R., 2014. A Case Study of a Learning Game about the Internet. In: S. Göbel and J. Wiemeyer, eds., *Games for training, education, health and sports*. Berlin, Heidelberg: Springer. pp.47–58.

Kim, J.H., Gunn, D.V., Schuh, E., Phillips, B., Pagulayan, R.J. and Wixon, D., 2008. Tracking real-time user experience (TRUE): A comprehensive instrumentation solution for complex systems. In: *SIGCHI conference on human factors in computing systems*. Florence. 5–10 April. New York: ACM.

Kosslyn, S.M., 2006. *Graph design for the eye and mind*. New York: Oxford University Press.

Kranstauber, B., Smolla, M., 2014. move: Visualizing and analyzing animal track data (1.2.475). [computer program] Available at: <http://cran.r-project.org/web/packages/move/index.html>.

Kriglstein, S., Wallner, G. and Pohl, M., 2014. A user study of different gameplay visualizations. In: *SIGCHI conference on human factors in computing systems*, Toronto. 26 April – 1 May. New York: ACM.

Kruskal, J.B. and Wish, M., 1978. *Multidimensional scaling*. Beverly Hills: Sage Publications.

Lampe, O.D., Kehrer, J., and Hauser, H., 2010. Visual analysis of multivariate movement data using interactive difference views. In: *Vision, modeling and visualization workshop*. Siegen. 15–17 November. Eurographics Association.

Lewis, C. and Wardrip-Fruin, N., 2010. Mining game statistics from web services: a World of Warcraft armory case study. In: *5th international conference on the foundations of digital games*. Monterey. 19–21 June. New York: ACM.

Macdonald-Ross, M., 1977. How numbers are shown. *AV Communication Review*, 25(4), pp.359–409.

Marselas, H., 2000. *Profiling, data analysis, scalability, and magic numbers: Meeting the minimum requirements for Age of Empires II: The Age of Kings*. Gamasutra. Available at: <http://www.gamasutra.com/view/feature/131546/profiling_data_analysis_.php>.

McCormick, B.H., DeFanti, T.A. and Brown, M.D. eds., 1987. Visualization in scientific computing, *Computer Graphics*, 21(6).

Medler, B., John, M. and Lane, J., 2011. Data cracker: developing a visual game analytic tool for analyzing online gameplay. In: *SIGCHI conference on human factors in computing systems*. Vancouver. 7–12 May. New York: ACM.

Medler, B. and Magerko, B., 2011. Analytics of play: Using information visualization and gameplay practices for visualizing video game data. *Parsons Journal for Information Mapping*, 3(1), pp.1–12.

Medler, B., 2012. *Play with data-an exploration of play analytics and its effect on player experiences*. PhD. Georgia Institute of Technology.

Mirza-Babaei, P., Wallner, G., McAllister. G. and Nacke, L.E., 2014. Unified visualization of quantitative and qualitative playtesting data. In: *SIGCHI conference on human factors in computing systems*, Toronto. 26 April – 1 May 2014. New York: ACM.

Moura, D., El-Nasr, M.S. and Shaw, C.D., 2011. Visualizing and understanding players' behavior in video games: discovering patterns and supporting aggregation and comparison. In: *ACM SIGGRAPH symposium on video games*. Vancouver. 10 August. New York: ACM.

Mueller, C., Martin, B. and Lumsdaine, A., 2007. A comparison of vertex ordering algorithms for large graph visualization. In: *International Asia-Pacific symposium on visualization*. Sydney. February. IEEE.

Nielsen, J., and Pernice, K., 2010. *Eyetracking web usability*. Berkeley: New Riders.

Nintendo, 1985. Super Mario Bros [game]. NES. Nintendo.

North, C., 2005. Information Visualization. In: G. Salvendy, ed. 2005. *Handbook of human factors and ergonomics*. 3rd ed. Hobokon: John Wiley & Sons, pp.1222–1246.

Osborn, J. and Mateas, M., 2014. Visualizing the Play of Arbitrary Games. In: 9th *International Conference on the Foundations of Digital Games*. Royal Caribbean Liberty of the Seas Cruise Ship. 3–7 April 2014. SASDG.

Persson, M., 2008. Infinite Mario [game]. Web.

Pfeiffer, T., 2010. Tracking and visualizing visual attention in real 3D Space. In: *Biannual meeting of the German society for cognitive science*. Potsdam. 3–6 October 2010. Potsdam: Universitätsverlag Potsdam.

Pfeiffer, T., 2012. Measuring and visualizing attention in space with 3D attention volumes. In: *Symposium on eye tracking research and applications*. Santa Barbara. 28–0 March. New York: ACM.

Phillips, B., 2010. Peering into the black box of player behavior: The player experience panel at Microsoft Game Studios. In: Games Developers Conference 2010. Available at: < http://www.gdcvault.com/play/1012646/Peering-into-the-Black-Box >.

R Development Core Team, 2014. R (3.1.0). [computer program] Available at: <http://www.r-project.org/>.

Shamoon, E., 2012. *How Call of Duty Elite evolved*. Available at: <http://www.polygon.com/2012/11/27/3682896/how-call-of-duty-elite-evolved>.

Shamoun-Baranes, J., van Loon, E.E., Purves, R.S., Speckmann, B., Weiskopf, D. and Camphuysen, C.J., 2012. Analysis and visualization of animal movement. *Biology letters*, 8(1), pp.6–9.

Schoenblum, D., 2010. Zero to millions: Building an XLSP for Gears of War 2. *In: Game developer conference 2010*. Available at: <http://gdcvault.com/play/1012456/Zero-to-Millions-Building-an>.

Sony Online Entertainment, 2004. *EverQuest II* [game]. MS Windows. Sony Online Entertainment

Splash Damage, 2003. *Return to Castle Wolfenstein: Enemy Territory* [game]. MS WIndows. Activision.

Thawonmas, R., Kurashige, M. and Chen, K.T., 2007. Detection of landmarks for clustering of online-game players. *The International Journal of Virtual Reality*, 6(3), pp.11–16.

Thompson, C., 2007. *Halo 3: How Microsoft Labs invented a new science of play*. Available at: <http://www.wired.com/gaming/virtualworlds/magazine/15-09/ff_halo>.

Tory, M. and Möller, T., 2004. Human factors in visualization research. IEEE *Transactions on Visualization and Computer Graphics*, 10(1), pp.72-84.

Tremblay, J., Torres, P. A., Rikovitch, N. And Verbrugge, C., 2013. An exploration tool for predicting stealthy behaviour. In: *2nd workshop on artificial intelligence in the game design process*. Raleigh. 15 October 2013. Palo Alto: AAAI Press.

Ubisoft Montreal, 2010. *Assassin's Creed: Brotherhood* [game]. Xbox 360. Ubisoft

Unity Technologies, 2014. *Unity—Game Engine*. Available at: <https://unity3d.com/>.

University of Vienna, 2013. *Internet Hero* [game]. Web. N.p.

Valve Corporation, 2006. *Half-life 2: Episode Two stats*. Available at: <http:// www.steampowered.com/status/ep2/ep2_stats.php>.

Valve Corporation, 2007a. *Half-Life 2:Episode Two* [game]. MS Windows. Valve Corporation.

Valve Corporation, 2007b. *Team Fortress 2* [game]. MS Windows. Valve Corporation.

Valve Corporation, 2012a. *The science of Counter Strike: Global Offensive*. Available at: <http://blog.counter-strike.net/science/maps.html> [Accessed 31 March 2014].

Valve Corporation, 2012b. *Counter-Strike: Global Offensive* [game]. MS Windows. Valve Corporation

van Wijk, J.J., 2005. The value of visualization. In: *IEEE visualization*. Baltimore. 23–28 October. Washington: IEEE.

Visceral Games, 2011. *Dead Space 2* [game]. MS Windows. Electronic Arts

Wainer, H., 1984. How to display data badly. *American Statistician*, 38(2), pp.137–147.

Wallner, G., and Kriglstein, S., 2010. DOGeometry (Web). [browser game] N.p.

Wallner, G. and Kriglstein, S., 2012a. A Spatiotemporal visualization approach for the analysis of gameplay data. In: *SIGCHI conference on human factors in computing systems*. Austin. 5–10 May. New York: ACM.

Wallner, G. and Kriglstein, S., 2012b. DOGeometry: Teaching geometry through play. In: *4th international conference on fun and games*, Toulouse. 4–6 September. New York: ACM.

Wallner, G. and Kriglstein, S., 2013. Visualization-based analysis of gameplay data: A review of literature. *Entertainment Computing*, 4(3), pp.143–155.

Ward, M.O., 2002. A taxonomy of glyph placement strategies for multidimensional data visualization. *Information Visualization*, 1(3–4), pp.194–210.

Ware, C., 2004. *Information visualization: Perception for design*. San Francisco: Morgan Kaufmann.

Williams, D., Yee, N. and Caplan, S.E., 2008. Who plays, how much, and why? Debunking the stereotypical gamer profile. *Journal of Computer-Mediated Communication*, 13(4), pp.993–1018.

Zoeller, G., 2010. Development telemetry in video games projects. In: *Game Developer Conference 2010*. Available at: < http://www.gdcvault.com/play/1012434/Development-Telemetry-in-Video-Games>.

Structural equation modelling for studying intended game processes

MATTIAS SVAHN AND RICHARD WAHLUND

Pervasive games are games extending into the real world (spatial expansion), where they involve others than the primary players (social expansion) and are played without any time delimitations (temporal expansion) (Montola, Stenros and Waern, 2009). Persuasive pervasive (PP) games are pervasive games with the intention of influencing the primary players' and sometimes even secondary players' attitudes, beliefs or behaviours in a specific direction. Thus they can be used for educational or marketing purposes.

The purpose of this chapter is to explain and show how structural equation modelling (SEM) can be used for studying the persuasive processes resulting from playing PP games. The main reason for such studies is to better understand the persuasive processes of PP games as part of the evaluation of such games, yielding indications of improvements for meliorating intended results. SEM may in fact be used for the evaluation of any game, to better understand how it works in the minds of the consumers and to what extent playing it results in a positive or negative experience of or attitude towards the game.

What is Structural Equation Modelling?

Structural Equation Modelling (SEM) is a method for studying causal relationships between numbers of variables assumed to be directly or indirectly (structurally) causally related to each other, thus including independent, intermediary and dependent variables. A structural equation model consists of a theoretical model with latent variables (constructs), depicting the causal structure of the latent variables, and a measurement model with manifest variables, the latter being measured indicators of the latent variables. The latent variables are similar to factors in a factor analysis, but defined within the structural equation model when it is estimated and tested.

Since an intended persuasion process is a causal process, we propose that SEM can be used for studying such processes by estimating and testing the assumed causal effects through the process, depicted by a structural causal model. In this chapter we present the SEM method, focusing on the persuasion processes of playing (pervasive) games. We also present a case where it is applied. The aim of the case is to find out if, and if so, show how SEM can be used for studying the flow of persuasion stemming from the persuasive game.

SEM has found common use in consumer behaviour studies (e.g., Verhagen and Van Dolen, 2009; Sarstedt and Wilczynski, 2009; Wahlund, 1991), but much more rarely in game research. Just to mention one example where it can be useful is for studying the extent to which a player's amount of previous game play in a genre (independent variable, survey data) impacts the learning (intermediate variable, server data from a tutorial level) and the game play behaviour (intermediate variable, server data), and to what extent these in turn explain the appreciation of the game (survey data, dependent variable).

SEM can be used for confirmatory or exploratory research. In the former case the researcher models a structure of causal relations deductively from theory and then tests this structure—the proposed model. In the case of exploratory research there are no strong validated theories about the causal structure or the constructs, as is often the case in game research (cf. chapter 10). SEM is, when applying an exploratory approach, developed through hypothetical theoretical reasoning, then tested, evaluated, adjusted, redeveloped and re-tested in several iterations, trying to optimize the model to reflect the reality of the data, while still making theoretical sense (Svahn, 2014).

SEM ESTIMATION TECHNIQUES

One well-known technique for estimating and testing a structural equation model is LISREL (*Linear Structural Relations*), developed by Karl Jöreskog (1969; 2001; 2006) and Dag Sörbom (Jöreskog and Sörbom, 1979) and based on maximum likelihood. This method offers great theoretical freedom when imagining the model structure, but places high demands on data distribution. Another well-known technique is PLS (*Partial Least Square* or *Projection to Latent Structures*), developed by Herman Wold (1966; 1981; 1985) and Svante Wold (Wold, Sjöström and Eriksson, 2001) and based on partial least squares (as indicated by its name).

This chapter is about the Partial Least Square technique for SEM (PLS-SEM). The primary objective of PLS-SEM is to maximize explained variance in dependent constructs. Some of the advantages of PLS-SEM are that it can work efficiently even when complex models are built on small sample sizes and when there is multicollinearity (Hair, et al., 2013, pp.124-126). Moreover, it does not assume the data to be multivariate normally distributed.

MANIFEST AND LATENT VARIABLES

As already mentioned, the theoretical structural model consists of latent variables which reflect abstract concepts that cannot be measured directly, like factors in a factor analysis. Instead, a latent variable is made of groupings of measured variables, that is manifest variables, each considered to reflect a facet of the abstract concept. The group of manifest variables covers the abstract concept in a way a single measurement cannot. A typical latent variable in game research could be immersion, a knotty construct that can be realized only with several combined measurement items (cf. Ermi and Mäyrä, 2005; Wirth, et al., 2007; Waern, Montola and Stenros, 2009).

A latent variable can be exogenous, that is an independent variable, not influenced by any other latent variable in the model, or endogenous, that is intermediate or dependent, explained by the model. The final variable or variables intended to be influenced through the persuasion process are termed the focal variables.

Latent variables can be either formative or reflective, each of which represent a slightly different conceptional perspective.

Reflective latent variables are underlying constructs to and thus measured by manifest variables. The construct is interpreted based on the factor loadings, which are the correlations between the manifest variables and the latent variable. Thus, if the construct theoretically is meant to reflect the presence of an existing idea, then it is a reflective latent variable. Therefore, internal consistency is an important issue for a reflective latent variable, and its key numbers should always be closely observed.

A sign of reflective nature of a latent variable is if it is possible to remove one or several manifest variables from the latent variable without the researcher finding a change in its meaning (Hair, et al., 2011; 2013). The immersion variable mentioned above would most likely be a reflective latent variable, as would attitude or belief variables.

Formative latent variables are causal indicators of the construct, which is sometimes termed a combination variable (Maccallum and Browne, 1993) or composite variable (MacKenzie, Pedsakoff and Jarvis, 2005). This means that the measures cause the construct and that the construct is fully derived by its measurement. It is therefore graphically represented by ingoing arrows from the manifest variables. Interpretation is made from the regression weights of the manifest variables onto the latent variable.

The theory of a formative latent variable is that the ingoing manifest variables together form a construct. That makes internal consistency into a non-issue for a formative latent variable. A rule of thumb on formative latent variables is to consider if the removal of one manifest variable changes the meaning of the construct the latent variable represents, then that latent variable has a formative nature (Hair, et al., 2011; 2013). In game research, "player behaviour" or "play experience" could be formative latent variables.

EVALUATING THE MEASUREMENT MODEL

The first criterion of the evaluation of the measurement model concerns the internal consistency. One of the measures of internal consistency of the manifest variables that make up the latent variables is *Cronbach's Alpha*. Cronbach's Alpha is a measure of the extent to which the manifest variables are consistent with each other. The calculation of Cronbach's Alpha presumes all manifest variables of a latent variable are equally reliable, that is that all manifest variables have equal outer loadings and the same strength in their relations to the latent variable they comprise.

The latter is unlikely ever to be the real case, so another measure is the *composite reliability*. That measure takes into account different outer loadings of manifest variables. Both measures are interpreted in the same way and sensitive for semantic redundancies in the manifest variables, that is questionnaire items that respondents found too similar. The presence of semantic redundancy can only be ascertained by the researcher taking an active role in the interpretation.

Average Variance Extracted (AVE) is a measure of convergent validity. It is the mean value of the squared loadings of the manifest variables. It is equivalent to the communality of a construct (Hair, et al., 2011; 2013). These three measures only apply to reflective latent variables.

The *cross loadings* table is another important tool for evaluation of the measurement model. It gives the distribution of factor loadings of all manifest variables across all the latent variables of a PLS-SEM. It is desirable to see all the manifest variables of a latent variable load strongly onto the latent variable they belong to, and only onto that latent variable. If all the manifest variables load strongly onto their latent variable and only onto that one, then the measurement model is mathematically sound. If not it needs to be rethought. The cross loadings are considered to be a liberal evaluation criterion (Hair, et al., 2011; 2013). It also has the strength of illustrating the measurement model in full detail.

The *Fornell-Larcker Criterion* is considered to be a more conservative estimate than the cross loadings. It compares the square root of the AVE values with the latent variable correlations. The square root of each construct AVE should be greater than its highest correlation with any other construct. The logic of this method is based on the idea that a construct shall share more variance with its associated indicators that with any other construct (Hair, et al., 2011; 2013).

ASSESSING THE STRUCTURAL MODEL

While the measurement model is about finding the right groups for the manifest variables, the structural model instead is about hypothesizing the causal structure of the latent variables. These hypotheses are represented graphically by a structure of unidirectional arrows between latent variables (Hair, et al., 2011; 2013).

One element in the evaluation of a structural model is to observe the *path coefficients* (similar to Beta coefficients in regression analysis, and also denoted β) of the relations between the latent variables. The path coefficient comes from calculating the degree to which one independent or intermediate latent variable is related to another intermediate or a dependent latent variable. A path coefficient assumes a value from -1 via 0 to +1. The closer to -1 or +1, the greater the influence of the explanatory variable on the explained variable, the sign showing the direction of the influence.

The *R-squared value* is a measure of the extent to which all independent or intermediate latent variables that are hypothesized to directly influence another intermediate or a dependent latent variable succeed in this, in other words the variance explained in an explained variable. Exogenous or independent latent variables have an R-squared value of zero since they are not influenced or explained by any other variables in the model.

A further way to evaluate a PLS-SEM is to calculate and read the *total effect* estimates. In a complex model with many latent variables and paths there may be more than one possible route by which an explanatory variable influences a dependent variable. A total effect estimate is the combined direct and indirect influences of one latent independent or intermediate variable on a dependent variable, through all paths between the variables.

The most common test of path coefficients is the *t-test*. The *p-values* of the t-values are used to assess the "level of unusualness" that the researcher sets as the satisfactory level. Each statistical test has an associated value of the likelihood that a pattern observed in the test would occur due to mere chance. In other words, it is a measure of the power or sensitivity of the statistical test, the probability that it correctly rejects the null hypothesis.

A commonly used p-value is 0.05. The reason for this is that 0.05 historically has been accepted as the standard (Pallant, 2010). That consensus has been criticized for being gratuitous and having a potential for misinterpretation (Schervish, 1996; Dienes, 2011; Yates, 1984). It is true that the p-value should be set in relation to the research context, when testing the enjoyment of a game in an explorative context, liberal p-values can be allowed, while when doing a clinical drug trial very strict p-values need to be set.

The researcher applying PLS-SEM should finally take all estimated parameters of the measurement and theoretical structural models into account and make a holistic evaluation relating to theory and the research questions when interpreting the PLS-SEM results. The PLS-SEM results are only a mathematical artefact that has no voice in itself. That which gives the researcher insight is to weigh the results from calculating the model against the research questions and the theory.

Some authors argue for the use of overall goodness-of-fit indices such as Root Mean Square Error of Approximation (RMSEA), Standardized Root Mean Square Residual (SRMR), and the Comparative Fit Index (CFI), for example Fey, et al. (2009), while others argue against the use of such indices, for example Hensele and Sarstedt (2013).

THE PLS-SEM WORK PROCESS AND A SOFTWARE TOOL

A common general work process for a PLS-SEM is to first set up the theoretically simplest causal model and then add hypothesised influencing factors consecutively until the theory is fulfilled, or the resulting output values start breaking down. Another work process is to first set up a theoretical model with all the paths and indicators supposedly imaginable and then remove one path or indicator per iteration until the key numbers have been maximized, while not losing sight of the original theory.

The software Smart PLS (Ringle, Wende and Becker, 2005) was used for the analyses in the case reported later in the chapter. The data are imported into Smart PLS as a .csv file. The measurement and structural models are drawn in a graphical interface into a hypothesized model. That model is drawn on the basis of ideas stemming from theory or theoretical reasoning. The manifest variables are added to the model one by one via a drag-and-drop interface. When the researcher is satisfied s/he presses the calculate button and the software calculates the model turning it from a hypothesized model into an estimated model.

There is no need for the researcher to write any code herself. The software provides the researcher with the key numbers in output files in the form of tables. Hair, et al. (2013) gives detailed instructions about how to import data, set up a model and evaluate it. There are several tutorials on Smart PLS to be found on Youtube (e.g., Gaskin, 2012), the quality of which however is varied.

CONSIDERATIONS FOR THE DATA COLLECTION

When the researcher is to collect data for PLS-SEM, one strategy is to apply the constructs narrowly but stringently (i.e., collect few data points and have confidence in that these can represent the theory). That would, when it works, give a clear and traditional work process when setting up the measurement model, the structure model, and iteratively purifying the PLS-SEM (Hair, et al., 2013, chapters 3–6). The risk then is that the data might not be able to capture the experience of the theoretical constructs.

Another choice is to design the data collection to cast a theoretically inspired but very wide data capturing net, admittedly with a lesser degree of precision in the theoretical constructs. This second process would capture a large amount of data and have large amounts of noise (i.e., spuriously caught data in relation to the signal). However, there would be a greater chance of capturing relevant phenomena.

The amount of noise in the data in the latter case would make the process of PLS-SEM difficult, in particular the process of iteratively optimising the model in conjunction with the continuing holistic application of theory. Still a wide data collection approach could be carried through if the reduction and purification process is kept within theoretical bounds (i.e., manifest variables could be dropped one by one as long as all the original theoretical constructs remain represented in the final data set that underlies the PLS-SEM).

The second route is considerably more laborious than the first route, but it yields a better chance that data pertaining to the interrelationships of the constructs will be captured than the first route (i.e., a lesser risk that the data collection work will be for nought).

STRENGTHS AND WEAKNESSES OF PLS-SEM AS TO GAME RESEARCH

In this section we discuss the strengths and weaknesses of PLS-SEM when it comes to game research. Compared to other sciences, game research have relatively little of established and validated constructs that have been through iterations of mathematical and empirical validation, so the work process of PLS-SEM for game research needs thoughtful and aware consideration.

When aiming to find out what the persuading process from playing a pervasive persuasive game looks like, and what the influencing effects in such a process are, the strength of PLS-SEM (and SEM in general) is obvious, in particular the ability to take even a rather vague construct, and measure its impact through several other variables on the final dependent variable. Whenever a design or experience quality of a game can be isolated and expressed numerically, the PLS-SEM can give insights. PLS-SEM fits well into for example game design pattern theory (Björk and Holopainen, 2004; Lankoski and Björk, 2007).

PLS-SEM is at its best as an evaluation tool, for example, if a researcher wants to know the impact of design qualities such as of *Competition* or *Player Killing* on the amount of time spent in a game (Björk and Holopainen, 2004). Then players can be queried in a survey on their experiences of those qualities, and data for playing time can be assessed from the servers based on the player ids. All these variables may in turn be used to explain the learning from a serious game, also measured in a survey.

One of the main downsides of SEM as a method in game research is that it assumes constructs that are theoretically defined and preferably validated. The quality of the measurements model is dependent on the latent variables being distinct expressions of theoretical ideas and also clearly distinct from each other. In game research, this is not yet always the case. For example, there is no agreed upon and validated construct for the experience of breaching the magic circle (Huizinga, 1949).

A case study: Agents Against Power Waste

We have applied PLS-SEM in a study of the persuasive process from playing the pervasive persuasive game Agents Against Power Waste (AAPW). It is both a prototype game and a real persuasive communications campaign. The aim of the game was to make families become more conservational with electricity (Larsson, 2011; Svahn, 2014).

The pervasive-game design included social, spatial and to some extent temporal expansion (cf. Montola, Stenros and Waern, 2009). The spatial expansion was included by the game system taking into account the real life electricity consumption of the households involved, via a back-end game system that incorporated the players' electricity company's billing data, which were sent to the electricity company once a day.

The social expansion was included by the electricity contract being one shared resource for the whole household, making all household members, whether they wanted to or not, into game players, when one household member (the primary player) played AAPW (the other household members being secondary players). The temporal expansion was included by letting the previous days´ game actions influence the following day's game play (Svahn, 2014).

The intention of the game design was to persuade the players—primary and secondary—via a process that is called the *Systematic route of thinking* in the Heuristic-Systematic model of persuasion, HSM (cf. Chaiken and Eagly, 1989; Chaiken, Lieberman and Eagly, 1987; Svahn, 2014).

The study was carried out as a field experiment within the context of the design research project "Young Energy", one of the research projects within the Energy Design Studio of the Interactive Institute—Swedish ICT (Anon, n.d.). The point of departure for Young Energy was to impact the energy awareness of youth through, adapting to how they live their lives, more specifically their use of information technology such as digital games or mobile phones (Torstensson, 2005).

The field experiment with AAPW was carried out in 2010 with 126 players, pupils in middle and high schools aged 13–15 years old and living in families. The families were recruited through contact with local schools. Field experiment was the chosen method since AAPW is a pervasive game and hence takes place in the respondents' real world. A further specific reason for the choice of field experiment was the open nature of pervasive games. When the game takes place in real life, anything that can happen in real life can happen in the game. Hence field experiments can capture emergent behaviours not foreseen at the outset.

For some pervasive games, the consequence of the necessity to interface with the everyday erases the difference between the game and the play session (Björk and Holopainen, 2004). The game is either only staged once, or every staging meets different everyday worlds that in turn lead to different interfaces with them. Therefore, the games cannot be quite exactly the same each time (Björk and Holopainen, 2004; Stenros, et al., 2012). As such, only a field experiment allows both players and researchers to see a pervasive game design fully enacted.

AIM AND HYPOTHESES FOR THE CASE STUDY

AAPW was meant to be one part of a larger effort towards answering a series of research questions (cf. Svahn, 2014). The aim of the case study presented in this chapter is to show how a persuasion process from playing a persuasive pervasive game can be described, measured, estimated and tested by employing PLS-SEM.

The focal variables—the intended final outcomes of the persuasion process—in the case of AAPW are attitudes toward saving electricity of both primary and secondary (parents) players (the latter within the social expansion of AAPW). Two hypotheses as to the focal variables are:

- H1: Playing AAPW will lead to more positive attitudes toward saving electricity among the primary players.
- H2: Playing AAPW will lead to more positive attitudes toward saving electricity among the secondary players—the parents.

The research question following the hypotheses then is: How does the persuasion process towards changed attitudes of both primary (pupils) and secondary (parents) players to energy saving look like?

REASONS FOR CHOOSING ELECTRICITY AS THE TOPIC

The topic of AAPW—electricity saving—was chosen due to the ecological, political and economic problems arising from the increased consumption of electricity in the world (Svahn, 2014; Gustafsson, 2010). Electricity consumption was also chosen because there is a low general knowledge about electricity and low awareness about one's daily electricity consumption. The reason for the latter is insufficient consumer information about the use and actually purchasing of electricity in everyday life, and that electricity is socially consumed, (i.e., most homes are used by several individuals of differing ages and incomes, yet it has only one contract with an electrical company as a shared resource for all household members). A pervasive game that applies social expansion (Montola, Stenros and Waern, 2009) could perhaps consider social consumption, not as a problem but instead as an element of the game play and of a persuasion process. The involvement of secondary players is included in this case study of AAPW.

THE PERSUASIVE PERVASIVE GAME AAPW

AAPW was an adventure and role-playing styled pervasive-persuasive game centred on social team play, with the player receiving quests in the form of secret agent missions. AAPW was a slow play turn based game with a mission to conserve household electricity. AAPW let players compete in teams and learn hands-on how to conserve electricity in their homes. The household was the unit of team membership, not the player. The player had to build cooperation as well within the team of three as within his/her own real life household. The missions were given in text (see figure 1). AAPW was played in a mobile first person perspective.

FIELDWORK AND DATA COLLECTION OF AAPW

AAPW was run as a controlled field experiment in 2010 in the Swedish city of Eskilstuna. The team recruited four school classes with pupils aged 13–15 years. Their parents were asked to take part. The parents became the secondary players that participated through social expansion. The children and their families took part in the game for 28 consecutive days and data were gathered from 126 households.

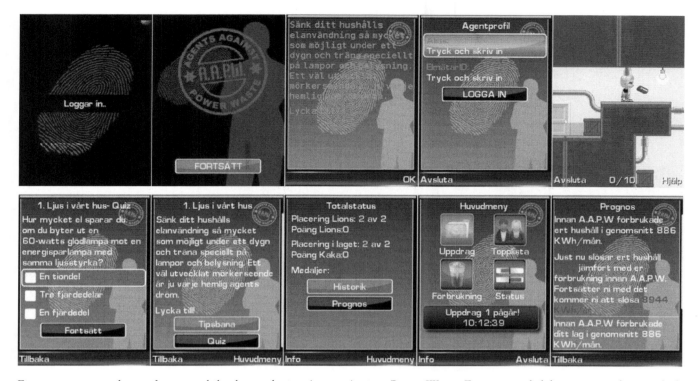

Figure 1. 10 screen dumps from a mobile phone playing Agents Against Power Waste. From upper left login screen, login-splash screen, presentation screen, agent profile/player profile, practice run in the form of a simple labyrinth game, a quiz, a mission presentation, a status screen, a navigation menu, and an end prognosis screen giving the player info on how much the player would save if the player continues living in the same way as during play.

There were pre-and post-game questionnaires towards test and control groups about attitudes, beliefs etc. regarding energy and electricity issues.

As measurements in the questionnaires, statements were used with seven point Likert scales anchored at each end of the scale. Data were also collected through log files from the game servers. The way the game server was connected to the electricity meter of the homes expanded the play space from the mobile phone screen to the entire household. It should be noted that this afforded an almost infinite number of ways that actions could influence the game. For example, buying a new dishwasher could be an in-game action.

Svahn (2005) developed a taxonomy of persuasive games based on the extent to which a game was dominated by its message(s), or dominated its message(s), a taxonomy further developed by Wahlund, et al. (2013). The main point of the taxonomy was to identify to what extent the game was unrelated to the message it carried, or the game being the message. In those terms, AAPW was the message (cf. McLuhan and Fiore, 1967). In that situation, any thought about the game or the game experience was inseparable from thought about the message. The design was meant to give the player little room to think about the game or the game play experience without thinking about saving electricity.

We first present the final structural model that resulted from applying PLS-SEM to AAPW, including the tests of the two hypotheses specified. We then make an evaluation of the model arrived at.

RESULTS FROM APPLYING PLS-SEM TO AAPW

The final estimated structural model is presented in figure 2. The model has 56 manifest variables loading on eleven latent variables (Svahn, 2014, table A11), of which four are exogenous and seven endogenous, connected with 16 paths. The model converged in 16 iterations.

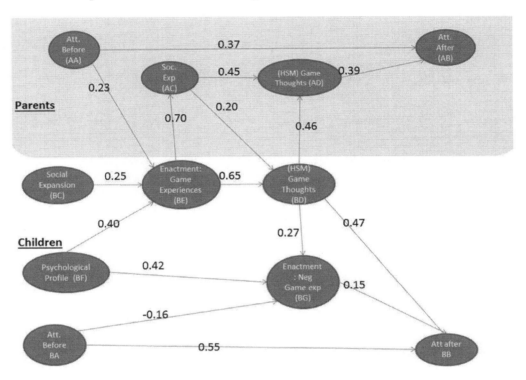

Figure 2. The final PLS-based structural equation model for AAPW, showing the found causal relations and their path coefficients.

As indicated by the model in figure 2, there is a clear effect on both the primary (the pupils) and the secondary (the parents) players. The hypotheses that there was an effect on the focal variables were also tested by comparing the means of the indexed variable "Attitudes toward saving electricity" before and after playing AAPW for the primary and secondary players, respectively, using t-test. The hypotheses were further tested by comparisons with the control group.

As to H1, the result is that the primary players (the pupils) were 6 percent more positive toward electricity saving after than before playing AAPW ($p < 0.01$), which supports the hypothesis. As to H2, the result is that the secondary players (the parents) were 8 percent more positive toward electricity saving after than before playing AAPW ($p < 0.01$). Also H2 was thus supported.

The hypotheses were also tested by comparing the mean attitudes of the primary and secondary players after AAPW against the control group, also after AAPW. The result concerning H1 shows that the primary players were 7 percent more positive toward saving electricity after playing AAPW (p < 0.01) than the control group at the same point in time. The result concerning H2 shows that the secondary players were 6 percent more positive toward saving electricity after participating in AAPW than the control group at the same point in time (p < 0.01). These results further support H1 and H2.

THE PERSUASION PROCESS BEHIND THE CHANGED ATTITUDES OF THE PRIMARY PLAYERS

As to the research question, how, then, did these changes come about? Looking at the influence on the focal variable children's attitudes towards electricity after AAPW, that is their "post-play attitudes", the corresponding attitudes before AAPW, that is their "pre-play attitudes", had the largest total effect (0.53), with a high direct effect of $\beta = 0.55$. This means that pre-attitudes matter, and becomes more positive by playing AAPW. At the same time, there was a slight countervailing negative effect via children's "Enactment: negative game experiences". The latter had a direct and total effect on the children's post-play attitudes of $\beta = 0.15$. See Svahn (2014, Table A12) for t-values of all path coefficients.

The next most influential variable on children's post-play attitudes was their "(HSM) game thoughts", with a total effect of 0.51 and a direct effect of $\beta = 0.47$. This effect was increased by an indirect effect via children's "Enactment: negative game experiences" (as are the children's pre-attitudes). Thus, the more systematic processing and the more negative the children are towards the game itself, the more positive toward electricity saving are the children after playing AAPW.

The third most influential variable on the children's post-attitudes was their "Enactment: game experiences", the indirect total effect being 0.41. The influence went via the children's "(HSM) game thoughts" and "negative game experiences" as described above, but also via the parents' involvement (their level of "social expansion") and its effect on the children's "(HSM) game thought". Thus, the more one played and the better it went, the more positive post-attitudes among the children toward electricity saving.

Other variables that were found to have an indirect positive total effect on children's post-attitudes are parents' pre-attitudes (0.09) and their level of social expansion (0.10), as well as the children's level of social expansion (0.10) and their "psychological profile" (0.10). The latter is a rather complex but still coherent variable made up of four manifest variables relating to need for achievement and being respected (Table A10 in Svahn, 2014). All these effects on children's post-attitudes were thus positive and the intended.

THE PERSUASION PROCESS BEHIND THE CHANGED ATTITUDES OF THE SECONDARY PLAYERS

As to the focal social expansion variable "parents' post-attitudes toward electricity saving", the variable with the highest total effect (0.43) was "parents' pre-attitudes toward electricity saving", with a direct effect of $\beta = 0.37$, which was enhanced by indirect effects via children's "Enactment: game experiences", "parents' level of social expansion" and both the children's and the parents' "(HSM) game thoughts". The children's "Enactment: game experiences" and "(HSM) game thoughts" were thus stimulated by the parents' pre-attitudes and level of social expansion.

The second most influential variable on "parents' post-attitude toward electricity saving" was parents'

"(HSM) game thoughts" (β = 0.39, which was also the total effect), in turn effected by the "parents' level of social expansion" (β = 0.45, with a total effect of 0.54) and children's "(HSM) game thoughts" (β = 0.46).

The third most influential variable was children's "Enactment: game experiences", the total effect being 0.26 via "parents' level of social expansion", children's "(HSM) game thoughts" and parents' "(HSM) game thoughts", with the parents' "level of social expansion" being the fourth most influential variable (a total effect of 0.21), followed by children's "(HSM) game thoughts" (a total effect of 0.18). The level of interactions between the primary and secondary players when playing AAPW, that is the social expansion of AAPW, thus clearly had an effect on both players' focal attitudes in the intended direction.

AS TO THE FINDINGS CONCERNING HSM AND SOCIAL EXPANSION

The HSM is a theory applicable for describing the underlying mental processes of playing AAPW. It is included in the AAPW model by two latent variables, the parents' "game thoughts" and the children's "game thoughts". These are both intermediate latent variables meaning that while they have an incoming impact from other variables, they also impact other latent variables in turn.

The parents' "game thoughts" influences parents' "attitudes after" with a direct effect of β = 0.39. Children's "game thoughts" effects the latent variable children's "attitudes after" with β = 0.51. These impacts are high and is an indication that the more effortful and conscious the thoughts about the game, that is the more systematic the thinking, the more positive the attitudes.

As mentioned above, the children's "Social Expansion" had a rather small indirect total effect on children's "post-attitudes" (0.10), and an even smaller indirect total effect on parents' "post-attitudes" (0.07). The children's "Social Expansion" did, however, have notable influencing effects within the persuasion process on parents' "Social Expansion" (0.18), via the children's "Enactment: game experiences" (β = 0.25) and further on parents' "(HSM) Game Thoughts" (0.17). The indirect total effect of the children's "Social Expansion" on their own "(HSM) Game Thoughts" was 0.20.

The parents' experience of social expansion (AC) had a large total effect on their "(HSM) Game Thoughts" (0.54) and from there on their "post-attitudes" (0.21). It also had an effect on the children's "(HSM) Game Thoughts" (0.20) and then a somewhat lower total effect on the children's "post-attitudes" (0.10). Social expansion thus obviously play a role in the persuasion process, somewhat strengthening the persuasion in the intended direction.

EVALUATION OF THE AAPW STRUCTURAL EQUATION MODEL

As to the proposed latent variables of AAPW, the results were that the AVE was greater than 0.5 for five of the nine latent variables where the AVE-measure was applicable (Svahn, 2014, table A8). Average Variance Extracted was not an applicable measure for the two formative latent variables children´s "Enactment: Game Experiences" and children´s "Enactment: Negative Game Experience". The Composite Reliability values were in the range of 0.77–0.92, and the Cronbach's Alpha values were in the range of 0.71–0.89 (Svahn, 2014, table A8), all indicating an acceptable discriminant validity for the latent variables.

That four out of the nine latent variables for which AVE was applicable had an AVE lesser than 0.5 is troublesome. It indicates an uncertainty as to whether the variance captured by the latent variables really is larger than the variance due to the measurement error. It appears that the unidimensionality and convergent validity of the constructs to some degree is in flux. The problem is to some degree alleviated because two of the four weak constructs are the attitudes toward saving electricity of both parents and children of the family *before* playing AAPW. These variables were constructed based on the "best" corresponding constructs for attitudes *after* playing AAPW, in order to make them comparable.

What an initial explorative factor analysis found was that the attitude constructs and thus the attitudes themselves were more indefinite *before* AAPW than *after* AAPW. This means that playing AAPW had an effect on the quality of the attitudes toward saving electricity, making them more distinct after than before playing AAPW. This was an unforeseen but interesting finding. Altogether, the overall degree of internal consistency in the measurement model as measured by Cronbach's Alpha and Composite Reliability is acceptable.

The path coefficients presented in Figure 1 are generally quite high. The R-squared values are also rather high (Svahn, 2014, table A8). The t-values were calculated using the *bootstrap method* with the "no sign changes" setting applied in Smart PLS. It is the most conservative setting. If the significances err, they err on the side of false negatives rather than on the side of false positives (Hair, et al., 2013, p.164).

The t-values of the path coefficients in the model are very high (Svahn, 2014, Table A12), the highest (t = 11.4) being for the path from the latent variable Children's "Enactment: Game Experiences" to the latent variable Parents´ "Social Expansion". That is in itself an interesting result as it gives support to social expansion being an important element in the persuading process. The combined measures of the measurement model—the sizes of the path coefficients and the acceptable t-values—give the overall impression that both the measurement model and structural model of AAPW are acceptable.

The Fornell-Larcker test results (Svahn, 2014, table A9) indicates that all the square roots of the AVE measures exceed the construct inter-correlations, thereby strengthening the discriminant validity of the measurement model expressed by the AVE values. The cross loadings (Svahn, 2014, table A10) show that loadings within constructs exceed loadings outside the constructs, also indicating acceptable discriminant validity.

Summing up

Relating to the hypotheses stated and the research question asked concerning AAPW, the results from applying PLS-SEM to AAPW show not only the intended and expected effects on the focal variables in the intended direction, but also give a picture of the persuasive process behind the changes in the focal variables, both as to the players' post-attitudes toward saving electricity, and the parents' post-attitudes toward saving electricity.

The results also indicate that social expansion of playing AAPW does play a role in the persuasive process, influencing other variables in the process in the intended way. The same is true for type of mental process: the more systematic and less heuristic the thought process of both primary and secondary players, the more positive the post-attitudes of both primary and secondary players toward saving electricity.

As to the purpose of this chapter, it has been explained and shown how structural equation modelling (SEM) can be used for studying the persuasive processes resulting from playing persuasive pervasive games, resulting not only in a better understanding of a persuasive process from playing such a game, but also in the actual causal effects through the process. It has thus been shown that PLS-SEM can be used for evaluation of such games, yielding indications of improvements for meliorating intended results.

We argue that SEM thus also can be used for the evaluation of any game, to better understand how it works in the minds of the consumers and to what extent playing it results in a positive or negative experience of or attitude towards the game as such. The only thing needed to achieve this is to measure the experiences, attitudes etc., which we have shown is quite possible, and to follow our example.

Recommended readings

- Hair, J.F., Hult, T.M., Ringle, C.M., and Sarstedt, M., 2013. *A primer on partial least squares structural equation modelling (PLS-SEM)*. 1st ed. California: SAGE.
- Hair, J. F., Sarstedt, M., Ringle, C.M., & Mena, J.A., 2011. An assessment of the use of partial least squares structural equation modelling in marketing research. *Journal of the Academy of Marketing Sciences*, 40, pp.414–433.
- Svahn, M., 2014. *Pervasive Persuasive Games. The Case of impacting energy consumption*. PhD. Stockholm School of Economics.
- Gaskin, J., 2012. SmartPLS basic SEM path analysis. Available at: <https://www.youtube.com/watch?v=6G9MfgImWCw>.

References

Anon, (n.d). Interactive Institute Eskilstuna. Available at: <https://www.tii.se/groups/energydesign>.

Björk, S. and Holopainen, J., 2004. *Patterns in game design*. Florence, KY: Charles River Media.

Chaiken, S., 1987. The heuristic model of persuasion. In M. P. Zanna, J.M. Olson and C.P. Herman (Eds.), *Social influence* the Ontario Symposium. 5th ed. Hillsdale NJ: Lawrence Erlbaum Associates, p. 3.

Chaiken, S., Lieberman, A. and Eagly, A., 1989. *Heuristic and systemic information processing within and beyond the persuasion context*. In: J. Uleman, and J. Bargh, eds., *Unintended thought*. New York, NY: Guilford, p.212.

Dienes, Z., 2011. Bayesian versus orthodox statistics: Which side are you on? *Perspectives on Psychological Science*, 6, pp.274–290.

Ermi, L. and Mäyrä, F., 2005. Fundamental components of the gameplay experience: Analysing immersion. In: Proceedings of the DiGRA 2005 Conference: *Changing views: Worlds in play*. Vancouver. June.

Fey, C.F., Morgulis-Yakushev, S, Hyeon Jeong Park, H.J. and Björkman, I., 2009. Opening the black box of the relationship between HRM practices and firm performance: A comparison of MNE subsidiaries in the USA, Finland, and Russia. *Journal of International Business Studies*, 40(4).

Gaskin, J., 2012. SmartPLS basic SEM path analysis. Available at: <https://www.youtube.com/watch?v=6G9MfgImWCw>.

Gustafsson, A., 2010. *Positive persuasion – designing enjoyable energy feedback experiences in the home.* PhD. Gothenburg University and Chalmers University of Technology.

Hair, J.F., Hult, T.M., Ringle, C.M. and Sarstedt, M., 2013. *A primer on partial least squares structural equation modelling (PLS-SEM).* California: Sage.

Hair, J.F., Sarstedt, M., Ringle, C.M. and Mena, J.A., 2011. *An assessment of the use of partial least squares structural equation modelling in marketing research.* Journal of the Academy of Marketing Sciences, 40, p.433.

Hensele, J. and Sarstedt, M., 2013. *Goodness-of-fit indices for partial least squares path modeling.* Computational Statistics,, 28(2), pp.565–580.

Huizinga, J., 1949. *Homo ludens: A study of the play-element in culture.* 2009. London: Routledge.

Jöreskog, K.G., 1969. A general approach to confirmatory maximum likelihood factor analysis. *Psychometrika, 34,* pp.183–202.

Jöreskog, K. G., 2001. A general method for analysis of covariance structures. In: D.M. Titterington and D.R. Cox, eds., *Biometrika: One hundred years.* Oxford: Oxford University Press, pp.345–357.

Jöreskog, K. G., 2006. LISREL. Encyclopedia of statistical sciences. Hoboken: Wiley. Available at: <http://onlinelibrary.wiley.com/doi/10.1002/0471667196.ess1481.pub2/pdf>.

Jöreskog, K.G. and Sörbom, D., 1979. *Advances in factor analysis and structural equation models.* New York: University Press of America.

Lankoski, P. and Björk, S., 2007. Gameplay design patterns for believable non-player characters. In: *Situated play.* Tokyo. September. pp.416–423.

Larsson, C., 2011. *SLUTRAPPORT PROJEKT—unga utforskar energi.* (Official No. Prj.nr: 32255-1). Sweden: Energikontoret i Mälardalen.

Maccallum, R.C. and Browne, M.W., 1993 The use of causal indicators in covariance structure models: Some practical issues. *Psychological Bulletin* 114(3), pp.533–541.

MacKenzie, S.B., Podsakoff, P.M. and Jarvis, C.B., 2005 The problem of measurement model misspecification in behavioral and organizational research and some recommended solutions, *Journal of Applied Psychology* 90 (4), pp.710–730.

McLuhan, M. and Fiore, Q., 1967. *The medium is the message.* Harmondsworth: Penguin.

Montola, M., Stenros, J. and Waern, A. eds., 2009. *Pervasive games: Theory and design.* Germany: Morgan Kaufman.

Pallant, J., 2010. *SPSS Survival Manual.* 4th ed. Berkshire: Mc Graw Hill.

Ringle, C.M., Wende, S. and Becker, J.-M., 2014. Smartpls 3. Hamburg: SmartPLS. Available at: <http://www.smartpls.com>.

Sarstedt, M. and Wilczynski, P., 2009. More for less? A comparison of single-item and multi-item measures. *Die betriebswirtschaft*, 69 (2), p.211.

Schervish, M.J., 1996. P values what they are and what they are not. *The American Statistican*, 50(3), pp.203–206.

Svahn, M., 2014. *Pervasive Persuasive Games. The case of impacting energy consumption.* PhD. Stockholm School of Economics.

Svahn, M., 2005. Future-proofing advergaming: A systematisation for the media buyer. In: *Proceedings of the Second Australasian Conference on Interactive Entertainment.* New York: ACM, pp.123–187.

Stenros, J., Waern, A. and Montola, M., 2012. *Studying the elusive experience in pervasive games. Simulation and Gaming*, 43(3), pp.339–355.

Torstensson, C., 2005. *En förstudie för att utreda förutsättningarna för forskningsprojektet Young Energy.* Eskilstuna: Sweden: Interactive Institute.

Verhagen, T. and Van Dolen, W., 2009. Online purchase intentions: A multi-channel store image perspective. *Information & Management* 46(2), pp.77–82.

Waern, A., Montola, M. and Stenros, J., 2009. *The three-sixty illusion: Designing for immersion in pervasive games.* In: Proceedings of the SIGCHI conference on human factors in computing systems (CHI '09). New York: ACM, pp.1549–1558.

Wahlund, R., 1991. *Skatter och ekonomiska beteenden.* PhD. Stockholm School of Economics.

Wahlund, R., Rademaker, C., Nilsson, P. and Svahn, M., 2013. *Mediernas roll i marknadskommunikationen*, in G. Nygren, and I. Wadbring eds., *På väg mot medievärlden 2020*. Lund: Studentlitteratur.

Wirth, W., Hartmann, T., Böcking, S., Vorderer, P., Klimmt, C., Schramm, H., Saari, T., Laarni, J., Ravaja, N., Ribeiro Gouveia, F., Biocca, F., Sacau, A., Jäncke, L., Baumgartner, T. and Jäncke, P., 2007. A process model of the formation of spatial presence experiences. *Media Psychology*, 9(3), pp.493–525.

Wold, H., 1966. Estimation of principal components and related models by iterative least squares. In Krishnaiaah, P.R., ed., *Multivariate analysis.* New York: Academic Press. pp.391–420.

Wold, H., 1981. *The fix-point approach to interdependent systems.* Amsterdam: North Holland.

Wold, H., 1985. Partial least squares. In Kotz, S. and Johnson, N.L., eds., *Encyclopedia of statistical sciences* 6. New York: Wiley, pp.581–591.

Wold, S., Sjöström, M. and Eriksson, L., 2001. PLS-regression: a basic tool of chemometrics. *Chemometrics and Intelligent Laboratory Systems* 58(2), pp.109–130.

Yates, F., 1984. Tests of significance for 2 × 2 contingency tables. *Journal of the Royal Statistical,* 147, pp.426–463. DOI=10.2307/2981577.

PART IV

MIXED METHODS

16. Mixed methods in game research

Playing on strengths and countering weaknesses

ANDREAS LIEBEROTH AND ANDREAS ROEPSTORFF

What we observe is not nature itself, but nature exposed to our method of questioning (Werner Heisenberg, 1958).

A diversity of imperfection allows us to combine methods not only to gain their individual strengths but also to compensate for their individual weaknesses (Brewer and Hunter, 2006, p.17).

Games are a tricky phenomena to study. They exist both as artifacts and practices, and sometimes have consequences reaching far beyond the play context. Fittingly, game researchers are also scattered across disciplines, which means we rarely use the same tools or vocabulary. From a mixed methods standpoint, this is an upside.

Designers and researchers who only observe a game through one instrument—be it surveys, brain-scans, ethnography, or something else—will pick up on a limited fraction of the information available. If we are interested in both players and games, as well as the moments where they merge into play, a mixed methods approach is called for.

In this chapter, we illustrate how play can be studied at different levels: in-game, in-room, and in-world (Stevens, Satwicz and McCarthy, 2008), and now also in-body (Haier, Karama, Leyba and Jung, 2009; Jarvela, Kivikangas, Katsyri and Ravaja, 2013; Spapé, et al., 2013; Weber, Ritterfeld, and Mathiak, 2006). Mixed methods is, however, more than mixing methods up. It is a planned process where a different line of sight towards a chosen object of inquiry—be it a game or a psychological concept such as aggression or learning—are drawn up through a progression from hypothesis formation, over data collection and analysis, to the integration of the multiple data streams. The latter is typically known as triangulation.

The chapter presents a post-disciplinary view on how to pick and combine methods, drawing on our own work and on illustrative examples from the rapidly growing cache of literature. In the words of legendary designer Sid Meier, complexity is central to making games interesting (Camargo, 2006), and may even be conducive to learning compared with relatively simpler designs (Golas, 1981; Squire, 2006). But studies of game complexity rarely touch upon all the practical social and psychological things that go on around gaming, from the room where the console is situated, to ideas recruited from the player's life world.

The chapter presents a post-disciplinary view on how to pick and combine methods, drawing on our own work and on illustrative examples from the rapidly growing cache of literature. In the words of legendary designer Sid Meier, complexity is central to making games interesting (Camargo, 2006), and may even be conducive to learning compared with relatively simpler designs (Golas, 1981; Squire, 2006). But studies of game complexity rarely touch upon all the practical social and psychological things that go on around gaming, from the room where the console is situated, to ideas recruited from the player's life world.

While in no way a complete review of the mixed methods traditions or the many competing voices therein (cf. Johnson, et al., 2007; Östlund, et al., 2011 or Brewer and Hunter 2006), the goal of this chapter is to pick up on the main tenets as they relate to games, especially in relation to the unique facets that make gaming an ideal case for illustrating the upsides of mixed methods work, namely gameplay trajectories as they emerge in the meeting between player and game, and the multiple levels at which games and their consequences can be observed.

Example 1: The living room lab

In a very good example of mixed methods research, Jo Iacovides, et al. (2011, 2013) studied eight people playing in a lab environment which mimicked the comforts of home including, in true English fashion, tea and biscuits. The researchers combined real-time observations and biometric measurements with think-aloud prompts, surveys, post play-interviews and three weeks of play diaries to find indices of breakdowns and breakthroughs, which they were interested in studying as drivers of gameplay and in-game learning. Breakdowns were understood as "observable critical incidents where a learner is struggling with the technology, asking for help, or appears to be labouring under a clear misunderstanding" while breakthroughs are "observable critical incidents which appear to be initiating productive, new forms of learning or important conceptual change" (Sharples 2009, p.10 cited in Iacovides, et al., 2011 p.4).

Video recordings captured what was going on in-game and in-room while participants were playing some games they had brought from home. Players were fitted with electrodes to record electrodermal activity in the fingers (GSR, galvanic skin response), heart rhythm (EKG, electrocardiography), and facial muscle activity (EMG, electromyography) on the jaw (indicative of tension) cheek (indicative of smiling), and forehead (indicative of frowning) (Iacovides, et al., 2013, p.6). Such technologies have been used in an array of gameplay studies (e.g., Jarvela, et al., 2013). In order to assess what the participants did when they became stuck in everyday play: who they talked to about games, when they visited websites, and whether they thought they had learnt anything from their activities (p.7). The participants also kept play diaries over several weeks.

The researchers used these many streams of data to understand how the participants played in everyday settings and critically to triangulate information about significant game events emerging concurrently in-room, in-game and in-body, that might indicate breakdowns and breakthroughs. The biophysical patterns were taken as proxies for psychological events. However, on closer scrutiny the complex sen-

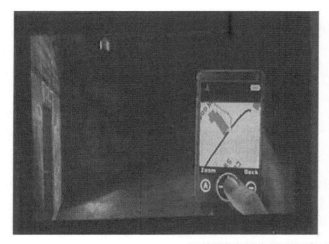

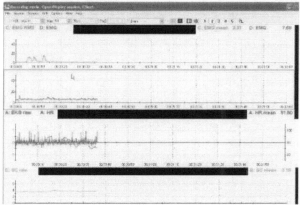

Figure 1. Three streams of data from Iacovides's living room lab.

sor data did not correspond very well to the observed in-game and in-room occurrences. The video-feeds were thus crucial to contextualize and interpret the concurrently-collected biological data.

Example 2: Mobile learning

Mixed methods researchers are rarely treated to such controllable conditions as the English living room lab. In a different study we planned a two-year investigation of the mobile audio drama The Chosen (Hansen, Kortbek, and Grønbæk, 2008; 2010; 2012), where sixth–ninth grade students are guided though a series of outside locations through an interactive "eco horror story" to conduct science tasks. The experience is not unlike a museum audio guide, but it has both an overarching narrative and a set of challenges scattered through the scenes. We wanted to know if the unique and slightly scary game-play would create "autobiographical landmarks" (Lieberoth and Hansen, 2011; Lieberoth, 2012; Shum, 1998), which could facilitate students' access to the semantic and procedural information related to the unique episode. Initially, we planned to test this hypothesis using fMRI scans of players answering quiz questions about the story and the curriculum 12 weeks after The Chosen.

Before running a complicated and costly scanner-study, however, we needed to confirm that some kind of episodic remembering would be going on at recall. Extensive fieldwork at the beginning of the project allowed us to explore the play setting, sample teachers' motives, identify typical activity trajectories, spot common incidents, and to marvel at the social dynamics of groups of young kids on a day out. A quiz and survey were used to measure learning outcomes and address measure potential predictors of memory such as immersion and intrinsic motivation. This was, however, all completed at the time of play, with no obvious link to the school setting. We therefore did post hoc interviews in two classrooms about the kids' experiences, meaning-making, perceived learning outcomes, and recall strategies. By adding this qualitative dimension to an otherwise neuro-scientific approach, we learned that participants were able to describe events in quite some detail after several months, but had fuzzy memories about the story arc.

These qualitative findings allowed for critical tweaks to our hypotheses and important adjustments to the quantitative instruments used. Being present to observe kids filling out quizzes in the play area revealed that everyone thought the questionnaires were too long, and they would often hunker down together and cross-check their results (a huge source of potential bias). The more unruly students, who might have benefitted most from an alternative learning frame, were most unlikely to complete the surveys.

Given the richness of this mixed methods information, and the complexity of inter-individual experiences discovered, we decided against an fMRI study before we could to fine-tune the quantitative setup.

The two cases catch the main tenets of mixed methods nicely. Different styles of research, along with their disparate techniques, empirical logics and accompanying sub-hypotheses (Brewer and Hunter, 2006), are brought to bear on a single theoretical problem. In our study of the mobile learning game The Chosen, the mix occurred in the interest of developing a primary methodology, while the living room lab study examined several tracks of parallel data with a common goal in mind. Both also deployed methods to probe beyond the immediate situation, into subjects' everyday lives, thus following more complex trajectories of activity and effect than would otherwise have been possible.

Levels of observation

Reed Stevens and his collaborators (2008) identified three levels of activity that are worth observing when studying games: In-game, in-room and in-world. Looking to the examples, we might add in-body.

In-game means the things that go on as part of the game interface, for example, at game-mechanical, interactional and narrative levels. This can, for instance, be recorded using screen- or mouse-capture, aggregated player movement heat maps (figure 7), or turn-by-turn analysis of players' positions in a board game. There are many possible distinctions within this level, for instance between a game's core loops and structural gameplay chat streams and animated sequences.

In-room literally means what transpires moment to moment between things and people in the room. The term is a bit deceptive, because it applies equally to all gaming arenas from the gridiron, over Live Action Role Playing (LARP) forests, to psychology labs. Data is usually gathered with participant observation, video or audio recordings, and can be codified quantitatively or qualitatively (Dow, MacIntyre and Mateas, 2008). This is often a central dimension to understanding players, gameplay, and cognitive processes alike.

In-body implies bodily states that accompany play—which can be measured with technologies like biosensors, brain-scanners, or eye-trackers—and used as indications of cognitive processes which are not directly observable. This is a difficult but rewarding domain to work with, because of the work necessary to interpret data as proxies for cognitive and psychological phenomena. Measurements can happen in many situations—from fMRI labs to roaming with wearable sensors—and add an extra level of information that cannot necessarily be picked up through subjective reports or qualitative observations.

In-world refers to all the elements in real life which somehow touch upon the gameplay or vice versa. Prior knowledge and experiences may influence gameplay strategies, just like gaming may be conducive to learning or reinterpretations of life events. For instance, Stevens and colleagues present a nice vignette (2008, pp.53–62) where two siblings' play spawns a conversation about the general real world concepts of cheating and fairness, which in turn affect their attitudes toward the game. In-world relationships might be picked up from talk during play sessions, as well as ethnographical observations or quantitative effect measures in the world beyond (cf. chapter 11).

Each of the four levels draws attention to different units of observation and analysis, and has ideal methods attached. Entrenched research styles with little sensitivity to the complexity of games tend to emphasize only one.

For instance, a much-cited *Nature* study of dopamine level changes during video game play (Koepp, et al., 1998) managed to ignore all other levels than their in-body focus. The article never reports which game the participants had been playing in the PET-scanner, or if there were nuances in how individuals progressed though the game, except giving a vague description:

> [The task] involved moving a 'tank' through a 'battlefield' on a screen using a mouse with the right hand. Subjects had to collect 'flags' with the tank while destroying 'enemy tanks'. Enemy tanks could destroy the three 'lives' of the subjects' tank. If subjects collected all flags, they progressed to the next game level[...] (Koepp, et al., 1998, p.267).

This stands in stark contrast to how Iacovides and colleagues (2011; 2013) used in-body measures as just one stream of information about the gameplay, concurrent with in-game and in-room data.

OTHER LEVELS OF ANALYSIS

It is perhaps worth mentioning that the idea of levels is not unique. In fact, there are many possible ways of slicing this cake, depending on your focus. For instance, Elias, Garfield and Gutschera's Characteristics of games (2012) supplies a plethora of lenses which can be found at agential levels involving human practice or more design-based systemic levels. Similarly, Cowley and colleagues (2014) suggest that game design patterns, the interplay of game context with player traits, and in-body measures of experience are fruitful levels of observation and analysis.

Looking more to behavior and attitudes, Doug Gentile and his colleagues proposed five dimensions along which video games can have effects—the amount, content, context, structure, and mechanics of play. In this view, level-approaches explain how research findings that initially appear contradictory are actually sometimes congruent, resting on the premise that games and the ways people interact with them are multidimensional, with each dimension likely to be associated with specific types accessible data (Anderson, Gentile and Dill, 2012, p.253; Gentile and Stone, 2005; Gentile, 2011).

COMPLEXITY ACROSS LEVELS

Stevens and colleagues (2008) warns us against falling into a "separate worlds view". People bantering in the room, what goes on on-screen, neurons firing, hearts pounding, and how gaming becomes a conduit for thought about the real world, are obviously not hermetically sealed off from each other—except as a convenient heuristic to help us talk about where and when to deploy which empirical tools. Just delimiting the temporal scope of play in preparation-rich miniature games like Warhammer 40.000 (Carter, Gibbs and Harrop, 2014) or chess tournaments (Fine, 2012; Tarbutton, 2010) can be challenging and requires sensitivity to the relationship between in-room incidents and in-world phenomena.

Fixtures of mixed methods research

Mixed methods approaches are especially popular in fields like education (Johnson and Onwuegbuzie, 2004; Shakarami, Mardziah, Faiz, and Tan, 2011; Yin, 2006) nursing (Kroll and Neri, 2009; Östlund, et al., 2011) and social work (Brewer and Hunter, 2006; Lietz, Langer and Furman, 2006), which are defined by their close marriage to practice rather than rigid methodological traditions. Game research is a similarly practical field now emerging at a high pace with industry stakeholders, fandoms and university researchers clamoring to claim territory.

BEYOND QUALITATIVE VERSUS QUANTITATIVE

Without a bit more to go on, it could sound like mixed methods research primarily endeavors to bridge the age-old trenches between qualitative and quantitative research. Indeed, the most commonly published kind of mixed design simply combines survey and interview data. Fifty-seven per cent of social science studies use this approach, while another 27% only co-analyze open and closed survey items (Fielding, 2012, p.131).

The strong suit of qualitative inquiry is the ability to take advantage of naturally occurring data (Silverman, 2001), as long as they are observable as part of physical and social practice—including artifacts and documents. While ethnographers do not take steps to control their variables the same way experimentalists do, they have unique opportunities to be surprised, study the interrelationships between complex dances of elements, reactively gaining access to tacit systemic logics. The reliability of qualitative data and analyses can, however, be challenged at the levels of generalizability and refutability. Causal conjectures derived from unique situations are hard for other scientists to test empirically (as per Popper, 1963), and the complexity of any in-room or in-game event makes it difficult to claim that what happens in one study truly compares well to another unless a strict multi-case setup like that used by Iacovides is employed.

Quantitative tools, on the other hand, are scalable and efficient once developed, but often lack in contextual information and risk painting pictures of non-existent averages. In essence, quantitative methods only give researchers information about variables they have explicitly front-loaded into their study and found a way to quantify. When we studied The Chosen, being present for about 20–30% of the actual episodes where the data came from gave a fair view of the big differences between all the school classes that came out each week. For instance, some immigrant children did not master the Danish language well enough to complete surveys and quizzes in time, which lead to considerations of the generalizability of the data across demographics. This is a nice example of how concurrent ethnography in a complex real world setting can support design and interpretation of quantitative data in a strong and practical way.

Divisions other than the quantitative-qualitative chasm may, however, encapsulate much more central blind spots. There may, for instance, be very good reasons to combine types of qualitative work (e.g., participant observation followed by interviews) or quantitative sources of data collection: for example cross-sectional studies in a main population to identify systematically deviating properties of an effect study cohort, (cf. chapter 11). Mixed methods approaches can thus appear within general logics, or serve to bridge between them.

MORE IS NOT ALWAYS BETTER

One might also come to believe that mixed methods work on a more is better or more advanced is better principle. Although many studies integrate their data by an additive logic (which we shall see is often suboptimal), each additional method is costly in terms of data-gathering and especially data analysis and integration, which can end up combining a seemingly unending barrage of parallel problems including artifacts and missing data (Iacovides, et al., 2013), not to mention challenges to ecological validity stemming from mounting self-report measures, prying eyes and sticky electrodes. Most approaches can usually add a little perspective to most studies, so the method is not one of addition, but one of coming up with clever ways to meaningfully integrate a minimally-costly but maximally-informative combination of data tracks (Brewer and Hunter, 2006; Fielding, 2012). A good theoretically grounded hypothesis, followed by pragmatic considerations of opportunities to collect and compare data, should reveal which research styles are ideally suited to explore a particular game or test particular hypotheses.

FROM ADDITION TO EXPLORATION OR INTEGRATION

As a rule, mixed method studies come in three varieties: additive, integrative, or explorative work.

Additive approaches are sometimes frowned upon (Fielding, 2012; Johnson and Onwuegbuzie, 2004; Sui and Zhu, 2005), because many work from a 'more is better' assumption This can lead to a kind of confirmatory triangulation (see below), where overlaps or novel findings are interpreted on one main method's terms. At their worst, however, additive approaches end up resembling parallel studies that might as well have been published separately. This is not scientifically wrong, but it is important to be explicit if some methods were included to generate auxiliary data or if several researchers were doing their own thing all the way though.

Integrative studies are rarer, but demonstrate the merits of formulating specific questions or hypotheses, and then mapping out what methods can be conjointly used to answer or test them, and what is needed to sufficiently document settings and relations surrounding the construct. In such approaches, methodology and congruency allows styles to speak together at chosen junctures, from hypothesis generation, over data collection, to analysis and final integration.

Finally, and apparently unnoticed in many treatments, methods may simply be mixed because researchers are embarking on an exploratory journey, unsure of what they are looking for or how to operationalize a particular theoretical construct. This may be the case in sequential work, where piloting or several open avenues of inquiry is needed to formulate hypotheses or to streamline a research design. In our opinion, each of these varieties can have their legitimate place in research, but it is important to be clear about such distinctions in your work.

FROM MIXING METHODS TO MIXED METHODS

Thus, moving from just mixing methods to doing mixed methods research involves being explicit about how the multiple methodological styles work together, including relative weightings such as explicitly stating reasons for disseminating some data thoroughly while leaving others in the background to address auxiliary hypotheses, bridging between the levels of observation, or adding perspective to causal claims. We will discuss these challenges in the remaining parts of this chapter.

Temporal aspects

As alluded to in the discussion of additive, exploratory and integrative approaches, methods may be deployed at different temporal stages, from data collection, over data integration and raw analysis, to the more interpretative parts of a research project (Kroll and Neri, 2009; Östlund, et al., 2011).

EVENTS AND INCIDENTS DEFINE SETTINGS

Settings come to explicitly define space and time coordinates in the research. According to Brewer and Hunter's (2006) multi-method framework, events can be defined as the larger units of time like a gaming session or chess tournament (Fine, 2012), while incidents are the smaller units that occur and reoccur across events, which will often be observed at several points, and can then be systematized into theories about systemic properties and processes. When we were studying The Chosen, quizzes, gameplay observations, and surveys always took place in the same setting with classes and students as the interchangeable units of observation. But apart from a few pilots, follow-up measurements took place in diverse non-observed classrooms, which created a need to integrate space and time in the final data analysis. Indeed, complex hierarchical regression techniques confirmed that variations in classroom membership are one of the strongest predictors of both experiences and quiz performance.

PARTICIPATION TRAJECTORIES

Gameplay processes can be understood in terms of activities within gradually unfolding, bounded possibility spaces. This process can be observed at the four levels discussed above, but researchers will also find very different information depending on where in a play trajectory they decide to collect data.

For instance, chess has been analyzed as a complexity tree with more than 10^{43} possible positions with accompanying variations in tactical choices (Shannon, 1950), and that only accounts for what is going on the board—not in player's heads or conversations over the table. Characters in World of Warcraft (Blizzard Entertainment, 2004) roam much more freely, but game elements like level abilities and quests unlocked diminish the actual trajectories available through Azeroth. If we view gameplay as a possibility space with many different potential trajectories, we realize that each player can have varying experiences, and will be guided by many different elements.

Framing and structuring are often neglected in especially psychological or educational discussions, but they are central to understanding how games change everyday activities into something that is playful and engaging, and how to research player trajectories through a game space. To illustrate this open world, Henriksen modeled role-playing paths with an arrow (the player trajectory) winding its way through a circle (the overall game frame) containing many other circles (potential situations which may or may not be realized) (Henriksen, 2004) (figure 2) making RPGs and LARPs a more complicated affair to study than the choice-trees of chess. The model bears strong resemblance to the overview of posts visited in The Chosen (figure 3), but perhaps inadequately describes how game mechanics and framing devices guide players on particular routes, as it was conceived for LARPing.

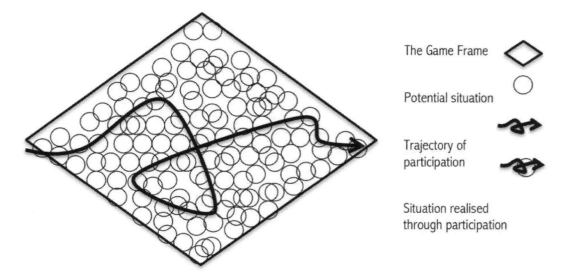

The Game Frame

Potential situation

Trajectory of participation

Situation realised through participation

Figure 2. Henriksen's gameplay trajectory model for open worlds

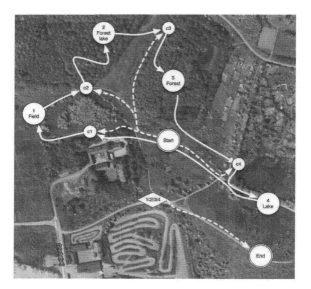

Figure 3. Posts distributed in the outside area hosting The Chosen.

Apart from being a central observational dimension, time can also delimit shifts from tinkering, exploration, and pilot studies, to main investigations. Although this implies an external movement from explorative research to tightly planned hypothesis testing, both benefit from iterative deployments. In an excellent review of mixed methods reporting in nursing practice, Östlund (2011) and colleagues found that most researchers do not report the exact practical and analytical relationship between methodological styles employed, and whether they appeared sequentially, concurrently or in parallel. It is often also unclear if some methods were peripheral or ancillary to a dominant style (Johnson and Onwuegbuzie, 2004).

To give an example, the study of The Chosen was planned out in a sequential fashion to support a primarily in-body study. However, work in the field gradually became a concurrent feature as more and more information was needed to reach an adequate design. Later, the methodology also became deployed in parallel studies, and we started working on more games.

To catch different instances and player trajectories, Lieberoth would sometimes trail groups of students around the outside play area, and sometimes camped out at particular posts to observe how groups approached a challenge. Only with this process of piecemeal interceptions could it be identified which instances, such as students trying to compare our surveys, were systematically recurrent features of the broader events (see figure 4).

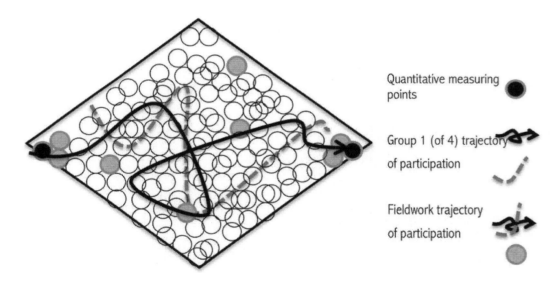

Figure 4. Fieldwork trajectory specific to studying for The Chosen.

Iacovides and colleagues' streams of lab data are stereotypically concurrent, but the study included sequential elements to bridge into everyday life. Sensitivity to the temporal dimensions in any empirical project allows game researchers to strategically move back and forth between observational levels, and to end or revisit different research styles as time progresses.

Having discussed data collection and mixed methods philosophies at some length, we need to consider how to integrate findings and a priori method choices via triangulation.

The tricky business of triangulation

Mixed methods are set apart from just mixing methods by systematic data integration. By mixing methods, we put several kinds of findings about the same object into dialogue (Fielding, 2012) but without data integration, findings from multiple channels will just be parallel tracks of information that might as well be part of separate research projects serendipitously aimed at the same subject matter.

The metaphor of triangulation stems from the trigonometry principle by which gunners, surveyors, and navigators mathematically locate unknown points in space by drawing up a triangle based on sides and angles they already know, and then calculating the unknown's position as the third corner.

In mixed methods, the metaphor is used to describe combinations of two or more kinds of data to reveal information about some more elusive third construct. Historically, the term has been applied quite loosely and often inconsistently (Bazeley and Kemp, 2011, p.57), most commonly seen in additive studies where patterns discerned from mounting information is used to support conclusions from a particular angle, rather than for testing assumptions and mapping settings.

The triangulation metaphor is a bit deceptive as there may be more than two methods, while a single object of inquiry is usually preferable. Triangulation has, for instance, been used to mix statistical data, interviews, and videotape focus groups to dissociate several ways to play (Kallio, Mäyra and Kaipainen, 2010). Game researchers have also mobilized the term when supplementing qualitative data with self-report scales (Hoffman and Nadelson, 2009) and for stepwise disconfirmation of alternative causal hypotheses in studies of games' in-world effects (Anderson, et al., 2012).

EACH METHOD SUPPLIES A LINE OF SIGHT

The central tenet of triangulation is that having two well-known vantage points allows you to hone in on a third and less-observable object.

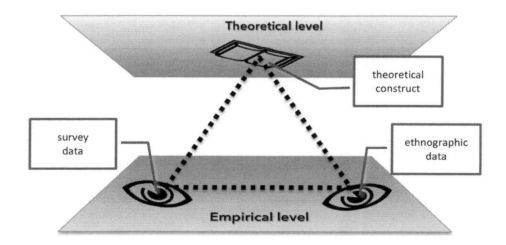

Figure 5. Triangulation (adapted from Östlund et al., 2011).

Each line in the triangle in figure 5 presents a potential line of sight:

1. toward the object of inquiry

2. between research methods.

Lines of sight toward the theoretical object (e.g., *arousal* or *paratelic engagement*) denote ways of gathering data on that construct, ideally along with hypotheses about which indicators to look for (e.g., above baseline EKG-readings or. desire to continue play without pay). Each line should reveal separate viable information as discussed in our treatment of observation levels and time, including being equally able to reject a strong hypothesis or describe unique elements of the setting. But a line can also serve legitimate confirmatory purposes (e.g., if focus group participants express similar opinions when interviewed during play) or to enrich interpretation (e.g., stories peripheral to the main research question might bridge in-world and in-room elements). If no immediate value is discernible, they should be considered redundant to the research design.

Each line between research methods allows you to consider the unique contributions and blank spots of your chosen tools from the philosophy that every method has blind angles. However, because one line of sight might yield better results or grant more perspectives on the other data streams, data integration and triangulation may not always be quite symmetrical. The trick is to report these relationships clearly, so the contribution of each method is made clear on its own terms. If afforded due attention, the full combination of lines facilitates the necessary interaction between different streams of data, including their inherent scientific philosophies and assumptions. In good triangulation reporting, all lines should be discussed and preempted in the methods section: not blotted out by the best emerging story. Figure 6 demonstrates to readers how participant observation served both as a scaffold for the study design and later interpretation of the quantitative data in The Chosen, while the interview data collected after a few weeks bore more directly on the construct of *landmark events* in memory recall.

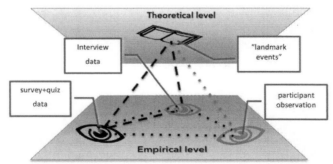

Fig 6: triangulation with interview data as bridge in *The Chosen*

Figure 6. Triangulation with interview data as bridge in The Chosen

Integration of data is, however, a complex matter where there is no one recipe to rule them all. Some mixed methods gaming studies do not use the triangulation term at all, instead preferring the trappings of grounded theory (in the case of Dow, et al., 2008 concurrently coding in-game data in a pool with retrospective interviews and survey data). Triangulation is thus mainly an important metaphor that forces us to describe the relationships between data sources. This is necessary for mixed methods to be a worthwhile endeavor, and the process creates insights beyond just piling on more data and referencing them in sequence.

TECHNOLOGIES FOR DATA INTEGRATION

Software like N-vivo (e.g., Welsh 2002) represents the typical way of coding of ethnographic data and interviews into numerical formats. This redescription of qualitative units into quantitative data represents the dominant direction in mixed methods. The only way of moving in the opposite direction has been with infographics and narrative framing, which are already basic trappings of quantitative data interpretation.

With much happening in-game new ways of recording, representing, and integrating data are emerging.

Figure 1 illustrates how wave oscillations from several in-body sensors can be displayed with in-room and in-game video data. Having this aggregated image of data streams allowed Iacovides and colleagues to conclude that their physiological data did not in fact easily predict breakdowns and breakthroughs in gameplay. In our experience, in-room observations are often the best indicators of anything cognitive, meaning that the current push for neuro-imaging or biosensor data is something of a double edged sword, in that it can only be properly used through stepwise bridging from their clinical origin domains and data triangulation with in-game and in-room factors. An example of tools for this process is biometric storyboards (Mirza-Babaei, et al., 2013), where designers first hypothesize where in a gameplay trajectory players will encounter different emotional experiences, and players' actual curves are then plotted onto the same graph. This creates a clear and nicely narrative way of seeing in-game with in-body events emerge together, and a way to test hypotheses with complex biometric data.

Figure 7. Heat map of player movements in the educational game Fair Play (Gutierrez, et al., 2014). Used with permission from Games, Learning and Society, University of Wisconsin, Madison.

Logging data in-game similarly allows for new and interesting ways of working with 3D space, turning the game world itself into data documents. Figure 7 demonstrates how a development tool conceived by Games learning and society at University of Wisconsin, Madison, makes it possible to beautifully aggregate the spatial junctions where players on average tend to spend more or less time in a 3D environment. Mappings like these allow us to figure out where to deploy different methods to triangulate data on processes and experiences, but figuring out how to make data work together in their modalities is the true promise of the added technological dimensions offered by in-room sensors and recorders, in-body measures and digital objects of inquiry. For instance, the heat map could just as well indicate emotions emerging in the player, as the avatar occupied different sections of the gamescape.

Discussion

As you can tell from the way we have moved many pieces around in this chapter, mixed methods has much to offer any study of games and gaming, and vice versa. But doing mixed methods research instead of just haphazardly mixing methodological styles places a great deal of responsibility on the scientist.

Since methodological skills are often scattered across disciplines, it is safe to assume that mixed methods researchers need to spend time learning the ropes in research environments other than the one they were originally trained in, or (even better) establish trans-disciplinary teams and arenas for exchange and collaboration.

Open-minded mixed methods workers who are internally and externally well-connected are prime candidates for the attribute of organizational boundary spanners for their fields and research units (Burt, 2004; Fleming and Waguespack, 2007; Tushman and Scanlan, 1981). Indeed, loving and understanding games is a nodal point where skilled people from disparate disciplines can find common ground, and quickly reach a level of shared language to traverse disciplinary traditions (Clark and Marshall, 1978). You should take transdisciplinary work as not just a practical and theoretical endeavor, but also a cultural challenge that allows games researchers to usher in post-disciplinary thinking.

When we coined the in-body level of observation, we must admit being tempted to dub it in-mind. But in truth, factors going on in each person's private experience and cognitive processes are only available through proxy. In-body data allow us to get very close to biological factors preceding or resulting from particular cognitive events, but without a record of in-game events and the in-room context, including interpretative talk, it is very hard to guess exactly from where a spike in skin conductance or added blood flow to cerebral regions normally associated with episodic memory arises, and what it means to both the player and the researcher's hypothesis. Instead, these proxy observations together allow us to triangulate our way towards latent factors of mind and experience, such as frustration or exhilaration which can both occur in measures of arousal when a player encounters a tricky in-game problem, and might delimit very different dimensions of the same psychological gameplay trajectory. It is, however, notoriously easy to over-interpret data from e.g. brain imaging technologies, and many have fallen into statistical and logical traps created by underpowered studies and attempts to make reverse inferences. Avoidance of such traps requires that brain imaging data be collected in the context of well-designed and tightly controlled experiments, which are sufficiently bridged to the real-world context they address. This is why the quantitative and qualitative studies of recall strategy were so important to the study of The Chosen; we could not run fMRI studies before we were absolutely sure of what we were measuring, and if out theories could be tested outside the scanner. The problem highlighted here is even greater for anthropology than for psychology as we need to include culture, experience, and behavior in studies of the brain (Roepstorff and Frith, 2012, p.3). Thus, especially when employing tantalizing new technologies, the pragmatic question you need to ask at every step of the way while looking at your study's lines of sight is this: "Are all these methods informative? Do we know how to integrate the data streams? Can we simplify our work somehow? Or have we created new blind angles which we need to cover in-game, in-room, in-world, or in-body?"

Conclusions

Mixed methods must not be confused with an anything goes approach where more is better. Too many researchers employ a mix of methods, but forget to state how the data collection and analysis played together, and if they had a priori plans for this process or let methodological shifts unfold in an exploratory manner. Mixed methods takes each method seriously in itself, and allows for varying levels of detail as long as the research project as a whole makes sense from a planned methodological point of view. It uses its different lines of sight (to borrow a gaming trope) to illuminate both the field and the other methods used.

In game research, the tradition emerging around mixed methods has the benefit of not being married to any particular theoretical style with implicit views of what is a proper empirical approach to that subject matter. Such pragmatic challenges to traditional disciplinary boundaries are healthy to students and universities alike, and encourage us to not just employ different methods in the lab or field, but also to try out different theoretical perspectives.

Recommended reading

- Iacovides, I., Aczel, J., Scanlon, E. and Woods, W., 2013. Making sense of game-play: How can we examine learning and involvement? *Transactions of the Digital Games Research Association*, 1(1), pp.1–17.
- Brewer, J., and Hunter, A., 2006. *Multimethod research: A synthesis of styles*. 2nd ed. Thousand Oaks: Sage
- Creswell, John W. 2015 *A concise introduction to mixed methods research*. London: Sage
- Östlund, U., Kidd, L., Wengström, Y. and Rowa-Dewar, N., 2011. Combining qualitative and quantitative research within mixed method research designs: a methodological review. *International Journal of Nursing Studies*, 48(3), pp.369–83. DOI=10.1016/j.ijnurstu.2010.10.005.

Acknowledgements

Andreas Lieberoth would like to thank Reed Stevens, Jo Iacovides, and Dennis Ramirez for their friendship and hospitality at Northwestern, University College London and the University of Wisconsin-Madison. Challenging conversations about games and methods—mixed or otherwise—make us collectively wiser one bite at the time.

References

Anderson, C.A., Gentile, D.A. and Dill, K.E., 2012. Prosocial, antisocial, and other effects of recreational video games. In: D. G. Singer and J. L. Singer, eds., Handbook of children and the media. 2nd ed. Thousand Oaks: Sage, pp.249–272.

Bazeley, P. and Kemp, L., 2011. Mosaics, triangles, and DNA: Metaphors for integrated analysis in mixed methods research. Journal of Mixed Methods Research, 6(1), pp.55–72. DOI=10.1177/1558689811419514.

Brewer, J. and Hunter, A., 2006. Multimethod research: A synthesis of styles. 2nd ed. Thousand Oaks: Sage, p.216.

Burt, R.S., 2004. Structural holes and good ideas. American Journal of Sociology, 110(2), pp.349–399. DOI=10.1086/421787.

Camargo, C., 2006. Interesting complexity: Sid Meier and the secrets of same design. Crossroads: The ACM Student Magazine, 13(2), p.4.

Carter, M., Gibbs, M. and Harrop, M., 2014. Drafting an army: The playful pastime of Warhammer 40,000. Games and Culture, 9(2), pp122–147. DOI=10.1177/1555412013513349.

Clark, H., & Marshall, C., 1978. Reference diaries. In D.L. Waltz, ed., Theoretical issues in natural language processing (vol. 2). New York: ACM, pp.57–63.

Cowley, B., Kosunen, I., Lankoski, P., Kivikangas, J. M., Järvelä, S., Ekman, I., Kemppainen, J. and Ravaja, R., 2014. Experience assessment and design in the analysis of gameplay. Simulation & Gaming, 45(1), pp.41–69. DOI=10.1177/1046878113513936.

Dow, S., MacIntyre, B. and Mateas, M., 2008. Understanding engagement: A mixed-method approach to observing game play. In: User Experiences in Game (CHI '08). Florence. New York: ACM, pp.5–10.

Elias, G.S., Garfield, R.S. and Gutschera, K.R., 2012. Characteristics of gmes. Cambridg: MIT Press.

Fielding, N.G., 2012. Triangulation and mixed methods designs: Data integration with new research technologies. Journal of Mixed Methods Research, 6(2), pp.124–136. DOI=10.1177/1558689812437101.

Fine, G.A., 2012. Time to play: The temporal organization of chess competition. Time & Society, 21(3), pp.395–416. DOI=10.1177/0961463X12458733.

Fleming, L. and Waguespack, D.M., 2007. Brokerage, boundary spanning, and leadership in open innovation communities. Organization Science, 18(2), pp.165–180. DOI=10.1287/orsc.1060.0242.

Gentile, D.A., 2011. The multiple dimensions of video game effects. Child Development Perspectives, 5(2), pp.75–81.

Gentile, D.A. and Stone, W., 2005. Violent video game effects on children and adolescents: A review of the literature. Minerva Pediatr, 57(57), pp.337–358.

Golas, B., 1981. Complexity and learning in business policy games. Simulation & Gaming, 12(3), pp.295–306. DOI=10.1177/104687818101200303.

Gutierrez, B., et al., 2014. A video game designed to address implicit race bias through active perspective taking. Games for Health Journal, ahead of print. DOI=10.1089/g4h.2013.0071.

Haier, R.J., Karama, S., Leyba, L. and Jung, R.E., 2009. MRI assessment of cortical thickness and functional activity changes in adolescent girls following three months of practice on a visual-spatial task. BMC Research Notes, 2, p.174. DOI=10.1186/1756-0500-2-174.

Hansen, F.A., Kortbek, K.J. and Grønbæk, K., 2008. Mobile urban drama: Setting the stage with location based technologies. In: U. Spierling and N. Szilas, eds., Proceedings of 1st joint int. conf. on interactive digital storytelling. Berlin: Springer, pp.20–31. DOI=10.1007/978-3-540-89454-4.4.

Hansen, F. A., Kortbek, K. J. and Grønbæk, K., 2010. Mobile urban drama for multimedia-based out-of-school learning. In: MUM '10. Limassol. December.

Hansen, F.A., Kortbek, K.J. and Grønbæk, K., 2012. Mobile urban drama: interactive storytelling in real world environments. New Review of Hypermedia and Multimedia, 18(12), pp.63–89. DOI=10.1080/13614568.2012.617842.

Heisenberg, W.,1958. Physics and philosophy. 1989. London: Penguin.

Henriksen, T.D., 2004. On the transmutation of educational role-play: A critical reframing of the role-play in order to meet educational demands. In: M. Montola and J. Stenros, eds., Beyond role and play: Tools, toys and theory for harnessing the imagination. Helsinki: Ropecon ry, pp.107–130.

Hoffman, B. and Nadelson, L., 2009. Motivational engagement and video gaming: a mixed methods study. Educational Technology Research and Development, 58(3), pp.245–270. DOI=10.1007/s11423-009-9134-9.

Iacovides, I., Aczel, J., Scanlon, E. and Woods, W., 2011. What can breakdowns and breakthroughs tell us about learning and involvement experienced during game-play? In: 5th European conference on games based learning, Athens. October.

Iacovides, I., Aczel, J., Scanlon, E. and Woods, W., 2013. Making sense of game-play: How can we examine learning and involvement? Transactions of the Digital Games Research Association, 1(1), pp.1–17.

Jarvela, S., Kivikangas, J.M., Katsyri, J. and Ravaja, N., 2013. Physiological linkage of dyadic gaming experience. Simulation & Gaming, 45(1), pp.24–40. DOI=10.1177/1046878113513080.

Johnson, R.B., Onwuegbuzie, A.J. and Turner, L.A., 2007. Toward a definition of mixed methods research. Journal of Mixed Methods Research, 1(2), pp.112–133. DOI=10.1177/1558689806298224.

Johnson, R.B. and Onwuegbuzie, A.J., 2004. Mixed methods research: A research paradigm whose time has come. Educational Researcher, 33(7), pp.14–26. DOI=10.3102/0013189X033007014.

Kallio, K.P., Mäyrä, F. and Kaipainen, K., 2010. At least nine ways to play: Approaching gamer mentalities. Games and Culture, 6(4), pp.327–353. DOI=10.1177/1555412010391089.

Koepp, M.J., et al., 1998. Evidence for striatal dopamine release during a video game. Nature, 393(6682), pp.266–8. DOI=10.1038/30498.

Kroll, T. and Neri, M., 2009. Designs for mixed methods research. In: S. Andrew and E.J. Halcomb, eds., Mixed methods research for nursing and the health sciences. Chichester: Wiley-Blackwell, pp.31–49.

Lieberoth, A., 2012. The science of memory: And how it should affect design of games for outside education. In: S. Berg and A.D. Rasmussen, eds., Eco-education handbook: Research in and experience with teaching/learning Methods. Aarhus: Aarhus University, pp.9–13.

Lieberoth, A. and Hansen, F., 2011. Can autobiographical memories create better learning? The case of a scary game. In: D. Gouscos and M. Meimaris, eds., Proceedings of ECGBL 2011: The 5th European conference on games based learning, pp.350–357.

Lietz, C.A., Langer, C.L. and Furman, R., 2006. Establishing trustworthiness in qualitative research in social work: Implications from a study regarding spirituality. Qualitative Social Work, 5(4), pp.441–458. DOI=10.1177/1473325006070288.

Mirza-Babaei, P., Nacke, L.E., Gregory, J., Collins, N. and Fitzpatrick, G.A., 2013. How does it play better? Exploring user testing and biometric storyboards in games user research. In: Proceedings of the CHI '04 Conference on Human Factors in Computer Systems. New York: ACM, pp.1499–1508.

Östlund, U., Kidd, L., Wengström, Y. and Rowa-Dewar, N., 2011. Combining qualitative and quantitative research within mixed method research designs: a methodological review. International Journal of Nursing Studies, 48(3), pp.369–83. DOI=10.1016/j.ijnurstu.2010.10.005.

Popper, C. (1963). Conjectures and refutations. In: T. Schick, ed., Readings in the philosophy of science. Mountain View: Mayfield Publishing Company, pp.9–13.

Roepstorff, A. and Frith, C., 2012. Neuroanthropology or simply anthropology? Going experimental as method, as object of study, and as research aesthetic. Anthropological Theory, 12(1), pp.101–111. DOI=10.1177/1463499612436467.

Shakarami, A., Mardziah, H.A., Faiz, S.A. and Tan, B.H., 2011. Remembering differently: Use of memory strategies among net-generation ESL learners. Educational Research and Reviews, 6(4), pp.350–357.

Shannon, C.E., 1950. XXII . Programming a computer for playing chess 1. Philosophical Magazine, 41(314), pp.193–204.

Shum, M.S., 1998. The role of temporal landmarks in autobiographical memory processes. Psychological Bulletin, 124(3), pp.423–42.

Silverman, D., 2001. Interpreting qualitative data: methods for analysing talk, text and interaction. 2nd ed. London: Sage.

Spapé, M.M., Kivikangas, J.M., Järvelä, S., Kosunen, I., Jacucci, G. and Ravaja, N., 2013. Keep your opponents close: social context affects EEG and fEMG linkage in a turn-based computer game. PloS One, 8(11). DOI=10.1371/journal.pone.0078795.

Squire, K., 2006. From content to context: Videogames as designed experience. Educational Researcher, 35(8), pp.19–29. DOI=10.3102/0013189X035008019.

Stevens, R., Satwicz, T. and McCarthy, L., 2008. In-game, In-room , In-world: Reconnecting video game play to the rest of kids' lives. In: Salen, K., ed.,The ecology of games. Cambridge: MIT Press, pp.41–66.

Sui, J. and Zhu, Y., 2005. Five-Year-Olds Can Show the Self-Reference Advantage. International Journal of Behavioral Development, 29(5), 382–387.

Tarbutton, M., 2010. Twin City chess club: A visual ethnographic examination of chess. In: Outstanding Ethnographic Research Projects. Available at: <http://digitalcommons.iwu.edu/anth_ethno/1/>.

Tushman, M. and Scanlan, T., 1981. Boundary spanning individuals: Their role in information transfer and their antecedents. Academy of Management Journal, 24(2), 289–305.

Weber, R., Ritterfeld, U. and Mathiak, K., 2006. Does playing violent video games induce aggression? Empirical evidence of a functional magnetic resonance imaging study. Media Psychology, 8(1), pp.39–60. DOI=10.1207/S1532785XMEP0801_4.

Welsh, E., 2002. Dealing with data: Using NVivo in the qualitative data analysis process. Forum: Qualitative Social Research, 3(2).

Yin, R., 2006. Mixed methods research: are the methods genuinely integrated or merely parallel? Research in the Schools, 13(1), pp.41–47.

17. Systematic interviews and analysis

Using the repertory grid technique

CARL MAGNUS OLSSON

When assessing game-oriented work, researchers and designers alike are faced with a difficult choice. On the one hand, an interview session with players could focus on specific game mechanics and design ideals behind them, which the researcher has defined to be of particular relevance. On the other hand, it may also be in the interest of researchers to minimize the direct impact they have during the interview phase itself in order to allow the players to drive, emphasize, and reflect on what they perceive as particularly relevant. This chapter focuses on presenting the flexibility of the repertory grid technique (Kelly, 1955) when used as an interview technique in game-oriented research. Furthermore, the chapter covers some of the systematic tools for analysis—statistical, numerical, and interpretative—that the technique has been extended with over the years.

Personal construct theory

The repertory grid technique is a methodological extension of the personal *construct theory* (Kelly, 1955). Personal construct theory argues that individuals make sense of their world through the construction of dualities that allow the individual to place a particular experience (from an object, an action, or another person) on the scale that the duality creates. For instance, when asked to describe someone, the response could be in terms of how tall or short, relaxed or anxious, and smart or annoying, that this person is perceived to be by the respondent. Noteworthy is that the terms themselves have a particular and highly subjective meaning to each respondent. Furthermore, the duality is formed between the two concepts that make sense to nuance between. Personal construct theory stipulates that constant testing of conscious experiences, individuals build an ever-evolving network of dualities that they apply to make sense and create meaning.

The foundation Kelly (1955) uses for this, is his argument for "man-the-scientist" (today perhaps more appropriately expressed human-the-scientist), that is that this construing of the world is no different than what any scientist might use.

> Man looks at his world through transparent templets which he creates and then attempts to fit over the realities of which the world is composed. The fit is not always very good. Yet without such patterns the world appears to be such an undifferentiated homogeneity that man is unable to make any sense out of it. Even a

poor fit is more helpful to him than nothing at all [...] Let us give the name constructs to these patterns that are tentatively tried on for size. They are ways of construing the world." (Kelly, 1955, p.8–9.)

Constructs are used for predictions of things to come, and the world keeps on rolling on and revealing these predictions to be either correct or misleading. This fact provides the basis for the revision of constructs and, eventually, of whole construct systems. (Kelly, 1955, p.14.)

These constructs are, given the subjective nature of them, what Kelly refers to as the personal constructs. Implicitly, the pairing of two phenomena into a scale also indicates their relation to a third phenomenon, which does not fit into this scale (Bannister and Fransella, 1985). This third phenomenon could however be related to a fourth phenomenon as part of another construct, which in turn is different from a fifth phenomenon, and so on—subsequently yielding an intricate network of personal constructs which dictates the sensemaking process of environments, social interaction and artifacts.

Implied by the focus personal construct theory has on individuals and individual perceptions is a phenomenological stance towards meaning creation (cf. Husserl, 1900). Phenomenology is the study of how conscious experiences give rise to meaning. By arguing that personal construct theory is inherently phenomenological, we interpret for instance the 'man-the-scientist' example above as an expression of conscious sensemaking. This implies that subjectiveness is recognized and embraced by the repertory grid technique, and that generalization must be done carefully as an expression of the context rather than as evidence of an objective truth (i.e. what a more Kant, 1781, inspired theoretical view of perception and meaning creation would argue). In simpler terms, the repertory grid technique is a tool that strives to open the doors to an individual's meaning creation process related to a specific experience.

As Bannister and Fransella (1985) argue, the two phenomena in a personal construct may—and typically are—related to other phenomena. This implies that a larger network of related personal constructs make up what Heidegger (1927) would refer to as an ontology of objects in the world, that is the set of elements through which meaning is created in any given situation. As with personal constructs, ontologies are re-negotiated over time as new experiences and objects test their applicability and relevance.

This change process is similar to the role of coupling within phenomenology. Coupling is an expression of the effectiveness to convey intentionality, that is, the meaningfulness of a particular action. Originally, Brentano (1874) described intentionality as a human actor's ability to express meaning through action, while derived intentionality (Dourish, 2001) has since been described as the interpretation of meaning that an observer makes (based on her own experiences) as another actor performs (or records, as in the case of a game mechanics that a game developer implements, for instance) an action. As the coupling between an action and the meaningfulness of this action becomes questioned, existing ontologies are challenged and re-assembled in new ways to compensate for the change in (experienced or derived) intentionality. Similarly, as personal constructs are situated dualities related to a particular context, changes in the context implies that the personal constructs may also change in order to compensate for new experiences of action and new meaning of this action.

While the focus on personal construct theory is individual, this does not mean that comparisons between different sets of personal constructs cannot be made. On the contrary, just as intersubjectivity (Schutz, 1932)—the creation of shared meaning between two or more actors—is of significant relevance to phenomenology, shared sets of personal constructs between several actors speak to the strength of the coupling between an experience of action and the intentionality of this action. While even cases of strong coupling (as all experiences) are subject to change over time, such cases may still be considered particularly suitable to for instance further analysis, development of design principles to support them, or as guide for product development prioritization. In this regard, comparisons between the personal constructs of several individuals could even be argued as one of the core opportunities afforded by personal construct theory.

The repertory grid technique

Through the methodological technique referred to as the repertory grid technique, personal construct theory identifies and systematically analyzes the captured personal constructs—individually for in-depth understanding of a single meaning creation process, or in comparison with other individuals to recognize cases of particularly strong coupling.

The repertory grid technique has been used in a wide array of fields, including information systems research (cf. Hunter, 1997; Moynihan, 1996; Tan and Hunter, 2002; Olsson and Russo, 2004), clinical psychology (Shaw, 1980; Shaw and Gaines, 1983; 1987), organizational dynamics and organizational design (Dunn and Ginsberg, 1986; Wacker, 1981), and human computer interaction (Easterby-Smith, 1980; Fallman, 2003; Fallman and Waterworth, 2010). Given the suitability and use of the repertory grid technique in other research fields, the technique has significant support for its applicability as a general research tool and subsequently may safely be embraced in game-oriented research as well.

Through a number of illustrations related to game-oriented research, this chapter will exemplify how to use repertory grids as methodological tool of inquiry. Before we can move to these illustrations, however, we must first establish what the main components are in the technique and how they are used to empirically elicit and evaluate peoples' subjective perceptions. The three main components involved in developing repertory grids are elements, constructs, and links (Tan and Hunter, 2002).

ELEMENTS

The elements represent that which is being examined, and could for example be different architectures, or different social groups. Elements may be *supplied* by the researcher (Reger, 1990) — which is common when using theory to guide element selection (e.g. using Lund, 2003, to explore the material aspects of a particular environment) — or *elicited* from the participants (Easterby-Smith, 1980) — using scenarios, pools of potential elements, or discussion with the respondent. Several rules apply for what makes valid elements, e.g. that they should be discrete (Stewart and Stewart, 1981), homogenous (Easterby-Smith, 1980), non-evaluative (Stewart and Stewart, 1981) and representative (Beail, 1985; Easterby-Smith, 1980).

CONSTRUCTS

The constructs are used as the assessment basis for the elements under examination, and could in a comparison of social groups include for example «small–large», «passive–active», «hierarchi-cal–empowered», and «local–distributed». A technique known as laddering is commonly employed during elicitation, where neutral and probing questions such as "why [...]", "in what way [...]", and "can you elaborate on [...]" are asked to insure that the researcher understands well the context of the labels used by the respondent (Reynolds and Gutman, 1988).

There are four ways to approach respondents with constructs.

1. Constructs may be supplied by the researcher in order to control the exploration, and allow for statistical analysis of similarities and differences among the respondents (Latta and Swigger, 1992).
2. Constructs may be elicited based on triadic comparison of elements. This approach randomly presents three elements at a time to the respondent, who points out which of the three is different than the other two, and what this difference is. Labeling differences and similarities is entirely done by the respondent, without researcher intervention. This process is repeated over all possible combinations of elements or using a pre-determined set of combinations between elements. A combination of supplied and elicited constructs may be used if a certain degree of freedom as well as control is important (Easterby-Smith, 1980).
3. Group elicitation of constructs is essentially a workshop format of normal elicitation (Stewart and Stewart, 1981). Subjective meaning of each individual respondent is somewhat lost as the group discusses and agrees on what best represents them as a whole. However, comparing individually elicited constructs with group elicited constructs can in itself capture which parts overlap between the individual and the group.
4. Full context form may also be used to elicit constructs. This implies leaving it to the respondent to sort through all elements and place them in any number of piles, where each pile has a specific meaning to them, and where all elements in each pile have the same aspects associated with them. Once the sorting is done, the respondent is asked to give two or three words that capture the unique meaning of each pile. This has been used in cognitive psychology (Reger, 1990) and to find shared meaning in organizational contexts (Simpson and Wilson, 1999). This fourth alternative uses its own way of linking elements with constructs through statistical analysis of the groupings and relationships between them (rather than the more common approach detailed below).

LINKS

The links between elements and constructs are provided by finally asking the respondent to *rate* each element on a scale using the constructs. Odd number scales such as one to five, one to seven, one to nine, and one to eleven have been successfully used (Tan and Hunter, 2002). It has been suggested that retest reliability is likely to be lower when using a scale of more than one to five (Bell, 1990). Those in favor of larger scales argue that this offers greater freedom in rating to the respondents, and recommend a rating scale larger than the number of elements that are being compared (Hunter, 1997). Alternatively, respondents may *rank* all elements between the labels of each construct. Using ranking, respondents may however feel forced to find differences between elements that they do not subscribe to. As a result, rating is the most common technique used (Tan and Hunter, 2002).

Using repertory grids in game-oriented research

For game-oriented research, the potential use of the repertory grid technique of course depends on the research interest first and foremost. The technique is inherently comparative, regardless if treating them as idiographic or nomothetic entities. The notions of idiographic and nomothetic grids are explained further in the latter part of this text, but in brief—an idiographic grid focuses on the subjective experiences of the individual, while a nomothetic grid focuses on the comparison of individual or group grids. The comparative nature stems from the set of elements that are being compared and drive the rating (and possibly entire elicitation process) of constructs. In the case of idiographic grids, both elements and constructs may be elicited, while nomothetic grids require that either elements or constructs (or both) are supplied by the researcher.

The highly structured interview technique lends a strong support to researchers. This process may (if so desired) be almost entirely free from researcher bias, but is still flexible enough to allow respondents to define the language (through construct elicitation) that they themselves feel is most appropriate given their subjective experiences and meaning creation process while playing. For instance, if the interest lies in understanding player styles over different map designs in *StarCraft 2* (Blizzard Entertainment, 2010), each map is an element candidate. The researcher may then chose the sample type and sample size they expose these elements to, for example, players of all races, only Zerg players, only Terran players, only Protoss players, players recognized as rush/timing attack players, players recognized for their late-game prowess, etc. Similarly, if the researcher interest is to compare different implementations of for instance player-vs-player combat in MMOs, the different MMOs become the elements used to elicit constructs. The selected MMOs must of course all have some form of player-vs-player element in order to be representative (cf. Beail, 1985; Easterby-Smith, 1980)—as listed earlier in the rules for element selection.

If, on the other hand, the research focus lies in testing the applicability of research hypotheses, it may be relevant to supply constructs rather than elicit them to increase researcher control over the direction of the results. Research hypotheses can be developed in many ways, but are commonly defined through a literature review, based on a pre-defined theoretical research framework, or through best-practice review of de facto patterns used in industry or by end-users. An example of this could be hypotheses related to the common argument for continuous playtesting as important during all stages of game design and development (cf. Fullerton, 2008). Through literature review of effective playtesting techniques, a set of related hypotheses could be generated for what 'should' be useful at different stages of design and development. By conducting repertory grid sessions with designers and developers in game developing organizations—using the identified playtesting techniques as elements—researchers may test extant research understanding versus actual use and impact in industry.

Constructs are not the only ones that may be elicited however. Using formal analysis (see chapter 3), gameplay design patterns (cf. Björk and Holopainen, 2004; Holopainen, 2011), or game design mechanics (cf. Järvinen, 2008; Sicart, 2008), recognized patterns and mechanics may be used as sources for supplied constructs, that respondents are asked to elicit game support for. As argued earlier, elicitation may also be in part supplied and in part elicited. If we for instance start from a pre-defined set of constructs related to gameplay design patterns to elicit game support for these, it is feasible to include a second repertory grid phase where additional gameplay design patterns within the elicited set of games are elicited. This would make the study in part nomothetic as it starts from a pre-defined set of constructs, and in part idiographic as it allows each respondent a chance to add constructs based on the individually elicited elements. If the researcher, prior to the second elicitation phase, would combine all elements elicited from the respondents during the first phase and expose all respondents to the full set of elements, the study would be nomothetic and allow for comparison between participants.

As an effect of the comparative nature of repertory grids, results typically lead to a set of characterizing constructs that may be discussed in relation to the particular research focus. As illustrated by Olsson (2011), the grid results themselves do not have to be the end result of a study. Instead, the results may for instance be used as foundation for theory development by applying a theoretical framework to the grid results to further contextualize the results and identify gaps between theory and grid results. Such games imply research opportunities that in themselves are contributions and potentially end result of the study, or may be viewed as opportunities for design and development activities. Such activities may then be assessed either using repertory grids again later, or through other assessment techniques based on researcher needs and relevance for the study.

Analyzing repertory grids

As earlier discussed, repertory grids are founded on the personal construct theory and subsequently hold particular interest in the individual perspective. A result of this is that repertory grids are commonly analyzed individually, and we will therefore begin this section by outlining common approaches for such analysis. Following this, we present analysis techniques focusing on commonalities in order to capture coupled experiences that are shared between sets of individuals. This section presents a subset of the analysis techniques described in Tan and Hunter (2002) with related links to the free-to-use WebGrid tool (WebGrid, 2014) where applicable. The reliance on WebGrid illustrations of this chapter is motivated by the tool being free-to-use and its steady development over the last decade (maintained by the University of Calgary and University of Victoria). A considerable body of research has furthermore been developed in relation to it, which is also shared on its website (RepGrid, 2014) together with links to both the free web based WebGrid tool (WebGrid, 2014) and RepGrid stand-alone applications available in limited personal free-to use and full research/enterprise licenses (Center for Personal Computer Studies, 2014). Analysis techniques not covered by WebGrid that are presented below are still equally relevant to consider, but starting by familiarizing oneself with the free analysis tools is a good way to get into repertory grids.

INDIVIDUAL GRID ANALYSIS

Content analysis implies identifying the most common tendencies through simple frequency count. This means that the researcher counts how many times particular elements or constructs are discussed by the respondents (Hunter, 1997; Moynihan, 1996). Alternatively, categories of similar constructs or elements may be identified and counted (Stewart and Stewart, 1981). This may be particularly useful if the object being counted (constructs or elements) were elicited from the respondents, as this reduces the likelihood that the same constructs are mentioned more than once.

Rearranging repertory grids (Bell, 1990; Easterby-Smith, 1980) is done by reordering elements and constructs so that constructs that are similarly rated are placed close to each other. As much as possible, this is then repeated for the elements in order to position similarly interpreted elements as close to each other as possible. When rearranging repertory grids, visual focusing (Hunter, 1997) can be performed. This means that construct poles may be reversed if this aids identification of similar constructs or elements. The reason for this is that patterns in the ranking of elements are in this case the focus and not the order in which respondents identified the poles (Hunter, 1997). An illustration of this process may be found in Stewart and Stewart (1981). WebGrid (2014) supports automatically rearranging and visual focusing as part of the FOCUS cluster (Shaw and Thomas, 1978) transformation analysis.

Transformation is a common approach for analyzing repertory grids. This includes FOCUS cluster analysis (Shaw and Thomas, 1978), where clusters of similarly rated elements and constructs are placed in linked groups. These links show the level of numerical similarity between the elements and constructs. Highly similar ratings for two constructs may signify that they are in fact the same aspect but with minor nuance differences. As elaborated in for example Fallman (2003) and Olsson (2011), it is recommended to semantically review clustered elements and constructs in order to verify that the similarities are likely because of a shared fundamental aspect rather than coincidental similarity. Olsson (2011) and Olsson and Russo (2004) complement this semantic review with qualitative interpretations of the laddering process (Reynolds and Gutman, 1988) used during the interview session to increase the validity of the semantic review. FOCUS cluster analysis is the main form of analysis supported by WebGrid (2014), although additional analysis tools have been added in the later versions of WebGrid as a complement to FOCUS cluster analysis.

Decomposing repertory grids implies breaking the grids down to the fundamental structure. PrinGrid analysis is an example of decomposing which WebGrid (2014) supports. It uses the decomposition technique of *principal component analysis* together with the popular factor analysis (Bell, 1990; Easterby-Smith, 1980; Leach, 1980). This implies that each construct is treated as a vector to permit vector analysis to be used in order to rotate constructs as much as needed in n-space to present the constructs (vectors) as separated as possible from each other in a two-dimensional figure. Elements are then mapped onto this two-dimensional image to show which construct poles (vector nodes) are closest to them, or in simpler terms which construct poles are central to each element, and the relative distance between each element.

Cognitive content analysis may be measured in three ways: element distance, construct centrality, and element preference. Such measurements are possible to compare across individuals and are part of the original propositions by Kelly (1955). They have been widely reviewed in extant literature on personal construct theory (Dunn, et al., 1986; Fransella and Bannister, 1977; Fransella, et al., 2003; Slater, 1977).

1. *Element distance* measures the distance between elements and represents the respondent's perceived similarity between them. Elements that have construct ratings that are similar on all constructs are considered closely related while those rated differently on all dimensions are considered different. This simple definition implies that elements with high similarity are interpreted as sharing the same underlying meaning for the respondent. The FOCUS cluster analysis (Shaw and Thomas, 1978), which WebGrid (2014) supports, performs element distance measurements as part of its analysis. It is based on Reger's cluster analysis technique (Reger, 1990).

2. *Construct centrality* describes what Kelly (1955) theorized as constructs that are central to an individual in relation to all other related constructs (hold a high correlation to all other constructs). Identifying the correlation strength may be done with a simple correlation matrix or as part of factor analysis (Reger, 1990). The PrinGrid analysis of WebGrid (2014) is an example of construct centrality analysis.

3. *Element preference* refers to the desirability of each element in relation to the other elements being compared, as perceived by the respondent. This is calculated by the average score of each column of a repertory grid, where the highest average signifies the most preferred element. Care must be taken if element preference will be used as analysis technique, as the context of the grid session must clearly be stated as the preference of one element over the other(s) (depending on if using a dyadic or triadic elicitation process). If the context is to identify nuanced descriptions of differences between elements that all have merit, element preference analysis is not suitable. In addition, construct pole reversal via visual focusing (Hunter, 1997)—which is part of the WebGrid (2014) FOCUS cluster analysis—cannot be used as this would affect the calculation of column average for an element. Fortunately, element preference is simple to calculate manually (or by using a spreadsheet) based on the original repertory grid, before any other analysis is used to for instance rearrange, transform or decompose it.

Cognitive structure analysis may be measured in three ways: cognitive differentiation, cognitive complexity, and cognitive integration. The use of univariate analysis for all three measures has been reviewed widely (Dunn, et al., 1986; Fransella and Bannister, 1977; Fransella, et al., 2003; Slater, 1977). The multivariate analysis that for instance factor analysis (Reger, 1990) performs shows complexity and integration.

1. *Cognitive differentiation* describes the number of constructs used for the element analysis. Many constructs imply that the cognitive differentiation is high, while low differentiation means that only a few constructs were used. This is measured by simply counting the number of constructs elicited (or supplied).
2. *Cognitive complexity* refers to the correlation level of the different constructs. The greater the correlation level is, the greater the similarity between constructs are, which implies that the constructs are similar in meaning. Starting from a high number of constructs (large cognitive differentiation), and inspired by Fallman (2003), Olsson (2011) uses multiple stages of analysis where highly correlated constructs in each stage are grouped into single constructs in order to identify a set of constructs that best describe the full (read: high) cognitive complexity of his study.
3. *Cognitive integration* describes the degree of linkage between constructs. It is therefore the opposite of cognitive complexity and thus measured in the same way. As illustrated in the multiple stages of Olsson (2011), the cognitive integration itself provides an insight into the richness of meaning creation of respondents and the many facets that go into this process. High correlation between constructs implies a highly integrated system of interpretation (and subsequently lends support for clustering constructs together).

COMMONALITY ANALYSIS

Analyzing repertory grids from multiple respondents allows researchers the chance to identify commonalities. This may be achieved in at least two ways, and the purpose of the study directs which approach should be pursued.

Element commonality analysis focuses on identifying commonalities between the elements in question, such as for Fallman (2003) and Olsson (2011), the constructs from each respondent may simply be added to one large summative repertory grid. For traceability, it may be relevant to index constructs from each respondent as they are placed in the summative repertory grid (which in practice is a group repertory grid), in order to preserve the ability to return to for instance laddering questions as semantic review is done during FOCUS cluster analysis. This is important as constructs may semantically appear to be the same for two or more respondents, but still be paired with different construct nodes and subsequently may imply different meaning. Correlation analysis coupled with laddering should be used in such cases to increase the reliability of the semantic review. This form of commonality analysis is in principle the same as an individual repertory grid analysis, save the added care which must be taken during possible clustering of constructs.

Respondent commonality analysis focuses on identifying commonalities between respondents rather than between elements, there are three main approaches that may be used (Ginsberg, 1989): linguistic analysis, mapping techniques, and multivariate techniques.

1. *Linguistic analysis* is a formal process used by Walton (1986) which classifies respondent expressions as part of well-established and stable construct categories within a discipline. The focus lies on minimizing researcher bias during interpretation and is a somewhat cumbersome process (Tan and Hunter, 2002).
2. *Mapping techniques* include Q-type factor analysis and multidimensional scaling (MDS). These may be used to map collective meanings from individual respondents or groups of respondents. Q-type analysis results in clusters of individuals that are closest to each other, as per their ratings of the elements. Meanwhile, MDS analysis results in elements that are most frequently rated becoming placed closer together. This yields a normative map that shows which of the elements provide best-fit for the respondents.
3. *Multivariate techniques* include for instance variance analysis, regression analysis and discriminate analysis. Such techniques are applied to each individual repertory grid and the resulting structure is compared. The goal here is to identify groups of respondents that show a similar structure in their individual repertory grids, as such similarity hints towards a similar cognitive understanding of the elements. Due to the focus on structure for groups of respondents, multivariate techniques allow for testing of hypotheses and are useful to understand group behavior, such as organizational work patterns or end-user patterns.

Further commonality analysis techniques are available in Tan and Hunter (2002), but the above are among the more common. Element commonality analysis was added to this chapter, despite not being listed by Tan and Hunter, as it is an example of recent adaptations of repertory grid commonality analysis. An attractive aspect of both individual repertory grid analysis and commonality analysis is the potential for multi-stage analysis, using complementing forms of analysis to enrich the cognitive understanding.

Repertory grid research design

SAMPLE SIZE

Repertory grid sessions and analysis is a highly intensive exercise, where researchers must have prepared well and ideally test (cf. Olsson and Russo, 2004; Olsson, 2011) the intended process against a few respondents to validate and adapt the process before executing it on the full set of respondents. The focus on detail is high and data is treated carefully which leads to a relatively small sample size needed. Based on the findings of Dunn, et al. (1986) and Ginsberg (1989), Tan and Hunter (2002) argues that 15 to 25 respondents within a comparable population is likely to be sufficient in order to generate constructs that approximate a *universe of meaning* for the specific repertory grid foci. At this point, further constructs from additional respondents may use different words semantically but tend to represent the same cognitive meaning. From a game-oriented perspective, comparable population means that researchers must carefully consider if the respondents may be placed in one group without risk for the results to become conflicting. For instance, can novice players be mixed with hardcore players given the research objective? If the research concern is something that is not likely to be affected by the level of experience, the two can be combined. On the other hand, if the level of experience may affect the results it is instead better to use two sample populations if both groups of players are of interest. This would mean having one group of experienced players and one group of novices, ideally 15 to 25 in each if the goal is to define a generalizable set of constructs for the elements in question.

In the case of Dunn, et al. (1986), 17 respondents were used to generate a total of 23 unique constructs. Interestingly, these constructs were identified already after the tenth interview. Of course, in cases were the focus is not on identifying a universe of meaning, such as when conducting assessments of group behavior patterns in an organization, the relevant sample size may be smaller. An example of this is the shared understanding between the respondents lies in focus, perhaps as part of a change or innovation process. Using a smaller set of respondents to generate input to a more broadly distributed questionnaire is furthermore possible.

PREVIOUS EXAMPLES OF USE

Before deciding on the design of a new repertory grid study—and particularly if this is the first time conducting one—reviewing some existing studies is a good idea. While this is of course always a good idea when using a tool or technique, it is of particular value for the repertory grid technique due to the sheer number of options that the flexibility of the method provides. Some hands-on examples of use may therefore provide useful guidance and furthermore illustrate contrasting options that allow informed methodological reflections to be developed.

As repertory grids presently lacks diffusion in game-oriented research, five examples from the information systems (IS) domain will be used instead. The first four examples of table 1 are adapted from Tan and Hunter (2002) while the fifth example is from chapter five of Olsson (2011) in order to show a more recent example of extended use. Incidentally, Olsson (2011) contrasts a context-aware game for passengers in cars with other context-aware applications used in cars. As Olsson's work is positioned towards IS rather than game-oriented research, the game itself is not in focus. Rather, his focus was on the interaction patterns that the game created which were contrasted with other in-car applications to better understand the mediation process between human and non-human agents in dynamically changing contexts. The work illustrates, however, that games are also relevant as study objects in other research streams than the strictly game-oriented outlets, and that using games is also accepted in those research streams.

	Hunter (1997)	Moynihan (1996)	Phythian and King (1992)	Latta and Swigger (1992)	Olsson (2011)
Research objective	Explore the qualities of 'excellent' systems analysts	Identify situational factors from the planning and running of new IS development projects	Develop rules for an expert system to support customer tender evaluations	Validate the grid in modeling communal knowledge regarding design of system interfaces	Initial data analysis prior to applying a theoretical mediation framework for context-aware applications
Research perspective	Qualitative	Qualitative	Quantitative	Quantitative	Mixed
Nature of repertory grid	Idiographic	Idiographic	Nomothetic	Nomothetic	Nomothetic
Key findings	Several themes considered as qualities of excellent systems analysts	Identified themes over and above literatureDifferences in project managers' construction of project contexts	Identified key factors and rules influencing tender decisionsExpert system improved consistency	Commonality of constructions support the use of the grid to model group knowledge	15 characterizing aspects of context-aware systems in cars8 mediation types after individual element analysis
Element selection	Systems analysts with whom participant has interacted	Systems development projects on which participant has worked	Previous customer tender enquiries	Components of online bibliographic retrieval systems	Ten context-aware systems related to travel by car
Construct elicitation	ElicitedQualities of 'excellent' systems analysts	ElicitedSituational factors influencing risks in new systems projects	SuppliedKey factors and rules influencing tender decisions	SuppliedAttributes of system interface design	SuppliedBased on the Olsson (2011) mediation framework
	Minimum context form (triadic sort) and laddering	Minimum context form (triadic sort)	Minimum context form (triadic sort) and laddering	Minimum context form (triadic sort) and supplied constructs	Constructs not perceived as relevant may be declined Laddering
Linking	Rating	None	Rating (grid)Ranking (elements)	Rating	Rating
Grid analysis	Content analysisVisual focusing	Content analysis	Cluster analysis (FOCUS)Correlation	Cluster analysisCorrelation	Multi-staged FOCUSCluster analysis
	COPE and VISA		Mathematical modeling		Semantic review and laddering

Sample and size	53 users and IT professionals from two insurance companies	14 systems development project managers	Two manager experts involved in assessing tender enquiries	Instructor and students who completed an information search and retrieval course	11 interviewees with experience from embedded systems development

Table 1. Five examples of how repertory grids have been used within information systems research (adapted from Tan and Hunter, 2002, and Olsson, 2011).

RESEARCH APPROACH: QUALITATIVE, QUANTITATIVE, OR MIXED METHODS?

Repertory grids lend themselves well for qualitative as well as quantitative analysis, or a mix of the two to increase the richness of possible interpretation. Two of the five examples in table 1 rely on qualitative analysis. In the case of Hunter (1997), content analysis was used to interpret aspects of 'excellent' systems analysts. The content analysis included visual focusing and computer software (COPE) to assist the identification of emerging themes. Meanwhile, Moynihan (1996) used repertory grids to guide the decision-making process for projects working with external clients. In this case, individual repertory grids were created for each respondent and content analysis used to identify themes based on the elicited constructs.

The quantitative approaches used by two of the five examples in table 1 rely on mathematical or statistical analysis of their repertory grids. Phythian and King (1992) used FOCUS cluster and correlation analysis on individual respondent's repertory grids, and on combined grids for all respondents. This was used to identify key factors needed for a systematic decision-making process support tool. Latta and Swigger (1992) used cluster analysis (and Spearman's rank order correlation—see Latta and Swigger [1992] for further details) to identify similarities in interpretations among students after interface design lectures, and the correlation strengths of these similarities.

A mix of quantitative and qualitative analysis techniques may also be used. In the example of Olsson (2011), a multi-stage process for identifying unique constructs of rich meaning was developed. In each stage, FOCUS cluster analysis was used to identify clusters of constructs with similar cognitive meaning to the respondents. These suggested clusters were then reviewed semantically to ensure that the clustering did not include falsely positive matches or contradictions that laddering responses could not explain. The quantitative FOCUS cluster analysis was subsequently reviewed qualitatively using semantic review and qualitative laddering responses to increase reliability of the identified clusters. The mix of quantitative and qualitative techniques for analysis allowed Olsson (2011) to identify unique constructs with rich meaning that capture the complex and dynamic mediation process that human actors perceive while using context-aware systems and interacting with others during travel by car. Using only quantitative analysis, Olsson would likely have had to reject and dismiss many suggested construct similarities as it would otherwise have been impossible to separate falsely similar constructs from those that laddering elaboration could support as related. Vice versa, relying only on qualitative analysis, researcher bias and sheer number of constructs would likely have prevented many of the rich constructs to be even considered.

Repertory grids are either idiographic or nomothetic in their nature. *Idiographic* implies that the focus is on the individual and her subjective experiences, with results subsequently presented as expressions of the individual cognitive meaning. If the research instead focuses on comparing repertory grids of individuals or groups of individuals, such grids are considered *nomothetic*.

For ideographic grids, and as was the case for Hunter (1997) and Moynihan (1996), the elements being compared are not shared between all respondents. If constructs are elicited rather than supplied, this means that generalization over the entire sample of respondents become impossible to do, which leads researcher focus towards depth of analysis rather than breadth. Themes that are common—despite the different elements (and possibly different constructs as well)—between the respondents *may* emerge, but this cannot be taken for granted or forced out of the data. Any such themes must clearly be rooted in the individual respondent's construct elaborations, which implies that using techniques such as laddering during interview sessions are recommended.

Tan and Hunter (2002, p.52) stress, however, that "researchers interested in the idiographic characteristics of individual unique RepGrids are not restricted to analyzing the elicited RepGrid data purely from a qualitative perspective". They note that research on strategic management holds examples where quantitative analysis has been performed on idiographic RepGrids. For instance, in a study by Simpson and Wilson (1999) a list of key success factors for effective strategies was used as elements. The studied companies supplied the factors and the resulting data was analyzed using multidimensional scaling, correlation, and cluster analysis.

Research that focuses on comparing repertory grids of individuals or groups of individuals are instead considered *nomothetic* in their nature. In order to allow comparisons, elements or constructs must be shared between the respondents (Easterby-Smith, 1980). As noted by Tan and Hunter (2002), this form of research tends to be quantitative, but the mixed approach by Olsson (2011) illustrates how quantitative and qualitative analysis may be used in combination during nomothetic repertory grid studies. While all three nomothetic examples in table 1 use supplied elements as well as constructs, it is sufficient if either of these is supplied (cf. Fallman, 2003; Olsson and Russo, 2004) and the other is elicited.

Concluding reflections

The above examples illustrate potential use of the repertory grid technique and should be interpreted as such. They were selected as they show different research agendas, as well as different approaches to the use of the repertory grid technique. For more in-depth examples of specific studies, simply following up by reading the referenced studies listed above is recommended. As the focus of such reading is on how the repertory grid technique was used, it does not matter that the studies come from non-game research. In fact, the support from multiple research domains that they illustrate strengthens the argument that the technique is likely to be useful within game-oriented research as well.

An advantage of the repertory grid technique as data collection tool is the relative ease with which the research process can be tested before exposing it to the full set of respondents. Using colleagues and associates with at least a rudimentary understanding of the problem domain in question, allows researchers the opportunity to both practice with the technique itself and informally validate the design of the grid process. The extensive flexibility of the repertory grid technique—ranging from element selection or elicitation, via construct selection or elicitation, as well as how to approach the actual interview session and in particular the laddering process, to the number of options for analysis—means that dry-run tweaking is advisable.

Finally, Tan and Hunter (2002) make two important points about the use of repertory grid that bears repeating. First, the repertory grid technique can be used together with other research methods, for instance to validate other techniques, or as a pre-study phase that directs further investigation. Second, the repertory grid technique is part of the personal construct theory, which itself is one of several theories in cognitive science (Berkowitz, 1978). Specifically, this chapter has emphasized the inherent phenomenological assumptions that the personal construct theory relies upon, beyond what Tan and Hunter (2002) elaborate on.

The impact of the philosophical foundation that the personal construct theory—and subsequently the repertory grid technique—relies upon is important. Mixing the use of repertory grids with methodological techniques that are neither neutral in stance (such as mathematical and statistical analysis—neither of which were part of Kelly's original analysis techniques, but were included above), nor share the phenomenological foundation, is problematic as the findings and chain of arguments of such a mix would not be internally consistent. This is of course always the case of any mixed method approach, and as such is not to be considered a flaw in the research method, but rather a precaution for the use—rather than abuse—of the method.

Recommended reading

- Bradshaw, J.M., Ford, K.M., Adams-Webber, J.R. and Boose, J.H., 1993. Beyond the repertory grid: New approaches to constructivist knowledge acquisition tool development. *International Journal of Intelligent Systems*, 8(2), pp.287–333.
- Coshall, J.T. 2000. Measurement of tourists' images: The repertory grid approach. *Journal of Travel Research*, 39(1), pp.85–89.
- Enquire Within 2014. Helpful hints for using the repertory grid interview. Available at: <http://www.enquirewithin.co.nz/hintsfor.htm>.
- Jankowicz, D., 2003. *The easy guide to repertory grids*. Chinchester: Wiley.

References

Bannister, D. and Fransella, F., 1985. *Inquiring man*. 3rd ed. London: Routledge.

Beail, N., 1985. An introduction to repertory grid technique. In: N. Beail, ed., *Repertory Grid Technique and Personal Constructs*, Cambridge: Brookline Books, pp.1–26.

Bell, R.C., 1990. Analytic issues in the use of repertory grid technique. *Advances in Personal Construct Psychology*. 1, pp.25-48.

Berkowitz, L., 1978. *Cognitive theories in social psychology*, New York: Academic Press.

Björk, S. and Holopainen, J., 2004. *Patterns in game design*, Boston: Charles River Media.

Blizzard Entertainment 2010. *Starcraft 2: Wings of liberty* [game]. Blizzard Entertainment. Available at: <http://us.blizzard.com/en-us/games/sc2/>.

Brentano, F., 1874. *Psychology from an empirical standpoint.* English translation 1995, New York: Routledge.

Center for Personal Computer Studies 2014. *Rep 5* [computer program]. University of Calgary. Available at: <http://repgrid.com/>.

Dennett, D., 1987. *The intentional stance.* Cambridge: MIT Press.

Dourish, P., 2001. *Where the action is: The foundations of embodied interaction.* Cambridge: MIT Press.

Dunn, W. N., Cahill, A. G., Dukes, M. J. and Ginsberg, A., 1986. The policy grid: A cognitive methodology for assessing policy dynamics. In: W.N. Dunn, ed., *Policy analysis: Perspectives, concepts, and methods.* Greenwich: JAI Press, pp.355–375.

Dunn, W.N. and Ginsberg, A., 1986. A sociocognitive network approach to organizational analysis. *Human Relations,* 40(11), pp.955–976.

Easterby-Smith, M., 1980. The design, analysis and interpretation of repertory grids. *International Journal of Man-Machine Studies,* 13, pp.3–24.

Fallman, D., 2003. In romance with the materials of mobile interaction: A phenomenological approach to the design of mobile interaction technology. PhD. Umeå University.

Fallman, D. and Waterworth, J.A., 2010. Capturing user experiences of mobile information technology with the repertory grid technique. *Human Technology: An Interdisciplinary Journal on Humans in ICT Environments,* 6(2), pp.250–268.

Fransella, F., and Bannister, D., 1977. *A manual for repertory grid technique,* New York: Academic Press.

Fransella, F., Bannister, D. and Bell, R., 2003. A manual for repertory grid technique, 2nd ed., Chichester: Wiley-Blackwell.

Fullerton, T., 2008. *Game design workshop: A playcentric approach to creating innovative games.* 2nd ed. London: Elsevier.

Gaines, B.R. and Shaw, M.L.G., 1993. Eliciting knowledge and transferring it effectively to a knowledge-based system. *IEEE Transactions on Knowledge and Data Engineering.* 5(1), pp.4–14.

Ginsberg, A. 1989. Construing the business portfolio: A cognitive model of diversification. *Journal of Management Studies,* 26(4), pp.417–438.

Heidegger, M., 1927. *Being and time.* Translated 1962. New York: Harper & Row.

Holopainen, J., 2011. Foundations of gameplay. PhD. Blekinge Institute of Technology.

Hunter, M.G. 1997. The use of RepGrids to gather interview data about information systems analysts. *Information Systems Journal.* 7, pp.67–81.

Husserl, E., 1900. *Logical investigations.* Translated 1970. London: Routledge.

Järvinen, A. 2008. Games without frontiers: Theories and methods for game studies and design. PhD. University of Tampere.

Kelly, G., 1955. *The psychology of personal constructs.* Vol 1 & 2, London: Routledge.

Latta, G.F. and Swigger, K., 1992. Validation of the repertory grid for use in modeling knowledge. *Journal of the American Society for Information Science.* 43(2), pp.115–129.

Leach, C., 1980. Direct analysis of a repertory grid, *International Journal of Man-Machine Studies,* 13, pp.151–166.

Lund, A. 2003. Massification of the intangible: An investigation into embodied meaning and information visualization. PhD. Umeå University.

Moynihan, T., 1996. An inventory of personal constructs for information systems project risk researchers. *Journal of Information Technology.* 11, pp.359–371.

Olsson, C.M., 2011. Developing a mediation framework for context-aware applications: An exploratory action research approach. PhD. University of Limerick.

Olsson, C.M. and Russo, N.L., 2004. Evaluating innovative prototypes: Assessing the role of lead users, adaptive stucturation theory and repertory grids. In: *Proceedings of IFIP WG 8.6.* Dublin. pp.1–25.

Phythian, G.J. and King, M. 1992. Developing an expert system for tender enquiry evaluation: A case study. *European Journal of Operational Research,* 56(1), pp.15–29.

Tan, F. B. and Hunter, M. G. 2002. The repertory grid technique: A method for the study of cognition in information systems. *MIS Quarterly.* 26(1), pp.39–57.

Reger, R. K., 1990. The repertory grid technique for eliciting the content and structure of cognitive constructive systems. In: A.S. Huff, ed., *Mapping Strategic Thought.* Chicester: John Wiley & Sons, pp.301–309.

RepGrid, 2014. *Rep 5.* Available at: < http://repgrid.com/>.

Reynolds, T. J. and Gutman, J., 1988. Laddering theory, method, analysis, and interpretation. *Journal of Advertising Research.* 28(1), pp.11–31.

Shaw, M.L.G., 1980. *On becoming a personal scientist: Interactive computer elicitation of personal models of the world.* New York: Academic Press.

Shaw, M.L.G. and Gaines, B.R., 1983. A computer aid to knowledge engineering. In Proceedings of the British Computer Society Conference on Expert Systems, pp.263–271.

Shaw, M.L.G. and Gaines, B.R., 1987. KITTEN: Knowledge initiation & transfer tools for experts & novices. *International Journal of Man-Machine Studies.* 27(3), pp.251–280.

Shaw, M.L.G. and Thomas, L.F., 1978. FOCUS on education: An interactive computer system for the development and analysis of repertory grids. *International Journal of Man-Machine Studies*. 10, pp.139–173.

Schutz, A., 1932. *The phenomonology of the social world*. Evanston: Northwestern University Press.

Sicart, M., 2008. Defining game mechanics. *Game Studies*, 8(2). Available at <http://gamestudies.org/0802/articles/sicart>.

Simpson, B. and Wilson, M., 1999. Shared cognition: Mapping commonality and individuality. *Advances in Qualitative Organizational Research*. 2, pp.73–96.

Slater, P., ed., 1977. *Dimensions of intrapersonal space: Volume 1*. London: John Wiley & Sons.

Stewart, V. and Stewart, A., 1981. *Business applications of repertory grid*. London, UK: McGraw-Hill.

Wacker, G. I., 1981. Toward a cognitive methodology of organizational assessment. *Journal of Applied Behavioral Science*. 17, pp.114–129.

WebGrid, 2014. *WebGrid 5*. Available at: <http://webgrid.uvic.ca/>.

Walton, E.J., 1986. Managers' prototypes of financial terms, *Journal of Management Studies*, 23, pp.679–98.

18. Grounded theory

NATHAN HOOK

Grounded theory (GT) research method discussed in this chapter was developed by Barney Glaser and Anselm Strauss (1967). Rather than reviewing previous literature, developing a hypothesis and then testing it, the GT process starts with data collection, gradually building up categories and forming a theory, before linking that theory to previous literature at the end. GT does not set out test an existing pre-defined hypothesis, but instead has the aim of developing new theory.

The term GT itself derives from the notion that theory should be grounded firmly in data. Critics have argued this is misleading as it is a method, not a theory. Charmaz (2006) uses *grounded theory method* which produces *grounded theories*. I prefer the terms used by Hammersley and Atkinson (2005): *ground theorizing* to refer to using this method, and *grounded theory* to refer to the product of the activity; that is, grounded theorizing produces grounded theory. In any case, this method abbreviates to GT for short.

Brief description of the GT process

KEY POINTS OF GT IS THAT:

- It is a process for developing a new theory, not for testing an existing theory.
- It is data-driven and inductive. That is, a process is followed which is led by and constantly refers back to the data. It is then a systematic way to analyze qualitative data, comparable to the systematic methods used for quantitative data.
- The process of analysis is not separate to data collection; the analysis is conducted as data is collected.

Overview of the process of GT

What follows below is a brief description of the general process of carrying out GT analysis. It is provided here to offer an outline of the general structure, followed by further details of the core steps and then detailed examples from game research to provide the details of how the process actually works in practice.

1. Identify your substantive area, often including one or more groups of people to research. For game research typically this might be a subgroup of players, but could also be game developers or game journalists.

2. Collect data. This often includes:
    ◦ Making observations of an activity. For game research, this might include observing play.
    ◦ Accessing pre-existing records (e.g., photographs, artistic works, biographies, news reports, survey data, organization documents). For game research, this might include game manuals and game journalism.
    ◦ Conversing with individuals or a group of individuals. This can include face-to-face or remotely, in real-time or off-line; that is interviews or surveys.
3. Carry out *open coding* as data as is collected. This is an ongoing process alongside collecting data. Items can be coded in multiple ways. Concepts gradually emerge from codes, and higher categories emerge from the concepts. Eventually while doing this a core category, which explains behavior in the substantive area, emerges.
4. Write memos throughout the entire process. Writing memos records challenges along the way and eventually becomes the basis for the method chapter in the final write-up. Most important are memos about codes and their relationship to other codes.
5. Once the core category and the main concern is recognized, move to *selective coding*—only coding for the core and related categories.
6. Find the *theoretical codes* that best organize the substantive codes.
7. Now review other literature and integrate with your theory.

Some presentations of GT analysis imply there are a standard series of steps to follow. Hammersley and Atkinson (2005) call these presentations "vulgar accounts" and reject this notion. Under GT, data is not viewed as material to manipulate but material to *think with*. GT researchers expect to operate with a certain amount of creative chaos.

It is important to grasp that in GT, analysis of data is not a distinct phase. Data is gathered, analyzed and the results used to guide further data collection. This iterative process is ongoing, with data being gathered strategically as the process develops rather than according to a predetermined plan.

This is the method of doing the research, not the sequence to follow for the presentation of the research. GT research is still presented in a fairly traditional sequence, with a literature review or previous research discussed early on in the write-up. One small difference is the post-analysis discussion section is often longer for GT research than other research, as it includes more extensively relating the findings to previous theory.

THE CODING PROCESS

As soon as data is collected the process of *open coding* begins. To carry out the coding, the GT researcher goes through the data line by line, noting possible meanings, associations and nuances. If recorded interviews have been used, then making the transcript of interview material can be part of this close reading activity. A GT researcher approaches each line as an indicator for a new concept to be identified as specifically as possible.

The notes on each section of data are recorded in what GT technically terms a code; the code often is just a phrase or single word. Glaser and Strauss (1967) do not explain how to do this, or what the researcher is looking for. Strauss and Corbin (1998) recommend using free association for this; make notes without looking back, and label each expression afresh.

For example, one participant told Brown and Cairns (2004) that they keep playing games when there is "the chance to achieve things and unlock new abilities/items." This line might produce a code such as "achieving" or "unlocking".

While it is intended that the research should try to analyze one line at a time, in practice, the sections of data can often be bigger than this. As another example, Turner (1981) analyses their field notes paragraph by paragraph.

The primary indication to stop further data collection and open coding is when additional coding no longer producing new concepts. Glaser (1978) terms this *theoretical saturation*. Unlike some other research methods, there is not a stage of data collection after this point looking for deviant cases.

As a rule of thumb for the quantity of data to aim for, Strauss and Corbin (1998, p.281) suggest that: "Usually, microscopic coding of 10 good interviews or observations can provide the skeleton of a theoretical structure" but they go on to add "This skeleton must be filled in, extended, and validated through more data gathering and analysis, although coding can be more selective."

THE CONCEPTUALISING PROCESS

The next stage is to bring the many codes together to form concepts. Strauss and Corbin (1998, p.103) define a concept as "an abstract representation of an event, object, or action/interaction that a researcher identifies as being significant in the data."

Codes with commonality are grouped together. Glaser and Strauss (1967, p.37) warn against looking for ideas established by other researchers, as this "hinders searching for new concepts." For example, Brown and Cairns (2004) brought together codes including the one from the previous example, into the concept "achievement".

THE CATEGORIZING PROCESS

After conceptualizing, the GT researcher will have many concepts. The GT researcher needs to integrate these into a smaller number of more inclusive groupings. This process involves looking for commonalities and categories into which the concepts can be grouped. Strauss and Corbin (1998, pp.124) explain that a category "stands for a *phenomenon*, that is, a problem, an issue, an event, or a happening that is defined as being significant to respondents."

The aim is to move from many concepts to fewer categories. It is not useful to get too caught up in the definitions of what a concept, category or phenomenon are relative to each other.

After forming categories, the next step is to try to connect these categorizes and narrow down to a small number of core categories; some writers refer to one core category and other related categories. Turner (1981, p.232) openly points out that which category is useful depends on "the investigator's interests and upon the pattern of subsequent data."

Continuing the previous example, Brown and Cairns (2004) constructed three core categories from their many different categories (described in detail below). The "achievement" concept became a sub category of the first of these, the core category of "engagement."

The theorising process involves finding the relationship between the core categories, and other categories and concepts form the new theory. This is developing by looking further at the data.

Coding of further data after the core category has been identified is referred to as *selective coding*. The term *closed coding* is also used to refer to coding limited to only codes related to the core category.

The researcher might explore different aspects of the core category—is it part of a bigger process or can be broken down into parts? Glaser (1978) calls this stage *theoretical coding* and lists different *coding families* to support this process. Here are some of his coding families that are likely to be relevant to games research.

- Process (Stages, phases, phasing, transitions, passages, careers, chains, and sequences).
- Strategy (Strategies, tactics, techniques, mechanisms, and management)
- Interactive (Interaction, mutual effects, interdependence, reciprocity, symmetries, and rituals).
- Identity-Self (Identity, self-image, self-concept, self-evaluation, social worth, and transformations of self).
- Cutting-Point (Boundary, critical juncture, cutting point, turning point, tolerance levels, and point of no return).

See Böhm (2004) for a discussion of this in more detail.

Development and variations of GT

Since its original development, GT has split into different traditions as the two founders each separately developed it further. What has been presented above is an attempt to present a simplified generic version. There are also inconsistencies within each writer's work, as their views have changed and developed. GT was developed in the 60s, and Glaser himself is still publishing new material about GT in 2014.

Glaserian GT remains close to the original form of GT. It is based on the principle that *all is data* so it uses both qualitative and quantitative data. This could include observations, interviews, literature data, and even fiction. It emphasizes induction or emergence as methods of reasoning. Glaser's terminology includes a strong distinction between substantive and theoretical coding.

Strauss's version of GT developed further away from its original form. It focuses more strongly on qualitative data and is more formalized and systematic; Glaser calls this version of GT "qualitative data analysis." (QDA). Strauss' terminology places more emphasis on the distinction between *open coding* (discovering categories), *axial coding* (discovering concepts) and *selective coding* (discovering the core concept).

According to Strauss, there are three basic elements of the GT approach:

- theoretical sensitive coding, creating concepts from data
- theoretical sampling, deciding what to interview or observe based on the analysis of the data gathered so far
- comparing between phenomena and contexts.

Detailed examples below show both Glaserian and Stausian versions of GT applied to game research. Galserian GT is particularly appropriate to games research due to the use of a variety of media as data; in a game research context that could include reviews and articles about games, and the game-as-fiction itself. For example, if researching the experience of playing a game based on a film, it might be appropriate to include the original film itself as data.

There are other later versions of GT, one of which is *constructivist grounded theory* (CGT) which was developed by other researchers based on the Strausian tradition. CGT is based on the belief that data and theories are constructed by the researcher and participants, rather than being discovered. One practical difference is that CGT strives to maintain the involvement of the participants throughout the research process. For more information on CGT, see Mills, Bonner and Francis (2006).

GT is sometimes taught as part of ethnography, but is in fact a distinct method. The data collection techniques of the two methods can be similar, and in both methods the collection of data is guided strategically by analysis of earlier gathered data. However they differ in that ethnographic research usually seeks to produce descriptive accounts and descriptive theory; GT seeks to produce new explanatory or predictive theory.

STRENGTHS AND CRITICISMS

Since GT actively avoids conducting a literature review early in the research process, it naturally lends itself to research of new topics where there is little or no academic literature on which to base research. While game research is relatively young as a formal academic discipline, GT may be a useful method to consider. It can also be useful for a less experienced researcher without prior exposure to the literature—lack of past exposure makes it easier to literally ground oneself in the data and follow where it leads, rather than seeing a previously learnt model or theory in data.

GT has elements which are similar to the implicit parts of more typical qualitative research. For students of research methods, studying GT is a way to learn the implicit points and understand the related criticisms of qualitative research generally. For example, the qualitative method Thematic Analysis developed out of GT but limits itself to picking out themes, rather than developing theory. Learning GT then is a solid basis for learning and using other qualitative methods.

Böhm (2004) argues that GT is more difficult to learn than other methods, because it is a *Kunstlehre* (art) that demands creativity in its use. In contrast to this, Thomas and James (2006) argue that GT is too formulaic in nature to be creative. Certainly GT is more systematic than some other qualitative methods, which can be a strong point when a researcher is demonstrating the rigor of their approach. . GT is open about the agency of the researcher as part of the process; that could be regarded as a strength or a criticism, depending on your own perspective.

At a practical level, examples of GT research often tends to focus on interview data and transcript analysis. This contrasts with original claims it can be used with a wide variety of types of data. Approaches to transcription are generally not discussed as a part of GT; for example, Strauss and Corbin (1998) quote speakers word for word but actually tidy up irregular speech into grammatical sentences and do not record pauses in speech. The approach to transcription should at least be considered and discussed.

Also at a practical level, the fine-grained line-by-line analysis is clearly not feasible for a large-scale project (although because each line is analyzed as a discrete unit, a transcript can be broken up to have an entire class of students work on it). It is likely that for practical purposes some unacknowledged form of selection is applied to the data or early concepts to make the process manageable. Dey (1999) suggests the GT approach of considering small section of data loses the benefit of a more holistic view and can miss connections operating on a larger scale.

A practical strength of GT is that analysis can start early; speaking in 2002, Glaser said it can even start during the first interview. The data collection process, especially waiting for participants to respond, can hold up some other parts. If conducting a research project with limited time and a looming deadline, the ability to start analysis early is clearly useful.

At an epistemological level, Denzin (1997, p.17) locates traditional GT (as opposed to CGT) in the modernist phase of ethnography, using "rhetoric of positivist and post-positivist discourse." This position opens GT up to two criticisms:

- It is unclear whether GT analyses the world or interpretations of the world. That is, is the data the participant's experience, or participant's worldview or interpretation (which would capture cultural and symbolic meanings)?
- Do the patterns identified correspond to patterns out in the world? As can be seen from the examples below, GT inherently tends to develop branching tree structures in the theory it produces. In some cases, connections may be multiple and fluid, beyond the ability of a two-dimensional branching diagram to represent.
- Combining both practical and epistemological issues, is it also possible for an experienced researcher to challenge the concept of approaching data without any preconceptions? An experienced researcher may already be familiar with the literature of the topic. Some would say it is better to reflect on, acknowledge and explicitly state your own theoretical assumptions rather than try to deny them.

Examples

The rest of this section will review some real examples of grounded theory applied to game research, to illustrate how it is applied in practice.

THE PLAYER ENGAGEMENT PROCESS: AN EXPLORATION OF CONTINUATION DESIRE IN COMPUTER GAMES

Schoenau-Fog (2011) used GT to investigate engagement: the desire of players to keeping playing. He collected data using a qualitative survey of 41 players. This consisted of open-ended questions about general gaming experiences, with questions such as "What in a game makes you want to continue playing?" and "What in a game makes you want to come back to play?" He then analyzed it to develop "a process-orientated player engagement framework consisting of objectives, activities, accomplishments and affect."

The data collection produced 205 answers. After removing empty, incomprehensible and overly broad answers, the remaining answers were separated to produce 312 statements. These statements were then organized and coded for "triggers of player engagement." An example from this process provided by Schoenau-Fog is the statement 'being able to battle others' was fitted into the category 'socialising.'

The codes were finally grouped into 95 categories. These categories were then re-evaluated for comparisons with each other, resulting in 33 tentative categories. Another iteration of this process reduced this to 18 conceptual categories (or concepts as they are termed in the description above), such as "interfacing" and "socialising". These were finally structured into four "main components" (their term for core categories):

- Objectives: intrinsic or extrinsic
- activities: interfacing, socializing, solving, sensing, experiencing the story and characters, exploring, experimenting creating and destroying
- accomplishment: achievement, completion and progression
- affect: positive, negative and absorption.

Schoenau-Fog created a circular diagram, theorizing that objectives lead to activities which lead to accomplishments which lead to affect which lead to further objectives, with an additional connection that activities can also lead directly to affects. This is a good example of how GT does not always result in branching tree diagram theories.

After the first survey, Schoenau-Fog conducted two further surveys to verify this new theory. No new components or categories emerged from doing this. In GT terms, saturation had been achieved.

Schoenau-Fog also applied a form of quantitative analysis, counting the number of statements that relate to each category and ranking them accordingly; these findings should not be considered an actual quantitative method, and no claims are made that the results generalize. Instead this can be viewed a simple descriptive way to present the data set to an interested reader, just as the participant's ages are presented in quantitative terms of range and mean.

Schoenau-Fog's paper includes an extensive section comparing the results to other theories, including discussing the relationship between engagement and flow. Compared to other methods, this kind of discussion in the write-up of GT research can be notably longer and more in-depth.

WHERE DO GAME DESIGN IDEAS COME FROM? INVENTION AND RECYCLING IN GAMES DEVELOPED IN SWEDEN

Hagen (2009) used GT to investigate the process of game development in 25 games including AAA titles such as the *Battlefield* series (e.g., *Battlefield 1942*, Digital Illusion, 2002), from four different development studies. He used artifact analysis of the games themselves and interviews with the game designers as his primary data. Secondary data included published interviews with the designers by others, a range of web sites and game reviews in magazines. This is a good example of how GT attempts to bring together a wide range of different kinds of material and data sources. Many other research designs would only consider a small subset of this array of data.

For example, a description of the game *Battlefield 1942* used in the data set included:

> A common explanation for the success is that the games in the Battlefield series allow the player not only to control the player character, but also a lot of different vehicles (military cars, tanks, boats, air planes etc.). This feature could be said to represent a loan from the so-called vehicle simulation genre. (Hagen, 2009, p.6.)

This was coded and eventually contributed to forming the category "from another game genre." (p. 6)

Being led by the data, or "bottom-up from the data" as Hagen calls it, he developed a model of the *game concept*, the collection of design ideas that make up the game. The *game concept* consists of a recycled part and inventive part. Design ideas can be drawn from:

- The game domain: from the game's dominant genre, from another game genre, from another game or brand.
- Narratives and visual art: from cinematography and film, from books, from other narratives.
- Other human activities: from sports, from playful activities, from war and warfare.
- Human technology and artifacts: from historical or contemporary society, predicting future technology.

This example lends itself well to showing how a GT can work in practice. One can imagine a researcher interviewing designers and going through a range of other data sources, coding the data along the way, and gradually arriving at these categories. Had the researcher used more conventional interviews with thematic analysis, they would have excluded all the other data sources. In addition by coding as part of the data gathering process, the later interviews were done in a more informed way, perhaps meaning that less interviews are needed overall.

AN INVESTIGATION OF GAME IMMERSION

Many players, designers and researchers discuss immersion, but the meaning is unclear. Brown and Cairns (2004) used GT to develop a grounded theory of immersion. They interviewed seven regular gamers after they played their favourite digital game for thirty minutes. They also videoed the players while playing, but found so little physical action this was not worthwhile.

Brown and Cairns are open that this study is small, and that "the majority of the analysis was through open coding, identification of concepts and categories of concepts, and some axial coding, identification of relationships between categories." They used Straussian GT; this is not discussed explicitly, but their reference section includes Straus and Corbin (1998), but not any work by Glaser.

The resulting theory consists of three different levels of involvement, which each require the removal of barriers to reach. The barriers open the way to players achieving that level of immersion, but do not ensure it is achieved. Summarizing the theory briefly, these levels and barriers are:

The first level is engagement, the barriers to which are:

- Access: which covers liking the general type of game, and the game controls being usable.
- Investment, which covers investing time in the game, and energy and effort learning how to play.

The second level is engrossment, the barrier to which is:

- Game construction: when game features combine in such a way that the gamers' emotions are directly affected by the game. This includes visuals, tasks and plot.

This engrossment level causes a high level of emotional investment, leads to feelings of being drained when not playing. It includes less awareness of the players' surroundings.

The third level is total immersion or presence, being cut off from reality such that the game is all that mattered. The barriers to this are:

- Empathy, which is the growth of attachment to the game. Gamers who did not feel this talked of a lack of empathy. Games that removed this barrier were mostly first person games, and also role-playing characters where gamers assume a character.
- Atmosphere is created from the same elements as game construction, but has relevance to the actions and location of the characters.

This research then creates a scale for different kinds of immersion. After presenting this model, Brown and Cairns relate it back to variety of other writers and concepts, such as flow. While we might question whether these concepts really make up a scale, it certainly seems an improvement of previous scattered and conflicting notions of what immersion is, and an attempt to bring different concepts together.

In terms of writing style, Brown and Cairns include many direct quotes from the research participants in their paper, demonstrating how the theory is firmly grounded.

Moreover, their research is a good example of a more modest and manageable application of GT—analysis of only seven interviews. It shows how a close reading of a small data sample can develop a new theory.

A SOCIAL PSYCHOLOGY STUDY OF IMMERSION AMONG LIVE ACTION ROLE-PLAYERS

This example comes from my own early research as a social psychology student, published in Hook (2012). It is included here to demonstrate how general principles (rather than the exact process of GT) can inform research, and as an example of how an early stage researcher can use it.

For my MSc dissertation, I investigated the relationship between player identity and character identity and how emotions bleed in and out of fictional player experiences in live action role-play games (larp). I collected data using email interviews of 41 live action role-players and I had intended to use thematic analysis and template analysis for this. However, many of the replies also discussed immersion, which I had not prepared a prior literature review for. At the time I was unaware of Brown and Cairns (2004)'s research discussed above into computer game immersion.

While I used my intended methods for other parts of the research, I addressed this topic of immersion by an informal grounded theory approach, looking at player-participant notions of what immersion was. Immersion ended up forming a third part in the results section and a slice of the discussion section of the dissertation, and later a separate paper.

My use of email interviews (written questions, inviting lengthy free text replies) for data collection was a design choice that treated the participants as experts in their own activity, even if they lack a formal terminology. Compared to live interviews, it allows participants to be more reflective rather than being put on the spot. It also removes the need for transcription, which means more participants can be included.

Statements were extracted from the (sometimes) lengthy replies. Memos and codes were created, in practical terms using the MS Word comment functions. This then produced a series of categories, with the core category in the paper being "immersion".

For example, one participant said "the whole point of role-playing (larp and tabletop) is to immerse yourself in your character and in another world/time [...] the ability to 'feel' the things my characters feel[s]" while another participant said "My ideal, which I achieve occasionally, is to "become" the character fully—I'm just a little background process watching out for OOC [out-of-character] safety concerns and interpreting OOC elements of the scene for [the characters], they are in the driver's seat; I feel their emotions, have their trains of thought and subconscious impulses, and they have direct control of what I am doing, subject only to veto." Both of those were coded on "immersion as goal," which ended up becoming a category. Note the second quote is somewhat long—the email interviews produced sometimes long verbose answers. To make this manageable my units of analysis were a little bigger than literally line-by-line.

Another participant said, "You need to start thinking like the character, and when you feel the way they would, you have mastered that character." This produced two codes, both the "as goal" code again and "like the character". This ended up contributing to a category of "first person vs. third person."

Categories that emerged were:

- immersion as a goal for some players
- immersion as strong emotion
- immersion as possession, even when not playing.
- inner psychological immersion vs. outer realism immersion.
- first person vs. third person thinking
- frequency for immersion, from almost never to only being oneself for short moments.

I then reviewed the data again to try to develop these categories into a theory. I did not produce a tree structure, but instead presented the theory more informally as four key points:

- Some participants seek to achieve immersion during play as a goal.
- Immersion as a term is used to refer to both inner psychological experience and to outer realism. The latter assists in achieving the former and helps players experience strong emotion during play.

- The frequency of immersion into character is a point of personal difference, one that normally remains invisible.
- A few participants experience exceptionally strong immersion into their characters, which we might term a sort of "possession" that takes hold sometimes even while not playing.

This was not the most formal use of GT, and not the best developed of theories. However, it does show how useful observation can be extracted by following the general principles (even without the specifics) of GT, even by a novice researcher.

My notion that outer realism (e.g., the use of props and costume) supports inner immersion fits with Brown and Cairns (2004) notion of the barrier of "atmosphere" to achieving "total immersion." However, Hook (2012) goes slightly further in suggesting it actively support immersion, rather than being only a requirement. This subtle difference may reflect a difference between immersion in computer games and immersion in larp.

In documenting this study (both my dissertation and the paper), I used many direct quotes from the participants. My motive at the time for this was the social and critical psychology perspective of letting participants speak in their own voice, but it also fulfills the GT perspective of solidly grounding the concepts in the data and making the analysis transparent. I mostly avoided correcting typing or grammatical errors in quotes for this reason.

There are many conflicting uses of the term immersion among researchers, especially in the Nordic larp literature. This analysis tried to induce what meanings the term holds for players. Notably, it revealed points of personal difference in the way players think about their character, with some thinking in the first person and some in the third person, and a personal difference in how often different players feel themselves to be immersed.

Conclusion

Few other methods advocate trying to clear your mind of any preconceptions and start your research with data collection. Even if you do not intend to use GT, it is worth reflecting on how much you agree with the positions on which GT is based.

As I hope the examples here have demonstrated, GT can be a powerful tool when tackling new ground and trying to develop new theories. GT does not require identifying hypotheses, offers the flexibility in data collection and usage of the ethnographic method with the strength of being able to actually discover (or create) new theories that carry predictive power, theories that can then be tested by more traditional methods.

Recommended reading

- Dey, I., 1999. *Grounding grounded theory: Guidelines for qualitative inquiry*, San Diego: Academic Press.
- Strauss, A. and Corbin, J., 1998. *Basics of qualitative research: Grounded theory procedures and techniques*. Newbury Park: Sage.

Acknowledgements

Thanks to Christian Jensen Romer and Jori Pitkänen for their feedback on drafts of this chapter.

References

Brown, E. and Cairns, P., 2004. *A grounded investigation of game immersion.* in CHI'04 extended abstracts on Human factors in computing systems pp.1297–1300. New York: ACM.

Böhm, A., 2004. Theoretical coding: Text analysis in grounded theory. In: U. Flick, E. Kardorff and I. Steinke, eds., *A companion to qualitative research.* London: Sage Publications, pp.270–275.

Charmaz, K., 2006. *Constructing grounded theory.* London: Sage Publications.

Denzin, N.K., 1997. *Interpretive ethnography: Ethnographic practices for the 21st Century.* Thousand Oaks: Sage.

Dey, I., 1999. *Grounding grounded theory: Guidelines for qualitative inquiry,* San Diego: Academic Press.

Digital Illusion, 2002. *Battlefield 1942* [game]. Electronic Arts.

Glaser, B. and Strauss, A., 1967. *The discovery of grounded theory: Strategies for qualitative research,* London: Cambridge University Press.

Hagen, U., 2009. Where do game design ideas come from? Invention and recycling in games developed in Sweden. In: *Breaking new ground.* London. September. Available at: < http://www.digra.org/wp-content/uploads/digital-library/09287.25072.pdf >.

Hammersley, M. and Atkinson, P., 2005. *Ethnography principles in practice.* 3rd ed. London: Routledge.

Hook, N., 2012. A social psychology study of immersion among live action role-players. In: S. Bowman, ed., *Wyrd Con Companion Book 2012,* Orange. pp.106–117.

Mills, J., Bonner, A. and Francis, K., 2006. The Development of constructivist grounded theory. *International journal of qualitative methods,* 5(1), pp.25–35.

Thomas, G. and James, D., 2006. Re-inventing grounded theory: some questions about theory, ground and discovery. *British Educational Research Journal,* 32 (6), pp.767–795.

Turner, B.A., 1981. Some practical aspects of qualitative data analysis: One way of organising the cognitive processes associated with the generation of grounded theory. *Quality and Quantity,* 15, pp.225–247.

Strauss, A. and Corbin, J., 1998. *Basics of qualitative research: Grounded theory procedures and techniques.* Newbury Park: Sage.

PART V

GAME DEVELOPMENT FOR RESEARCH

19. Extensive modding for experimental game research

M. ROHANGIS MOHSENI, BENNY LIEBOLD AND DANIEL PIETSCHMANN

This chapter covers the topic of *extensive modding* in the area of experimental game research. In simplified terms, modding a computer game means changing specific aspects of how the game looks and feels to the user. This also includes applying minor changes to the game, such as changing the appearance of just a few objects, which does not require a high degree of expertise. Solely relying on making minor changes, however, severely limits the type of research questions that can be addressed. Therefore, we advocate extensive modding, which refers to modifications of a large extent that allow researchers to examine almost any research question imaginable. Extensive modifications may range from major content extensions or replacements, like new tasks or quests, game environments, characters or game mechanics, to total conversions, like changing the game scenario or theme, or the game genre. To apply these changes, researchers have to know which modding tools are available for a given game and how to use them properly. Advanced modifications, such as changing the behaviour of the game world and its inhabitants or even the fundamental mechanics of the game, often require deep knowledge of the game, game design, the modding community and—depending on the game—a certain level of programming skills.

The chapter assists researchers to make informed decisions for modding videogames and to avoid typical pitfalls, especially in laboratory experiments. Although it cannot provide all the knowledge needed to create advanced modifications, it will provide 1) a thorough discussion how experimental studies with videogames can benefit from extensive modding, 2) best practice guidelines, and 3) online supplementaries, especially a list including more than ninety modifiable games and their respective modding tools as well as web links to modding communities and tutorials in order to provide a starting point for extensive stimulus design.

Extensive modding

Scacchi (2010) gives a broad explication of the term *modding*, including 1) user interface customizations, 2) game conversion mods, 3) machinima and art mods (i.e., cinematics and art created using games), 4) custom gaming PCs (i.e., PCs with custom design or extreme performance), and 5) game console hacking (i.e., removing manufacturer's protection from one's gaming console). As we focus on game research, we are not interested in the latter three kinds of modding, but rather in the former two, namely user interface customizations and game conversion mods. *User interface customizations* change the way the user interacts with the game without changing the game content itself, therefore restricting which actions players can perform within the game and how much information about the current game state is available. Researchers could, for example, choose to manipulate players' problem solving strategy by preventing the use of weapons (e.g., Mohseni, 2013a), to manipulate players' risk perception by withholding information about players' health and constitution, or to manipulate navigational cues within the game by deactivating the overlay of maps and compass information (e.g., Pietschmann, et al., 2013).

Game conversion mods, on the other hand, change the content of the game, namely the environments (e.g., custom levels or maps[1]), objects, characters, scripts[2], game rules, and game mechanics. Creating *custom maps* allows researchers to create environments, which are especially designed for the proposed research question. For some questions, it might be sufficient to extend standard maps and place new architectural objects within the existing game environments (e.g., Hartmann and Vorderer, 2010, study 1). Other research questions might require the creation of larger areas that are loaded separately from the main game content and feature completely new environments (e.g., Pietschmann, et al., 2013; Mohseni, 2013a). Creating custom maps also enables researchers to minimize the impact of confounding variables, because every element in the custom environment can be controlled. In other cases, it might be of interest to change certain *objects* or *characters* of the game. These changes can range from fairly simple appearance changes of 3D models (e.g., Hartmann and Vorderer, 2010, study 2) to changes which affect the way an object or character operates within the game (e.g., Mohseni, 2013a). For example, if the research question involves non-violent problem solving, a weapon could repel enemies instead of causing damage (e.g., Elson, et al., 2013)—more so, the weapon does not even have to look like a weapon (e.g., Kneer, Knapp, and Elson, 2014). Modifying existing game scripts is another crucial method to change the core game mechanics of a game. This again can range from small changes (e.g., triggering simple events upon pre-defined player actions) to rather complex modifications, for example creating scripted quests (Mohseni, 2013a).

Game conversion mods can go as far as "total conversions [creating] entirely new games from existing games of a kind that are not easily determined from the originating game" (Scacchi, 2010). *DOTA 2* (Valve Corporation, 2013) is an example of a popular game originating from a total conversion of *Warcraft 3: Reign of Chaos* (Blizzard Entertainment, 2002), which uses completely different game mechanics, ultimately changing the genre of the game.

In our perspective, *extensive modding* refers to the extent and the amount of applied modifications to achieve an experimental manipulation required for a given research problem, and not the specific type of a modification employed. It includes large-scale changes of the user interface, content extensions or replacements, and total conversions.

MODDING VS. CLASSIC APPROACH

Typically, game effects studies use one game for each experimental condition with pre-tests ensuring that the games only differ in the aspect that is to be experimentally manipulated. This is what we call the *classic approach*. But while this approach only requires the time to find suitable games, modding additionally requires time to create the mod, which necessarily includes the preceding acquisition of in-depth expertise on technical game details. This process can be rather time consuming: Mohseni (2013a),

---

1. Maps are visual representations of an area, which may include roads, buildings, plants, animals, non-player characters etc.
2. Scripts are short sequences of programming code.

for example, invested approximately six man-months to create one extensive mod. Apart from the required development time, modding can also have side effects. For example, changing central aspects of the game in order to raise internal validity (e.g. modding an open world game to create a linear pathway forcing all participants to use the same path) may lead to a decrease in external validity, as the modified and unmodified versions of the game lead to completely different playing experiences.[3]

Considering the effort required to modify a game, it can still prove to be a worthwhile endeavour. According to Hartig, Frey and Ketzel (2003) and to McMahan, et al. (2011), the best approach for studying games is to realize all experimental conditions within the same game. If the sample size is sufficient and participants are randomly assigned to the conditions, it can be expected that potential confounders influence each condition equally. Also, realizing all conditions within the same game has the benefit that it is much easier to study combinations of independent variables. Trying to achieve this by using separate games would require the researchers to find at least one game for each experimental condition, while these games would have to be maximally different in regard to the independent variables, but at the same time maximally indifferent in regard to all other variables. Following this approach leads to several quality-reducing drawbacks: First, the more potential confounders (i.e., unwanted differences between the games) have to be controlled at the same time, the harder this is to achieve. Second, potential confounders must be measurable in an objective, reliable, and valid way. Third, unknown confounders cannot be controlled for. Therefore, this approach cannot rule out that unknown confounding variables influence experimental findings, leading to misinterpretations of data and false conclusions. Consequently, the classic approach comes with the risk of turning games research into "a series of case studies comparing individual titles with each other" (Elson and Quandt, 2014, p.3), which is especially true for experiments where combinations of two independent variables are represented by different games. Consequently, modding provides the best quality-to-effort ratio for high-quality experimental studies.

MODDING VS. RELATED APPROACHES

If researchers conclude that modding is worthwhile, they have several options to select from: 1) Develop a completely new game, 2) change the source code of an existing game, and 3) mod an existing game using an editor.

Theoretically, by developing a game from scratch, all research problems imaginable can be investigated. Practically, developing a new game is much more time-consuming than modding and can take a full professional game development team several years. Therefore, professionals sometimes license the engine[4] of a competitor's game to reduce their own effort. However, even when using an already existing engine, the remaining programming effort is substantial. Developing a less complex kind of game (e.g., a simple flash-based browser game or a game using a game creation tool kit) can be a viable solution to further reduce the effort. However, this approach introduces its own set of problems. First, due to technical limitations, the simplicity of these games often restricts the type of interaction processes and game mechanics and therefore limits what kinds of research questions can be addressed. Second,

3. Questions relating to validity are discussed by Landers and Bauer (chapter 10) and Lieberoth, Wellnitz and Aagaard (chapter 11).
4. A game engine is "a large software program infrastructure that coordinates computer graphics, user interface controls, networking, game audio, access to middleware libraries for game physics, and so forth" (Scacchi, 2010). Some available engines can be used freely for non-commercial purposes.

games developed by small-budget research teams are less likely to be well-balanced, rich in content and engaging (chapter 12). Third, in terms of ecological validity it is questionable if findings obtained using such games can be generalized to the rather complex commercial games.

All problems mentioned above can be avoided by adapting an existing commercial game. This can be done by directly changing the source code of the game (e.g., Hartig, Frey and Ketzel, 2003) or by using a ready-made editor. The former is usually impossible, because most publishers only make the source code of a game public in case the game is no longer of monetary value. However, even if the source code is publicly available, it can be hard to edit. Modern games are complex programs that may consist of more than a million of lines of code in different programming languages. This may be the reason why game studios began creating editors to make content creation more feasible.

Game editors are tools that change certain aspects of a game. Some editors allow to apply changes to the player character, while most at least enable players to create their own maps or levels, which can include the placement of objects, light sources, and sound effects (e.g., *Valve Hammer Editor 3* for older Valve games; *Far Cry 3 Map Editor* for Ubisoft's *Far Cry 3*). More advanced editors allow players to create new quests, new non-player characters (NPCs), new (voiced) dialogues, and sometimes even facial expressions (e.g., *The Elder Scrolls IV: Construction Set* for Bethesda's *TESIV*; *The Elder Scrolls V: Creation Kit* for Bethesda's *TESV*; *Valve Source Software Development Kit* for newer Valve games). By using scripts within these editors, it is possible to adjust the behaviour patterns and dialog sequences of NPCs, to set stages of quests, to change features of the player character, and to even change the rules of the game including game mechanics. Some game editors (e.g., *Crysis 3: Sandbox 3* for Crytek's *Crysis 3* and the already mentioned editors for *TESIV* and *TESV*) also offer tools to import textures or models from external 3D-editors (e.g., from Blender Foundation's *Blender* or Autodesk's *3ds Max*), which makes it possible to add new graphics to the game (e.g., high-definition textures, new backgrounds, and new game character visuals).

To sum it up, powerful editors can apply nearly any imaginable changes to a game's content, rules, and mechanics. Editors can even apply changes that formerly needed a direct alteration of a game's source code while being much more efficient. However, not every game provides an editor, and most of the powerful editors are only available for the genres of (first-person) shooters (FPS) and role-playing games (RPG). Even if an editor is provided, it may have drawbacks like restricting what parts of the game can be changed, being inconvenient to use, being badly documented, having no debugger, or even having flaws like unstable functions or defective compilers. In addition, as most editors are standalone programs, in order to test intermediate versions of the mod, the editor has to be closed and the game to be loaded for every single test, which can make testing small changes inefficient.

EXAMPLES OF EXTENSIVE MODDING

In this section, we demonstrate the scope of stimulus manipulations through modding by providing examples of existing studies. Thus, we will focus on technical details, especially the tools that were used to create the stimulus material. The presented selection of studies is mostly based on Elson and Quandt (2014), who discuss many studies conducted with modded videogames. For those examples that are not discussed in full detail, a thorough summary can be found in the online supplementary. In addition to this list, three studies by the authors are presented in more detail.

Changing the source code

Only few studies exist where the source code of a game was changed. Probably the first one was conducted by Hartig, Frey and Ketzel (2003; for an English version see Frey, et al., 2007), who wanted to find out if they could modify *Quake 3 Arena* (id Software, 1999) to be usable for psychological experiments. The purpose of their study was to check if the software was reliable and if participants with and without experience in 3D-games were able to solve tasks of differing complexity, focusing on participants' navigational problems and negative outcomes, such as cybersickness. To achieve this, they used id Software's *qeradiant* level editor to create five maps of differing complexity including a practising and a training ground and changed the source code to log players' position every time they reached a checkpoint. Other examples are a study by Chittaro and Sioni (2012) using a Whac-A-Mole game and a study by Klimmt, Hartmann and Frey (2007) using a Java-based game.

Using an editor

Most of the researchers employing mods were using an editor for a *first-person shooter* (FPS) game. An exception to this is a relatively early study by Carnagey and Anderson (2005), who wanted to examine the effects of rewarding and punishing violent actions in videogames on later aggression-related variables. For this purpose, they created three versions of the racing-car game *Carmageddon 2* (Stainless Software, 1998): one rewarding kills of pedestrians, one punishing kills, and one making kills impossible.

Another exceptional study comes from Dekker and Champion (2007), who used players' biometric data to dynamically change the playing experience in order to investigate how real-time low-budget biometric information can enhance gameplay. For this purpose, the authors modified *Half-Life 2* (Valve Corporation, 2004) using Valve's *Source SDK*. The authors chose the pre-existing level Ravenholm and extended it with the goal to create an immersive horror scenario. The mod affected speed of movement, sound level, game shaders, screen shake, NPC spawn points, and NPC behaviour. It featured several modes like a bullet time mode, an invisibility mode, an excited mode, and a black-and-white mode.

The rest of the studies were all investigating the effects of violent video games by modding a FPS. Within this group of studies, the work presented by Van den Hoogen, et al. (2012) stands out, as it is one of the few studies carrying out the stimulus manipulation using mods as a within-subjects factor design. Van den Hoogen, et al. investigated the effect of player-death on game enjoyment. Their goal was to find out if players smile after their character died because of stress relief or because of challenge feedback. To test this, they created gameplay situations that allow for episodes of tension relief with positive and negative valence. *Half-Life 2* (Valve Corporation, 2004) was used as a basis, for which they created a new map.

An example of a study using only pre-existing mods comes from Staude-Müller, Bliesener and Lutmann (2008), who investigated if playing violent videogames leads to desensitization. For this purpose, they used several pre-existing mods for *Unreal Tournament 2003* (Epic Games, 2002), which were taken from the Internet and videogame magazines. Using these mods, they created two experimental conditions that differed concerning the instruction of the game, the explicitness of violence displays, and their impact on the gameplay.

A couple of thematically related studies were conducted by a researcher group around Hartmann, who investigated the effects of virtual violence and moral disengagement. These studies include Hartmann and Vorderer (2010) as well as Hartmann, Toz and Brandon (2010). Hartmann and Vorderer (2010, study 1) investigated the effect of virtual violence against (non-)human opponents and opponent blameworthiness on guilt, negative affect, and enjoyment. They modified an already existing map of *Half-Life 2* (Valve Corporation, 2004) using Valve's *Hammer Editor 4*. The opponents' human appeal was manipulated by swapping the original character models with either human soldiers or zombie-like creatures. Blameworthiness was manipulated by an in-game cover story stating that enemies had invaded the streets and were only protesting or were shooting at civilians. Blameworthiness was further manipulated by influencing the aggressiveness of the opponents; they were set either to attack the player and other civilians at first sight or to attack the player only when fired upon. In study 2, they used *Operation Flashpoint* (Bohemia Interactive, 2001) to manipulate the portrayal of consequences, whereas they used the *FPS Creator* (The Game Creators, 2005) in Hartmann, Toz and Brandon (2010) to have more control over the stimulus.

In a thematically related study, Elson, et al. (2013, for an extended version see Elson, 2011) wanted to find out if pace of action and displayed violence in computer games have an effect on aggressive behaviour and autonomic arousal. For this purpose, they modified *Unreal Tournament 3*[5] (Epic Games, 2007) in several regards. First, they installed the already existing mod *UT3 Speed Modification Mutator* (Chatman, 2008) in order to create two conditions of pace of action. Second, they used Epic Games' *Unreal Engine 3 Editor* and *UnrealScript* in order to create a non-violent condition in which the explicitness of displayed violence was decreased. They tried to achieve this by creating a new "death animation" in which the display of blood and gore was changed into the characters dropping their weapons, freezing, and becoming invisible, and by changing the player's weapon to look and sound like a tennis-ball shooting nerf gun. Further, they disabled the pain screams of the player character and of all opponents and removed aggressive language by deactivating the verbal messages from the computer-controlled characters and by editing the on-screen messages (e.g., after killing an opponent). In a second study, Kneer, Knapp and Elson (2014) studied the (interacting) effects of difficulty and explicitness of displayed violence on arousal as well as aggressive cognitions, emotions, and behaviour, using *Team Fortress 2* (Valve Corporation, 2007).

The study of Mohseni (2013a) also falls into the category of an FPS-based aggression study, with the exception that the employed game is usually regarded as a Role-Playing Game (RPG) in First-Person perspective. The author addressed the question if situations of violent helping behaviour in the game increase violent and helping behaviour. In-game violence and in-game help were manipulated as independent variables by modifying *The Elder Scrolls 4: Oblivion* (Bethesda, 2006) using Bethesda's Construction Set. Participants had to solve a quest[6] given within the game. The first independent variable *in-game violence* was manipulated by making the quest only solvable either by fighting against six bandits (violence condition) or by stealthily traversing the map (no-violence condition). The second independent variable, *in-game help*, was manipulated by making the quest only solvable by either saving the quest giver (help condition) or going on a treasure hunt (no-help condition). These two independent variables were combined, which resulted in a 2×2 experimental design with four conditions, namely

5.   *Unreal Tournament 3 was formerly known as Unreal Tournament 2007, and is the 4th instalment of the series. Its numeration is based on the version of the engine.*

6.   Video recordings of the quests are available at YouTube on emergency assistance condition (Mohseni, 2013b) and treasure hunt condition (Mohseni, 2013c).

emergency assistance (violence and help), *killing* (violence and no-help), *helping* (no-violence and help), and *treasure hunt* (no-violence and no-help). The game started with an in-game tutorial in which players learned the controls. After that, players were given the quest within the game, which ended after the quest was solved (in approx. 20 minutes). A number of measures were taken to heighten immersion. First, all in-game dialogues were fully voiced and lip-synced. Second, NPCs were not just standing around, but instead performed different tasks like eating while sitting at a table, patrolling the area, working in a magical laboratory, fighting against crabs, and switching levers to randomly teleport a quest item. Third, traps were placed within the dungeon. Fourth, several pre-existing mods were employed to improve the quality of the graphics. Fifth, an additional mod was installed to create visual feedback when the player was hit. Last, the game music was replaced with scores from the film *Conan the Barbarian* (Pouledouris, 1982). Internal validity was also improved by several measures. First, player character death was circumvented, because this would have ended the game, rendering it impossible to finish the quest. Instead, as soon as the player character's health went below a certain threshold, he/she went unconscious, i.e. the character was instantly immobilized, fell on the floor and was teleported to the last checkpoint where the quest was resumed. Second, the mod checked if any irregularities occurred (e.g., counting if six bandits were killed). Third, pathways were mostly linear to prevent players from losing direction and to create a more comparable gaming experience. Fourth, a plugin was installed that made it impossible to activate the in-game console, rendering cheating impossible. Fifth, a mod was used to prevent players from using game features like blocking, casting, quick saving, quick loading, moving automatically and changing the point of view. Last, another mod fixed known bugs. Three pre-tests were conducted to optimize the quests' usability (e.g., by reducing the number of message boxes that have to be clicked on) and to check for several confounders, namely interestingness, excitation, enjoyment, frustration, difficulty, perceived arousal, presence, the graphic's closeness to reality, and the explicitness of displayed violence.

Pietschmann, et al. (2013) also employed a RPG, but instead of looking into aggression, they studied the effects of video game GUIs and player attention on game enjoyment and presence. They built a new map in *The Elder Scrolls V: Skyrim* (Bethesda, 2011) using Bethesda's *Creation Kit*, which placed the player in the position of an adventurer, trapped in a dangerous tomb, trying to escape from tomb raiders. In the cover story, the players had to collect gold to bribe the raiders' guards when they reached the exit of the tomb. In fact, there were no tomb raiders at the exit, the game just ended when players reached the door leading to the surface. Gold coins were placed both in map areas that were related to the players' goals (risky situations, crossroads) and in areas unrelated to the players' goals to manipulate attention processes while performing secondary tasks. The map required players to perform typical game tasks, which were ultimately aiming at spatial information processing. The map was designed as a typical cavern labyrinth, filled with traps and puzzles, similar to the design of the dungeons that can be found in the original game (figure 1). The mod *Immersive HUD*[7] (Gopher, 2013) was employed to render the GUI significantly less intrusive. Additionally, the authors first decompiled and then modified the GUI file using Adobe Flash. To create the experimental condition with the GUI completely turned off, Pietschmann, et al. swapped the existing GUI elements with transparent textures and then recompiled the GUI file into the correct file format.

In a thematically related unpublished study, Pietschmann and Liebold used *The Elder Scrolls V: Skyrim*

---

7. *A head-up-display (HUD) is the part of the GUI that does not display the 3D-world itself, but constantly provides information to the player about his health, his ammunition, the enemy's power etc.*

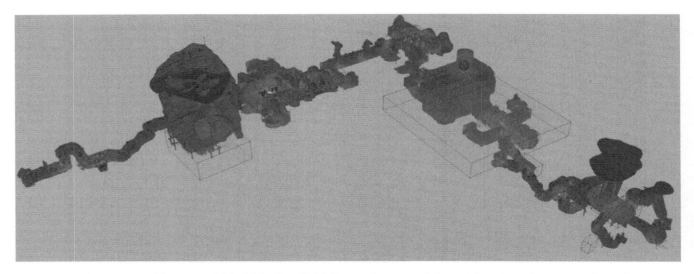

Figure 1. Map layout resembling typical The Elder Scrolls V: Skyrim dungeons (adopted from Pietschmann, et al., 2013)

to study the effects of image and graphics quality on the construction of spatial situation models in a 2×2 between-subjects factor design, varying image quality and attention allocation on two levels each[8] A custom level of an island with a small village was built using Bethesda's *Creation Kit*. Players started at the beach and were greeted by an NPC who guided the players towards the village. The NPC was fully voiced and part of a custom quest to explore the island. The players' task was embedded within a narrative: As a consultant sent by the local king, their objective was to assess the damage done to the village buildings by a recent bandit raid. The NPC was their contact on the island and was tasked to show them around the village. A recognition test of objects on the island measured memory performance after completion of the game task. Thus, it was important to control the amount of time each player was exposed to certain game objects (i.e., the buildings). The self-designed quest contained the experimental sequence and timing, so each player could be presented the same game objects in the same time frame. The NPC guide commented on and pointed at some buildings (thus making them relevant to the narrative). This allowed the manipulation of users' attention processes. In another experimental condition, the custom level was modified to accommodate a dual task to further manipulate attention processes: The NPC guide told players that in addition to the bandit raid, the village suffered from a rat infestation. The NPC asked players to help him count the rats on their way to be able to estimate how much traps and poison are needed to fight them. Several dozen rats were placed along the path of the players through the village, so they could spot them every couple of seconds. Behaviour scripts were added that made the rats flee from players when discovered. This manipulation proved successful to draw players' attention away from the buildings of the game world. The graphics quality conditions were realized using pre-existing modifications. In the high quality condition, graphics were tweaked with various mods developed and continually improved by the game's community, resulting in state of the art graphics (figure 2). In the low quality condition, the configuration files were modified to disable shadows, lighting effects, and dynamic vegetation. Additionally, the texture LOD adjustment of the graphic card driver was set to a very high level so that textures were not loaded in the game, resulting in a very minimalistic cell shading look. Overall, using two computers and two different versions of the custom level, Pietschmann and Liebold could implement a clean 2×2 experimental design.

8.   For two-factorial and between-subjects design, refer to Landers and Bauer (chapter 10).

Figure 2. Resulting visual styles of the improved version (left) and simplistic version (right) of a dimly lit environment in The Elder Scrolls V: Skyrim by Pietschmann and Liebold

Best practice

After describing several studies that employed mods, the goal of the following section is to provide important general guidelines for the design of game mods as stimulus material. If researchers are willing to profit from the advantages of modding, the first decision they have to make is whether it is more feasible to create a new game or to modify an existing one. If they decide to create a new game, the list of game and mod creation toolkits included in the online supplementary (Mohseni, et al., 2014) provides a good starting point as it provides an overview of today's game creation toolkits. Researchers are advised to first decide which genre (FPS, RPG, strategy game, etc.; see Smith, 2006) best represents their research question and then to pick a toolkit supporting this genre. Additionally, game taxonomies may be helpful to make an informed game choice. A number of taxonomies can be found in Järvelä, et al. (chapter 12). If researchers decide to modify an existing game instead of creating a new one, the list of modifiable games within the online supplementary may come in handy, because it provides a table of more than ninety games including its genre, year of publication, engine, editor(s) and information where to download the required tools.

CHOOSE THE GAME

Several aspects are worth considering when choosing a game for a modding project.

1. The game should be up-to-date: A modern game can be more immersive[9], but may need better (and as a result of that, more expensive) hardware. High-end hardware is known to often produce unwanted noise and heat, and dealing with these side effects may also raise the costs.
2. The game should have an active modding community: A vivid community may have created valuable resources which can be used in one's own mod in order to minimize development efforts. For example, Mohseni (2013a) as well as Pietschmann and Liebold used several pre-existing mods to fix bugs, to improve the quality of graphics, to prevent player characters from dying, or to make cheating impossible. A vivid community may also be willing to answer questions regarding the implementation of the modifications. Community members can

---

9. We use the term immersion in accordance with Wirth, et al. (2007), who conceptualize spatial presence as the experiential counterpart of immersion, which means that immersion is a technological quality of the stimulus that causes feelings of spatial presence.

inform about undocumented functions and known bugs in the editor and are sometimes even willing to help locating bugs in the created mod. This can be especially useful to researchers, who are often inexperienced in creating mods.

3. The game should provide a setting that is suitable for the research question: Displaying violent acts in a medieval scenario might have different effects on the player compared to a modern warfare scenario.

LEARN THE GAME

Because "[k]nowing how a game is used is a necessary step before undertaking any research design", Williams (2005, p. 459) recommends researchers to play the game. According to the author, knowledge about the game is also helpful for estimating the generalizability of one's findings, that is, external validity. Järvelä, et al. (chapter 12) further point out the value of knowing the game for the internal validity of the experiment: Especially researchers that are personally less familiar with games risk to overlook how seemingly unimportant game features may combine and influence the playing experience, possibly confounding the main effect. Therefore, the authors recommend playing the potential game to get a feeling for the tasks involved and to spot factors that might influence the tasks participants are requested to perform. We want to add another recommendation of how to learn the game, namely to consult the designers of the game in question (e.g., via forum), its modding community, and its experienced players. These groups have extensive expert knowledge about the games they play or even create, which would take researchers months or even years to catch up with.

SETUP THE PLATFORM

The next step after learning the game is setting up a development platform, on which the game and the editor are installed. It is advisable to choose a system that resembles the experimental hardware as close as possible. Unwanted issues such as (black, grey and white) screens of death, crashes, low frame rates, and loading delays, can be caused by the hardware and its drivers, because mods often render games less stable compared to the vanilla version. This minimizes the risk that the mod only runs smoothly on the development platform, but not on the experimental equipment. Of course there are exceptions to this rule: Even if the mod should only run on a single display during the experiment, creating the mod is much easier if two or more displays are installed, because most editors feature multiple windows that should stay open simultaneously (e.g., TES4 has one window for scripts, one for 3D-models, one for quests, and one for the render preview).

MAXIMIZE INTERNAL VALIDITY

While creating mods, researchers should try to maximize *internal validity* by creating comparable stimuli. Apart from this, researchers should make in-game cheating impossible. For example, most games offer a game-internal debugging console, which can be started anytime from within the game. These consoles often offer the possibility to remove objects, to kill non-player characters, to transport the player character to another place and so on. The mod should make sure that participants are not able to use these options during the experiment. Additionally, the mod should make sure that the game is not interrupted during the experiment. For example, a lot of videogames display a game over screen if the player character dies, and some of them automatically resume a previous game state. Researchers could therefore prevent player characters' deaths (e.g., Hartmann, Toz and Brandon, 2010, Study 1; Mohseni, 2013a), however, this may negatively affect the game experience. Games can also contain fancy loading screens. If these negatively affect the intended manipulation, they should be deactivated or replaced by neutral versions like black screens. Moreover, if possible, the mod should include some kind of manipulation check (e.g., checking if the game was played as planned, how many non-player characters were killed). Manipulation checks within the game should be given preference, as they are harder to circumvent, but external checks can be used as a supplement where internal checks are not feasible. For example, Carnagey and Anderson (2005) watched and recorded the number of kills, while Kneer, Knapp and Elson (2014) used an age restriction rating, a violence rating and a difficulty rating as manipulation checks. Others used subjective rating scales, for example, Hartmann, Toz and Brandon (2011), Hartmann and Vorderer (2010), Elson, et al. (2013), and Mohseni (2013a). Provisions like these can help to rule out cheating participants, broken playing sessions and other issues.

CREATE COMPARABLE STIMULI

Creating comparable stimuli can be achieved by equalizing player samples, dynamically adapting difficulty, reducing game complexity, controlling variation in confounders, and conducting pre-tests. Järvelä, et al. (chapter 12) address most of these issues[10], although their chapter implicitly focuses on unmodified games. Nonetheless, their suggestions are of equal importance to the use of modded game versions. Most of these measures can be combined in one way or another, but some of them depend on the decision to let novices participate in the study.

EQUALIZE PLAYER SAMPLE

In videogames, interactive stimuli change according to participant actions. Experienced players likely progress further in a given time, use more diverse and effective playing styles or access more advanced game items (chapter 12), and have more knowledge about the controls of the game (Frey, et al., 2007). Dekker and Champion (2007) report that inexperienced players are struggling with learning the gameplay and get confused more easily by the virtual surroundings. These struggles even influence biofeedback assessment. Novices need a lot of time to learn the game at the expense of the time they have for solving the given task (Hartig, Frey and Ketzel, 2003; Dekker and Champion, 2007). Järvelä, et al. (chapter 12) state that if novices were given too little time to learn the controls, this would likely influence the quality of the data. They therefore suggest recruiting participants with some (ideally genre specific) experience unless the research specifically addresses learning. The drawbacks to this solution are that it can be hard to find experienced players, especially females (chapter 12; Mohseni, 2013a; cf. Quandt, et al., 2013 for sex differences in videogame usage), and that results may not be generalized to inexperienced players. However, if researchers want to investigate the population of typical players, this is no problem at all. If recruiting experienced players only is not an option, researchers can 1) include a training phase (e.g. Hartig, Frey and Ketzel, 2003; Elson, et al., 2013) and a tutorial (e.g., Hartig, Frey and Ketzel, 2003; Mohseni, 2013a; Hartmann and Vorderer, 2010) respectively, and 2) measure differences in gaming experience (e.g., Staude-Müller, Bliesener, and Lutmann, 2008; Elson, et al., 2013; Mohseni, 2013a).

---

10.   Järvelä, et al. (chapter 12) discuss the problems of equalizing player samples, dynamically adapting difficulty, reducing game complexity, and controlling variation in confounders, but they do not recommend to conduct pre-tests. The latter may be due to their strong focus on unmodified games.

Additionally, they can dynamically adapt the game's difficulty, reduce the game's complexity, and control unwanted variation between conditions.

DYNAMICALLY ADAPT DIFFICULTY

A problem related to differences in player skills is that of game difficulty. According to Järvelä, et al. (chapter 12), modern games implement routines that automatically and continuously adapt the difficulty to that of the player's ability level. The authors suggest that if the goal is to create similar experiences, researchers should make use of automatically adapting difficulty, as it can be useful in creating equally challenging gaming experiences. Mohseni (2013a), for example, scripted enemies to be the less challenging the less health the player character has. This ensured that even inexperienced players could finish the given task. The drawback of this approach is that pre-tests are needed to check for over- and under-adaptation. Therefore, using a difficulty setting that reflects players' skills, but that stays static for the whole game, can be a time-saving alternative to dynamical adaption. For example, Elson, et al. (2013) adjusted difficulty by assessing players' abilities during the warm-up rounds. In contrast to the dynamical approach, this strategy poses the risk that the assessment is inaccurate. In principle, experienced players could dissimulate their skills and get a low difficulty setting, while inexperienced players could win more than usual due to pure luck and get a high difficulty setting. Therefore, Elson, et al. (2013) used multiple warm-up rounds for a more reliable assessment. However, this does not solve the problem of dissimulation. As a result, if researchers expect participants to dissimulate, they are advised to employ a dynamic adaption of difficulty. On the other hand, if the goal is to use the same content for all participants, Järvelä, et al. (chapter 12) suggest avoiding automatic difficulty adjustments. This may be hard to realize, as internal adaptation routines are often hard to detect and hard to modify.

REDUCE GAME COMPLEXITY

An additional approach to create comparable stimuli is to reduce complexity so that novices do not suffer from their inexperience: An in-game tutorial can be created to introduce the game mechanics (especially the controls), multi-way paths can be changed to linear paths, and in-game equipment and player character skills can be reduced to a minimum. Reduced complexity is quite common in the beginning phase of modern games, where players are slowly introduced to the different game mechanics in order to prevent early frustration. Complexity reductions are also achievable through modding. For example, Hartmann and Vorderer (2010, study 2) surrounded their level by a wall so players could not get lost. Hartmann and Vorderer (2010) as well as Hartmann, Toz and Brandon (2010) also made player characters invincible and provided them with only one weapon with unlimited ammunition. Elson, et al. (2013) used pre-existing mods to remove unwanted weapons and power-ups, while Hartig, Frey and Ketzel (2003) removed displays of players' health and ammunition, and restricted players' movements to forward, backward, and turning around.

However, the latter study demonstrates that even a major complexity reduction may not suffice to enable novices to play the game. Although participants could only move forward, backward and turn around, novices still struggled to navigate the map, and some of them even suffered from cybersickness. In addition to this, any major changes pose a risk of compromising game quality (cf. chapter 12). For example, if unimportant objects like room decorations are removed from the experimental level so that players do not meddle with them, this may lead to a rather boring level design. However, feeling stimulated and challenged is a prerequisite for engagement (Van den Hoogen, et al., 2012). For example, Dekker and Champion (2007) found that their immersive audio effects had a large impact on engagement. So if researchers strip the game of elements that seem superfluous to them, like audio effects or room decorations, this may result in reduced player engagement, which in turn may decrease the overall effect of the stimulus. Even worse than this, extreme changes may reduce *external* validity, as they may lead to a totally different kind of game. Therefore, when applying extreme changes, it is absolutely essential to conduct pre-tests in order to check for side effects.

CONTROL CONFOUNDER VARIATION

Another way to ensure a comparable playing experience is to control for unwanted variation in potential confounders. For example, in the experiment by Mohseni (2013a), the manipulation could have led to unwanted differences in confounding variables like player activation (Van den Hoogen, et al., 2012) or different perceptions of difficulty (Klimmt, 2001; Klimmt, Hartmann and Frey, 2007), competition (Adachi and Willoughby, 2011), frustration (Breuer, Scharkow and Quandt, 2013), entertainment (Klimmt, 2006), presence (Klimmt, 2006; Tamborini and Skalski, 2006), pace of action (Adachi and Willoughby, 2011, Elson, et al., 2013) and others. Of course, within the modding approach, the impact of these confounders is probably less problematic compared to the classic approach. Nonetheless, the mod was fine-tuned in pre-tests to have an equal impact of these confounders[11] on all experimental conditions, and the confounders were also measured at the end of the experiment itself. Other examples are Carnagey and Anderson (2005), who let participants rate the videogame on various dimensions (e.g., difficulty), Hartmann and Vorderer (2010, study 1), who assessed the number of opponents' shots, and Elson, et al. (2013), who measured game experience regarding gameplay, graphics, and emotional impact.

CONDUCT PRE-TESTS

The first and foremost reason for pre-tests is to find out if the manipulation works as expected. For example, in a "violent" condition it is advisable that the mod helps to make sure that participants have no alternative to acting violent, while in a non-violent condition, participants should have no opportunity to act violently. Researchers should make sure to test prototypes of the mod every now and then to detect flaws as soon as possible. The second reason is to check for unwanted variation in potential confounders caused by the manipulation, as already mentioned. The third reason is to find problems within the experimental setting. For example, it is also advisable to check for side effects of the hardware, because modern games are very demanding. It is possible that high-end computers produce heat to such an extent that participants in later sessions are faced with an up-heated room, which in turn can lead to drowsiness and to an up-heated noisy computer, which may lead to difficulty in concentration. Another problem can be the lighting conditions. Dark rooms often lead to better visuals (see Dekker and Champion, 2007; Mohseni, 2013a), but may also impede inexperienced players from finding individual keys on the keyboard. Experienced players, however, can be impeded by normal type input devices as they are often used to play with special equipment like mechanical keyboards and low-latency mice. Additional problems may arise from using biofeedback devices. For example, Dekker and Champion (2007) reported that players were impaired by these devices and could not properly use the mouse.

11. With the exception of competition and pace of action, but with the addition of graphic's closeness to reality, and the graphic's level of displayed violence.

Normally, it is advisable to record participants' in-game behaviour, as it can potentially confound the effects under observation. In some cases, participants' behaviour within the game can also be part of the research question. Ideally, recording behaviour is possible by letting the game automatically log each and any event. For example, Van den Hoogen, et al. (2012) automatically logged game events together with the system time as they needed to synchronize the game events with continuous EMG measures, while Kneer, Knapp and Elson (2014) recorded players' performance using log files from which kills and deaths were extracted. The drawback of this solution is that it can result in large and confusing log files, which have to be analysed by special tools, and that most games do not offer this kind of logging. For example, Elson, et al. (2013) had to install a logging mutator to automatically log in-game events. An alternative approach is to include script code in one's mod which logs important events. For example, Mohseni (2013a) logged the number of times players died and how many enemies players killed. A further alternative mentioned by Järvelä, et al. (chapter 12) is to use external logging systems like key loggers, screen capture videos and mouse-click recorders.

If logging is not feasible at all, the video signal can be recorded. According to Järvelä, et al. (chapter 12), this method has two drawbacks: it produces additional effort to identify critical events by reviewing the recordings, and not every event of interest (e.g. attention focus) can be identified in the recordings. Another drawback of the method is that additional hardware is needed to create high-quality recordings. As software-based solutions have to be installed on the experimental PC where they can have detrimental effects on the PCs performance if the recording quality is set to high levels, we recommend using a second recording PC with a suitable capture card installed.

Further reading

- Elson, M. and Quandt, T., 2014. Digital games in laboratory experiments: Controlling a complex stimulus through modding. *Psychology of Popular Media Culture*, ahead of print. DOI=10.1037/ppm0000033.
- McMahan, R.P., Ragan, E. D., Leal, A., Beaton, R.J. and Bowman, D.A., 2011. Considerations for the use of commercial video games in controlled experiments. *Entertainment Computing*, 2(1), pp.3–9. DOI=10.1016/j.entcom.2011.03.002
- Mohseni, M.R., Elson, M., Pietschmann, D. and Liebold, B., 2014. Modding for digital games research. Available at: <http://www6-medkom.hrz.tu-chemnitz.de/modding>.
- Ravaja, N. and Kivikangas, M.J., 2009. Designing game research: Addressing questions of validity. In: U. Ritterfeld, M. Cody and P. Vorderer, eds. 2009. *Serious games: Mechanisms and effects*. New York: Routledge. pp.404–412.

References

Adachi, P.J.C. and Willoughby, T., 2011. The effect of violent video games on aggression: Is it more than just the violence? *Aggression and Violent Behavior*, 16(1), pp.55–62. DOI=10.1016/j.avb.2010.12.002

Autodesk, 2012. *3ds Max* [computer program]. MS Windows. Autodesk.

Bethesda, 2006. *The Elder Scrolls IV: Oblivion* [game]. MS Windows. 2K Games.

Bethesda, 2011. *The Elder Scrolls V: Skyrim* [game]. MS Windows. Bethesda.

Blender Foundation, 1994. *Blender* [computer program]. MS Windows. Blender Foundation.

Blizzard Entertainment, 2002. *Warcraft 3: Reign of Chaos* [game]. MS Windows. Blizzard Entertainment.

Carnagey, N.L. and Anderson, C.A., 2005. The effects of reward and punishment in violent video games on aggressive affect, cognition, and behavior. *Psychological Science*, 16(11), pp.882–889. DOI=10.1111/j.1467-9280.2005.01632.x

Bohemia Interactive, 2001. *Operation Flashpoint* [game]. MS Windows. Codemasters.

Breuer, J., Scharkow, M. and Quandt, T., 2013. Sore losers? A reexamination of the frustration-aggression hypothesis for colocated video game play. *Psychology of Popular Media Culture*, ahead of print. DOI=10.1037/ppm0000020.

Chatman, B., 2008. *UT3 speed modification mutator* [computer program]. MS Windows. Available at: <http://www.moddb.com/games/unreal-tournament-3/downloads/speed-modification-mutator>.

Chittaro, L. and Sioni, R., 2012. Killing non-human animals in video games: A study on user experience and desensitization to violence aspects. *PsychNology*, 10(3), pp.215–243. Available at: <http://www.psychnology.org>.

Crytek, 2013. *Crysis 3* [game]. MS Windows. Electronic Arts.

Dekker, A. and Champion, E., 2007. Please biofeed the zombies: Enhancing the gameplay and display of a horror game using biofeedback. In: B. Akira, ed., *Situated play*. Tokyo. September. Tokyo, Japan: DiGRA. Available at: <http://www.digra.org/digital-library/publications/please-biofeed-the-zombies-enhancing-the-gameplay-and-display-of-a-horror-game-using-biofeedback>.

Elson, M., 2011. *The effects of displayed violence and game speed in first-person shooters on physiological arousal and aggressive behavior*. Diploma. University of Cologne. Available at: <http://www.malte-elson.com/files/elson_diploma_thesis.pdf>.

Elson, M. and Quandt, T., 2014. Digital games in laboratory experiments: Controlling a complex stimulus through modding. *Psychology of Popular Media Culture*, ahead of print. DOI=10.1037/ppm0000033.

Elson, M., Breuer, J., Van Looy, J., Kneer, J. and Quandt, T., 2013. Comparing apples and oranges? Evidence for pace of action as a confound in research on digital games and aggression. *Psychology of Popular Media Culture*, ahead of print. DOI=10.1037/ppm0000010.

Epic Games, 2002. *Unreal Tournament 2003* [game]. MS Windows. Atari.

Epic Games, 2007. *Unreal Tournament 3* [game]. MS Windows. Midway Games.

Frey, A., Hartig, J., Ketzel, A., Zinkernagel, A. and Moosbrugger, H., 2007. The use of virtual environments based on a modification of the computer game Quake III Arena in psychological experimenting. *Computers in Human Behavior*, 23(4), pp.2026–2039. DOI=10.1016/j.chb.2006.02.010.

Gopher, 2013. *Immersive HUD* (Version 1.1) [computer program]. MS Windows. Gopher. Available at: <http://www.nexusmods.com/skyrim/mods/3222>.

Hartig, J., Frey, A. and Ketzel, A., 2003. Modifikation des computerspiels Quake III Arena zur durchführung psychologischer experimente in einer virtuellen 3D-umgebung. *Zeitschrift für Medienpsychologie*, 15(4), pp.149–154. DOI=10.1026//1617-6383.15.4.149.

Hartmann, T., Toz, E. and Brandon, M., 2010. Just a game? Unjustified virtual violence produces guilt in empathetic players. *Media Psychology*, 13(4), pp.339–363. DOI=10.1080/15213269.2010.524912

Hartmann, T. and Vorderer, P., 2010. It's Okay to shoot a character: Moral disengagement in violent video games. *Journal of Communication*, 60(1), pp.94–119. DOI=10.1111/j.1460-2466.2009.01459.x.

id Software, 1999. *Quake 3 Arena* [game]. MS Windows. id Software.

Klimmt, C., 2006. *Computerspielen als handlung: Dimensionen und determinanten des erlebens interaktiver unterhaltungsangebote*. Cologne: Herbert von Halem Verlag.

Klimmt, C., Hartmann, T. and Frey, A., 2007. Effectance and control as determinants of video game enjoyment. *CyberPsychology and Behavior*, 10(6), pp.845–848. DOI=10.1089/cpb.2007.9942.

Kneer, J., Knapp, F. and Elson, M., 2014. Challenged by rainbows: The effects of displayed violence, difficulty, and game-performance on arousal, cognition, aggressive behavior, and emotion. In: ICA: *64th conference of the international communication association*. Seattle, May.

McMahan, R.P., Ragan, E.D., Leal, A., Beaton, R.J. and Bowman, D.A., 2011. Considerations for the use of commercial video games in controlled experiments. *Entertainment Computing*, 2(1), pp.3–9. DOI=10.1016/j.entcom.2011.03.002

Mobile3D, 2010. *YUGame* [game]. iPhone. Mobile 3D. Available at: <https://itunes.apple.com/us/app/yugame/id351890205?mt=8>.

Mohseni, M.R., 2012. Virtuelle nothilfe. Selbstlosigkeit oder Selbstgerechtigkeit. In: W. Kaminski and M. Lorber, eds., 2012. *Gamebased learning: Clash of realities 2012*. Kopaed: Munich, Germany. pp.243–258.

Mohseni, M.R., 2013a. *Virtuelle nothilfe: Ein experiment zum effekt von virtueller hilfe, gewalt und nothilfe auf hilfe- und gewaltverhalten*. PhD. Osnabrück University. Available at: <http://repositorium.uni-osnabrueck.de/handle/urn:nbn:de:gbv:700-2013072311013>.

Mohseni, M.R., 2013b. *Oblivion nothilfe-bedingung*. Available at: <http://youtu.be/3TNkWTRNNYE>.

Mohseni, M.R., 2013c. *Oblivion schatzjagd-bedingung*. Available at: <http://youtu.be/CoAY3AN5kI4>.

Mohseni, M.R., Elson, M., Pietschmann, D. and Liebold, B., 2014. Modding for digital games research. Available at: <http://www6-medkom.hrz.tu-chemnitz.de/modding>.

Pietschmann, D., Liebold, B., Valtin, G., Nebel, S. and Ohler, P., 2013. Effects of video game GUIs on the construction of rich spatial situation models and spatial presence. In: F. Schwab, A. Carlous, M. Brill and C. Henninghausen, eds., *Proceedings of the 8th conference of the media psychology division of the german psychological society*. Würzburg, September.

Pouledouris, B., 1982. *Conan the Barbarian*. [CD]. Paris: Milan.

Quandt, T., Breuer, J., Festl, R. and Scharkow, M., 2013. Digitale Spiele: Stabile Nutzung in einem dynamischen Markt. *Media Perspektiven*, 10, pp.483–492.

Ravaja, N. and Kivikangas, M.J., 2009. Designing game research: Addressing questions of validity. In U. Ritterfeld, M. Cody and P. Vorderer, eds., 2009. *Serious games: Mechanisms and effects*. New York: Routledge. pp.404–412.

Scacchi, W., 2010. Computer game mods, modders, modding, and the mod scene. *First Monday*, 15(5). DOI= 10.5210/fm.v15i5.2965.

Smith, B. P., 2006. The (computer) games people play. In P. Vorderer and J. Bryant, eds., 2006. *Playing video games. Motives, responses, and consequences*. Mahwah: Lawrence Erlbaum, pp.43–56.

Stainless Software, 1998. *Carmageddon 2* [game]. MS Windows. SCi Games.

Staude-Müller, F., Bliesener, T. and Luthman, S., 2008. Hostile and hardened? An experimental study on (de-)sensitization to violence and suffering through playing video games. *Swiss Journal of Psychology*, 67(1), pp.41–50. DOI=10.1024/1421-0185.67.1.41.

Tamborini, R. and Skalski, P., 2006. The role of presence in the experience of electronic games. In: P. Vorderer and J. Bryant, eds., 2006. *Playing video games. Motives, responses, and consequences*. Mahwah, NJ: Lawrence Erlbaum, pp.225–240.

Ubisoft, 2012. *Far Cry 3* [game]. MS Windows. Ubisoft.

The Game Creators, 2005. *FPS Creator* [computer program]. MS Windows. The Game Creators.

Valve Corporation, 2002. *Valve Hammer Editor* [computer program]. MS Windows. Valve Corporation.

Valve Corporation, 2004. *Half-Life 2* [game]. MS Windows. Valve Corporation.

Valve Corporation, 2004. *Source SDK* [computer program]. MS Windows. Valve Corporation.

Valve Corporation, 2007. Team Fortress 2. [game]. MS Windows. Valve Corporation.

Valve Corporation, 2013. Dota2. [game]. MS Windows. Valve Corporation.

Van den Hoogen, W. M., Poels, K., IJsselsteijn, W. A. and de Kort, Y. A. W., 2012. Between challenge and defeat: Repeated player-death and game enjoyment. *Media Psychology*, 15(4), pp.443–459. DOI=10.1080/15213269.2012.723117.

Washburn, D., 2003. The games psychologists play (and the data they provide). *Behavior Research Methods*, 35(2), pp.185–193.

Williams, D., 2005. Bridging the methodological divide in game research. *Simulation & Gaming*, 36(4), pp.447–463. DOI=10.1177/1046878105282275.

Wirth, W., Hartmann, T., Böcking, S. Vorderer, P., Klimmt, C., Schramm, H., Saari, T., Laarni, J., Ravaja, N., Ribeiro Gouveia, F., Biocca, F., Sacau, A., Jäncke, L., Baumgartner, T. and Jäncke, P., 2007. A Process Model of the Formation of Spatial Presence Experiences. *Media Psychology*, 9(3), pp.493–525.

20. Experimental Game Design

ANNIKA WAERN AND JON BACK

One way to understand games better is to experiment with their design. While experimental game design is part of most game design, this chapter focuses on ways in which it can become a method to perform academic enquiry, eliciting deeper principles for game design.

Experimental game design relies on two parts: varying design, and doing some kind of studies with it. In this chapter we limit the discussion to experiments that involve *people* that play the game.

Design science

The approaches we discuss in this chapter are best framed within the context of design science (Cross, 2001; Collins, et al., 2004). This research paradigm has two faces: it is the scientific study of design concepts and methods (Cross, 2001) but also encompasses the use of design as a research method (research *by* design) (Collins, et al., 2004; Kelly, 2003).

It is well known that design experiments are part of the design process for most games. Game designers tend to experiment throughout the design process; by adding and deleting components, changing rules, balancing, modifying themes and changing the way the game interacts with players. They also play-test their designs. Zimmerman (2003) writes exquisitely on how playing a game is part of the iterative design process, and how new questions about the design grows out of each play session, and Fullerton (2008) develops a full-fledged methodology for integrated playtesting and design.

What then, makes design experimentation a scientific research method? The short answer is that firstly, scientific experimentation must be done with some level of rigour, and secondly, it must be done to answer questions that are somewhat more generic than just making a singular game better. Experimental design is a research method when the aim is to understand something generic, some more fundamental aspect of game design. Thus, the way we discuss experimental game design in this chapter straddles both perspectives on design research: it is a way to, through designing, understand more about design principles for games.

While this chapter focuses on design experiments involving players, playtesting is not completely necessary in experimental design. Many dynamic aspects of game design can be tested without players. Seasoned game designers often use Excel or similar tools to calculate game balance (Clare, 2013). Joris Dormans has developed machinations (Adams and Dormans, 2012) as a useful tool for simulating the dynamics of resource management in games, and game theory presents theoretical tools to understand some of the dynamics of multi-player gaming (Osborne, 1994). It is also possible to experiment with games using simulated players (Bjornsson and Finnsson, 2009).

All of these methods are valuable tools for game design, and have potential to also be valuable in experimental game design research. The problem is that they all rely on abstracting the player. They require that we already know something about how players are expected to behave. But this is seldom true in game design research—rather, we are looking to explore the link between game design and player's behaviour and experience. Hence, while calculations and simulations may help us trim and debug the game we want to experiment with, the research results will emerge from testing the game in practice, with players.

When is a game design experimental?

We have already established that the experimental game designs we are looking at, are such that serve to elicit something interesting about design principles for games. Hence, it is not the status of the game design that marks it out as experimental or not. Experimental game designs can be sketchy, consisting of bare-bone game mechanics and interface sketches, or they can be full-fledged games or prototypes that are made publicly available for weeks or months. It is not the format of the game or the trial that determines whether it is experimental but the kind of experiment we plan to perform with the game. We can distinguish between classical, *controlled* experiments that aim to provide answers to descriptive or evaluative questions, and more open forms of experimentation where the aim is to explore and develop innovative solutions. The latter form of experimentation can concern game fragments as well as full games. Below, we distinguish between *evocative* and *explorative* design experiments, which both support more open design investigations.

CONTROLLED DESIGN EXPERIMENTS

The classical approach to empirical experimentation is to use controlled experiments. In a controlled experiment, you contrast multiple setups against each other, to measure the effects of varying a small set of parameters. One performs a controlled experiment where one either subjects different participants to different conditions (inter-subject comparison) or each subject experiences all conditions (and within-subject comparison) (cf. chapter 10, experimental research designs). Applied to experimental game design research, this corresponds to varying one or more design factors in a game, and subject players to different versions of the same game.

Controlled experiments have their role in game research in general; and have for example been used in studies that explore how people learn to play games and in studies that investigate the gameplay experience. They have also recently got an interesting use in the context of online games. In A/B online testing, two versions of a game are launched in parallel to different parts of the player population and evaluated based on desirable responses. If one version makes players, say, pay more, then that version may later on be launched as the new standard.

Still, there are many pitfalls in using controlled experiments in the context of design research (cf. chapter 12). The obvious one is that in order to enable experimentation at all, the game must exist and run fairly smoothly. If your aim is to study variants of a computer game and must develop the game to be able to study it, you end up with a very expensive experiment. It is sometimes possible to use game mods for this purpose (cf. chapter 19).

The most challenging factor is directly related to experimenting with design. A game is a complex web of design decisions, making it hard to isolate and vary a particular factor without fundamentally changing the game. The only option is often to construct an experiment setup where the game works optimally in one of the conditions, and the other one is a crippled version of the original where a particular design feature has been disabled. This problem is aggravated by the fact that it makes little sense to do a controlled experiment, unless the factor that you are varying teaches us something interesting about game design. But if it *is* interesting, chances are that the factor is tightly integrated with the core design choices for the game, and is impossible to vary without drastically changing the game.

Furthermore, controlled game experiments suffer from the fact that the immediate effect of varying a game design is typically that people start to play the game differently. Salen and Zimmerman (2004) describe this as games being *second order design*. The player experience does not arise from the game as such, but from the game session in which the player has participated. As most games can be played in several ways, a small change in design can have a huge impact on how people play the game. While this is in itself worthy of study, many studies do not take this aspect into account, but only aim to capture the player experience. A confounding factor is that whereas game design certainly has an effect on player engagement, so do a host of other things: including how players were recruited to the study and whom they are teamed up with.

Finally, controlled experiments with design must be repeated several times over in order to yield reliable results. Unless experiments are repeated over several games, we know very little about the generalizability of results. In the particular game that you used it may be true that varying factor A leads to results B. However, will the same be true for another game? Are the results specific to a game genre? Where are the limits—what are the design factors that delimit the validity of the results? No single study can answer these questions. Refer to chapters 12 and 19 for more detailed discussion.

The example we will use to illustrate this approach is from applied psychology. Choi, et al. (2007) report on a rather well executed design experiment, concerning modes of collaboration in a MMORPG. The goal of this study was to investigate how reward sharing interacts with how dependent you are on grouping up to achieve a task. The authors tested for experiences of flow, satisfaction, and sense of competence. Essentially, the result was that if players could achieve a goal independently of each other (despite the fact that they played in a group), they had more fun, experienced more flow and felt more competent if they also received rewards independently of each other. And conversely, if the players were dependent on each other they had more fun, experienced more flow, and felt more competent if they also shared the rewards.

This experiment avoids several of the potential pitfalls. First of all, the experiment was done with a pre-existing game, rather than a game prototype developed for the purpose of the study, short-cutting the issue of having to develop a full game. The game was modified (cf. chapter 19) to generate the experiment conditions, and multiple versions of the game were installed at local servers. Secondly, the goal of the study was *not* to study the game with or without a given design feature. Instead, the study explored how two varied factors interacted with each other (solo or group goal achievement, solo or group reward), avoiding the comparison of an optimal setup with a suboptimal one. Finally, the factors that were varied were at the game mechanics level and as such represented core design factors, while still sufficiently isolated so that they could be varied without rewriting large parts of the code.

Despite this, the study still fails to convince. The main problem is that in the setup where players could achieve the goal on their own without help of each other, the game also became significantly *easier*. Hence, it is possible that players changed their play style under this condition. Maybe they dispersed to do different challenges in parallel; maybe they just sat back and took turns in defeating the enemies. The article does not present any information on the gameplay strategies that developed under the different experiment conditions.

From a game design perspective, the topic of the article can also be challenged. Choi, et al. (2007) claim that interdependency is an important concept in MMORPG design. While this may be true, the results of the study come across as trivial. Most likely, any MMORPG player or game designer would dismiss the results of the paper as self-evident. It is significant that the article has been published in applied psychology rather than as a game research article; it says something about social psychology applied to games, but little about game design.

Finally, the article uses a rhetorical trick to inflate the generalizability of the study—it never mentions which game that is studied! The game is discussed only as "a MMORPG". This tacitly implies that the results would hold for any game in the genre, an over-generalization that any game design researcher should be wary about.

EVOCATIVE DESIGN EXPERIMENTS

Most of the informative design experiments in game design research are much less rigid than the controlled experiments discussed above. Essentially, they fulfil a similar role as iterative play testing does in the practice of game design; they are done to iteratively refine an innovation. The difference is that in design research, the design experiments are not about refining a particular game—they are done to elicit more abstract qualities about games.

The distinction is important, because experimental design research can have completely different objectives than looking for optimal design solutions. The games need not be meant to be good games, and the experiments may focus on other factors than player satisfaction. The overarching goal for this type of design experimentation is to explore the design space of game design, by understanding more about the behaviour and experiences that a design choice will evoke in players. Hence, we can call this class of design experiments *evocative*.

Evocative design experiments tend to be rather open. Even if designers typically already have an idea of how a particular design choice will affect player behaviour and experience, the unexpected effects tend to be even more important. Schön (1983) describes how most design practices include design sketching, such as the drawings used in architecture. When the design manifest in material form it 'talks back' to the designer, highlighting qualities of the idea that were previously unarticulated or even unintended. Since game design is second order design, games do not manifest in sketches, but by being played.

It may or may not matter who plays the game. Zimmerman (2003) describes a game design process where the early game play sessions were carried out within the designer group. The argument for designers playing the game is that it provides them with the full subjective experience of being a player. The argument against this approach is that internal playtesting very easily turns into designers designing for themselves, rather than for an intended audience. Both designer play and early user group playtesting have a function in game design research, and the choice depends on the design qualities you are exploring. Design experimentation is typically first done within the designer group, but if the core research questions are intrinsically related to the target group, it might be better to involve players from the target group from start.

It is often possible to do evocative game design experiments with very early game prototypes. The game mechanics for computer games can be tested early by implementing them in a board game (Fullerton, 2008) or by simulating them in *Wizard of Oz setups* (Márquez Segura, et al., 2013). An interesting option is *body-storming* (Márquez Segura, et al., 2013), which can be used when you wish to study the social or physical interaction between players in a computer or otherwise technology-dependent game. In body-storming, players are given mock-up technology that they *pretend* is working. This means that the rules of the game are not enforced by the technology, but through the social agreement between players. An interesting aspect of body-storming a game is that its rules need not even be complete, as players may very well develop their own rules while pretending to play the game.

While evocative design experiments are considerably simpler to perform than controlled design experiments, they still present some pitfalls. First of all, the games need to be rather simple. To enable experiments that elicit something about the design factor tested, the game needs to be stripped of as much as possible apart from this factor. This requirement may be difficult to reconcile with the fact that the game also must be playable, and that the game must have a way to manifest. Game structures cannot be tested without some kind of surface structure—there must be something that players can interact with.

In an on-going project (Back and Waern, 2013; 2014) a range of evocative game design experiments were performed, and two in particular serve well to illustrate the opportunities and pitfalls of evocative game design experiments. The game under development, *Codename Heroes*, is a pervasive game (cf. Montola, et al., 2009). It is played on mobile phones in public place as well as with hidden physical artefacts. The core game mechanics center on virtual messages that players move between the artefacts by walking from place to place. The game is developed as a research prototype. The research goals for this project are two-fold: one is to develop game mechanics and thematic aesthetics that can be engaging for young women and encourage them to move more freely in public space (Back and Waern, 2013). The second goal is to develop pervasive game mechanics that can scale to large number of players over large areas (Back and Waern, 2014), while the game can still manifest physically rather than being confined to the mobile phone display. In order to understand better how the different aspects of the game worked to fulfil our design goals, the game was deconstructed and tested it in parts, in the form of meaningful mini-games.

Game test 1: pen-and-paper prototyping

An early game test with Codename Heroes focussed on developing an understanding of the types of gameplay that would emerge from the core game mechanic, the message passing system. This playtest focussed on the experience of moving physically to transport virtual messages: and delivering them to other players and to specific locations.

This design experiment was done very early during the design process, and while the end result would be a game on mobile phones, no implementation was running at the time of the test. Hence, we had to somehow simulate the core game mechanics, that of physically carrying—and potentially also *losing* – messages. In order to make message passing an interesting challenge, messages can be lost in *Codename Heroes*. If a message is carried too far or for too long time, a team may lose it and other teams may pick it up. We needed to simulate this function in the playtest. It was simulated using coloured envelopes: every team had a colour, and could only carry messages in envelopes of their own colour. A location tracking system from a previous development project was repurposed to enable tracking the participants. If a team would travel too far in one direction the game masters would send them a text message, telling them to change the envelope of a message and leave it at their current location.

It is important to emphasise that while this function was simulated, other parts of the game design were not. In particular, the play experiment was done with actual movement (as seen in figure 1)—we did not test the game mechanics in the form of a board game, which easily could have been done. Since a core design goal of *Codename Heroes* is to encourage and empower young women to move in public space, we specifically did not want to take away this aspect. Players walked—and ran—considerable distances in this play test, and part of the game was located in an area that we thought could make players feel uncomfortable. It was also important to recruit players from the target audience to this test—most of the players were young women.

Several things were learned from this game test. Firstly, the experiment supported the assumption that the spy-style message passing game mechanics indeed was attractive to the participating young women representing our core target group. We also found that the game indeed had the potential to encourage the participating women to move about in public space. We could observe that by teaming up and making the movement part of a game, the participants selected to move about in areas they otherwise would have avoided, and also that this was a positive and empowering experience (Back and Waern, 2013).

The design experiment also talked back to us in a slightly unexpected way. Despite the quite clumsy way that players had to simulate some of the game functionality, the physicality of messages and envelopes added greatly to the game experience. For example, on one occasion a group of players came across a message that another group had been forced to leave. When spotting the envelope from afar they shouted out in joy, and reported this as one of the highlights in the playtest.

This playtest also exhibited an element of body-storming in that not all of the game rules were given. In particular, we did not tell the groups whether they would be competing or collaborating. The rule mechanic of leaving and picking up messages from each other could be interpreted either way. At the end of the game, the three groups came together to solve a riddle, but we had also used a scoring system to calculate scores for the individual teams. Players were not informed about this before starting to play. The reason was that we wanted to test how the participating young women would interpret the situation. Would they collaborate, or compete? In the end, we saw elements of both. The groups did a bit of collaboration on finding messages, in particular towards the end, but mostly played separately. When asked about it after the game had finished, they decided that they had been doing both. One of the participants articulated this as "we won together, but *they*" (the group that had got the highest score) "get to sit at the high end of the table".

This is a good example of an evocative game experiment. It used a stripped-down game design with a partial implementation, letting players simulate some of the functions that later were to be implemented. Furthermore, while one of the reasons for doing the experiment was to test if the core game mechanics (carrying messages around) was sufficiently engaging, we left parts of the game underspecified and looked for how the participants would interpret the situation. We studied the activities and experiences that the game evoked, and, some of the core insights came from unexpected aspects of the experiment design, such as the high value of the physical aspects of message passing.

Game test 2, testing the artefacts

In subsequent design experiments, we focussed specifically on the physical aspects of the game. While the message passing system is virtual and supported by a mobile phone app in *Codename Heroes*, the game includes physical artefacts that can affect its function.

In order for the game to scale to arbitrary space and arbitrary numbers of users, the number of artefacts must also scale. This is why the game primarily relies on players constructing the artefacts. The construction, activation and physical distribution of artefacts constitute the second core game mechanic in *Codename Heroes*, and more general is an interesting game mechanic. While the example of *Geocashing* (cf. by Neustaedter, et al., 2013) shows that it is fun to both hide and find artefacts in a treasure hunt style game, *Codename Heroes* is not a treasure hunt game. Hence, it was not certain that the experience would be the same. Furthermore, it was important to understand under which conditions the activity of constructing a game artefact would be an attractive game activity in itself.

Again, we constructed a mini-game, this time with focus on artefact construction and distribution. We let players build artefacts in a workshop, and use them to search for and distribute messages (see figure 2). However, we left out the challenges related to messages: players could not lose messages and there was no challenge related to finding a particular set of messages.

Figure 2. Artefacts being built during the construction game test.

While the activity of building artefacts in a workshop was engaging and rewarding, the rest of the experiment suffered from a lack of game mechanics. In particular, it was unclear to players if there was any progression towards some kind of goal. The effect was that we ran into difficulties both with recruiting participants to the experiment, and with players not completing the game.

The setup illustrates a risk with the mini-game approach, in that not every game mechanic can run in isolation. In our strife to at the same time avoid testing the message passing over again and not creating a hide and seek game, we had unintentionally created an interactive experiment that was not a game at all.

EXPLORING A GAME GENRE

An ambitious objective for experimental game design is to explore a novel game genre. Although such experiments still can be small and focussed, this ambitious goal will sometimes require the development of full-scale and sufficiently complex games, and study them extensively. An example of an ambitious project that aimed to explore design for an entire game genre was the European project *IPerG: the Integrated Project on Pervasive Games*. The project included several large-scale experiments with a fairly novel and under-researched genre, that of pervasive games (Montola, et al., 2009).

Needless to say, this form of design experimentation is time- and resource-consuming. There is very little difference in effort between developing a full-scale game in order to research it, and launching it as a commercial or artistic product. A large-scale game experiment will typically go through the same design process, with multiple design iterations and playtesting, an alpha and a beta phase, etcetera. While the process may end after beta testing rather than include a commercial launch (as that falls outside the scope of research), the final experiments can be large-scale and come across as open beta testing to the players (McMillan, et al., 2010).

The differences again lie in how the game is designed, and in how the testing is done. An experimental game needs to emphasise the factors that are interesting from a design research perspective. For example, the pervasive game *Momentum* was extreme in its attempt to merge role-play with everyday life (Stenros, et al., 2007; Waern, et al., 2009). This research was ethically challenging, as it meant that role-players would meet and interact with people who were not themselves playing and that might not even be aware of the game. A major result from this research was a deepened understanding of the ethical challenges of pervasive games in general (Montola and Waern, 2006a; 2006b).

The emphasis on trialling specific design factors can come in conflict with the designers' desire to also make an interesting and attractive game. This is less of a problem in evocative design experiments as these are smaller and also often done early, as part of the design process for a larger game. In full-scale design experiments, the balance between experimenting and creating an attractive game can lead to conflicts within the research group as well as cumbersome compromises in design. Montola (2011) discusses this in particular in relationship to technology-focussed research questions. If one of the purposes of the project is to develop and test new technology, this can very easily come in conflict with the designers' wish to make a good game, if the technology is not ready on time, or is buggy or slow.

Studying large game experiments presents its own challenges (Stenros, et al., 2011), in particular with understanding something about the relationship between specific design choices and the play behaviour and experiences that players exhibit. This is the reason why a typical game experiment will look rather different from an ordinary beta test. The game experiment requires extensive documentation, both in terms of filming, recording and logging play behaviour, and player's active reporting of their game play activities and experiences. It may be necessary to emphasise quality over quantity in data collection (Stenros, et al., 2011). Rich data is necessary in order to be able to deconstruct the play behaviour to identify instances of play that reflect particular game design elements. These can then be scrutinized in detail, to understand something about their effects on player behaviour and experience.

The study of experimental games is thus a complex and expensive interpretative process, which can be very rewarding if the game is innovative or focussed on interesting design qualities. In total, the process of experimentally developing a design understanding of a game genre is very expensive, in design and development as well as in testing, and can only be recommended when genre in question is novel, important, and under-researched.

Best practices and considerations

There are many similarities between game design research, and the practice of game design. In particular, game design research will often use explorative and interpretative experiments rather than classical controlled scientific experiments. However, there are also some important differences. In particular, there is a difference in the goals—experimental game design should aim to explore design factors that are novel or may be problematic, rather than strive to generate good games. This difference underlies the best practice recommendations summarized below.

In order for a *controlled experiment* to be relevant in game design research, it must be possible to vary the game in a way that does not cripple it. Furthermore, the design factor that is varied must be sufficiently interesting. As argued by Zimmerman, Forlizzi, and Evenson, (2007), design research is judged by its relevance to design rather than its repeatability.

Trialling a specific game design factor can also be done in *open and evocative design experiments*. These can even be done with incompletely designed or implemented games. But evocative design experiments must still be properly documented, and open for the fact that they can yield unexpected results. Also, it does not work to trial just any random idea – the game must be understandable and be playable by the participants.

Even *large-scale and fully developed games* can be developed for the purpose of explorative design research, if the goal is to trial innovative game design solutions in underexplored game genres. These experiments face particular challenges in data gathering and hypothesis testing, as it becomes difficult to attribute player behaviour to particular design factors. This is discussed in more depth in Stenros, Waern and Montola (2011).

Concluding remarks

While this chapter has focussed on experimental game design as a scientific paradigm, many of the practices are similar to those of user-centred game design as a practice. Tracy Fullerton's book *The game design workshop* (2008) is hence an excellent resource for developing a good overall process also in experimental game design.

The concept of *design science* was originally proposed by Herbert Simon (1981) in his book *science of the artificial*. It has been under intense debate ever since. Nigel Cross (2001) presents a nice summary of the different perspectives, advocating a paradigm that lies close to the one of this article.

There exist very little meta-level discussion of the kinds of knowledge that is the result of design research on games. However, there has been an intense discussion in the field of interaction design research that also is relevant for design research on games. Zimmerman, Forlizzi and Evenson (2007) argue that the designs produced within design science is a contribution in themselves, but stress a requirement that the results must be relevant for future design projects. Adopting a more theory-focussed perspective, Höök and Löwgren (2012) instead argue that design research should aim to produce 'strong concepts', as loose description of design theories that are at the same time scientifically defendable and relevant in the design process. Lim, et al. (2007) present one such concept that may be particularly well suited to trial in experimental game design; a framework for aesthetically pleasing interactivity.

Finally, proper data gathering is central to maintaining scientific rigor also in design science, but data gathering can be tricky in particular in large design experiments. Stenros, Waern and Montola (2011) present an overview of data gathering methods for pervasive games. While the article focuses on games that are played over large physical areas, most of the issues presented in the article apply to a wide range of games.

Further Reading

- Fullerton, T., 2008. *The game design workshop: A playcentric approach to creating innovative games*. Boca Raton: CRC press.
- Cross, N., 2001. Designerly ways of knowing: design discipline versus design science. *Design issues*, 17(3), pp.49-55.
- Zimmerman, J., Forlizzi, J. and Evenson, S., 2007. Research through design as a method for interaction design research. In: *Proceedings of the SIGCHI conference on human factors in computing systems, CHI '07*. New York: ACM, pp.493–502.
- Lim, Y., Stolterman, E. Jung, H. and Donaldson, J., 2007. Interaction gestalt and the design of aesthetic interactions. In: I. Koskinen and T. Keinonen, eds., DPPI, *Proceedings of the 2007 conference on designing pleasurable products and interfaces*. Helsinki. August. New York: ACM, pp.239–254.
- Stenros, J., Waern, A. and Montola, M. 2011. Studying the elusive experience in pervasive games. *Simulation & Gaming*, 43(3), ahead of print. DOI=10.1177/1046878111422532.

References

Adams, E., and Dormans. J., 2012. *Game mechanics: Advanced game design*. Berkely: New Riders.

Back, J. and Waern, A., 2014. Codename Heroes: Designing for experience in public places in a long term pervasive game. In: *Foundations of digital games (FDG)*. Fort Lauderdale. April.

Bjornsson, Y., and Finnsson, H., 2009. Cadiaplayer: A simulation-based general game player. *IEEE Transactions on Computational Intelligence and AI in Games*, 1(1), pp.4–15.

Choi, B., Lee, I., Choi, D. and Kim, J., 2007. Collaborate and share: An experimental study of the effects of task and reward interdependencies in online games. *CyberPsychology & Behavior*, 10(4), pp.591–595.

Clare, A., 2013. Using Excel and Google Docs for game design. *Reality is a Game* [blog]. 4 April. Available at: <http://www.realityisagame.com/archives/1819/using-excel-and-google-docs-for-game-design/>.

Collins, A., Joseph, D. and Bielaczyc, K., 2004. Design research: Theoretical and methodological issues. *Journal of the learning sciences*, 13(1), pp.15–42.

Cross, N., 2001. Designerly ways of knowing: design discipline versus design science. *Design issues*,17(3), pp.49-55.

Fullerton, T., 2008. *The game design workshop: A playcentric approach to creating innovative games*. Boca Raton: CRC press.

Höök, K. and Löwgren, J., 2012. Strong concepts: Intermediate-level knowledge in interaction design research. *TOCHI*, 19(3), pp.23:1–23:18. DOI=10.1145/2362364.2362371.

Kelly, A. E., 2003. Research as design. *Educational researcher*, 32(1), pp.3–4.

Lim, Y., Stolterman, E. Jung, H. and Donaldson, J., 2007. Interaction gestalt and the design of aesthetic interactions. In: I. Koskinen and T. Keinonen, eds., DPPI, *Proceedings of the 2007 conference on designing pleasurable products and interfaces*. Helsinki. August. New York: ACM, pp.239–254.

Márquez Segura, E., Waern, A., Moen, J., and Johansson, C., 2013. The design space of body games: technological, physical, and social design. In: ACM, *Proceedings of the 2013 ACM annual conference on Human factors in computing systems* New York: ACM, pp.3365–3374.

McMillan, D., Morrison, A., Brown, O., Hall, M. and Chalmers, M., 2010. Further into the wild: Running worldwide trials of mobile systems. *Pervasive Computing*. Helsinki, May. Berlin: Springer Berlin Heidelberg, pp.210–227.

Montola, M., Stenros, J. and Waern, A. 2009. *Pervasive games: Theory and design*. San Francisco: Morgan Kaufmann.

Montola, M., 2011. A ludological view on the pervasive mixed-reality game research paradigm. *Personal and Ubiquitous Computing*, 15(1), pp.3–12.

Montola, M. and Waern, A., 2006a. Ethical and practical look at unaware game participation. In: Manthos, S., ed., *Gaming realities. A challenge for digital culture*. Athens: Fournos Centre for the Digital Culture, pp.185–193.

Montola, M. and Waern, A., 2006b. Participant roles in socially expanded games. In: Strang, T., Cahill, V. and Quigley, A., eds., PerGames 2006 workshop of pervasive 2006 conference *pervasive 2006 workshop proceedings*. Dublin. May. Dublin: University College Dublin, pp.165–173.

Neustaedter, C., Tang, A. and Judge, T.K., 2013, Creating scalable location-based games: lessons from Geocaching. *Personal and Ubiquitous Computing*, 17(2), pp.335–349.

Osborne, M.J. and Rubinstein, A., 1994, *A course in game theory*. Cambridge: MIT press.

Salen, K. and Zimmerman, E., 2004. *Rules of play: Game design fundamentals*. Cambridge: MIT press.

Schön, D.A., 1983. *The reflective practitioner: How professionals think in action* (Vol. 5126). New York: Basic Books.

Simon, Herbert A., 1981. *The sciences of the artificial*. Cambridge: MIT Press.

Stenros, J., Montola, M., Waern, A. and Jonsson, S., 2007. Play it for real: Sustained seamless life/game merger in Momentum. In: Akira, B., ed., 2007. *Situated Play*. Tokyo: September. pp.121–129.

Stenros, J., Waern, A. and Montola, M., 2011. Studying the elusive experience in pervasive games. *Simulation & Gaming*, 43(3), ahead of print. DOI=10.1177/1046878111422532.

Waern, A., Montola, M. and Stenros, J., 2009. The three-sixty illusion: Designing for immersion in pervasive games. In: *Proceedings of the SIGCHI conference on human factors in computing systems, CHI'09*. New York: ACM, pp.1549–1558.

Zimmerman, E., 2003. Play as research: the iterative design process. In: B., Laurel, ed., *Design research: Methods and perspectives*. Cambridge MA: MIT press.

Zimmerman, J., Forlizzi, J. and Evenson, S., 2007. Research through design as a method for interaction design research. In: *Proceedings of the SIGCHI conference on human factors in computing systems, CHI '07*. New York: ACM, pp.493–502.

About the contributors

Jesper Aagaard is a PhD fellow at the Department of Psychology and Behavioral Sciences, University of Aarhus, Denmark, where he does qualitative research on the relationship between technology, multi-tasking, and attention.

Dr. Suellen Adams is an adjunct professor in library and information studies who teaches regularly for a number of institutions including the University of Southern Mississippi, the University of Rhode Island and the University of Alabama. Dr. Adams career has included business as well as information education. Highlights include being a founding partner of the video game programming company Westlake Interactive. She currently does some work for Maverick Software LLC, an iPhone app development company. Her research interests lie in the intersection of information and leisure pursuits. She is also the author of *Crash course in gaming for libraries*.

Jon Back, PhD candidate in Human Computer Interaction at Uppsala University, is a researcher with a love for the breaking point between it is just a game and the moment when real feelings and experience becomes part of it. He studies design for technology-enhanced play outside of the computer, focusing on how to create engagement, feelings and experiences in public place. Previously he has designed both live action roleplaying games and published board games, both for serious use and entertainment.

Dr. Kristina N. Bauer is an Assistant Professor of Psychology at the University of West Florida. She earned her MS and PhD in Industrial/Organizational Psychology at Old Dominion University. She holds a BS in psychology from the University of Pittsburgh and an MA. in Human Resource Management from the George Washington University. Her primary research interests include self-regulated learning with an emphasis on technology enabled instruction and transfer of training. She also has a passion for research methods and statistics. Kristina has presented her work at several conferences, including the *Society for Industrial and Organizational Psychology*, the *Academy of Management*, the *American Psychological Association*, and the *Association for Psychological Science*, and her work has been published in *Military Psychology*, *Journal of Experimental Psychology: Applied*, *Academy of Management Learning & Education*, and *The Psychologist-Manager Journal*. In her free time, she enjoys yoga and trips to the beach.

Dr. Staffan Björk is a full professor at the department of Applied IT at Chalmers and Gothenburg University. He has a PhD in Informatics from Gothenburg University and conducts research within the areas of gameplay design, pervasive games, and interaction design. Exploring novel gameplay possibility through information technology has been a primary strand in his research, which often has been conducted within EU-funded projects such as IPerG and TA2. A common theme in his research is to develop a design language for gameplay design. A primary result of this work is the gameplay design patterns concept and the book "Patterns in Game Design" co-written with Jussi Holopainen and published by Charles River Media. He has been active in promoting game research as a research discipline, being one of the founders of the Digital Games Research Association.

Dr. **Ashley Brown** is a lecturer in Game Design at Brunel University London. She is the author of *Sexuality in Role-Playing Games* and an editor of *The dark side of game play: Controversial issues in playful environments*, both from Routledge. She is a board member of the Digital Games Research Association and an avid role-player.

Amanda Cote is a doctoral candidate in the Department of Communication Studies at the University of Michigan. Her dissertation work primarily draws on a critical exploration of industry practices, texts and themes, as well as in-depth interviews with female gamers, to explore why gaming is currently facing virulent gender issues, the forces that continue to support misogyny in gaming, and the benefits and challenges of playing games as a woman despite these factors. She is also broadly interested in the interaction of parenting styles and techniques with children's gaming habits.

Dr. **Lina Eklund** is a researcher in the Department of Sociology at Stockholm University, Sweden. Her doctoral thesis dealt with the practises and experiences of social digital gaming as a leisure activity. Her current work focuses on uses and practises of digital technologies in managing families as well as the impact of anonymity on digital sociality. Her research interests concern social life and gender issues in relation to digital games and technologies.

Inger Ekman currently works at the University of Tampere, researching design techniques for experience design, with a specialization on game sound design. She has published extensively on game design and user experience, in journals such as Gaming and Virtual Worlds, Simulation & Gaming, Computer & Graphics, books, and conference proceedings.

Dr. **J. Tuomas Harviainen** (MTh, PhD) is a postdoctoral contract researcher at the School of Information Sciences, University of Tampere, Finland, as well as a recent MBA student at Laurea University of Applied Sciences. His research currently focuses especially on games as information systems. Harviainen works as a Chief Information Specialist for the Vantaa City Library, edits two academic journals, and supervises doctoral students for three Finnish universities.

Nathan Hook is a British Social Psychologist and current PhD student at the University of Tampere, Finland. His main research interests are role-playing in games and how the psychology of players can be changed by ludic experiences playing roles. He has designed and published a series of game-like psychodrama larp scenarios under the *green book* series. Homepage: www.nathanhook.netii.net.

Dr. **Isto Huvila** is a senior lecturer in information and knowledge management at the School of Business and Economics, Åbo Akademi University, in Turku, Finland, an associate professor at the Department of ALM at Uppsala University in Sweden, and an independent consultant. His primary areas of research include information and knowledge management, information work, knowledge organization, documentation, and social and participatory information practices. He received a MA degree in cultural history at the University of Turku in 2002 and a PhD degree in information studies at Åbo Akademi University in 2006.

Simo Järvelä has a background in cognitive science and human resources management. His current research interests include physiological linkage, embodied cognition, psychophysiology, media experience, emotions, games, and social interaction.

J. Matias Kivikangas is a researcher at EMOID group and a graduate student at University of Helsinki. His dissertation presents an emotion theoretic view on the psychophysiology of the (local) social game experiences: how the different aspects of social interaction shape the personal experience of playing digital games, and how can they be interpreted from the perspective of emotions.

Dr. Simone Kriglstein studied computer science at the Vienna University of Technology and graduated in 2005. She received her doctorate degree from the University of Vienna in 2011. From 2005 to 2007 she worked as usability consultant/engineer and user interface designer. From 2007 until 2011 she was research assistant and teaching staff at the University of Vienna. Since 2011, she works for several projects at the University of Vienna and the Vienna University of Technology. From 2012 to 2014 she also worked as postdoctoral researcher at SBA Research. Her research interests are interface and interaction design, usability, information visualization, and games.

Dr. Richard N. Landers, PhD, is an Assistant Professor of Industrial/Organizational Psychology at Old Dominion University. His research program focuses upon improving the use of Internet technologies in talent management, especially the measurement of knowledge, skills and abilities, the selection of employees using innovative technologies, and learning conducted via the Internet. Recent topics have included gamification, game-based learning, game-based assessment, unproctored Internet-based testing, mobile devices including smartphones and tablets, immersive 3D virtual environments and virtual reality, and social media and online communities. His research and writing has been featured in *Forbes, Business Insider, Science News Daily, Popular Science, Maclean's*, and the *Chronicle of Higher Education*, among others. Homepage: www.rlanders.net.

Dr. Petri Lankoski is a senior lecturer in game research at Södertörn University. His research focuses on game design, character design, play experiences and development-based research. Lankoski received his doctoral degree in art and design at Aalto University. Homepage: www.iki.fi/petri.lankoski.

Dr. Andreas Lieberoth is an applied game psychology researcher at the Interacting Minds Centre, Aarhus University, and an associated researcher and game designer at the Centre for Community Driven Research (CODER). His PhD was in cognitive and educational psychology. He has (co-)designed several games, both digital and analogue. His academic work centers on the social psychology and cognitive neuroscience of gaming, especially in the context of game based learning and citizen cyberscience.

Benny Liebold graduated in media and communication studies and is a junior researcher and lecturer at the Institute of Media Research at Chemnitz University of Technology, Germany. His research interests include states of focused attention during media use, emotional virtual agents, media effects, game based learning, and media research methods.

Dr. Michael Mateas is recognized internationally as a leader in computationally-focused design and analysis approaches in playable media. He is currently faculty in the Computer Science department at UC Santa Cruz, where he holds the MacArthur Endowed Chair. He founded and co-directs the

Expressive Intelligence Studio, one of the largest technically-oriented game research groups in the world, and is also the founding director of the Center for Games and Playable Media at UC Santa Cruz. His research interests include interactive storytelling and autonomous characters, procedural content generation, AI-based interactive art, and software studies. He received his PhD in Computer Science from Carnegie Mellon University.

Dr. **Carl Magnus Olsson** is an associate professor of the Computer Science department at the University of Malmö, Sweden. His research interests lie in experiential computing and the challenges for designing consumer technologies and software products. His teaching focuses on game design at the game development bachelor program. He has spent time as guest researcher at Northern Illinois University, and has a PhD from the University of Limerick, Ireland. In his PhD, he explored the mediating role of context-aware applications by designing, developing and assessing the impact of a context-aware game for backseat passengers in close collaboration with three automotive and software development organizations.

Dr. **Raphaël Marczak** holds a PhD in game studies from the University of Waikato (New Zealand), two Master's degrees in Computer Science (Engineering and Multimedia) from the University of Bordeaux (France). He has spent the last three years developing a model for video game classification in New Zealand by identifying which quantitative data sets, from psycho-physiological data to gameplay metrics can be used to enhance the assessment of gameplay experience. Before this project, he worked at LaBRI (Bordeaux, France) on the VIRAGE project, a collaboration between science and art.

Dr. **M. Rohangis Mohseni** graduated in psychology at the University of Cologne in 2005. After that, he became a scientific assistant at Osnabrück University. Until 2011, he worked at the university's Teaching Evaluation Service Point, and after that at the Center for Information Management and Virtual Teaching. His diploma thesis about moral courage inspired him to write a doctoral thesis about virtual emergency assistance. His research interests include computer game research, e-learning, mobile learning, and forms of (im)moral behaviour like aggression, helping and moral courage.

Dr. **Frans Mäyrä** is the Professor of Information Studies and Interactive Media, with specialization in digital culture and game studies in the University of Tampere, Finland. Mäyra heads the University of Tampere Game Research Lab, teaching digital culture and games since early 1990s. He is widely consulted as an expert in socio-cultural issues relating to games, play and playfulness. His research interests range from game cultures, meaning making through playful interaction and online social play, to borderlines, identity, as well as transmedial fantasy and science fiction. He is currently leading the research project Ludification of Culture and Society. Publications include: *Demonic texts and textual demons* (1999), *CGDC conference proceedings* (ed., 2002), *The metamorphosis of home* (ed. 2005), *An introduction to game studies* (2008), and a large number of articles and conference papers.

Dr. **Daniel Pietschmann** is a research associate at the Institute for Media Research, Chair of Media Psychology, Chemnitz University of Technology, Germany. Research interests include psychological and physical aspects of experiencing digital media, virtual reality environments, computer game research, TV studies and Transmedia Storytelling.

Jori Pitkänen is a professional drama instructor and game educator, currently doing his doctoral dissertation about the thought processes of gamers in video games and roleplaying games (live and table-top).

In his theses at the University of Helsinki (MA in Education) and the University of Applied Sciences in Helsinki (BA in Theatre Arts) he researched the application of live action role playing games in teaching and theatre directing. He used the stimulated recall method to research the thought processes of sixth-graders to find traces of historical empathy and its development during gameplay. He also used stimulated recall when he researched the unique, gamified teaching environment at Østerskov Efterskole in Denmark.

Dr. **Niklas Ravaja** is a professor at the Department of Social Research, University of Helsinki, and director of research at the Department of Information and Service Economy, Aalto School of Business. His areas of research interest and expertise include the psychophysiology of attention, emotion, and temperament, and media psychology.

Dr. **Julia G. Raz** earned her PhD. in Communication Studies from the University of Michigan. Her dissertation research employed a textual analysis methodology to investigate exergames and the construction of women and motherhood. Her other projects drew on ethnographic research and in-depth interviews in public spaces and industry trade shows to study the meaning of casual games. Dr. Raz is currently part time faculty at Santa Monica College and the New York Film Academy of Los Angeles.

Dr. **Gareth Schott** PhD, is a Senior Lecturer at the School of Arts, Screen and Media Program at the University of Waikato, New Zealand. He was the principal investigator and grant holder of the Royal Society of New Zealand: Marsden Grant that funded the research disseminated in this collection. He has published widely in the field of game studies prior to, and since its inception in 2001. He is co-author of *Computer Games: Text, narrative and play* (Polity Press) and sole author of *Violent Games: Rules, realism & effect* scheduled for publication in 2015 (Bloomsbury Press)

Olle Sköld (MA) is a doctoral student with one leg in archival studies research and the other in the field of information studies. His research interests range from matters relating to archival appraisal and the preservation of videogames to the study of memory-making, knowledge production, and documentation in online gaming communities. Sköld currently pursues his PhD at the Department of ALM (Archival Studies, Library and Information Science and Museums and Cultural Heritage Studies), Uppsala University, Sweden.

Dr. **Mattias Svahn** received his PhD from the Stockholm School of Economics. He has in collaboration with the Interactive Institute Swedish ICT researched the media psychology of pervasive games, in particular the consumer/players´ experiences and reactions when exposed to pervasive persuasive games for learning and advertising. He consults to large Scandinavian media houses and has published and presented at many international conferences on the consumer psychology of ambient media and pervasive advertising. His work bridges consumer behavior sciences, game design science and play theory. He was also senior coordinator and research leader for business development of pervasive games at the EU IST framework programme 6 project Iperg that developed prototype pervasive games and ambient media (see www.svahn.se).

Dr. **Jose Zagal** is faculty at DePaul University's College of Computing and Digital Media and visiting faculty at the University of Utah. His research explores the development of frameworks for analyzing and understanding games from a critical perspective. He is also interested in supporting games literacy. His book *Ludoliteracy: Defining, understanding, and supporting games education* was published in 2010.

More recently he edited *The Videogame Ethics Reader* (2012) as an entry point for reflecting upon and discussing ethical topics surrounding videogames. Zagal is Vice President of the Digital Games Research Association (DiGRA) and received his PhD in Computer Science from Georgia Institute of Technology.

Dr. **Richard Wahlund** is the Bonnier Family Professor in Business Administration, focusing on media, at the Stockholm School of Economics (SSE). He is also Head of the Department of Marketing and Strategy and the Center for Media and Economic Psychology at SSE. His research projects are mainly in the intersection of marketing, media and economic psychology, and he has above 100 publications. His latest projects focus on media and sustainability issues. Professor Wahlund is a member of several boards within business and academics, and also a frequent guest lecturer within industry and society.

Dr. **Annika Waern**, professor in Human-Computer Interaction at Uppsala University, is a research by design academic with a background in computer science and human-computer interaction. She has dedicated the latest ten years of her life to understanding games, and more specifically, *pervasive games*. During 2004–2008, she acted as the coordinator of IPerG, Integrated Project on Pervasive Games, an EU-funded project with nine partners spread around Europe. She acts as editor in chief for ToDIGRA, Transactions of the Digital Games Research Association and frequently participates in programme committees for scientific conferences in the fields of human-computer interaction and game research.

Dr. **Günter Wallner** serves as senior scientist at the University of Applied Arts in Vienna. He holds a doctorate degree in natural sciences from the University of Applied Arts Vienna and a diploma degree in computer science from the Vienna University of Technology. His research interests include the design, development, and evaluation of digital games as well as computer graphics and visualization. Currently his research focuses on the analysis and visualization of game telemetry data. His work has been published in international journals and conferences, such as *Computers & Graphics*, *Entertainment Computing*, and ACM SIGCHI.

Kaare Bro Wellnitz is a PhD student at the Department of Psychology and Behavioural Sciences, Aarhus University, Denmark. His main research area is motivation and educational psychology, where he is currently investigating the relationship between ways of organizing school and student engagement using a combination of quantitative and qualitative research methods.

ETC Press is a publishing imprint with a twist. We publish books, but we're also interested in the participatory future of content creation across multiple media. We are an academic, open source, multimedia, publishing imprint affiliated with the Entertainment Technology Center (ETC) at Carnegie Mellon University (CMU) and in partnership with Lulu.com. ETC Press has an affiliation with the Institute for the Future of the Book and MediaCommons, sharing in the exploration of the evolution of discourse. ETC Press also has an agreement with the Association for Computing Machinery (ACM) to place ETC Press publications in the ACM Digital Library, and another with Feedbooks to place ETC Press texts in their e-reading platform. Also, ETC Press publications will be in Booktrope and in the ThoughtMesh.

ETC Press publications will focus on issues revolving around entertainment technologies as they are applied across a variety of fields. We are looking to develop a range of texts and media that are innovative and insightful. We are interested in creating projects with Sophie and with In Media Res, and we will accept submissions and publish work in a variety of media (textual, electronic, digital, etc.), and we work with The Game Crafter to produce tabletop games.

Authors publishing with ETC Press retain ownership of their intellectual property. ETC Press publishes a version of the text with author permission and ETC Press publications will be released under one of two Creative Commons licenses:

- **Attribution-NoDerivativeWorks-NonCommercial:** This license allows for published works to remain intact, but versions can be created.
- **Attribution-NonCommercial-ShareAlike:** This license allows for authors to retain editorial control of their creations while also encouraging readers to collaboratively rewrite content.

Every text is available for free download, and we price our titles as inexpensively as possible, because we want people to have access to them. We're most interested in the sharing and spreading of ideas.

This is definitely an experiment in the notion of publishing, and we invite people to participate. We are exploring what it means to "publish" across multiple media and multiple versions. We believe this is the future of publication, bridging virtual and physical media with fluid versions of publications as well as enabling the creative blurring of what constitutes reading and writing.

Printed in Great Britain
by Amazon